A Working Class in the Making

A WORKING CLASS IN THE MAKING

Belgian Colonial Labor Policy, Private Enterprise, and the African Mineworker, 1907–1951

John Higginson

The University of Wisconsin Press

The University of Wisconsin Press
114 North Murray Street
Madison, Wisconsin 53715

The University of Wisconsin Press, Ltd.
1 Gower Street
London WC1E 6HA, England

5 4 3 2 1

Printed in the United States of America

Publication of this book was made possible in part
by a grant from the Andrew W. Mellon Foundation.

Library of Congress Cataloging-in-Publication Data
Higginson, John, 1949–
A working class in the making: Belgian colonial labor policy,
private enterprise, and the African mineworker, 1907–1951 /
John Higginson.
328 pp.   cm.
Bibliography: pp. 279–295.
Includes index.
1. Miners—Zaire—History. 2. Mineral industries—Zaire—History.
3. Working class—Zaire—History. 4. Belgium—Colonies—Africa.
I. Title.
HD8039.M61Z284   1989
331.7'622'09675109041—dc20   88-40435
ISBN 0-299-12070-8   CIP
ISBN 0-299-12074-0 (pbk.)

*To my family—Mama Christine, John Farid, Joye, and Malaika—
and to the people of Zaire and southern Africa*

Contents

Illustrations and Maps

ILLUSTRATIONS

MAPS

Tables

Abbreviations

AGUFI	Association des Agents de l'Union Minière et Filiales
BCK	Compagnie du Chemin de Fer du Bas-Congo au Katanga
BTK	Bourse du Travail du Katanga
CEC	centres extra-coutumiers
CFK	Chemin de Fer du Katanga
CFL	Chemin de Fer du Grands Lacs
CIE	conseils indigènes d'entreprise
CSK	Comité special du Katanga
MOI/s	main-d'òeuvre indigène/specialisée
OCTK	Office central du Travail du Katanga
OSS	Office of Strategic Services
POB	Parti ouvrier belge
UMHK	l'Union Minière du Haut-Katanga

Acknowledgments

In the time it has taken to write this book I have chalked up a rather large debt. Like most people who borrow without paying sufficient attention to the hidden clauses of the repayment plan, I am the humbler for borrowing so much, so often. My friends — and my enemies — have been more gracious than they know.

Long before I started writing the dissertation that provided the necessary point of departure for this book, I became indebted to a set of friends and extended kin whose ideas have had a profound effect on my own. They will find something of themselves here, even as they shake their heads and declare that I have made a muddle of most of their ideas. Ibrahim Abu-Lughod, Eqbal Ahmad, Ernest Allen, Giovanni Arrighi, Roderick Aya, General Baker, Carol Banks, Harold Baron, John Bracey, Johnetta Cole, Johannes Fabian, Barbara Fields, Karen Fields, Leon Forrest, the late Milton Gardner, Victor Goode, Macee Halk, Eric J. Hobsbawm, Shirley Hune, C. L. R. James, Jeffrey Jones, Bernard Magubane, Jeffrey McNary, Congress Mbata, David Montgomery, Kodi Muzong, Otto Olsen, Carl Parrini, Payanzo Ntsumo, Eric Perkins, Mark Selden, Archie Singham, Nancy Singham, Roy Singham, Robert Starks, Dale Tomich, Glinder Torain, Immanuel Wallerstein, and Paul Young are among this category.

I must also thank that wise and patient group of people who ran interference for me while I took a rather circuitous route to completing the initial research for this work: N. Y. Burwell, Dorothy Carter, Albert Feuerwerker, Maxwell Owusu, Marshall Sahlins, Charles Tilly, Louise Tilly, G. N. Uzoigwe, and Eric Wolf. Thanks to you all.

Then there is what I call the Africa–California connection: Eyo Alabi, Arthé Anthony, Merle "Hurricane" Bowen, Henry Bowman, Caroline McWatt Bowman, Judy Bowman, Vernon Coleman, Kondíoura Drame, Joyce "the Tartan Terror" Euwen, Harold Forsythe, Marjorie Forsythe, Frankie Houchins, Sue Houchins, the late Phyllis Johnson, Francis Nyong, Thomas "Guguruhunde" Parrish, Anita Robinson, and Julie Saville. They make up a special collateral branch of my extended family. Without their encouragement, which assumed various forms in the United States, western Europe, and southern Africa, this book might never have been completed.

Burrowing through archives is a lot like what some Britishers call pub crawling. In fact, a little of both can make for a pleasant mix, as long as the two spheres of activity are kept more or less distinct. A number of archivists and librarians in Africa, Europe, and the United States have shown me how to make this distinction in a happy and civilized environment. I must thank particularly Ms. Onuma Ezera of the Congo Collection at Michigan State University in East Lansing, Michigan; Citoyen Mulunda Kalembi, the former Director of Personnel at the Lubumbashi seat of the *Générale des Carrières et Mines* in Zaire; Madame A. Lamal, formerly of *Archives africaines* in Brussels; Mr. Gotwell Motsi of the National Archives of Zimbabwe in Harare; and Mr. John Ralph of Tanganyika Holdings Limited in London.

I would still be agonizing about the motives of some of the more obscure personages in this book were it not for the intelligent criticisms of some of my more generous colleagues who read portions or various drafts of this manuscript. Milton Cantor, Melvyn Dubofsky, Bruce Fetter, Eugene Genovese, Deena Gonzalez, Allen Isaacman, Bogumil Jewsiewicki, Bruce Laurie, J. Carroll Moody, Nzongola Ntalaja, Terence Ranger, Sean Redding, Joan Scott, Jan Vansina, and Helena Wall readily come to mind. Dubofsky, Fetter, Genovese, Jewsiewicki, Nzongola, and Vansina in particular disabused me of erroneous ideas and infelicitous prose with great eloquence and generosity.

Dona Curry of the Claremont Colleges, Jean Nyakora of the University of California at Los Angeles, and Karen Blaser, Cheryl Fuller, and Helen Satterlee of Northern Illinois University helped me to translate the complex plight of the Congolese mineworkers into the binary code of various computerized word-processing systems. From now on, thanks to them, I will take a more all-encompassing approach to Alan Turing's devilish invention. I cannot thank them enough.

Obviously I could not have completed this book with my own meager resources. I wish to thank the Ford and Haynes foundations, the National Academy of Sciences, the Social Science Research Council, and the Wenner-Gren Foundation for subventing my research and release time from teaching. They have my deepest gratitude.

Phyllis Kawano, an excellent cartographer and a wonderful human being to boot, splendidly captured geographical realities that form part of the deep background of the miners' story. As a result of her fastidiousness, this book has been relieved of a number of potentially embarrassing errors. The same can be said of my editor, Robin

Whitaker, and of the humanities editor at the University of Wisconsin Press, Barbara Hanrahan. Thanks Barbara, Phyllis, and Robin.

Finally, I wish to thank those people in southern Africa who made their experiences accessible to me and who would prefer to remain anonymous and my immediate family. I extend a very special thanks to my mother whose childhood recollections of the small triumphs and big defeats of working people in the oil fields and sawmill towns of northern Louisiana have taught me so much. To my wife, Joye Bowman, who took time from her own book on the peasantry of Guinea-Bissau to help me run down obscure references and "to get the words right," I owe more than I can say. To my children, John Farid and Malaika, I owe much more than this book, but I hope they will let it stand as a partial payment on a better and more humane future.

Note to the Reader

I have chosen to use a rather streamlined approach to prefixes for the various Bantu languages and peoples mentioned in this book. While this may not satisfy language purists, it will make the text more accessible to readers who have no knowledge of the general rules of orthography in Bantu languages.

Some readers will also note that the map of Katanga combines place names and administrative divisions from before and after the draconian fiscal retrenchment of 1933, which effectively lopped off the northwestern region of Katanga to form the province of Kasai. I chose such a format because the recruitment of African workers at the Union Minière du Haut-Katanga continued to be informed by the pre-1933 administrative divisions in terms of chieftaincies and territories.

A Working Class in the Making

Introduction

THE CONTEXT OF WAGE LABOR'S ADVENT

> Now (the) Congo may play the role of Serbia. Except for the terror of nuclear power on both sides, we might easily slide into the 1914 situation.
>
> > British Prime Minister Harold Macmillan shortly after Patrice Lumumba's murder in Katanga in January 1961[1]

> To the mines? And what do you want to go there for? All they ever do is eat fish, get drunk, and run machines. You will find that they are very different people from us.
>
> > Bwelenge Ahmed, a peasant fish salesman on the Zambian side of the copperbelt in 1974[2]

Thus concluded two men who were part of the recent history of Shaba Province, Zaire, formerly Katanga Province, Belgian Congo. For Macmillan, the mining industry in the area he knew as Katanga was one of the dark alcoves in the corridors of power—out of which could come a hot rather than a cold war. For Ahmed, the workers and the industrial towns of Shaba were the very antithesis of civility; yet without them, he and his world, the adjacent countryside, would be very different indeed. Both made observations about the surface realities of Shaba which obscured its most powerful leitmotiv: that between 1907 and 1949 private industry and the Belgian colonial government attempted to proletarianize Africans without creating a working class.[3] This attempt failed. This study explains why it failed. But since the failure did not constitute a victory for the African workers, this study is also an account of what happened instead, why, and what the outcome has come to mean for the contemporary world.

The concerns of this book also derive from a demystified reading of Pierre Ryckmans' dictum "dominer pour servir."[4] For in the 50 years before Ryckmans' accession to the post of governor-general of the Belgian Congo in 1936, and throughout most of the years that followed, the Congolese people were largely misserved by Belgian rule. Despite Belgian domination, a considerable percentage of the

Congolese population came to understand the spirit of modern capitalism and how it might work for them. But the spirit's conjurers
were not always willing to follow where it led, much less to allow
the toiling masses of Africa to do so.

The history of the mineworkers presents a unique opportunity to
study the processes of class formation on both a macro- and
microlevel. A large fund of archival material exists in Zaire, Belgium,
England, and the United States. But only a small portion of it has
been exploited to establish better the causal link between changes
in the mineworkers' way of life before and after the Depression and
the Second World War. Put crudely, the problems presented by this
evidence are: (1) How did the workers' lodges and friendly societies
emerge out of precolonial mutual aid societies? (2) How did these associations reemerge as vectors of popular protest during the African
strike wave of 1941, after they had been apparently destroyed by the
provincial secret police during the labor unrest of 1931? (3) How did
the friendly societies and millenarian sects like African Watchtower
reflect changing African attitudes about work during the 1930s and
1940s? (4) How did the peasantry adapt to forced labor recruitment
and the imposition of cash crops like cotton? (5) To what extent were
agrarian instances of popular protest influenced by industrial ones
once the peasantry was drawn into the marketplace? (6) Was the
leadership of the African workers' organizations drawn from specific
strata of workers — factory operatives or underground workers rather
than surface workers, for example? In short, what was the relationship
between the African workers' social consciousness and the kinds of
organizations through which they expressed that consciousness?[5]

Macmillan was quite right to observe that local discontent could
not be merely local in content, that, remote as it seemed, Katanga
was part of his own world. By the same token Ahmed was quite right
to note the alienness of Shaba, close as it was to him geographically.
To the eyes of a villager, only the topmost layers of this world — the
running of machines, the apparently uncouth behavior of the
workers — were visible. But this world had several layers: an international market in money and commodities, which influenced local
operations and constrained the process of industrialization in techno-
logical terms and also in terms of investment decisions; a greedy royal
family and its Belgian and foreign financial allies, who determined
choices between short- and long-term profitability and were also the
catalysts for administrative changes in the form of colonial rule; a
local colonial administration and police force charged with maintaining order and containing the aspirations of black and white colonial

subjects; a highly differentiated mass of African colonial subjects, who attempted to protect their lives and, in consequence, to force certain decisions on the part of those charged with keeping them in check at the workplace and at their places of residence in the towns and villages.[6]

Perhaps 1 million or 1.5 million people in Katanga and the neighboring colonies were affected, directly and indirectly, by the events discussed herein—roughly 5 percent of the present Zairean population and somewhere between 8 and 13 percent of the population during the period in question.[7] Depending upon how one computes labor turnover during the first 30 years of the Union Minière du Haut-Katanga's existence, somewhere between 180,000 and 250,000 men were pressed into its service.[8] Consequently, one must ask how the African mineworkers managed to shape a community under such conditions, and how they were, in turn, transformed from mineworkers to mining proletariat.

DEMOGRAPHIC DISTORTION

Once the Congo was seized by Léopold II and his mercenary armies, its resources and population made its local affairs the world's business.[9] But its earlier, more parochial, history is worth sketching briefly to illustrate the demographic changes that colonial investment caused. Shaba is a savannah woodland cut off from more fertile lands in the northeast by the Kivu-Maniema highlands. In the west the Kasai River separates it from Angola. Lake Tanganyika separates it from Tanzania and Zambia, while the waters of the Lualaba River and its tributaries constitute a drainage system that accentuates the valleys and plateaus of its central and southern regions.[10] The soil and subsurface of Shaba are highly acidic latosols, except in the valleys, where alluvial soil from the riverbeds takes their place. A sparse human population took what it could from this indifferently endowed natural environment. Agriculture had a relatively low level of productivity. For most of the precolonial period, cultivation and the largest human settlements were confined to the valleys and shores of the larger lakes.[11]

At the end of the seventeenth century, the advent of new crops from America, most notably maize and cassava, and hardier strains of older ones from the Zambezi floodplain provoked a marked but brief agricultural revolution. Cassava, maize, rice, and more resistant strains of millet increased the amount of insurance that cultivators could build against famine and epidemic diseases. Famines and death did not disappear, however, and west of the Lubilash River they provoked a steady out-migration of Luba, Songye, and Lamba peoples from the periphery of the northern Luba-Lomami Kingdom and the southern Lunda Kingdom of Aruund. Dwindling food supplies in the respective heartlands of these two kingdoms compelled their rulers to embark upon military contests for the fertile valleys of central and southern Katanga. With military conquest came an infrastructure composed of roads, drained salt marshes, settlements of between 2,000 and 5,000 people, and newly opened mines of gold, copper, and iron. The free cultivators of the backland were transformed into peasants, at least partly so.[12]

The mid-nineteenth century brought a new wave of conquerors. The incursion of the Chokwe from the west and the Swahili and Nyamwezi from the east ushered in an era of broader and more consistent contacts between Katanga and the trading entrepôts of East Africa on one hand and Portuguese Angola on the other. The Nyamwezi and Swahili merchants had the most penetrating effect on the region. With firearms, Islam, and a cosmopolitan urban culture, these interlopers tied the people of Katanga to the rapidly changing world east of the inland ocean of Lake Tanganyika and to the global current of trade in the Indian Ocean. By the 1860s the Nyamwezi merchant adventurer Msiri established an administrative capital, Bunkeya, with a population of over 10,000, in the very center of Katanga and incorporated all the possessions of the Lunda Kazembe west of the Luapula River.[13]

Even though the first phases of industrialization reestablished the old pattern of underpopulation in some areas and overcrowding in others, peasant agriculture was not destroyed altogether. However, by compulsion or the dictates of the market, the peasantry was obliged to cultivate cash crops such as cotton and sesame.[14] These crops tended to encroach upon acreage set aside for subsistence. For as the stronger roots of cotton planted in May strangled those of food crops planted in December (the regular planting season), the peasantry was often faced with the real prospect of starvation.

The importation of food and manufactured goods also forced a transformation of the peasantry's notion of "subsistence." This transformation was often registered in metaphysical terms, for Katanga's indigenous peoples thought of the undulating central valley of the plateau, Kalukuluku, as a holy place. Village smiths surface mined its copper, and adolescent boys were initiated into manhood among its arbors and along the banks of the Lubumbashi River. But for the thousands of Africans who came to dig the copper out of the earth for the Union Minière and to lay ties of the rail lines, it was to become a place of death and malevolent magic. Disease, strange and unclean food, and corporal punishment compelled the workers to turn to *bwanga*, or protective magic, and a myriad of ethnic brotherhoods and mutual aid societies.[15] Industry and the colonial state did not articulate with the African agriculture but distorted it to the point of caricature. Meanwhile, industrialization did not proceed fast enough to absorb the people displaced. The industrial transformation of Katanga brought in its train the transformation of preindustrial agrarian redoubts into reservoirs of wage labor.[16]

HIGH FINANCE AND THE ORIGINS OF THE POLITICAL AND INDUSTRIAL ORDER

At the outset of the twentieth century an industrial working class was still in the making in southern Africa. The initial phases of its making, particularly the employer's transition from formal to substantive control over the workforce, were especially drawn out.[17] Once under way, however, industrial growth was exceedingly rapid. By 1907 many investors were convinced that Cecil Rhodes's dream of a "second Rand" — an industrial region that would stretch from Southern Rhodesia to Katanga Province, Belgian Congo — was well on the way to fruition.[18] Others were more skeptical. Pierre Paul Leroy-Beaulieu, perhaps the most eminent European economist of the era after Alfred Marshall, took a different view of the labor problem in the African colonies, particularly the Belgian Congo:

Commerce will grow and extend itself in this region of the world only insofar as the Europeans establish their effective authority and political suzerainty; where they will cause peace to reign with the support of a pliant and disciplined military force; where they will prohibit local wars, massacres, pillage, and slavery; where they will open lines of communications whether they be simple routes, canals or railroads; where, through the example and initiative of their own nationals, they will make the native peoples accustomed to having more needs — that is to say, to work more and to pay for goods with money. It has been rightly said that the most characteristic sign of civilization is the multiplicity of needs.[19]

Beaulieu maintained that, in the final analysis, colonization had to be directed by a "rational bourgeois state," and that the concession companies — the late nineteenth- and early twentieth-century analogues to free trade zones — were merely transitory forms of economic penetration. Beaulieu cautioned Belgium in particular to take the Congo out of Léopold II's hands or find itself victimized by the other European powers in Africa. For if the Congo became an international project, as one line of debate suggested in the early 1900s, there would be no means to raise public revenues through a system of customs and tariffs. Yet if the colony remained in Léopold's hands, its potential profits would be squandered by a corrupt and inept administration.[20] The outlook of the Belgian banks concurred with Beaulieu's. For them, the concession companies and Léopold's right of eminent domain over all of the Congo had discouraged business initiatives of an industrial sort and a more systematic concentration of existing enterprises. Consequently, in 1908, after the transfer of the Congo from Léopold II to the Belgian government, Belgian banks were extremely optimistic about solving the Congo's labor and investment problems.[21]

The industrial penetration of Katanga was accomplished by a discordant institutional arrangement.[22] National rivalries between Belgian investors, the Société générale de Belgique and the Comité special du Katanga (CSK), and Anglo-American ones, most notably Robert Williams' engineering firm, Tanganyika Concessions Limited, exacerbated policy debates over technical problems and labor management. After the First World War soaring labor costs and the dramatic devaluation of the Belgian franc against the pound sterling also fed the rivalry between Belgian and British interests.[23] In the meantime the commercial exploitation of the mines continued to expand. By the end of the war, the mining industry had become an ineffaceable presence in Katanga and in the neighboring parts of Angola and Northern Rhodesia.[24]

Having achieved a sufficient, though never complete, coordination, these entities made themselves felt in the villages through the Bourse du Travail du Katanga (BTK), a parastatal labor recruitment agency, the Force Publique, or colonial army, and private labor recruitment agencies. The BTK and the provincial administration attempted to co-opt African institutions such as the land chieftaincies. Where such institutions proved intransigent or hostile to the demand for labor, they were either usurped or obliterated, although this was not always an easy task.[25] A large portion of the Congo's African population — particularly in the Sankuru region of Kasai, the far northeastern corner of Equateur, and central and eastern Katanga — continued to resist Belgian encroachment. An illustrative case was that of the Yeke chieftain Kamba of Sakayongo. On 17 July 1925 Kamba had been removed from office and exiled to the southern border town of

Sakania. On 25 March 1926 Kamba was moved to a second place of exile at Bukama. While in route to Bukama, he and his military escort were obliged to pass through his former chieftaincy. A riot ensued subsequently and was brutally suppressed by the soldiers. The army and the BTK, agencies that frequently exchanged personnel in the midst of such operations, continued to impress and indenture a large percentage of African wage labor until the end of the 1920s.[26]

This coercive machinery was further buttressed by an ideology of racial superiority, which justified the use of force and strongly militated against African access to institutions of the state or to actual state power. For at the outset of Belgian rule almost all of the local European protagonists genuinely believed in the myth of African savagery and ruthlessly imposed their version of political order on the indigenous people. From an intellectual standpoint colonial racism marked the genesis of an illusion, but one which powerfully influenced the pace of colonial occupation and the perceptions of the home population. Listen to Edmond Picard, a socialist member of parliament on a visit to the Congo in 1896:

Like the ape, the black is an imitator. His facility for imitation is amazing. At the work sites of the European invaders one sees veritable squads of masons, blacksmiths, and mechanics who have learned their trade from practical experience. . . . Their dexterity is undeniable. And doubtless it has caused some to speculate, foolishly so, on the complete assimilation of the blacks. But such people do not comprehend the difference between the mere imitator and the creator. For the essential truth of the matter resides in that difference.[27]

To be sure, there were dissenting views, and none more vocal than that of Emile Vandervelde, Picard's left-of-center rival for the leadership of the Parti ouvrier belge (POB). During the parliamentary debate of 1900 on the Budja revolt in the Congo, Vandervelde said:

There is a solidarity within European capitalism in this respect, but the brutalities which he (Léopold) is responsible for with regard to the blacks at Budja encourage brutalities against white workers. Since the government has abandoned . . . the cause of humanity, it is the workers who must point it out . . . because that same inhumanity menaces them as well.[28]

But on the eve of the Congo's transfer to the Belgian government, the position of Vandervelde and other former leftwingers began to veer toward that of Picard. In the heat of the parliamentary debates of 1907–8 Vandervelde asserted that it would be the Africans who would suffer most if Belgium were to "cut the cable, cut the Gordian knot" between itself and the Congo.[29] Twenty years later few white workers in Belgium or Katanga would be at home with any of the earlier socialist reservations about the exploitation of African workers. Rather, they would probably agree more with Emile Rolus, the director of native personnel at the Union Minière in the 1930s, who asserted, "The black must be compelled to work by means of the most austere and strict discipline. Otherwise, he is like a ripe piece of fruit which cannot be picked."[30]

Katanga's industrial working class emerged under colonial rule and monopolistic economic organization. While the European working class acquired its basic contours during the social democratic upsurge of the last quarter of the nineteenth century, no comparable ideological dawning enhanced the expectations of African workers at the Union Minière. Racism had much to do with this, specifying as it did the conditions under which democratic ideals need not apply. Industrial growth did not have the manifold character of an England plunging into the crucible of Industrial Revolution at the end of the eighteenth century. There was also no fierce intraindustry competition, no full-throttled drive by the employers to achieve a maximum level of production on the basis of demand. The production process was labor-intensive and limited to a narrow range of exports. Few of its benefits found their way back to the African workers or the rest of the African population. None was directly related to the overall growth of the economy. And the amelioration of the condition of the workers was often gratuitous or the product of their own efforts.[31]

The first generation of African miners retained a strong attachment to the land and their villages. Drawn from ethnically diverse rural backgrounds, they were constrained to work without regard to place of origin, ethnicity, or potential skills. Yet they attempted to live as Bemba or Luba after the work day had been completed. Agrarian mores persisted because African living standards and work patterns shifted mercurially and because Belgian rule remained so indifferent to the initial increase in African wage labor. The emergence of the African lodges, or *bashikutu*, and the growth of particular ethnic enclaves within the larger African quarters of the industrial towns were partly the outcome of the mining company and government's indifference. The African laborers of Katanga sometimes chose to dance *kaonge* or *mbeni* — pan-ethnic expressions of the alienation and violence associated with wage labor — but they more often chose the dances from their own respective regions. They associated with and were buried by men who spoke the language in which they thought, and they attempted to protect themselves from death and disease by means prescribed by their forefathers. However, the workers' initial coping mechanisms were compelled to operate in a context of rapid but distorted industrial growth. In the ensuing attempt to maintain control over their persons and their labor, the workers moved steadily beyond the horizons of their forefathers.[32]

As African workers began to demand better living and working conditions and higher wages, the mining company responded with piece rates, motion time study, and other aspects of scientific management to constrain their demands. However, corporate strategy continued to be shaped more by coercion than by material and moral incentives: corporal punishment was seen as a practical solution to the African workers' restiveness, even though it was illegal after 1922;[33] labor legislation talked of "masters and servants" rather than of employers and workers;[34] trade unions were illegal, and the mining company and the state inordinately feared the workers' lodges and friendly societies.[35] Work routines were therefore the product of skirmishes between rulers and ruled as well as between capitalists and workers. This discontinuity reflected the hegemonic but uneven influence of the Union Minière over the colonial state.[36] Katanga's industrial revolution involved the creation of an industrial working class without the creation of an industrial society.

RECENT LITERATURE

The main deficiency of recent studies of Zaire's working class is the implicit assumption that it had no hand in its own making. Properly read, most of the evidence contradicts this assumption.[37] A more thorough analysis carries the investigation beyond the forms of working-class organization that the relatively freer environment of European industrialization permitted. Trade union activity, which was banned throughout most of the colonial period, is a case in point. After the Second World War, the consideration of trade unionism does have some value as a trace element for the changing aspirations of the workers, but is of little help in accounting for the entire range of worker aspirations. It is of virtually no help in illuminating the early manifestations of these aspirations. A more comprehensive picture hinges, therefore, on the character and persistence of pre-trade-union forms of organization.[38]

In Johannes Fabian's anthropological study of the mining towns of Katanga, *Jamaa*, the problem of organization among the workers, is put in the context of what Fabian himself calls "the world of the Union Minière" on the one hand, and that of *bwanga*, or protective magic, on the other. As with industrial workers elsewhere in the underdeveloped world, these two spheres are not mutually exclusive: the wage paid by the company is "barren wealth" and thus the very starting point of evil; yet Fabian claims that the mineworkers occasionally made use of both voluntary association and protective magic to turn evil into its opposite and to infuse industrial society with a more humane character.[39] But while he gives a most illuminating view of the pervasive importance of preindustrial forms of collective action in shaping the contours of the mineworkers' aspirations, Fabian tends to abstract the workers out of their "world" by focussing too closely on the syncretistic Christian cult of *jamaa*, or family.[40]

Fabian is aware of all this. He notes how *jamaa* subverts instrumental kinship in the urban areas with its notion of "spiritual kinship," thus reinforcing the colonial notion of "tribalism" but at a higher level of abstraction.[41] Indeed, the *jamaa's* original program was much altered by cultural compromises that its founder, Placide Tempels, could not anticipate; for unlike modern philosophy's newborn child, the African workers of Katanga were not simply a blank page upon which successive phases of industrial expansion and social engineering could impose themselves. Insofar as workers saw their membership in the *jamaa* in active terms, they undermined the sect's original purpose.

Charles Perrings' *Black Mineworkers in Central Africa* inadvertently resumes the discussion on the passivity of the workers by attempting to discern the structural determinants of industrial expansion and, more parenthetically, worker aspirations. But at crucial points, Perrings does not give us any more than a few hints about the particular idiom out of which working-class culture grew. Nor does he sufficiently explain how its emergence must have affected the relationship between the mineworkers and their rural kin.[42] He focusses much on management's justification of its economic policies and little on the workers' collective response to such policies. Perrings' examination of the workers' initial reactions to the Union Minière's stabilization program of the late 1920s and the labor unrest of 1931 are cases in point. Nor does Perrings attempt to show how an analysis of labor protest in the 1930s and 1940s might serve as a corrective to the biased manner in which the Union Minière organized statistical information. His silence detracts considerably from his explanation of the Union Minière's strategic objectives.[43]

Despite overwhelming evidence to the contrary—much of which he himself provides—Perrings contends that a mining proletariat in

Katanga was "stillborn." Although a great deal of evidence does indeed suggest that the lines of demarcation within the African working class of Katanga have only recently reached closure, and although there was a rapid transformation of formal job descriptions for African workers during the period in question, particularly at the Union Minière, the wage relationship had begun to occupy the center of the workers' universe long before.[44] The centrality of the wage, combined with the inherent inequality of the colonial situation and the growth of an urban army of unemployed workers, did indeed prevent the emergence of a full-blown labor aristocracy composed of the industrially trained artisans and the mining clerks; but it went a considerable way toward infusing the workers' social consciousness with an indigenous, homespun labor theory of value.[45]

One cannot assess the importance of the wage question, therefore, in isolation from the political contingencies imposed upon industrial production by colonial misrule. Throughout most of its history, the mining company believed that it could absorb the workers' expectations given the dramatic increases in production and profits. Yet the workers did occasionally consider their interests incompatible with those of the company, although most African-worker protest was enacted as a hedge against the more arbitrary features of company and state policy. While the workers did not possess a revolutionary consciousness, an African world of work, deference, and resistance was rapidly constructed in Katanga during the first half of the twentieth century.[46]

Katanga's African mineworkers were more resilient than the state or the Union Minière imagined. They often attempted to make choices about their lives in the face of daunting opposition. However, like common people everywhere, the mineworkers had little to do with the institutional framework that gave legitimacy to the act of choosing; for such arrangements were the products of their rulers' expectations or of social and cultural behavior whose original purpose had long since faded from the collective memory. Inasmuch as they rarely chose the terrain of battle, the workers were faced with a series of ready-made solutions that did not suit their original aspirations and which, time and time again, played into the hands of their rulers. At each such instance the workers attempted to stop just short of a direct, violent confrontation; for they recognized that death was the final choice in the world of the living. So they chose life — which, on occasion, was worth dying for.

By examining the opposing vantage points of the African workers

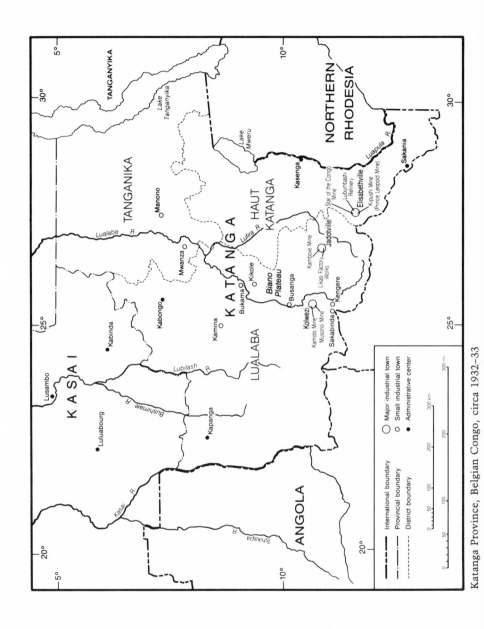

Katanga Province, Belgian Congo, circa 1932–33

14

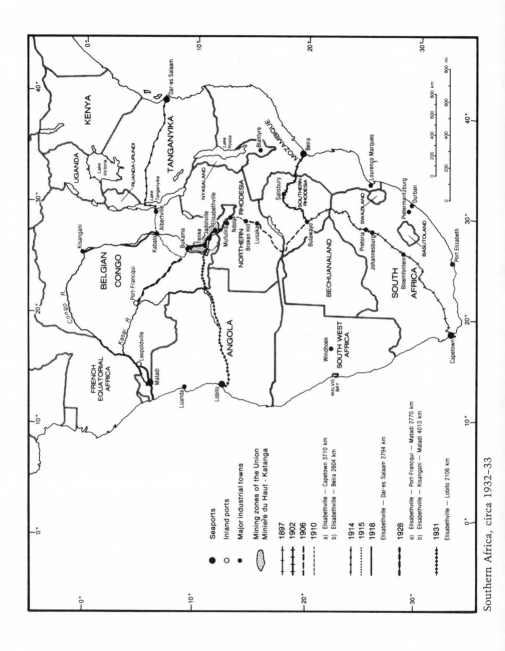

Seaports

Inland ports

Major industrial towns

Mining zones of the Union Minière du Haut - Katanga

1897	
1902	
1906	
1910	
a)	Elisabethville — Capetown 3710 km
b)	Elisabethville — Beira 2604 km
1914	
1915	
1918	
	Elisabethville — Dar-es Salaam 2794 km
1928	
a)	Elisabethville — Port-Francqui — Matadi 2770 km
b)	Elisabethville — Kisangani — Matadi 4013 km
1931	
	Elisabethville — Lobito 2106 km

Southern Africa, circa 1932-33

15

and the Union Minière, I will demonstrate how the workers caught a glimpse of what independence meant and how it changed their view of themselves. I will also show how a working class was made in the mines and industrial towns of Katanga, not as a mere precipitate result of Belgian and foreign capital, but as a social entity capable of pursuing interests that could threaten those of the mining company and the state.

PART ONE

Copper, Community, and Death

CHAPTER ONE

Getting on the Ground: The Practical Beginnings of the Union Minière du Haut-Katanga, 1907–1918

THE SEIZURE OF THE LAND

> The changes, which are going to be brought about in the economic regime of the Belgian Congo following the measures presently engaging our legislature, are looked upon favorably by the directors of the society. The changes will force the development of operations in Africa as large as the new circumstances will permit.
>
> > excerpt from an internal memo of the Belgian Banque d'outremer on the eve of the transfer of the Congo to the Belgian state, 18 January 1907[1]

> Have you noticed that every other native you see now has a gun and plenty of powder? There will be trouble one of these days.
>
> > Ralph Dixon, a pipefitter at the Lubumbashi works of the Union Minière to H. G. Robins, 1 August 1911[2]

In June 1907, H. G. Robins, a prospector for Robert Williams' Tanganyika Concessions Limited (TCL), was making his way north up the Lubudi River with a caravan of African bearers. He was trying to reach the point where the Lubudi joined the Lualaba River and where the plateau of southern Katanga gave way to the more habitable valleys: rumor had it that large deposits of diamonds and tin lay at the juncture of the two rivers. Robins was in a hurry. Most of the northern course of the river ran through a terrain where quartzite and iron were more plentiful than people; and he was anxious to exchange the African bearers he had brought from Northern Rhodesia for local ones before the outset of the rainy season.[3]

Much like other British prospectors and traders in Katanga during June of that year, Robins experienced great difficulty in hiring the local people, even though locusts, rinderpest, and long dry seasons had greatly depleted their food supplies. He tried every ploy he knew, including using his accumulated store of canned food as a lure. In September the rains came, a month earlier than expected, and Robins, still unable to find laborers, drove his homesick men with curses and threats of dispatching some of them with his revolver. But he took care not to travel too far too quickly, for African rebels as far south as the middle of the Lubudi River posed a direct military threat to Belgian sovereignty, and Robins' three rifles and one revolver were probably the extent of European power in the area.[4]

Despite the commencement of operations at the Union Minière in October 1907, the Belgian government thought the British presence in Katanga especially nettlesome. British firms like the Congo Trading Company sold local Luba people repeating Albini rifles rather than the less efficient breechloading ones; the government's soldiers did not have much better.[5] At the port town and future railhead of Bukama, Africans declared themselves universally in favor of trading with British firms.[6] And Britain continued to withhold its official recognition of Belgian sovereignty in Katanga — ostensibly because the new colonial regime could not prove that it had eradicated the excesses of Léopold II.[7] The Belgian administration rightly feared that the African population saw its rule as something less than permanent, and that a British occupation of the region would follow in its train.[8]

As early as 1907, territorial administrations saw the abolition of many of the larger chieftaincies as an important first step in derailing the agrarian economy and replacing tributary payments with the *impôt indigène*, or head tax, thus anchoring Belgian rule more firmly. Local chieftaincies often occupied a key position in regulating the precolonial economy. The undermining of African political authority was therefore indispensable to the garnering of wage labor, cash exchanges, and taxes.[9] But as the government sought to transform the context of village life between 1907 and 1917, the Yeke chiefs in central Katanga and the Luba paramount chiefs Kabongo and Kasongo Nyembo in north-central Katanga rose against it. A pliant and tractable African workforce was not immediately in the offing.

The territorial administration attempted to limit the physical mobility of the villagers while extracting more food and labor out of them than any paramount chief would have ever hoped to. This organizing principle of rural administration prevailed throughout the province and colony before the close of the First World War. It was an important complement to the mining company's attempt to acquire wage labor.[10] Such a policy did not work equally well in all places: At Mutombo Mukulu in Luba country, for example, Andre van Iseghem, the CSK *chef de poste,* tried desperately to get several "petty chieftains" and their subjects to relocate closer to the government fort between July and September 1908.[11] Earlier they had fled to the northern end of the Lubilash River, closer to the strongholds of the Luba insurgency.

Van Iseghem and his successor, P. Maroyez, worried that the smaller chieftaincies might become "infected" by the insurgents. But at the beginning of September 1908, one of the errant chiefs, one Sakadi, finally came into the post. Maroyez, the new *chef de poste,* was overjoyed. He peremptorily ordered Sakadi to reconstruct his village at a place called Songo Baraka, which was on the northwestern route to Kabinda, the territorial seat of Lomami. Songo Baraka served as one of a series of checkpoints for the administration in its attempt to confine the rebellion to the right bank of the Lubilash River.[12]

Sakadi's compliance seemed readily unconditional. Despite his initial elation, Maroyez wondered about the chief's motives. In his month-end report he observed that the situation in the region had in fact become more turbulent after Sakadi's return. Agricultural output, or more precisely, what the local peasantry deigned to bring to the fort, remained far below the administration's quotas. And there were rumors that no household in the territory would pay the head tax that year.[13] Rather than fleeing the insurgency, Sakadi had brought it within the administration's sphere, as Maroyez was to discover in October 1908. But Maroyez and his agents did not fully appreciate the scope of Sakadi's activities until the end of the year, when they counted the firearms they had seized in the villages near the fort—223 pistols and 66 rifles were confiscated between the time of Sakadi's return and December 1908. The government replaced Sakadi as hastily as it had appointed him.[14]

Between 1908 and 1911 more Luba chieftains fled with their people to the rebel strongholds in the semideserted stretches of land along the right bank of the Lubilash River. The rainy season came early between 1907 and 1909, so many people were less reluctant to settle on the sandy bank of the river. By 1911, 360 miles south of the forward rebel positions, prospectors for the Union Minière and Tanganyika Concessions were writing back to the Kambove office about the "disturbed state" of the Luba country.[15] In addition to insurgents, "marauding rubber traders" and agents of the newly formed Bourse du Travail du Katanga were scouring the country. Armed officials of the state—BTK labor recruiters, CSK policemen, and soldiers from the Force Publique—poured into central and northern Katanga from all directions.[16] In his bigoted but inimitable way, H. G. Robins, our prospector friend, put his slant on the events of the day in a letter to Sir Robert Williams in December 1910:

> There would be very great difficulty indeed, in getting any native within a wide radius of the "Star," more especially as the Smelter Plant will shortly be in course of erection and will require a considerable number of natives over and above those required for the mine.
>
> I believe that Waluba now get 10 shillings per month and their food at the "Star," therefore labour would be just as expensive or more so taking into account its quality for my work—than labour I could get in Rhodesia. I hear that there are a considerable number of private Rubber Traders and other irresponsible persons now traveling about between the "Star" and the Kasai River, and I expect that the natives are fully employed and being rapidly spoilt by Greeks, Dagos and other like characters.[17]

The insurgents had drawn a thin red line halfway through the center of the province, from Mutombo Mukulu to the headwaters of the Lubilash River. But after 1911 fewer people crossed over the line into the rebel zones. By 1912, in the face of the military buildup, Kabongo and his forces surrendered and sued for a separate peace. As a result, the head tax did not increase in Kabongo's lands and in the Yeke areas to the south. But in the Lomami and Tanganika-Moero districts the tax rose by 40 percent, to 6 and 10 Congolese francs, respectively.[18] Yet tax payment was not more forthcoming in any of the three regions. The villages were not completely at rest. Despite Kabongo's surrender, a sense of alarm persisted among local administrators and labor recruiters. For example, the BTK petitioned the colonial administration several times to allow it to impose its own special tax in the regions in question. Its requests were denied, however, since the local government did not have complete control over the BTK's activities.[19] The political situation in the center of the province remained uncertain.[20]

The state bore down on the peasantry in other ways as well. For example, 12.50 Congolese francs was the selling price of a 25-kilogram bag of locally produced salt.[21] Out of this selling price the African producer, who spent a large portion of the dry season and the first 1½ months of the rainy season producing five or six such bags, received 1.25 francs per bag, or roughly a week's wages for a porter or bearer.[22] Prior to 1907 salt in African measures had been exchanged for rifles, hoes, axes, and cloth; but as the state began to enforce cash equivalencies, African producers began to exchange salt for rubber. They would then exchange rubber for trade goods and rifles with Mbundu and mulatto traders in the far west and British traders on the Lubilash River and in Tanganika-Moero.[23] The peasantry saw such stopgap measures as a means to protect what the Russian economist Chayanov would have called the "effort price" associated with the production of items like salt. As the state's exactions began to exceed the peasant's subsistence threshold while also undermining simple commodity production, a significant portion of the peasantry found it less costly to rebel against the government than pay taxes or work for wages. Yet African resistance to specific state policies was not always tantamount to insurrection. The administration's strategy of fragmenting the larger chieftaincies was a kind of insurance against its becoming so.

Nature underwrote the unjust policies of the regime with crop failure, smallpox, and sleeping sickness during the long dry seasons of 1910, 1911, and 1912. Men and women who were left exposed by the deflated agrarian economy piled up in the chieftaincies and unclaimed open country like so many pieces of kindling wood — ready to be ignited by the slightest provocation from government-appointed chiefs, territorial administrators, or labor recruiters. The colonial administration ducked the issue by referring to those who departed as *flottantes* in official correspondence.[24] The largest segment of the peasantry in Lomami, Tanganika-Moero, and central Katanga remained on the land, however, particularly where the administration had not displaced local political leaders. Many such peasants sold food and palm oil on the work sites and had come to appreciate the value of money. But given the hardships of the two previous long dry seasons, labor impressment, and the new taxes, real prosperity and well-being remained elusive for the peasantry. Consequently, tax riots and other instances of unrest often swept through the villages.[25] The chiefs did not attempt to quell the unrest, since their control over labor and tributary revenue was also threatened by the new measures. As mobilization for the First World War began, the chance of combination became less remote among a restive but increasingly money-minded peasantry, the "floating population," and disgruntled chiefs.[26]

Of all the recalcitrant peoples, the Songye and their paramount chieftain Lumpungu put up the most effective resistance to the new measures.[27] Like the Yeke and Luba-Sanga near the work sites at Kambove, the Songye selectively catered for the food and manpower needs of the Europeans. By 1912, the Songye capital at Kabinda had also become the capital for the territorial government of Lomami.[28] Yet Lumpungu's power continued to extend deep into western Tanganika-Moero, and the colonial government was unclear about how to limit it.[29] Confusion over Lumpungu's intentions was pervasive within the administration. Even the physical landscape of Kabinda reflected the uncertainty of the political situation: Lumpungu's redoubt was on top of a mountain from which he and his lieutenants could look down on the Belgian fort and courthouse.[30] In 1917 Henri Segaert, a former magistrate of the territorial tribunal of Kabinda, assessed the test of wills between the Belgians and Lumpungu:

> The native quarter of Kabinda is right beside the white residences. Here the paramount chief Lumpungu still reigns as a quasi-absolute monarch. At Kabinda he presides over the destiny of almost 15,000 souls and most of the chiefs between the Lubilash (Sankuru), Lomami and the fifth parallel continue to pay tribute to him.
>
> Lumpungu is now an old man. He has lost one eye in the course of his stormy career, but he continues to look out on the world with a face that is a mask of energy, strength and even cruelty—characteristics that have shaped his indomitable will and led him to power. Presently his influence is still great, and one must resort to diplomacy in dealing with him, particularly since his racial and personal eccentricities have occasionally made it difficult for those charged with maintaining good and, for the moment, indispensable relations with this black sovereign. . . . Quite recently, for example, he furnished 1,000 military porters and a large amount of provisions and food-stuffs during the Tanganyika campaign.[31]

Having risen to power during the uncertain times of the Swahili invasion of the eastern Congo, Lumpungu had comprehended what the Belgians had accomplished, even if they did not: that although African guerrilla forces continued to have a certain nuisance value, the Belgians had quashed the stiffest resistance to their rule. Mobilization for the First World War, the northward expansion of the rail line and the mining sites, and the advent of the 1918 Spanish influenza pandemic gave the government a decided logistical advantage over the rebels.[32] Lumpungu was therefore the key to both the resistance and the peace. Kasongo Nyembo needed him in order to squeeze the Belgian forces between a set of pincers from the north and the west. The Belgians needed him in order to secure the north for labor recruitment and the expansion of the rail line. Lumpungu waited and chose neither. After Kabongo's surrender, Lumpungu was no longer in a position to join the rebellion, although he probably remained in communication with Kasongo Nyembo. Nor could he completely give in to the Belgians, despite his public declarations of loyalty and his hosting of the Belgian king in 1917.[33] Consequently, between 1912 and 1917 he attempted to bring as much of Tanganika-Moero as he could under his control, so that he could monopolize labor recruitment in that territory as well.[34]

Lumpungu thought the Belgians would choose a peace with conditions. They did not. Instead they chose, through the agency of the BTK and with guns and taxes, to continue to make war on a more or less pacified population in their relentless quest for labor. The future, at least the foreseeable portion of it, belonged to them.

THE WAGE QUESTION AND THE SEARCH FOR LABOR

Beneath the question of effective Belgian sovereignty lay the more complex one of how prospective workers were to be recruited and remunerated for their labor. As the most populous upcountry regions were brought to heel, the problem of labor recruitment and supply began to loom large in the thinking of government officials and the local management of the Union Minière and the rail line. Moreover, Elisabethville, the provincial capital and hub of the nascent mining industry, was beginning to expand.[35]

In 1907 Elisabethville had been a mere geographical expression which was overshadowed by the prospecting operations farther north at Kambove. But with the completion of the rail line coming from the south and the arrival of the first locomotive from Capetown on 27 September 1910, what had once been a mere beachhead against British influence became a town of 5,000 people.[36] Merchants hawked everything from pen knives and prospecting tents to women's underpants in the town's rutted streets. And as machinery, building materials, engineers, white miners, and prostitutes converged on it, Elisabethville's need for African labor grew by leaps and bounds. By 1911, a year after the arrival of the railroad, the Union Minière's Lubumbashi smelter works transformed over 9,000 tons of copper ore into 1,000 tons of blister copper or matte.[37]

Despite its growing sophistication, some features of life in Elisabethville remained unleavened: The municipal ordinance of 1912, which gave the *cité indigène*, or African quarter, a legal existence, was little more than a segregation ordinance that sought to stop death and disease just short of the European residential area. Serious gaps existed in the aggregate estimates of the African adult male working population, which ranged from 800 to 3,000. The only other outposts of European authority beyond the places of work were the police and the courts. And since the flow of labor was so discontinuous, Africans took and were grudgingly obliged a large amount of social space to reconstruct their lives.[38]

The colonial government attempted to engage the labor problems by forming the BTK, the parastatal labor-recruiting agency mentioned earlier. The BTK sought to meet Katanga's manpower needs with labor on-the-cheap.[39] Private labor recruiters—of which Robert Williams' Tanganyika Concessions Limited and the Portuguese Correa Freres were the most formidable—tended to frustrate the BTK's efforts, however, by offering higher wages and by hunting outside the confines of the Belgian Congo for laborers. By November 1911, for example, Tanganyika Concessions delivered 1,000 African recruits from Northern Rhodesia's Luapula-Mweru and North-Western provinces to the Union Minière's Elisabethville installation.[40] In turn, these recruits were joined by their brethren who, lured by tales of high wages and no tax collectors, crossed the border on their own initiative.[41] Although the British government stipulated that African laborers from Northern Rhodesia could not work north of the Star of the Congo Mine given the prevalence of sleeping sickness, hundreds were shifted to the Kambove mine and work sites farther north during 1912. By 1913 the BTK and Tanganyika Concessions were locked in bitter competition over these laborers once they completed their first six-month contract.[42]

There was a high premium attached to laborers from Northern Rhodesia: A British inspector of natives from Northern Rhodesia and three roving British vice consuls were part of the bargain. If these officials chose to be particularly energetic about observing working conditions—as did Inspectors H. G. Jones and H. Waterall and Vice Consul Campbell between 1911 and 1913—they could become inadvertent tribunes for African workers and egregious irritants for prospective employers.[43] As early as 5 September 1912 the government was circularizing employers about too many African workers, both Congolese and Northern Rhodesian, appearing to transfer effortlessly from one employer to another because of the intervention of the British inspectors and hastily drawn-up work permits which did not specify a given worker's place of origin or previous employment.[44] By the end of 1913 the Union Minière was so dissatisfied with the existing arrangements that it threatened to withhold its tax allotment to the government of Northern Rhodesia.[45]

The BTK appeared incapable of following up on its inherent advantage — an advantage that was further enhanced by the labor shortages caused by the opening of new work sites north of Elisabethville shortly after 1912. For example, the BTK retained a fixed wage rate of six to eight Congolese francs a month (somewhere between 40¢ and 45¢ in the American currency of the day) which did not vary from one kind of work to another.[46] Prospectors and rubber merchants often paid much more, and in hard currency, usually British sterling.[47] Coercion was therefore an important, though implicit, feature of the BTK's recruitment policies.

News of the BTK's armed forays caused many Africans to flee their homes before the recruiters arrived. Between 1913 and 1917 thousands of such refugees turned up in the rail and construction camps on the route between Elisabethville and Kambove.[48] They were the other, more precipitous result of the BTK's coercive recruiting tactics. Like the majority of Africans recruited by the BTK, most of them originated from a 27,000-square-mile area between the town of Pweto at the northern tip of Lake Mweru and the Lualaba River. What happened here determined the fate of thousands of Africans throughout Katanga until the close of the war.

Around the end of June the armed columns of BTK recruiters would start out from the government posts at Pweto and Kiambi.[49] If there were no obstacles such as rocks, boulders, or large trees, which would have to be blasted out of the way with dynamite, the columns could travel up to 14 miles a day, wading through the high grass and fording the muddy beds of dried up streams. In the back of their minds, as they scoured the country for men, would be the prospect of reaching the Lualaba River before the rains came; for with the commencement of the rains small streams would become swollen torrents and footpaths would disappear. All forward movement would cease because the rail line had not reached the river.[50]

If the BTK's agents had in fact met their quota of recruits, transportation to the work sites would have been that much easier once the river attained its normal level. If the quotas were not met before the rainy season, however, recruitment would become all the more difficult, for few men could be urged without threats and force to leave their crops and villages once the rains started. Timing was everything, and sometimes the columns could only inch along the paths. Villagers would often meet the recruiters before they reached a settlement with offerings of fruit, vegetables, and wild game, so that there would be no reason or opportunity for the column to stop and take a head count of the able-bodied men or cast roving, lascivious glances at the women and young girls. By September, a month before the rains came in a normal year, the recruiters would be desperate if they had not acquired enough men. Moreover, the land would be closing in on them as peasant farmers began to burn the forest and the bush for fertilizer in anticipation of the rains (if the previous year had been a bad one, peasants would start burning the forest as early as August or July). Chiefs and headmen would be hectored and women and children held in stockades until men were forthcoming. Such license often turned into murder, rape, and assault.[51]

The BTK's methods were plainly brutal and inefficient. As it dug in at its new headquarters at Kikondja, close to the Lualaba River and halfway between Kabongo's former chieftaincy and Tanganika-Moero, the number of refugees increased. Many proved refractory to the demands of colonial officials and potential employers. Few came specifically to work on the rail line or the newly opened mines.[52] Nor were they unmindful of the hazards of wage labor, particularly those to life and limb, or the choices that could be had among different employers. Wages had something to do with this, since most African laborers recruited by the BTK in 1916–17 were still on the 1911 wage rate, whereas Africans who made their own arrangements with either the rail line or the Union Minière were assured of a monthly wage of somewhere between 11 and 25 Congolese francs or the equivalent in sounder British currency.[53]

After 1917 the BTK's efforts to procure labor for the Union Minière and the rail lines inside Katanga were overshadowed by those of Tanganyika Concessions and by those of the Portuguese firm, Correa Freres. Moreover, as the rail line crept toward the BTK's headquarters at Kikondja, the agency became no more than a client of the rail line and its chief supplier of labor.[54] Similarly, in 1917, when the Union Minière bought most of the rail company's rolling stock and lent it a sum of money equal to its operating capital for the previous six years, both the rail line and the BTK were reduced to little more than instruments of the mining company's aspirations (see Table 1.1).[55]

By the close of the First World War the BTK's operations were confined to the more sparsely populated and removed areas of Katanga.[56] Yet it had helped to uproot the precolonial agrarian economy. As a result, the northern districts were primed for the advent of the mining industry well in advance of the rail line. The rail line did sunder the larger upcountry chieftaincies, but only after the BTK had emptied them of a good portion of their population. The rail line did replace the Lualaba River as the center of labor recruiting in Katanga, but only after the BTK had driven a large portion of the population of

Lomami and Tanganika-Moero south and west of the river. From the African vantage point, the world had been turned upside down.

THE POLITICAL ECONOMY OF LABOR SUPPLY:
CASUAL VERSUS PERMANENT LABOR

The Union Minière was not discouraged by the initial setbacks in the acquisition of a permanent workforce. Between 1907 and 1917 the permanent component of the Union Minière's African workforce — which, in the instance of the Lubumbashi foundry and the Star of the Congo Mine, had come largely from Nyasaland and the two Rhodesias — operated within an infrastructure created by casual and short-term contract labor from Katanga itself. Casual laborers did the basic development work at the mines and often with their bare hands dug out the rich outcropping of copper from the rockface of the open-pit mines. They acted as body guards, domestic servants, and orderlies; they dug ditches and furrows that became rail lines, sewers, and the foundations of buildings; they carried loads of food and machinery in regions where sleeping sickness, malaria, smallpox, and the absence of a rail line made conveyance by any other means virtually impossible. As Table 1.1 shows, their numbers grew rapidly, and, in so doing, powerfully mediated the process of industrialization; for the means of production and the division of labor did not yet anticipate increased mechanization despite the enthusiasm of Belgian banks and the feats of British engineers.[57]

By 1914 thousands of Africans flocked to the workers' camps for three- to six-month stretches. Despite the tremendous need for labor, there was no attempt to ensure the health of such laborers. Men who had escaped from sleeping sickness, malaria, or yellow fever in the hinterland were scourged by dysentery, typhoid, pneumonia, tick fever, tuberculosis, and influenza in the crowded and unsanitary conditions of the labor camps and the work sites. Thousands died — slowly at first, and then in great waves; for after 1916 the expansion of the mining industry overshadowed the construction of the provincial rail line while long dry seasons caused a conjuncture between downturns in the business cycle and a failing agrarian economy.[58] Unable to replenish their physical strength or increase their numbers through biological reproduction, numerous recruits languished in the workers' camps, while their rural kin slowly starved to death.[59]

The Union Minière, in hegemonic fashion, was beginning to subordinate all other economic interests to its own. In 1914, for example,

Table 1.1. Number and Percentage of BTK Recruits Employed in the Mining and
Rail Industries and as Casual Labor in Katanga, 1914–1921

	Actual Number of BTK Recruits	Percentage of the Total Number of Recruits
MINING INDUSTRY		
1914–15	8,000	35
1915–16	20,000	68
1916–17	36,700	70
1917–18	29,800	63
1918–19	25,500	65
1919–20	36,300	55
1920–21	42,000	47
RAIL INDUSTRY		
1914–15	10,000	43
1915–16	7,600	26
1916–17	9,150	18
1917–18	12,600	27
1918–19	12,800	33
1919–20	22,800	34
1920–21	40,700	45
CASUAL LABOR		
1914–15	5,200	22
1915–16	1,750	6
1916–17	6,150	12
1917–18	4,800	10
1918–19	950	2
1919–20	7,800	11
1920–21	7,600	8

Sources: AA, MOI no. 52 (3555), La Main d'oeuvre indigène, 11 juin 1921, Elisabeth-ville; TC/UM, 64, Annexe E, Chemin de Fer du Katanga (report on negotiations).

the rail line had laid 154 miles of track on a north-south axis, largely to service the needs of the mining company.[60] By 1916 the Compagnie du Chemin de Fer du Bas-Congo au Katanga (BCK) purchased new rolling stock worth 400,000 British pounds to deal specifically with the increased output at the Union Minière. Three hundred hauling cars and 20 locomotives constituted most of the new stock. In 1917, in order to prevent an increase in the freight rates, the Union Minière initiated a policy of paying the Chemin de Fer du Katanga (CFK) a subsidy of 60 francs for every ton of copper ore produced. Later in the year the Union Minière purchased a considerable amount of stock in the rail company and began to influence the rail lines' corporate policies directly, thus solving its problem of increasing freight rates altogether. By 1918 the rail company and the Union Minière arrived at special rates for the transport of ore, fuel, metals, machinery, timber, firewood, and food for African workers — the 60-franc bonus subsidy was dropped.[61]

Investing in the railway's growth gave the Union Minière a concrete means to consolidate and speed up the process of primary accumulation. And by 1917, the era of speculative investment in Katanga's mineral wealth had drawn to a close. At about the same time some of the smaller mines began to yield a considerable amount of ore for smelting and electrochemical concentration. Yet the Star and Kambove continued to be the mainstays of production until the opening of the underground Prince Léopold Mine at Kipushi in 1922.[62] Kambove's importance grew throughout the war. As of 1914 the relatively easy transport of ore from Kambove to the Lubumbashi foundry, combined with the expansion at the Star and the smaller mines, boosted production to dizzying heights. Between 1911 and 1914 the production of smelted blister copper went from a mere 998 to 10,772 tons. By 1918 the Union Minière was producing well over 20,000 tons of copper. This was all the more remarkable given the infant stage of the industry and chronic labor problems (see Table 1.1). Nevertheless, certain problems persisted. Derailments were frequent, and north of Kambove the rail lines were especially unsuited for large ore shipments.[63] But the problem of the rail lines was overshadowed by the more serious problems of labor shortages and the acquisition of a healthy and tractable workforce. Despite the transition from a particularly brutal mercantile capitalism to a burgeoning industrial one, a self-reproducing workforce remained elusive.[64]

INSIDE THE CHARNEL:
THE WORK SITES OF THE UNION MINIÈRE, 1914–1918

> One has the distinct impression that the administration (UMHK) is not too concerned about the health of those blacks who are no longer able to work, but in a previous period were a fundamental factor of the company's prosperity.
>
> Dr. Paul Polidori, a doctor for the provincial government of Katanga in a report on the sanitary situation at the Star of the Congo Mine, November 1916[65]

I am a Muluba and we Baluba do not do such work
(cleaning latrines and sanitary pits), for we would die
instantly. Moreover, as you can see, I am still ailing.
I went to explain all this to Tshanga-Tshanga [the
camp manager: the term means "disturber" in
Chiluba], but he beat me with a club for my troubles
and had a *capita* box my ears.

Lukwata, a worker at the Union
Minière's Star of the Congo Mine,
recounting his thoughts about work
to the king's barrister (*procureur du
roi*) shortly after an epidemic of
typhoid fever, 5 May 1917[66]

Between 1915 and 1919 the Union Minière absorbed over 60 percent
of the available African wage labor in Katanga, although its share of
recruits from Katanga itself fell sharply, going from 94 to 26 percent
between 1914 and 1916. The percentage of Africans from Katanga
working on the mines was often buttressed, however, by the sorely
pressed casual laborers of small independent contractors. With the
advent of the war an even greater percentage of casual labor was composed of Africans who simply slipped through the net of the BTK and
hired on directly with the mining company.[67]

The small percentage of Congolese workers belied their importance
to the Union Minière during the war period—a period when the company's profit margins rested largely on its ability to extract more of
the rich copper oxide from the open-pit mines at Ruashi and Kambove with a minimum of machinery. African casuals from Katanga,
as well as longer-term workers from Angola, composed the ill-starred
base of the Union Minière's expanding workforce.[68] After 1916, wages
for these workers did increase, but failed to keep pace with wartime
inflation.[69] For example, *capitas*, or "boss boys," at the larger mines
would often impose a one-franc surcharge for an adequate weekly portion of meat. Workers at those mines often spent as much as 80 percent of their wages on meat. Also, workers employed by private contractors could not be buried in the mining company's cemetery unless
the contractor paid the mining company a fee of 25 francs. Few contractors were much interested in paying such a fee.[70] Consequently,
a cynical policy of periodically cutting the cost of housing, food, clothing, and equipment for African workers became an implicit general
rule, even though the statutes of the mining company often expressly
forbade such procedure. High accident and mortality rates and flight
followed in this policy's wake, since so many workers at the bottom
rung of the company's workforce were not covered by its statutes.

A series of local epidemics – Elisabethville in 1912, the Star in 1916, and Kambove and Likasi in 1917 – provided the dress rehearsal for the terrible charnel that accompanied the end of the war.[71] In 1914 two doctors, André Boigelot and Paul Polidori, began two epidemiological studies of the *cité indigène* of Elisabethville and the Union Minière work sites at Kambove, Star of the Congo, and Lubumbashi. The separate findings of Boigelot, a company doctor for the Union Minière and a close collaborator of the Bureau of Industry and Commerce, and Polidori, an assistant medical officer in the bureau, were extremely disconcerting for the provincial administration, the BTK, and the Union Minière. Polidori's study was completed in 1915, but never experienced widespread public circulation. Boigelot, who began work early in 1914 at Lubumbashi and Kambove, made his findings public only after the beginning of the 1918 Spanish influenza epidemic. For obvious reasons, Boigelot stopped just short of an outright condemnation of the mining company. On the other hand, Polidori's report provoked a series of judicial inquiries about the living conditions in the workers' camps toward the end of the war.[72] Little in terms of medical policy actually changed.[73]

The worst of the local epidemics took place at Kambove. Adequate drinking water was a serious problem there throughout the war.[74] According to one industrial inspector on tour at the mine in October 1916, one pipe, which threatened to burst at any moment, was used to provide water for five steam shovels, two locomotives, and blasting and drilling equipment in the mine itself. The workers – 1,560 of them at the time – were obliged to line up before the workday commenced to get water from this same pipe and spigot. During the dry season the majority of the workers were compelled to rely on stagnant pools and narrow streams of muddy water at the bottom of riverbeds for drinking water. Enteritis and dysentery were the immediate results. Typhoid followed closely behind. Between 15 September and 15 October 1916, for example, 20 workers died from a combination of pneumonia, dysentery, and enteritis, and 38 more exhibited the symptoms of one or all of these ailments.[75]

Pneumonia, an indicator of overwork, was the major illness at Kambove, as it was at all the Union Minière work sites.[76] Although figures for Kambove were notoriously unreliable – none for any illness was reported for the first half of 1916, for example – the narrative evidence from the period clearly states that pneumonia killed off more workers at Kambove than any other work site. One interim report suggests that as many as 55 men per 1,000 died of pneumonia at Kambove in 1916. On an average, more than 38 men per 1,000 contracted pneumonia at some point during their stay with the company. At Lubum-

Table 1.2. Number of Men Ill at the Three Main Union Minière Sites in 1915–1916,[a] by Disease

	Lubumbashi		Star of the Congo		Kambove[b]
	1915–16	1916[c]	1915–16	1916[c]	1916[c]
Pneumonia	417	261	187	188	106
Phthisis and consumptive chest ailments	73	42	267	1	269
Dysentery and enteritis	202	251	21	15	53
Diarrhea	69	171	120	0	69
Typhoid	161	249	2	3	5
Malaria	10	5	4	–	9
"Mild" influenza	1,155	359	333	36	140
"Acute" influenza	1	4	4	–	11
"Fevers"	766	145	1,131	489	245
Syphilis	43	9	6	–	5
Scurvy	–	–	–	2	4
"Acute" exhaustion	39	120	13	–	–
Undiagnosed ailments	1,619	1,250	185	30	289

Source: AA, MOI 50 (3559), Service de l'Inspection de l'Industrie (section V Surveillance), 26 septembre 1916.

[a]The data are broken down for the two years involved by the following units of time: the 1915–16 column includes data for the last half of 1915 and the first half of 1916; the 1916 column includes data for the last half of 1916.

[b]No data are available for the 1915–16 period at the Kambove site.

[c]Mean number of workers at the three work sites in the last half of 1916: Lubumbashi – 2,142; Star of the Congo – 1,124; Kambove – 1,762.

bashi 677 men, or roughly 33 percent, of an average workforce of 2,000 men contracted pneumonia in 1916; at the Star 375 men, or 21 percent, of the workforce were stricken.[77] Between July and October 1916 an ever-increasing number of them, particularly those from villages between the towns of Pweto and Sampwe, chose to abscond.[78] These conditions were a result of machinery being valued more highly than the workers themselves. Dust and silicosis also contributed to the spread of pneumonia. The workers could endure such conditions for only so long.

Work and working conditions also contributed to workers' decisions to leave the camps. Workers rested for only 1½ days every two weeks at Kambove. No one escaped night work—which meant that many men worked two shifts in a given week. For every two weeks on the day shift there was one week of night work. The night shift began at 6:00 in the evening, when darkness falls on equatorial and southern Africa in one fell swoop. It ended in darkness as well—at 3:00 in the morning, three hours before daybreak. In 1916 the degree of artificial light that could have been mustered on the night shift would not have

Table 1.3. Mortality at the Three Main Union Minière Work Sites for Congolese and Foreign African Workers in the Last Half of 1916

	Number of Workers	Pneumonia		Dysentery		Other Causes[a]		Accidents		Total
		Cong.	For.	Cong.	For.	Cong.	For.	Cong.	For.	
		LUBUMBASHI								
July	2,399	3	2	0	0	0	0	0	0	5
August	2,351	1	2	0	0	0	0	0	0	3
September	2,249	5	4	0	0	1	0	0	0	10
October	1,854	5	19	0	3	3	1	0	0	31
November	1,883	2	1	3	6	3	0	0	0	15
December	2,116	1	10	4	6	1	2	0	0	24
										88
		STAR OF THE CONGO								
July	1,302	0	3	0	0	1	0	0	0	4
August	1,303	4	7	0	0	0	0	0	0	11
September	1,356	1	12	0	0	0	0	0	0	13
October	979	7	44	0	0	1	0	0	0	52
November	790	0	28	0	6	1	0	0	0	35
December	1,015	3	7	0	3	2	0	0	0	15
										130
		KAMBOVE								
July	1,847	7	1	1	0	8	1	0	0	18
August	1,935	4	0	0	0	4	0	0	0	8
September	1,904	4	0	2	0	7	1	0	0	14
October	1,542	14	3	0	0	19	4	0	0	40
November	1,644	1	0	1	0	5	0	0	0	7
December	1,699	0	0	1	1	2	2	0	1	7
										94

Source: AA, MOI 50 (3559), Service de l'Inspection de l'Industrie (section V Surveillance), 26 septembre 1916.

[a]Cholera, typhoid, etc.

made much impact on the darkness; for one of the factors holding up underground operations at Kambove was the dearth of electricity. Industrial accidents due to obscured vision combined with those resulting from fatigue. They made for an unremittingly grim picture of injuries to fingers, hands, feet, and eyes.[79]

By October 1918, 1,150 African deaths in the camps of the private contractors who supplied the Union Minière with supplementary hands were followed by approximately 1,100 instances of absconding by African workers.[80] Similar figures were amassed for the rail lines and the BTK. When the Spanish influenza epidemic reached the mining company's work sites at the end of October, health and social conditions were already very nearly at their worst.[81] Conditions declined further by the end of 1918. Work stopped for an entire month at Lubumbashi and the Star. By January 1919, 24 white workers had died from the epidemic, according to official sources. The toll of African deaths was reckoned in the thousands. Conflict between British camp managers and Belgian foremen on the work sites reached a boiling point. The implications of the escalating conflict were not lost on the African workers. As one company official put it:

The conditions under which they (the Africans) were working whereby the native had one master in the compound and another on the works, with a certain amount of uncertainty as to where the actual responsibility lay for any given condition, resulted at times in conditions which were undoubtedly not good for either the native or the work.[82]

Even where the worst conditions obtained, workers weighed the total set of circumstances before they decided to flee. For example, most of the nightsoilers, or latrine cleaners, at Kambove were Lozi from Barotseland. Their work directly exposed them to enteritis and dysentery—so much so that they were sometimes literally wading in blood and feces. This showed up in the mortality rates for the Lozi, which were higher than any other ethnic group in relation to their numbers. Yet they were the least inclined to flee, since they were over 200 miles from home.[83] In short, there was no direct, month-to-month correlation between mortality and illness and the decision to abscond. Such decisions were cumulative. The conditions of work, the distance between a given work site and their homes, whether their families were with them or not, as well as the contours of morbidity, entered into the workers' calculations. The workers did not rush blindly at the prospect of absconding.

What the workers themselves thought of these horrible living and working conditions surfaced occasionally in the reports of the industrial inspectors. Many of the inspectors would be accompanied by an African *greffier*, or clerk, who took down testimony in French and also in Swahili if the nature of the testimony seemed to warrant it. Of the 180 workers interviewed by Inspector S. Claessens at the end of October 1916 at Kambove, the testimony of the *capita* Mwanza Kashiri was the most revealing. Mwanza, who spoke on behalf of 140 workers from the Sampwe region and whose testimony was taken down partly in Swahili, said this:

The work here is hard. Moreover, the Europeans strike us with their hands and feet. When they discover that we have managed to acquire as much as

one loaf of bread beyond what we are rationed, they will refuse to check off
our ration ticket. Consequently, we are hungry and cannot work well. . . .
   The hospital treats disease with forced labor—fetching water and firewood
with which to boil it. Instead of receding, disease is, in fact, spreading. Miracu-
lously only one of us [1 out of the 140] has died. Longo-Longo [Jules Draux,
a BTK recruiter] did not tell us that we were to be hired for a year; he must
have written that in the little booklet [*livret du travail*] that we cannot read.
And he promised to return us to our village before the maize was a fifth of
a centimeter high.[84]

Mwanza's view of work at the mines was borne out by subsequent
testimony: Work was bad, but the hospital was worse; for it melded
work, punishment, and death into one horrifying and fatal experience. Workers were fixed on the designation of absconding from the
hospital as *se sauver* rather than *déserter*, when they could give direct
testimony. Such nuances—in some cases literally matters of life and
death—were only occasionally inscribed in the written record.[85]
   The grim working conditions of the African workers did not
improve in the years immediately following the war. The workers
were bound to a regime of long hours, back-breaking work, disease,
and low wages.[86] The permanence of the mining industry was conditioned therefore by two factors: the ability of the Union Minière to
weather the chaotic conditions of wartime business activity and, in
turn, to set the pace of Katanga's industrialization; and its ability to
increase both the actual and potential supply of African labor by deflat-
ing the economic carrying capacity of the surrounding countryside.
Violence and coercion carried out by the state and private labor
recruiters were indispensable for the latter factor, while passivity on
the part of the African workers, particularly with regard to wages,
was needed for the former. The mining company paid a high price
for this kind of control. Yet it did not come in a form that suited the
company. The result was an era of labor shortages for all industrial
enterprises in Katanga until 1927–28.[87]

CHAPTER TWO

Obstacles to Growth: The Union Minière in the Period Immediately Following the First World War

THE POSTWAR CRISIS AND THE PRODUCTIVE PROCESS

At the end of the First World War, Louis Franck, the Belgian minister of colonies, and other liberals in the Belgian government saw the Congo as a means to furnish Belgium with the industrial raw materials needed to rebuild its industrial economy.[1] The war and the German occupation caused widespread destruction to the physical plant of Belgian industry. The absence of returns on foreign investments or their complete loss further hurt the metropolitan economy. Speculation on stocks of raw materials and manufactured goods was widespread. Monetary problems and inflation caused prices and the cost of paper money to soar. Peace was followed by recession and eventual disillusionment with stopgap measures such as the Locarno Treaty which were designed to prevent economic collapse.[2] This chaotic situation in almost every sphere of economic life was capped by the postwar government's administrative and fiscal disorganization.[3]

The mining community of Katanga was fashioned in the aftermath of the chaos. The problem of the 1920s was not one of reconstructing the boomtown atmosphere of the interwar period, but rather of making industrial production a more integral feature of colonial society. The Ministry of Colonies was charged with altering the physical infrastructure of Katanga with an eye toward solving this problem. But the ministry's efforts were weakened by the refusal of the metropolitan government to match its enthusiasm for administrative change with more money for the colonial budget.[4] The metropolitan and colonial governments provided a few elements of an infrastructure for industrial growth in Katanga — electrification increased somewhat and there was talk of extending the rail line—but they were hardly enough to meet the expanded needs and expectations of the Union Minière.[5] The new mining technology, which came in the wake of the recession, was also a mixed blessing. At the Lubumbashi foundry works, and at some of the more mechanized mines like Kipushi, it became the catalyst for an ominous speed-up in the work routine.[6] More than easing the workload or improving the quality of output, the new furnaces, smelters, generators, and time-keeping machines gave rise to a growing number of African and white supervisors who, in addition to minding machines, were continuously on the lookout for ways to harness the pace of human labor to that of the machines.[7]

All this gave industrial growth a rather lopsided posture. At Lubumbashi virtually every machine worked at twice its normal capacity for a little over a decade—from 1917 to 1928.[8] About half of Lubumbashi's output was in the much inferior but marketable form of blister copper rather than ingots. The more modern refining plants at Panda and Shituru, which were completed in 1924, produced considerably less than overworked Lubumbashi. Consequently, expenditure for the repair of machinery at Lubumbashi was much larger than the maintenance costs for the newer refinery and leaching works.[9] Quality was altogether secondary to output.[10]

Even after global copper prices fell precipitously after the war, greater output and rapid labor turnover continued to determine company strategy.[11] The frequency of labor turnover meant that the question of how much freedom should be extended to African workers in bargaining with their employers became central to the proceedings of the local committees of the BTK, the Provincial Council, and the metropolitan Commissions du Travail.[12] One segment of Katanga's business and government leaders attempted to dissolve the Civil Code and reinstate corporal punishment and forced labor as a means of proscribing what the workers could do on their own behalf.[13] Camp managers, foremen, and labor contractors violated the code on a daily basis. Such violations demonstrated just how ineffectual the code was. Consequently, the attempt at legal reinstitution of corporal punishment was merely a formalization of an extant means of social control. Both the mining company and the state were concerned to contain the African workforce within well-defined limits, while assuming only the most inconsequential role in its reproduction.[14]

In tandem with the state's efforts to constrain the African workers, the Union Minière selectively borrowed South Africa's conceptions of mine and labor management.[15] Given the dearth of Belgian capital invested in the mines before 1924 and the unfavorable position of the Belgian franc against the British pound after 1919, the mining company and the provincial government were particularly eager to impose the new conceptions of management on that portion of the workforce that came from the British colonies to the south. The "franc crisis" had caused the wage rate of these workers to rise at an alarming pace—alarming, at least, from the vantage point of employers and tax collectors on both sides of the border.[16] Meanwhile real wages for Congolese workers were cut almost in half, while prices for manufactured goods rose almost 800 percent.[17] Following the Rand's lead, the Union Minière began to replace the smaller brick, straw, and iron dwellings with the dreaded Orenstein dormitories, or "bachelors quarters."[18] Each of these structures housed about 60 men. Pitched on a cement foundation and smelling of tar and lime, they resembled outhouses more than living quarters. Despite the cheapness and larger size of these dormitories, diseases were transmitted more readily. Rather than mitigating absenteeism and morbidity, the dormitories further aggravated them.[19]

What the Union Minière failed to realize was that the South African compound system in its most pristine form could work well only when there were no labor shortages—a situation that was rare, if not nonexistent, on most of the industrial work sites of southern Africa at the time. Moreover, the timing of the Union Minière's appropriation of the South African model was some 20 years too late, for it was this precise model that brought nearly 100,000 African mineworkers on the Rand out on strike between July 1918 and February 1919 and precipitated the Rand Rebellion of the white mineworkers in 1922.[20] Of course the various strata of provincial leadership, including the Union Minière's local executive, disagreed over the parameters of the postwar measures and whether one could really expect greater output from the African workers without combining physical coercion with higher living standards and wages. Whether to proceed on the basis of some kind of social engineering or not was a very open-ended question throughout the early and mid-1920s.[21] Two excerpts—one from an editorial that appeared in the bimonthly Notre Colonie on 15 November 1919 and the other from the second version of a speech given in 1923 and 1927 by the Apostolic prefect of Elisabethville and sometime bête noire of both the provincial administration and the Union Minière Monsignor Jean Felix de Hemptinne—illustrate the two extremes of official white opinion on this question. First, the editorial excerpt of 1919:

We have requisitioned porters, soldiers and workers from the native. The generation whose birth we have witnessed and the one that followed it have suffered terribly from the social and economic dislocation caused by our occupation. Future generations must collect some of the fruits of their fathers' suffering. They must enjoy, at least in part, some of the promised improvements.[22]

And then there was de Hemptinne with a bit of crude obfuscation:

I conclude, Monsieur le Procureur General, by recommending that you look closely at the Union Minière's new dispensation — one which is characterized by an unfashionable paternalism, by weakness and by measures that will do nothing but spoil the native. Little gifts of candy and cigarettes are given. Is this the kind of administration befitting a great industrial enterprise? Is this the wave of the future? In my view, this kind of regime will end with gunfire and bloodshed. In order to lead men, one must have a precise sense of their mentality.[23]

De Hemptinne's contemporaries were not to be outdone by him. "Everyone knows that the blacks detest work," declared Marcel Dufour, the head of the Bureau for the Inspection of Industry and Commerce at the Provincial Council meetings of 1926. Although in almost the same breath, and apparently oblivious to the way it undermined his initial assertion, Dufour claimed that the conditions in Katanga's prisons compared favorably with those on the work sites and in the workers' camps, according to the reports of his inspectors.[24]

As the concerns of those in power moved from the drinking habits of African workers to the likelihood of liaisons between African men and white women, racism in its crudest form often surfaced.[25] There was an echo of South Africa's "Black Peril" scares — which struck the industrializing Rand during the depression of 1905–7, and about which Charles van Onselen has written so ably — in many of the more important of their discussions.[26] As a result, the colonial administration promulgated article 36 of the ordinance of 8 July 1920. Article 36 invested any "responsible" white person with the powers of a policeman if a given situation seemed to warrant it. Its precedent was article 22 of the Charte coloniale, which stated that a missionary was in fact a state official.[27] Article 36 was equally particularistic: given the rampant Anglophobia of the colonial administration, no white person could be truly responsible unless he or she was also Belgian and Roman Catholic.[28]

Moreover, the recession of 1921–22 caused a sharp decline in the number of white mineworkers and foundrymen from South Africa in Katanga.[29] As early as 1919 white workers struck the Union Minière. The company and the government broke the strike with an added display of vindictiveness, since the majority of white workers were British subjects from South Africa. However, the local executive of the mining company did not anticipate that so many white workers would leave Katanga after the failure of the strike. At Panda almost a fourth of the white operatives left by July 1921. One Union Minière official half jokingly compared the exodus with that of the Boers from South Africa's Cape Province in the 1830s. Bankruptcy and the Anglophobia of local Belgian magistrates did not help matters, for many of those who left were facing prison sentences for bad debts.[30]

The departure of English-speaking workers further retarded the development of the new methods of management and production.[31] The global price structure, the bizarre make-up of the workforce, and its high rate of turnover combined to thwart the mining company's efforts at expansion. Consequently the mining company had to adjust to the postwar drop in copper prices in a peculiarly offhanded fashion. For while the most advanced machinery of the day was purchased to smelt the higher grade of copper oxides directly at Lubumbashi, the treatment of low-grade oxides, sulfides from the underground mine at Kipushi, radium, cobalt, and tin languished at the experimental stage until 1927. Various techniques to increase production, lower costs, and increase the pure metal content of the extracted ore (oxidation, leaching, and chemical and electrolytic concentration) were implemented, but not within a planned framework. All this mirrored the initial misgivings of the metropolitan government and Belgian investors about applying new techniques to the extraction of Katanga's ore.[32]

Despite the postwar recession, the Union Minière doubled its share of the world market and thus continued the haphazard expansion of its operations.[33] Although new mines were opened at Ruashi in 1921, technical innovation remained more or less nonexistent beyond the factories and the underground Prince Léopold Mine at Kipushi.[34] The number of African hands engaged in stockpiling low-grade ores at Kambove, the Star of the Congo, and the mining sites least accessible to rail transport increased markedly. Hours were long and rates of output no less than superhuman.[35] Consequently, the drive to recruit more African workers was pushed to unheard-of levels.[36]

THE CROOKED LINE OF MARCH

The Hinterland, Recruitment, and the Work Sites

> Up to 1924 no rule had been enunciated with respect to what was a judicious quota of recruited African labor. Recruiters propagandized an area as long as there were men ready to work. The quota was all those who desired to contract.
>
> Fernand Engels, former vice gov-
> ernor-general of Congo-Kasai Prov-
> ince, 1931[37]

Unlike the Africans who had come to work on the mines in the interwar years, the African workforce of the postwar period was primarily from the North-Eastern Province of Northern Rhodesia and the more remote northern territories of Katanga.[38] Some recruits were also drawn from the Chokwe who were streaming into Katanga from Angola after the collapse of the Congo-Angolan rubber trade between 1918 and 1923.[39] All these areas were more removed from the rail line and Katanga's commercial network than the target areas of labor recruitment in the previous decade.[40]

The destruction of the Aushi, Lala, and Lamba food-producing communities on the Belgian side of the Luapula Valley caused scores of Bemba, Bisa, and Lunda to flee into Katanga. Spurred on by hunger, sleeping sickness, and the sudden influx of Africans from the Belgian-held areas of the valley, they fanned out in northerly and westerly directions, using the blind spots along the borders as their points of entry into Katanga.[41] The trickle of casual labor from Northern Rhodesia which followed the rail line from 1911 to 1917 became a steady stream by the 1920s. It in fact complemented the shepherded movement of recruits to the mines.[42] By 1924 labor from Northern Rhodesia had become absolutely indispensable for the Union Minière's purposes.[43]

The recruitment levies of 1918 in Northern Rhodesia had given no hint of the sharp increase of 1919 and certainly none of the incredible one of 1920.[44] Two months before the outbreak of the Spanish influenza epidemic, agents for TCL had experienced the most extreme difficulty in acquiring a mere 1,200 men on the Northern Rhodesia side of the Luapula Valley. The company's agents and Portuguese subcontractors fared somewhat better in Angola, but only by resorting to a regime of cruelty that was unequalled in the immediate region until 1923. As early as 1918–19 the number of Angolan recruits at the Union Minière rose from 966 to 1,746. The real number of Angolan recruits for the period between 1919 and 1921 was much higher than the official figures suggested. Both the colonial government and the Union Minière, for their own respective reasons, failed to include the number of Angolans recruited by Portuguese subcontractors working for TCL.[45]

Diseases were often exported to the countryside by returning African workers. The rapid increase in population in those communities not affected by labor recruitment and work on the mines, particularly in Northern Rhodesia, was indirect evidence of the debilitating effects of mine labor. The population of Nsenga and Ngoni villages in Northern Rhodesia grew by as much as 20 percent, while those of the Bemba, Bisa, and Aushi, after having been inundated by private and government labor recruiters, stagnated or disappeared altogether. By the middle of the 1920s the footpaths crossing the lands of the latter peoples were called the trails of hunger by Africans living outside the region. The situation accelerated dangerously toward the middle of the decade.[46] According to the Annual Report for Northern Rhodesia of 1923–24, the spread of "tropical ulceration," which from its description was undoubtedly yaws, was occurring at alarming rates in these districts. Yaws was also a severe problem for the African communities in the immediate vicinity of the Union Minière work sites. By 1926 yaws, and to a lesser extent smallpox, had blanketed the southern end of Katanga and was filtering rapidly into the eastern and northern parts of Northern Rhodesia via columns of repatriated African workers.[47]

Despite the withering effect of epidemic diseases, the sheer volume of laborers gave all the European enterprises of the province the feeling that they were on the verge of a second wind.[48] African labor recruitment experienced a sharp increase after the influenza epidemic subsided at the close of 1919. As Table 2.1 shows, the BTK mission in Kasai alone pressed over 3,000 men, or about 250 a month, into the mining company's service. The number of BTK recruits increased steadily to a peak of 8,569 in 1922; in 1923 the total fell to 5,044, but rose to 8,648 the following year.

Part of the optimism about the future rested with the belief that the areas contiguous to Katanga, most notably Kasai and Maniema, could eventually furnish twice as many recruits as Northern Rhodesia and Angola combined. This view of the labor problem was tendered by the BTK's successful recruitment of laborers in areas like Kongolo on the northern edge of Tanganika-Moero.[49] Table 2.2 shows that in

Table 2.1. BTK Recruits for the Union Minière from Tanganika-Moero, Lubefu, Luluaburg, Kabinda, Lusambo, Lomami, and Kanda Kanda, 1918–1924

	Number of Men Recruited
1918–19	4,272[a]
1919–20	6,520
1920–21	7,500
1921–22	8,569[b]
1922–23	5,044[c]
1923–24	8,648[d]

Source: AA, MOI no. 52 (3555), Rapport du comité local pour l'exercice du 1er juin 1922 au 31 décembre 1923.
[a]3,465 recruited in 1919.
[b]1,414 died or fled.
[c]3,054 died or fled.
[d]2,615 from Kasai fled.

the second quarter of 1919 the number of BTK recruits from Kongolo going to the Union Minière went from 81 to 361, an increase of 470 percent. Yet Kongolo's share of the total number of recruits from Tanganika-Moero was little more than 15 percent. But its rate of increase was enough to catch the eye of the territorial administration, since the area had offered up no men for recruitment in the previous five years. Similarly Ankoro yielded 657 Africans in 1919 after five years of virtually no recruits.[50]

The twist with respect to the increase of African recruits at Kongolo was that the great mass of them had not come from Kongolo at all, but from Maniema and as far away as Kivu by virtue of their own energies and as a result of BTK coercion. This was evidenced by the unexplainable drop in 1920 to less than half of the 1919 count. The

Table 2.2. BTK Recruitment, Tanganika-Moero, 1917–1921

Territory	1917–18	1918–19	1919–20	1920–21
Kikondja	883	626	261	128
Pweto	539	74	96	664
Kiambi	261	163	177	9
Bukama	—	68	184	119
Sampwe	362	492	687	540
Ankoro	—	—	657	—
Kabongo	—	—	—	—
Kongolo	—	81	361	168
Kinda	—	—	—	—
Lukonzolua	—	61	—	—

Source: AA, MOI no. 46 (3351), B no. 374/719, Ministère des Colonies, 3 août 1926.

strongest proof, however, was the bitter and unanimous protest of the BTK recruiters in northeastern Tanganika-Moero, when the vice governor-general of Orientale Province prohibited further recruiting expeditions into areas under his jurisdiction because of the disruptive effect that recruiting had on the cultivation of cash crops such as rice and cotton.[51] Maniema was the area for which the vice governor-general was most concerned.

The written protests of the recruiting agents in the area reached the director of the BTK on 22 September 1920, just before the rainy season and the peak of the recruiting drive. They were remarkable for their inordinately confident tone. Their authors were apparently still basking in the triumphs of 1919. The letters depicted the vice governor-general as "naive" and possibly "incompetent" because he was either "ignorant of the needs of UMHK," or worse, he simply favored the spread of cash crops over the manpower needs of the mining company — in which case they strongly intimated that he be replaced.[52]

There was also a feeling that there should be some measure of improvement in the living standards of African workers, given the hardships they sustained during the war. Ironically the smaller enterprises and the European farmers, not the Union Minière and the rail companies, were the first employers to articulate these sympathies.[53] The mining company took such declarations rather lightly. Its spokesmen emphasized the fact that the wages paid to African workers in the agricultural and commercial sectors of the colonial economy were well below the official industrial median. They also pointed to the instances of violation of the colonial labor code of 17 August 1910, compiled by the Office for the Inspection of Labor and Industry between 1918 and 17 November 1919.[54] According to the statistics amassed by the office, European farmers and merchants were the most frequent violators of the stipulations of the code. From the mining company's line of reasoning, improvement was indeed long overdue, but in the agricultural and commercial sectors of the economy.

The company's policy with respect to meeting its tremendous manpower needs in this period was simply to have no fixed policy and to accept recruits from whatever sources appeared to be the most convenient and most promising. Of course, the recruitment missions in Angola and Northern Rhodesia were exceptions, but only contingently. The Angolan mission was quickly killed off once the amount of mortality and flight threatened to transform the Angolan presence on the mines into a financial liability in 1921–22. Moreover, the mass migration of Chokwe from Angola into Katanga in the early 1920s

made the Union Minière's large and highly visible recruitment network in Angola somewhat redundant. The enactment of the Kapanga
Convention in 1923 effectively erased the border between Angola and
Katanga where Lunda, Chokwe, and Luvale communities straddled
it. As a result, almost all the population of eastern Angola was placed
in an invisible labor reservoir which could be drawn upon by the
mining company in times of labor shortage.[55]

The only constant in the mining company's recruitment policy was
its dependence on laborers from the Rhodesias, the source of over 50
percent of its labor force until 1930. The company's adherence to a
purely Congolese strategy of African recruitment at this time was,
in most instances, opportunistic and, at best, a means to assure the
BTK officials and the colonial government that the company believed
in their combined abilities. Over the long run, despite the vast
increase in the number of Africans recruited by the BTK, the line of
supply varied in its reliability. As we shall see later, the revamped
recruitment efforts of the BTK in the 1920s were fraught with difficulties. In 1921–22, for instance, 1,216 out of the BTK's 8,569 recruits
for the Union Minière fled, while another 198 died before they reached
the work sites. In 1922–23 more than half of the recruits fled. Another
385 died on the way to the work sites or during the first 10 days of
work. In 1923–24, 2,615 of the recruits who fled came from territories
in the Kasai District. None of these grim factors was evident in 1919.[56]

By May 1920 the rosy projections of the previous year had darkened
considerably.[57] The number of recruits from the Kasai mission began
to fall off as early as the beginning of 1920 (see Table 2.1). A note
of pessimism was even sounded in the administrative offices of the
BTK itself. The collapse of the BTK's recruitment mission in Kasai
was the source of the growing pessimism. On 25 October 1920 the
commissioner-general of the BTK wrote to the minister of colonies
about the failure of the Kasai mission:

Monsieur le Ministre; You will observe that the BTK is unable to satisfy
the demands of the associated enterprises although the districts of Lulua and
Lomami have given satisfactory results. Tanganika-Moero has only furnished
us with 124 men for the month of August, while Lomami and Lulua have
supplied us with 334 and 259 respectively. The Kasai mission, which is in
the process of being abandoned, has supplied us with hardly any recruits.
Only six workers from here were sent to the work sites of UMHK in September 1920.

I must express here my regret that the efforts and money expended for the
success of the latter mission have gone for naught. The BTK proposes to

resume the operations undertaken by Jadot; but under the present conditions this organization cannot assume such a task. I would not be surprised if one of the consequences of this hiatus would be a long period of impasse among the natives of Kasai with respect to their contracting for hire with UMHK. . . . In this instance the reputation of the BTK will be gravely affected.[58]

The commissioner-general correctly assessed the future troubles of the BTK in Kasai and the districts and territories of Katanga proper. And after 1920, private recruiters, including agents of the BTK's chief competitor in Katanga, the Angola-based Portuguese firm of Correa Freres, often gained a foothold in areas where the BTK had lost ground. Previous sources of recruits, particularly those near the rail line, were intermittently closed off to BTK recruiters because of local epidemics of yaws, smallpox, and influenza, and the subsequent medical bans against recruitment. Private recruiters defied the medical bans, however, and quickly moved into the breach created by the withdrawal of the BTK's agents. The private agencies also pushed farther west into Lulua District.[59]

The BTK versus the Private Recruiters

As their letters to the Elisabethville and Kikondja offices clearly showed, the BTK's agents were especially agitated by the prospect of direct competition with the large private concerns. The conflict with Correa Freres began shortly after the war. By that time Correa Freres had managed to extend its operations successfully to three of Katanga's four districts—Lulua, Lomami, and Tanganika-Moero. By 1921 the firm had acquired more government contracts for African labor than the BTK itself, although its commission for a group of 10 Africans was 4.50 francs higher than that of the BTK. Because of the increased demands of the affiliated companies at the end of 1921, the rivalry between the BTK and Correa Freres became directly confrontational.[60]

By late 1920 Lulua District had become a virtual fiefdom of Correa Freres, according to local colonial officials. These circumstances were particularly uncomfortable for the BTK agents who were confined to the southern third of the district once Correa Freres and the other recruiting firms usurped their former spheres of influence at Sandoa and Kayoyo. Correa Freres's agents also reconstructed the terms of hire for African labor in the area along lines more favorable to themselves. This was done primarily by extending gifts and bribes to the retainers of local headmen as well as to territorial chiefs. This practice further complicated the succession crises in many of the chief-taincies of Lulua.[61]

The ease with which the private recruiting companies undermined the BTK throughout Katanga was partly due to their willingness to take on Africans as agents and contractors. Africans continued to be employed as contractors in the private agencies well into the 1920s, even though African names were conspicuously absent on the official rosters of recruiting agents attached to the BTK.[62] The BTK did continue to retain a handful of African contractors and recruiters; but they were confined to Elisabethville and, more likely than not, functioned more as compound police for the incoming recruits than as contractors.

The presence of African recruiting agents hardly suggested a more liberal policy in terms of the treatment that Africans received at the hands of the recruiting companies.[63] A respectable number of the African recruiters, or so it seemed from the names they gave to the licensing bureau — "Sale," or Dirty André, and "Kimputu," or Tick Fever Johnny, for instance — were roughly hewn and violent men. They were often strangers to the regions in which they operated, although they had a broader knowledge of local mores and customs than their European counterparts. This made them an even greater menace in the villages. The activities of Dirty André are cases in point. André was a mulatto recruiter for Correa Freres from a neighboring province. Between 1925 and 1926, in the Lulua District, he arbitrarily detained and intermittently beat three women — one of whom was a Chokwe medium called the Mwa Tshikwota — and recruited scores of Africans by force and, no doubt, by dint of his capture of the Mwa Tshikwota spirit medium.[64]

Competition between the BTK and private recruiters was especially intense in the Haut-Luapula District, particularly in the larger chief-taincies such as Mofimbi, Mopola, Kavalo, and Kindalo. Albert Delforge, the chief BTK agent in the region from 1918 to 1923, never ceased complaining about how ineffectual government initiatives were in reversing the situation. Delforge and his subordinates had extreme difficulty recruiting 27 Africans in Kavalo and Kindalo because the inhabitants fled across the border to Northern Rhodesia after raids by recruiters from Correa Freres.[65] The majority of Africans taken from the area were sent initially to the lumber camps of the Bas-Congo–Katanga rail line. By the end of 1921, however, almost half of the recruits had fled to the work sites of the Union Minière.[66]

According to Delforge, the soldiers and agents of Correa Freres had not only spirited away scores of the inhabitants, but had also commandeered almost all of the available supplies of cassava flour, maize, sorghum, and *bitoyo* (salt fish). This kind of extortion played havoc with the regional cash economy, while simultaneously coercing scores of Africans into the recruiters' columns by drying up food supplies. By the mid-1920s the dry season was universally understood to be the "hunger season" on both the Congolese and Northern Rhodesian side of the Luapula Valley.[67]

The activities of the private recruiting agencies and the BTK also affected the food supply for the African quarter of Elisabethville. Maize, cassava, and dried fish all fell into short supply as a result of speculation and the armed occupation of the most important areas of indigenous food production south of Elisabethville. Prior to 1920 merchants would often leave the rail station at Sakania and go for several days' march in search of foodstuffs. They would then resell these items in Elisabethville and the surrounding unincorporated African quarters. Although trade in food did not completely disappear, it was only a shadow of its former self after 1926 and clearly vulnerable to the forays of the recruiters.[68]

Hardly any information about the private recruiters exists beyond a surname and a place of residence, which were given when they applied for licenses to recruit Africans. If a given agent was in business for himself as opposed to one of the larger recruiting firms, the record is even murkier. Occasionally impressionistic discourses on the alleged moral character and mental capacities of an agent crept into the correspondence of an administrator or magistrate. More often than not, however, it was only a fleeting reference offered in haste and without exceptional importance to the author of the document.[69]

Most of the private recruiters were foreigners — Greeks, Italians, or Portuguese — although there were always a few Belgians among the private firms and agents. Many of the foreign recruiters had either been soldiers or ambulant traders in Angola or one of the other neighboring colonies before the war. The colonial administration viewed them with a great deal of suspicion given their "foreignness" and *déclassé* backgrounds.[70]

A greater amount of information exists for the agents of the BTK. There is at least enough to give one some idea of the probable motivations of the men who percolated into the different territories in search of recruits and why they stayed in spite of the shifting political fortunes of the agency.[71] Even the brief biographies of the men who were rejected by the BTK are revealing, because the rejections followed a pattern.

For example, Jules Victor Lotte was born in Louviere, a town in the Belgian province of Hainaut, in 1879. He had served as a chief clerk and later as a *chef de camp* at one of the Kilo-Moto gold mines in the northeastern Belgian Congo during the war. From 1918 to 6 June 1921 he worked for the Chemin de Fer du Katanga (CFK). The BTK failed to take Lotte on as a recruiter, however.[72]

Jules Joseph Pirson was also born in the relatively poor mining district of Hainaut on 23 August 1885. He was working in Belgium as a customs clerk at the time that he applied for a recruiting position with the BTK. Pirson had worked in the Congo before as a customs inspector at Kinshasa and Boma. In spite of his former services in the Congo, he too was rejected.[73]

Hector-Joseph Gillain had been a rubber agent in the Congo Free State from 1905 to 1909. His file says that he had risen rapidly through the ranks because of his great "zeal" — something that can only mean brutality given the circumstances of the era. Born in the Commune Saint Gerard in Namur on 21 June 1887, Gillain claimed on his dossier to be quite "familiar with the methods of the BTK" because a number of his former compatriots had worked for the BTK as recruiters. The BTK hired Gillain and shipped him to the Congo at the end of January 1922.[74] Similarly, Otto Walter, a Swiss citizen, applied for a position as a labor recruiter with the BTK in 1924. At the time, Walter was an officer in a military training camp in Lausanne, Switzerland. He was hired almost immediately.[75]

Albert Victor Delforge, the chief BTK agent, was born in the Commune Saint Gilles in Brussels on 5 January 1880. Delforge had been a lieutenant in the Force Publique in the era of the Congo Free State. He served in the Umangi-Bangala area and Maniema until 1905. From 1906 to 1908 Delforge functioned as the *chef de poste* at Mandungu in the Bangala region and had overseen the shipping of rubber from this backland station to Bumba, Buta, and Uele in the far northern Congo.[76] During the First World War, Delforge had been a commander of Belgian military forces at Ujiji, Tanganyika. Shortly after the war he was instrumental in enforcing the hut tax throughout the Belgian protectorate of Ruanda. On his accession to a post with the BTK he received the highest recommendation from his former commander, Edouard Tombeur, who, at the time, was also the state inspector of industry and commerce for Katanga.[77]

The only major difference therefore between most of the private European recruiting agents and those employed by the BTK was that the former were drawn from the dregs of the colonial armies in the Congo and elsewhere — drunkards, felons of sundry stripes, and deserters — while the BTK drew its men from those who had waded in uniform through the bloody circumstances of colonial occupation. Almost all of the BTK's white personnel had seen military action in

Africa. A large number of them would have had to return to the hard-bitten circumstances of the coal mining districts of Belgium if employment with the BTK had not presented itself. Service in the colonial army had been a means for upward mobility. Employment by the BTK gave them the opportunity to push the military metaphor beyond the particular circumstances of colonial occupation and war, while pursuing a career that was deemed "respectable" more out of necessity than convention.[78] With the advent of the labor shortages of the 1920s the services of such men could not be easily discouraged. For the increased demands of the BTK's clients, particularly the Union Minière, the collapse of the agency's Kasai mission, and the aggressiveness of the private companies put the future of the BTK into grave question by the end of 1924.[79]

Between 1920 and 1924 the workers' camps and work sites of Katanga were emptied of laborers faster than men could be recruited. By October 1921, the Union Minière's African workforce had fallen from 12,000 to 7,000 men. Although scores of Africans still continued to leave the deplorable conditions of the woodcutting camps of the rail line to hire on at the mining company, their numbers did little to stanch the hemorrhage of over 40 percent of the company's workers as a result of death or flight.[80] The countryside, particularly the Lunda areas and western Katanga, balked at the prospects of further recruitment during the course of the recession. Land chiefs often refused to send workers who had absconded back to the work sites. Others cut the labor supply at its source by refusing to exhort their constituencies on behalf of the recruiters. In Tanganika-Moero the recapture of fleeing workers was greatly hindered by groups of rural bandits who attempted to press such workers into their own ranks. By 28 October 1921 the BTK had issued a circular which claimed that the influence of workers who had fled to the villages had become a greater obstacle to further recruitment than the prospective recruits' fear of disease.[81]

In Lulua District, where a yield of 500 recruits for the year was described as "good" in 1921–22, the number of recruits that fled even before they were securely under foot was particularly striking. At the very moment that the results of recruitment in Lulua for July–November 1922 were being reported to the central office of the BTK, for example, Jules Drion, the second in command of the BTK mission in Lulua, was compelled to halt a recruiting mission at Dilolo in order to go in search of fleeing recruits. Flight was often a means of indicating work preferences. At Sandoa, the stronghold of the BTK in Lulua in 1922, entire caravans of workers became "uncontrollable" once they discovered that they were going to the Union Minière works at Busanga, according to the BTK recruiter A. Thibaut. Caravans going to the company's work site at Musonoi had to be completely suppressed by the end of 1922. Armed coercion availed nothing.[82]

The situation had not changed appreciably by 1924. An excerpt from a company force report that year reads almost exactly like the BTK report of 1921–22. Summarizing the response of Africans from Lulua once they arrived at Busanga, it said:

> The recruited Africans were taken principally to Busanga and after having complained excessively deserted *en masse* while putting up stiff resistance in the interior. It will take a little time to restore normal recruiting patterns.[83]

Oftentimes the search for malcontents led BTK agents into Angola. Jules Drion and Daniel Moltens, the BTK agents at Sandoa and Katanga, respectively, and Marcel Vervoot at Kinda and Kafakumba, several miles farther south, were all known to have made several forays into Angola in 1922, allegedly in search of fleeing recruits. What is more likely, though, is that the recruiters were simply bent on acquiring enough recruits to replace those who had fled. These manhunts eventually took their toll on the disposition of the local population. In 1923–24 the Chokwe population along the Angola-Katanga border rose against the predations of the recruiters.[84]

Table 2.3 shows that the number of men recruited in the Lulua District and the number actually delivered to Union Minière work sites often varied wildly between June 1922 and January 1923. The manhunts in Angola by BTK agents often bolstered parcels of recruits after severe losses, but obviously not with the original recruits. Between June and September 1922, for example, Jules Drion recruited 210 men in Lulua. Out of this number, 2 fled outright, and 21 more escaped or were released by the Union Minière because of illness or infirmity once they reached the work sites. Yet Drion was credited at the end of the period with having delivered 195 men to the work sites. Similar situations obtained for labor recruiters such as Marcel Bourette, Emile Zumwald, and Jules Moyaert (see Table 2.3).

The number of fleeing workers throughout Katanga was so high by 27 October 1922 that provincial officials writing to the Ministry of Colonies at the end of the year thought it best to describe the abscondings as a movement. The spread of pneumonia, influenza, and other diseases with more debilitating symptoms, like yaws, must have influenced the decision of some African laborers to flee.[85] But one must resist the temptation to make direct correlations between

Table 2.3. Escapees and *Réformés* among BTK Recruits from the Lulua District for the UMHK, 1922–1923

Recruiter	Number of Men Recruited	Number of Escapees	Number of *Réformés*	Number of Men Delivered to UMHK
1st SEMESTER, JUNE–SEPTEMBER 1922				
Moyaert	130	30	28	89
Lucas	51	3	22	10
Drion	210	2	21	195
Le Canne	7	–	2	5
Delforge	16	3	–	8
Zumwald	62	–	11	54
Bourette	52	1	16	48
Shoenecker	26	–	14	12
Vervoot	10	–	3	–
2nd SEMESTER, SEPTEMBER 1922–JANUARY 1923				
Moyaert	186	1	17	151
Lucas	170	23	11	120
Drion	71	12	18	51
Le Canne	51	–	–	41
Delforge	–	–	–	–
Zumwald	51	–	7	20
Bourette	56	20	4	32
Shoenecker	–	–	–	–
Vervoot	–	–	–	–

Source: AA, MOI no. 52 (3555), Recrutements (Lulua).

disease, mortality, and flight; for as previously mentioned, such a decision was a manifold process. Consequently, we must be content to describe the flight of large numbers of African workers in the 1920s as "silent protests," simply because we know so little about how the workers arrived at such a decision, and even less about how a core group passed the word on to thousands of other workers.[86]

The flight of African workers and recruits in the 1920s was partly due to the combined efforts of the BTK, the private recruiting agencies, and the large employers to impose longer terms of hire on African recruits. Before the recession, for example, six months had been the average length of time for an African laborer at the Union Minière. The mining company had not attempted to reinstitute the 18-month contract for most of its workers, since stinting on working and living conditions was, at this point, the most palpable way of cutting production costs. The short-term contracts remained in place until 1924, when the fact-finding mission of the Commission du Travail made nine months, or eight 30-day labor tickets, a much more palatable alternative for the company.[87]

The nine-month contract itself was a result of the way in which flight had changed the circumstances of labor supply. But while the nine-month contract was far from the earlier two-year ideal, except in the case of recruits from Northern Rhodesia and factory hands, it still had its drawbacks.[88] African recruits saw nine months of wage labor as fundamentally no different from conscription into the colonial army. And it had not been for soldiering that they had come to the work sites, but for money and cloth—items that could easily be translated into larger plots of land, young wives to work them, and increased prestige among their kin and village networks—for how else were they to be compensated for their long absence from the land.

By the 1920s, experience had taught rural Africans to question the recruiters' proverbial promise to have them back in their villages before the next planting season. Consequently, although the African recruits often brought their political leaders and notables to the work sites with them—no doubt the reason many such people were listed as labor contractors in the government's judicial bulletins—they seldom, if ever, brought their women or land chiefs.[89] When the length of their contract threatened to cut them off from the circumstances they left behind in the rural areas, withdrawal of their labor was often their only recourse.[90] Moreover, the hostile indifference of the chiefs toward the Union Minière reinforced the propensity to flee. Of the chiefs' attitudes, Martin Rutten, a former official of the Union Minière and governor-general of the Congo by 1926, said:

> Under the present conditions the attempt to find deserters is very difficult. The native chiefs do not inform the territorial authorities of the presence of deserters in their chieftaincies and employers are generally unscrupulous in employing Africans who could have deserted from other firms.[91]

There was also a rear guard of the sick, underaged, and infirm among the fleeing malcontents of the early 1920s. These Africans fled largely as a means of protest over workloads. At the Union Minière they were written up as *réformés* once they returned to the work sites or were recaptured by the recruiters. Many of them were adolescents. Others suffered from lingering and debilitating illnesses and were the hapless victims of unscrupulous recruitment methods. In 1922 and 1923, respectively, 236 and 403 of the workers fleeing the Union Minière were *réformés*.[92] Minimum medical standards in the selection of African recruits were nonexistent.

By 14 May 1924 the public stance of the Union Minière was that, given the prevailing labor shortages, it could not see itself undertaking the construction of new factories or any other project that involved a substantial outlay of capital until the problems associated with labor supply were solved. Two executives of the mining company, Jules Cousin and the ubiquitous Edgar Sengier, suggested that direct recruitment by the state should be resumed. As a matter of course, this would have entailed a complete overhaul of the organization and functions of the BTK.[93] Short of this, however, the Union Minière steadily increased its dependence on African labor coming from Northern Rhodesia, except in the instance of those mines most removed from the rail line. Between 1926 and 1928, the Union Minière assumed de facto control over the internal organization of the BTK. Table 2.4 suggests why the mining company might have chosen to assume more direct control over the Congolese labor supply at this point. As of October 1928 there was virtually no Union Minière work site that had less than 16 percent of its workforce incapacitated by illness. Among the Panda, Lubumbashi, Kisanga, and Musonoi work sites the lowest death rate was four men a month, well over in some instances.

The Union Minière and the other industrial companies of Katanga experienced a serious labor dearth from 1921 to 1928. Physical abuse and violence in the recruitment of African laborers were widespread. African workers frequently fled such conditions — partly because a sizable number of them, if not the majority, saw themselves as ill-starred peasant farmers rather than workers. The African workforce was hard put to reproduce itself on this basis, even though it was more capable of doing so than it had been before the First World War. Flight, death, and disease were the boundary markers of the African workers' conception of community at the end of the decade — so much so that

Table 2.4. Number of Deaths and Percentages of African Workers Unable to Work Because of Illness, by Work Site at the Union Minière, October 1928

Work Site	Number of Men	Deaths for the Month	Percentages of Illness
Lubumbashi	2,353	4	20.40
Star of the Congo	1,517	3	23.73
Prince Léopold (Kipushi)	1,109	2	21.64
Luishia	1,466	2	16.37
Panda	5,076	8	18.91
Kakontwe and Shinkolobwe	1,473	3	24.44
Kambove	916	2	26.20
Kisanga	743	12	19.81
Musonoi	1,053	6	68.38
Kikole	429	–	–

Source: AG, C8, MOI/DS, Réunion 1928, 12 décembre 1928.

several local committees of inquiry and two metropolitan *commissions du travail* in 1924 and 1928 attempted to show that such conditions were not in the long-range interests of the recruiting agencies and the industrial companies. Yet without the excessive demands of the mining company and the other industrial companies the violence associated with recruitment might have been less. Until 1928 the demographic spoilation of Katanga's countryside was without any real constraints. The conditions in the rural areas simply mirrored the conditions of industry and industrial policy.[94]

As a result of increased absconding, the company was compelled to take on large numbers of Africans who were without identity papers or who had to be hired under hastily drawn-up group contracts. Spontaneous forms of hire further aggravated the tendency toward absconding, since they left even fewer means of tracing disgruntled laborers. The collection of the head tax also became very nearly impossible in instances where workers were without identity cards or passbooks and circulated from work site to work site. These workers became soldiers in a driven army of wage labor. Despite these bleak conditions, a significant number of Africans chose to take their chances on the work sites of the mining company. For, in the instance of many recruits, the situation in their villages was even more bleak.[95]

The Union Minière's triumph over the circumstances of industrial growth was therefore a conditional one. The mining company's increasing use of terms such as *"déserteur"* and *"réformé"* and the absence of sustained technical growth enhanced the military cast of management and the workplace while imposing a harsh but inconsistent form of discipline on the workers. Although the mining company determined the pace of industrial growth, it could neither control nor foresee the consequences of its growth. It was not until the end of the 1920s, when the company began to withdraw from southern Africa's regional migrant labor system, that it achieved greater control over the social context of industrial production. By the middle of the decade, however, few doubted that such control would be achieved. As Maurice Robert succinctly observed:

In Katanga it will be different. Here every endeavor will have some relationship to the mining industry. The interests of mineral exploitation and of the mining companies must become dominant in the thinking of private citizens and colonial subjects. All other preoccupations are of secondary importance and must become directly or indirectly tied to the problems of the mining industry.[96]

For the remainder of the 1920s the mining company attempted to enhance its control over the African workforce.

PART TWO

The Quaking of a Generation: The African Mineworkers from 1927 to 1939

CHAPTER THREE

African Workers in the Industrial Towns, 1919–1930

THE PROSPECTS OF SOCIAL CONTROL

> The objectives of the colonizer in matters concerning indigenous unskilled labor should be to modify unrecognizably the natural division of the black population, in order to conclude a distribution of the latter so that the largest concentrations of Africans are around the centers of economic activity.
>
> Felix Varbeke, July 1921[1]

In the decade before the Depression a growing number of African workers attempted to form new communities and ways of life in Katanga's industrial towns. The rural world from which they had come was composed of wood, mud, and the prowess of their chiefs. The world of the mining towns and the factories was composed of iron and cement. Yet while these two worlds settled on different foundations, prospective African workers sought to use some of the cultural mores of their villages to redefine the constraints imposed upon them by town life and wage labor.

Town life had an air of desperation about it. Not a small amount of it was the result of real hunger and deprivation. The importation of manufactured goods aggravated the more basic needs of the workers.[2] Crime—whether against property, persons, or colonial notions of civility (open-air African dancing was illegal, for example) — and the workers' dependence on money sometimes articulated these needs. And alcohol and marijuana often disassembled the workers' social aspirations and inured them to the inequities of the social order.

Most colonial officials saw the teeming *cités indigènes* as breeding grounds of sedition and unrest—worlds in which the daily struggle among Africans and between Africans and Europeans for a measure of security could suddenly turn into an all-out war against civilization. For such officials an African in the dock represented more than just a gratuitous wrongdoer. He or she was a harbinger of distant rural unrest or an insubordinate voice at the workplace.[3] The courts, particularly the police tribunals, posited an automatic connection among certain occupations, ethnic groups, and the character of crime. The zones designated as the neighborhoods of foreign African workers (Northern Rhodesians, Nyasalanders, Angolans, etc.) were, in the jaundiced view of the authorities, nests of thieves, pettifoggers, and passport forgers; the Lamba and Bena Chisinga were thought to be upholders of religious unorthodoxy and mongerers of sedition and rebellion; the Chokwe were chronic humbuggers who were given to cannibalism, crimes of violence, and sorcery; Africans from Pweto and Tanganika-Moero were incorrigible drunkards and brawlers—the list of quirks and prejudices was endless.[4]

Up to 1918 the African sections of the towns were the legal responsibility of the governor-general in Boma. But colonial officials on the spot were strapped with the grim burden of managing a highly mobile and transient African population and setting up a barrier of residential ordinances between black and white. By 1919 the provincial administration began to think of the towns' African quarters as entities in their own right in order to disengage itself from any fiscal commitment to them.[5] This took the form of a ridiculous attempt to divide the urban African population into new chieftaincies, which were dreamed up especially for the towns and which were to be headed by men appointed by the administration. The rapid influx of Africans into the towns during and after the First World War demonstrated the bankruptcy of the plan, however; its failure propelled the colonial government and the urban African population toward the ambiguous circumstances of the 1920s.[6]

The early 1920s were a time of feverish construction, and many new projects—from buildings to roads—were undertaken to shore up the infrastructure of the industrial towns. The brickmaking and construction industries boomed. Hundreds of African bricklayers, carpenters, and masons changed the face of Elisabethville, Jadotville, and the smaller mining towns.[7] Moreover, the provincial administration became actively concerned to bring the situation in the African quarters of the towns within its purview and control. While its efforts did not equal those of the mining company, the potential results of such attempts at social engineering came to be much appreciated by both the provincial administration in Elisabethville and the governor-general's office in Léopoldville.[8] While such efforts increased after the rise of a liberal provincial government under Vice Governor-General Gaston Heenen in 1926, neither the mining company nor the colonial government met with much initial success in their attempts to transform African aspirations in conjunction with the physical landscape. Despite the reconstruction of Elisabethville's African quarter, the actual deployment of the African population continued to be a serious problem for the authorities.

By July 1921 Maurice Lippens, the governor-general of the Belgian Congo, had drawn the provincial administration of Katanga — albeit unwillingly — into a plan to reconstruct Elisabethville's *cité indigène* and thus ensure the African presence on the work sites and in the towns. The new *cité* was erected adjacent to the workers' camp of the Union Minière between the marsh, or *dembo*, of the Lubumbashi River and the rail line. It was here that the government hospital for Africans was built, as well as several schools and the central prison. Lippens entrusted the military to refurbish and rebuild the old *cité* with the aid of convict labor. By 1924 Avenue Sankuru was widened and a communication line, which later became Avenue Prince Léopold, was built. In 1927–28 a sewage and drainage system was completed for the entire town.[9] But between 1922 and 1927 the *faubourgs* and *quartiers ruraux*, or squatters' areas, grew literally under the nose of the administration. Conversely, the European sector of the industrial area at the northern end of the town remained in the direct line of crossing for Africans going to and from work.[10]

As early as 1922, less than a year after Governor-General Lippens had ordered the levelling and reconstruction of Elisabethville's old African quarter, official observers began to speak of the new *cité* in disparaging terms. One anonymous, official witness of the African groundswell spoke of it in these terms:

> In the vicinity of the larger European communities a large number of natives consisting of the servant class and employees of various enterprises are bound to congregate. Accommodations for them must be arranged. In the case of Elisabethville there are ten thousand such natives, and the quarter assigned to them has been allowed to impinge too closely upon the European quarter, and indeed in some instances penetrates between the streets of the European quarter. A minimum of one kilometer should be established between the European and African city. . . .[11]

What the governor-general's reconstruction scheme managed to achieve was something less tangible than absolute residential segregation but potentially more important as far as industry's future was concerned. This was the right to determine the parameters of the struggle for resources in the urban areas once the African masses had been compelled to join the competition. The new laws and ordinances imposed a stringent, cruel, and undemocratic dispensation on all Africans living in the towns. Consequently, African industrial workers often envied the lot of African domestic servants, who, by virtue of their proximity to Europeans, could acquire enough to eat as well as receive the cast-off garments of their employers. Food and clothing, or the lack thereof, were serious matters for those Africans who decided to remain in the towns.[12]

Once African workers became attached to the towns, a uniform standard of living became an absolute necessity. Its achievement became a perpetual source of conflict among the industrial towns' ethnically diverse African population. For despite the abolition of porterage over large areas of Katanga, the general condition of African labor experienced a marked decline between 1922 and 1927. Wage rates for the more skilled and higher paid African workers fell sharply, while those of the more unskilled and inexperienced workers increased slightly. The declining prestige of the upper strata of African workers — mining clerks, soldiers, policemen, and some categories of domestic servants — as a result of the general decline in their wage rate and its failure to keep pace with inflation, gave rise to numerous crimes against property such as embezzlement and forgery.[13] This loss of prestige among the elite strata of African workers manifested itself in other arenas besides the economic one. The wage and standard of living questions were often refracted into the other forms of competition. This was particularly so during the recession of 1921–22. The Musafiri Affair of July–September 1922 was a case in point.[14]

The facts of the Musafiri case were fairly straightforward: On 15 August 1922 Musafiri, an African domestic servant residing in the European quarter of Elisabethville, killed a white man whom he suspected of having an affair with his wife, Henrithé. Apparently the actual adulterer was the housemate of the murdered man, although it is not clear that the murder victim was free of any involvement; for rumor had it that the two white men, who both worked for the BCK, and Musafiri's wife had formed a *menage à trois* and were engaged in sexual acts that were considered unnatural and depraved by the town's African population.[15] Both Africans and Europeans seized upon each minute detail of the case. The actual court case moved with astonishing speed, going from the municipal court (*tribunal de premier instance*) to the appeals court (*cours d'appel*) in less than 12 days. Musafiri was arrested, tried, convicted, and executed within 2½ weeks of the actual murder.[16] His execution drew huge crowds and was the first and last public hanging in Elisabethville. It was meant to be a lesson. And to some Europeans, even some in official circles, and virtually all of the town's African population, it was no more than an officially sanctioned lynching.[17]

What the whites of Elisabethville were so incredulous about was the degree of premeditation in the murder. Apparently Musafiri had delayed taking action for some time before doing anything about his wife's infidelity; presumably he moved with caution and deliberation in confirming the allegation and deciding what to do about it because of the strong ties he had with his wife after nine years of marriage and a wrenching move from their home village. But in the minds of the magistrates, police officers, and employers, Africans simply did not merge thought and action in this way—in short, they were neither devious nor vindictive.[18] The colonial masters had been taken in by their own tendentious shopping list of racial stereotypes. One anonymous official in the vice governor-general's office admitted as much:

It is profoundly disturbing to think that there are perhaps hundreds of blacks among us who have grievances against Europeans similar to that of Musafiri's, and who hide their rage . . . under a mask of deference; it is disturbing to think that among the blacks so affected are numerous soldiers. And I fear that without direct and forthright measures, the situation might become worse. Judging from the reaction to the assassination [the choice of words is interesting here] in the press and in private conversation, few Europeans have the courage to recognize that the whole affair was precipitated by the fact that the situation between white employers and black households is not what it ought to be. . . .[19]

Then the official began to reflect on Musafiri himself and the choices he had before him:

One could say that several wrongs have been committed here: The black should not have taken matters into his own hands; that is obvious. But wasn't he obliged to seek some form of redress? The appeals court admonished Musafiri for not having sought the intervention of a magistrate. But wouldn't a magistrate have urged him to remain silent, chasten his wife and lick his wounds?[20]

Ultimately the competition of African and European men for African women in the urban areas degraded those women in particular and all the women of the colony in general. The disparity between African and European wages and living standards was an important foil of such contests, and, predictably, exacerbated an already vola-

tile social situation. White missionaries did not help matters by pros-
elytizing the urban African population about the merits of conjugal
fidelity and sexual continence.[21] In the wake of the Musafiri case
Governor Rutten urged the promulgation of two decrees that would
demonstrate to the African population that the government meant
to punish white adulterers and that it recognized the permanence and
legitimacy of urban African households. The decrees read as follows:

(1) Any European or individual of the white race who engages in sexual
    activity with a married native woman, even with her consent, will be
    liable to a fine of 100 to 500 francs (approximately 5 to 25 American
    dollars) or imprisonment up to 15 days. In the instance of a repeating
    offender, imprisonment will be mandatory.
(2) It will be considered an instance of entrapment in the urban areas if a
    married native woman engages in an intimate liaison with a European
    and does not produce written evidence indicating her marital status before
    the liaison commences.[22]

What was really being said here was a lot less lofty than the form
in which it was uttered: punishment for white male adulterers was
to remain, at best, cosmetic, and African women were enjoined to
follow a series of absurd prescriptions – even as they broke the law – to
cover the misdeeds of their European partner.

Had it not been for the subsequent allegorical uses that the colonial
administration made of this rather routine case of adultery, mistaken
identity, and murder, it would have passed unnoticed into the
administrative and judicial annals of the province. Instead, between
15 August and 15 September 1922, two telegrams were sent to Louis
Franck, the minister of colonies, from the offices of the governor-
general in Léopoldville and Governor Rutten in Elisabethville.
Franck's cabinet at the Ministry of Colonies in Brussels, as well as
the Provincial Council of Katanga, discussed the case for weeks at
a time.[23] By July 1923 the police tribunals were given the power to
convene and pass judgment on accused Africans without the intervention of a civil magistrate. All this was largely the result of
Musafiri's trial in Elisabethville and that of the millenarian prophet
Simon Kimbangu in Léopoldville.[24]

The growing number of domestic servants in Katanga's towns
further nuanced the demographic characteristics of the African
working class and caused the scissors of sexual and racial competition to cut in the opposite direction. For, like South Africa, the pre-
ponderance of black domestic servants in Katanga were male, and
by the middle and late 1920s many such servants were Lamba and

Bena Chisinga adolescents from the Haut-Luapula District and the adjacent territories of Northern Rhodesia. Most were experiencing the first flush of adult sexuality. But the conditions of their employment compelled them to suppress such feelings while they aided adult women with their daily toilet, washed the underwear and nightclothes of the master and mistress, changed bed linen, and were inadvertently privy to the indiscretions of their employers. All this made for a routinely explosive situation. The fact that most male African domestic servants could pursue their duties and avoid the shrapnel of such explosions was a testimony to the restraint and civility of most servants and a few of their employers.[25] But when a white female deliberately stepped across the line that divided her from her servants, the structures of deference and domination usually accompanied her. Intimacy with an inexperienced or uninitiated young man gave a palpable edge to his more experienced mistress and became yet another metaphor for his subordinate position. For the mistress was also his employer and could withhold the emblem of his value to her—his wage. Paradoxically, the African male servant risked all he had in such situations—including his life.

A white woman's fall from grace, when it could be shown that she freely entered into a relationship with a male African servant, was often rationalized in the courts as symptomatic of a natural lack of resolve or restraint in the female species, particularly at certain times of the month or during menopause.[26] On the other hand, the African male—even the uninitiated adolescent—was, in the eyes of the court, the purveyor of a crude, animallike sexuality which he was obliged to keep in check, even if he was not altogether aware of it. Throughout the industrial southern end of Africa, as in the American South, lynching seemed the most fitting method of enforcing such obligations.[27]

Private life for white industrial workers, as well as African workers, was often a tortured and fragmented affair. At the Union Minière divorces were frequent but nevertheless difficult to obtain given the impact of Roman Catholicism on civil law. The divorce suit brought against Jeanne Fournier by her husband, Auguste, was typical of the personal problems of white workers and their families. In December 1925 Auguste Fournier, a foreman at the Union Minière works at Likasi, filed for a divorce from his estranged wife, Jeanne, who had abandoned their household and returned to Belgium the year before with another European worker from the Likasi works. As of December 1926 Auguste had still not received his divorce from the court despite the absence of his wife. A week later he himself was taken before the district tribunal for public drunkenness and carrying a firearm.[28]

White industrial workers, who frequently amused themselves with alcohol and firearms, constituted a much greater threat to public safety than the courts and police cared to admit, since there were fewer institutional restraints on their destructive behavior pattern. Denied firearms and legal equality with whites, African policemen could hardly function as a restraining force for the often murderous consequences of the white workers' whiskey-fueled orgies of violence. Consider Jacob Hippolyte, a pipefitter for the Union Minière at the Lubumbashi works, who was arraigned for drunkenness and disorderly behavior on 5 January 1925. Hippolyte had fired on a group of Africans in the African quarter of Elisabethville a few days before his arraignment. Although he had wounded several Africans, he was charged with what amounted to only a misdemeanor in the colonial legal code. John Sisson, a Boer machinist from South Africa who worked for the Union Minière, was arrested on 17 June 1925 for assaulting an African worker named Dalamba Ilunga. At the time of his assault on Dalamba, Sisson was already under indictment for public drunkenness.[29] Unlike Hippolyte, Sisson appeared in court and did not flee the charges.

As the 1920s progressed, the web of moral assumptions and obligations governing the industrial workers became all the more complex. Obviously the African workers and the Union Minière saw the question of community somewhat differently, since the question of community was inseparable from that of social control for the mining company. The provincial government generally concurred with the Union Minière, although it often found itself walking a tightrope between the views of the mining company and those of the Catholic church's chief ideological policeman, Monsignor Jean Felix de Hemptinne.[30] The Commission for the Protection of the Natives — which was formed in 1923 but began to aid in regulating the affairs of labor and capital only after the League of Nations' censure of Belgian labor practices in the Congo in 1926 — put together an army of agents from the helping professions and missionary societies and sent them into workers' camps and African quarters not only with medicines to cure disease and stem infant mortality, but also with a warped vision of what the African worker's family and community should be. A special subcommission of the Commission for the Protection of the Natives, which was formed in December 1923 and met regularly throughout the 1920s, attempted to give a forum to the views of the state, Church, and industrial companies.[31] It acted as a kind of a vector, albeit an imprecise one, for the more self-serving aspirations of all three.[32]

By the mid-1920s, for reasons that will be discussed in the next chapter, the migrant labor system in Katanga was beginning to break down.[33] Moreover, African workers began to see the Union Minière's paternalistic but cost-effective response to its breakdown as no more than a European reiteration of their own desire to preserve the urban African communities.[34] By 1928, motorized vehicles and rail lines, which reached as far north as Port Francqui, 140 miles northwest of Luluaburg, and as far west as the coast of Angola, began to replace the recruiters' columns and the several-weeks-long forced march to the work camps.[35] Despite the attempts to keep women away from the urban areas, those of them who had made it to the towns by their own efforts and those who had accompanied their husbands or had been induced to come by the Union Minière were turning up more frequently in the African quarters of the towns and in the workers' camps, although single women were not always welcomed by the agents of the mining company and the state.[36]

The power of the previously mentioned police tribunals grew enormously after 1923 — so much so that in matters concerning Africans their power exceeded rather than seconded the civil magistracies.[37] There were checks on the power of the tribunals, however. And, as the Musafiri case suggests, the police were occasionally compelled to deal with African workers as men with aspirations not unlike their own, though informed by a different method of reasoning. Nevertheless, the police were obliged to present themselves as agents of order. Force was an integral part of their conception of order. As the thinking of the chief executives of the Union Minière and the leading government officials turned toward the prospect of creating a permanent, self-reproducing industrial workforce in the middle and late 1920s, the police tribunals served to undergird the new calculus of material incentives. The newly empowered tribunals, which prefigured the growth of the secret police, or *sûreté*, less than seven years later, also signified that the local administration was finally beginning to wrest some measure of formal control from the governor-general in its attempt to regulate the African quarters of the towns.[38] This was as it should have been, since over a third of the Union Minière's workers at this point still refused to move to the workers' camps.[39]

What one sees emerging from the police blotters and force reports of government and mining officials is a raw and unfinished corporate outlook. This outlook was laced with all the cruelty and greed that shaped the parameters of Belgian colonial society in the 1920s. Throughout all this, the failure to grasp the momentum of men and circumstances — succumbence to the sheer inertia caused by the flood of facts and statistics from the mining sites with no effort to seize upon their implications for overall policy and what was to be done in the specific situations — was tantamount to a cardinal sin for a police investigator or mining-company administrator.[40] The central administration of the Union Minière and the police magistracies were posted with resourceful and intelligent men. But the majority of them were desperately afraid of failure, and would resort to cruelty as well as imagination in the pursuit of the interests of their employers and their own personal advancement. Under such circumstances, and with the lust for profits as great as it was in the 1920s, management often became a simple matter of holding the line in the old way — with guns and men willing to use them on the flimsiest of pretenses.[41]

Yet there were important differences between the central office of the Union Minière at Elisabethville and those of the outlying work sites. The central office took a dim view of lapses in "discipline" at the outlying mines. It rarely saw such occurrences in terms of African responses to deteriorating conditions of life and work.[42] The central administration reasoned that such developments were inevitably due to the shortcomings of local administration: Jean Schroeven at Busanga and Kikole was a "boor and a dullard"; Edouard Cremion was petulant, fearful, and passive — "a man used to cringing"; and A. Deluuw in Lomami was a man "totally oblivious to his obligations," according to the secret memoranda of the central administration.[43] The world of the mining sites and factories closed in on these men and severely constrained their freedom of action. In like manner, without the benefit of a coherent plan until 1927, these officers sought to quash and stifle the aspirations of the African workers whenever such aspirations threatened to emerge.

KEEPING THE COUNTRYSIDE AT BAY: THE GROWTH OF
THE URBAN POPULATION AND THE BEGINNINGS
OF WORKER STABILIZATION

Between 1919 and 1927 the economic deflation of Katanga's country-side and the adjacent portions of Angola and Northern Rhodesia caused the African population of Katanga's towns to increase dramati-cally. The rural exodus threatened the stability of urban life at every turn during the first decade following the First World War. It also plunged the countryside into a state of profound stagnation, for the most immediate effect of the 1921 recession on the African popula-tion was the slump in the price of maize and other foodstuffs. De-prived of a large portion of the cash revenue brought by such commodities, still reeling from the loss of human life experienced during the 1918–19 Spanish influenza epidemic, and without a wage labor force upon whom they could foist their losses, African peasants found it increasingly difficult to adapt to the conditions of the market and capitalist competition.[44] Older men, chiefs, and headmen more frequently entered into polygynous relationships in order to increase the supply of available labor for their lands. Such relationships further aggravated the disjuncture in the rural social structure, particularly in the more densely populated districts and territories. At times the disjuncture set kin and village networks and young and old against each other in a violent way.[45] Although induced by outside forces, such violence often came dressed in regional drag. A case in point was that of Tshimanga Makassa.[46]

Tshimanga Makassa lived in the village of Bakwa Kisongo in the district of Lomami. On 21 May 1928 – after a long absence from his village – Tshimanga murdered a woman named Tshibwe, one of his father's younger wives, at the American Presbyterian Mission at Bibanga. He was condemned to death by the police tribunal at Kamina on 11 August 1928. Before imposing the death sentence on him, the tribunal described Tshimanga as "a very dangerous creature who had deliberately chosen to live on the margins of society knowing no other law than his own ferocious instincts."[47]

In his attempts to defend himself, Tshimanga said that he had killed Tshibwe because she had "killed" his infant son, Kitoba, with a spell or curse. Kitoba had, in fact, died several days before Tshimanga murdered Tshibwe. According to Tshimanga, he had consulted three oracles – Kabuya, Kadima, and Kaseya – before killing Tshibwe. All three had told him that his son's fatal illness was caused by the wife of his father who belonged to the Bena Shimba clan. What the oracles were saying in a backhanded way was that the advent of Tshimanga's father's new wife had snatched away a portion of Tshimanga's own inheritance – no doubt, the reason that he left home the first time. The death of the child was merely emblematic of the new arrangement between the living and the dead in Tshimanga's household.[48]

The flight of ever-increasing contingents of young men like Tshimanga Makassa – men who were infused with a fiercely independent spirit as a result of their collective disillusionment – followed hard on the heels of the older generation's attempt to make the best of a bad situation.[49] While describing the consequences of this burgeoning wanderlust, one observer said that the villagers between Lusambo and Pania Mutombo "dance no longer" – presumably because having been deprived of so much cadet labor, they had no time to dance.[50] Once these young men reached the urban areas many of them decided to stay. And after 1926, industry was able to draw a percentage of its workforce from the towns. Labor of a temporary sort—the "floating population" of the colonial censuses—was always at hand.[51]

Initially these men demanded little from town life and often received less than they expected. Disease persisted. Work was gruelling and accompanied by corporal punishment. And food was often inedible because of its quality or because it was foreign to their diets.[52] By 1923, in the camps of the Union Minière near Elisabethville, some green vegetables could be purchased by African workers, but the more familiar cassava leaves, a staple green vegetable of the region, were in short supply. One kilogram of fish and 50 kilograms of salt—items that were in short supply everywhere else—were part of the weekly rations in the Union Minière camps. Six kilograms of maize flour, one kilogram of rice, and one of meat completed the array of rations that African workers bartered away for more familiar foods, canned sardines, jerked beef, and warm clothing. When no other fare could be acquired, they lived on company rations. Although this diet was far from adequate, even in terms of the Union Minière's own nutritional standards, it was the best that could be had among the large companies.[53]

The vastness of the demand for African labor at the Union Minière suggested a return to the illegal methods of recruitment.[54] In order to meet the incessant need for labor, a rather unscrupulous campaign to bend the legal framework of the Congo, the Charte coloniale, ensued.[55] The ultimate aim of this campaign was to mold both the urban and rural African population to the vacuous specifications of industrial capital by foisting a large portion of the reproduction costs of the industrial workforce onto the shoulders of the unsuspecting peasantry. At the same time government and industry made a combined effort to keep the social problems of the hinterland, particularly those associated with excessive labor recruitment, at a safe distance from the work sites, or at the very least, confined to the squatters' areas on the periphery of the towns. For despite a marked increase in the number of African workers taking on three-year contracts, it was still necessary to recruit 10,000–12,000 men annually to maintain an effective workforce of 14,000.[56] Moreover, while the number of workers recruited from Katanga and the neighboring Congolese provinces rose throughout the 1920s—partly because of varying methods of bookkeeping—the rate of increase fell markedly, going from roughly 8,000 in 1921–22 to about 2,000 in

1927–28.[57] By the end of 1924 about 3,000 men from Elisabethville's African quarter were continuously employed by the Union Minière.[58] As their numbers grew, such men began to make their presence felt in both the towns and the workers' camps.[59]

Although the appreciation of the number of Africans in the towns of Katanga could be easily comprehended by any European clerk who had the patience to sift through the files of residence and work permits, the total impact of the African quarter on urban life in general was less easy to get at.[60] The colonial administration did not readily understand the web of African family and household life. That there was some semblance of family life in the African quarter was understood, but comprehending how it functioned and to what end was problematic for the administration. For example, in 1924, the territorial administration of Elisabethville estimated that there were 250 African children living in the African quarter of the town and in the workers' camps. Who took care of them and whether they had actually been born in Elisabethville, however, were two of the municipality's great imponderables. In the minds of the authorities the African family was a given in the countryside and very nearly nonexistent in the towns. Consequently, children were anomalies, and African women merely convenient objects of male sexual desire or, at bottom, prostitutes.[61]

According to the received wisdom, the urban African worker would have to become monogamous and live in a nuclear household; for how else would he come to appreciate the interrelated notions of wage labor and the accumulation of wealth. Any other pattern of family life, where duties and obligations extended beyond an immediate family group, was anathema because it would impede the output of African labor.[62] The two major religious orders in Katanga, the Salesian Fathers and later the Benedictines under Monsignor de Hemptinne's leadership, presented themselves as the chief proselytizers of this view in the provincial council and in local ad hoc committees on African labor.[63] After the First World War they proselytized both the rural areas and the towns. Better endowed financially than the Salesians, the Benedictines offered to aid the provincial administration in stanching the influence of Protestant missionaries over segments of the urban African community and to educate both Africans and Europeans in the industrial towns. As a result, the Benedictines acquired complete control over most of the educational institutions of Elisabethville, the outlying towns, and the workers' camps. Monsignor de Hemptinne especially directed their energies toward tightly rivetting the conceptual environment in which the African was habituated to the changing needs of industry, particularly those of the Union Minière. School curricula followed the path of big industry. On the other hand, the Salesians became responsible for monitoring adult African behavior and attitudes in the rural areas south of Elisabethville. With the exception of a feeble attempt to initiate voluntary associations among African workers, the Salesian presence in the towns virtually disappeared.[64]

Throughout the 1920s Elisabethville and Jadotville were the recipients of the majority of newcomers to the towns because of their larger fund of resources and institutions. By the end of the 1920s there were nearly 30,000 Africans in greater Elisabethville and about 14,000 at Jadotville. These figures represented an increase of over 18,000 people in less than seven years for Elisabethville, or a rate of official increase of a little over 2,000 people a year. Jadotville's rate of increase from 1921 to 1928 was not as great—fewer than 800 people annually—but respectable enough considering the deplorable state of housing in the town's African quarter.[65] Both towns grew in tandem with the increase in output at the Union Minière's factories and mines; and, as Table 3.1 shows, there was only a hint of predominance of births over deaths among the households of the Union Minière's workers. It is unlikely that the general urban African population was increasing primarily on the basis of births.[66] In fact, the rather slim margin of births over deaths among Union Minière workers—a margin that would not increase markedly for almost a decade—suggests that improvements in the quality of the workers' lives were more tentative than the mining company cared to admit. If the general infant population of Elisabethville and Jadotville rose at all during this period, it was probably because of municipal absorption of outlying squatters' communities and the smaller adjacent mining towns such as Karavia and Kambove.[67]

African workers accepted some aspects of the Union Minière's stabilization policy while rejecting others. In Elisabethville and Jadot-

Table 3.1. Birth and Death Rates per 1,000 Households at the UMHK, 1927–1930

	Birth Rates	Death Rates
1927	142.4	221
1928	144.6	169.5
1929	152.5	135
1930	192.87	156.03

Sources: Léopold Mottoulle, "Mortinatalité et natalité chez les enfants des travailleurs Union Minière" (camps industriels), *Bulletin médical du Katanga* 7ème année, no. 1 (1930); Engels, "La Province du Katanga," *Rapport de la Commission du Travail,* Province du Katanga, 1931, p. 92.

ville the prospective workers' adaption occurred in relation to a larger, more skewed field of European power and institutions in the form of the colonial courts, police, labor inspectors, social welfare agents, and priests.[68] This made for nuances in the execution of the new order of things that no one could have foreseen at the time. The relative increase in the number of infants and children in Katanga's towns and the Union Minière camps, for example, was probably due more to the workers' preventive measures than the mining company's stabilization plan.[69] The more observant government officials readily acknowledged these efforts. They suggested that the workers tended to accept those policies of the company that did not interfere with their access to kin and village networks, and which allowed them to negotiate town life and wage labor on their own terms to some degree. In 1930 Fernand Engels drew attention to some of the workers' probable aspirations in the Government Study Group report for that year:

The application of the law with respect to the workers' camps is full of difficulties. We maintain, moreover, that the native prefers to live in the *cité indigène* rather than a camp. In the *cité* he lives in his own house; in the camp he lives in the house of his employer.[70]

The reinterpretation of the law, as well as its controversion, helped the mining company to articulate how it wanted to reshape the workforce. The decree of 16 March 1922 was one of the three laws that provided the legal point of departure for worker stabilization. This law outlined the rights and obligations of "civilized masters" and "native employees." Initially the decree simply attempted to delineate definite standards of conduct for casual and domestic workers. Gradually, the implications of the law spread to industry.[71] By 1926 the decree had become a means of filling the "lacunae and imperfections" in the labor ordinances of 1910 and 1912. The change in terms of the language between 1910 and 1922, from *louage de service* to *contrat du travail*, was, in fact, a subtle recognition of more numerous categories of African labor. Despite periodic labor shortages, the legal structure of Katanga had to take into account the increase in the number of permanent proletarians.[72] But the law moved more slowly than the workers. Some divisions of management at the Union Minière thought that the decree was woefully inept in spite of its stipulation of fines for absenteeism and civil prosecution for unauthorized departures from work. And the law said nothing explicit about African workers who did not demonstrate "appropriate" or "enough" respect for Europeans. Nor was it very precise about work stoppages, illegal strikes, or the exercise of corporal punishment.[73]

After 1925 the chief agencies for enforcement of labor legislation in Katanga, particularly the law of 1922, were the Comités consultatifs du Travail et de l'Industrie, the former Office de l'Inspection du Travail et Industrie. Its inspectors were also considered judicial police officers and agents of the colonial *parquet*, or court. Each inspector was theoretically invested with the power to draw up a *procès-verbal* in instances of unsafe or unsanitary conditions or physical abuse of African workers at a given place of work. But as early as 1925, the performance of the industrial inspectors came under sharp criticism from both private and government quarters. On 26 November 1925 Antoine Sohier, the *procureur général*, or chief justice, of Katanga, stated in a meeting of the Provincial Committee of Katanga that, although he did not question the sincerity or devotion of the industrial inspectors, the persistence of "abuse" in recruitment and negligence in industry with respect to the obligations due African workers seemed to indicate that the inspectors could not make employers obey the law:

I have just indicated that it is through the existing personnel that control over the native workers must be assured. It behooves us to spell out precisely measures which could impose rigorous moral and financial guarantees on labor contractors and recruited natives alike. There should be a strict observance and control of visas in general; better census and statistical records should be kept and employers should be exhorted not to be late with information and forms that aid in these endeavors. . . .[74]

Sohier's "observations" led to a series of verbal and written protests by Chief Industrial Inspector Marcel Dufour, Chief Medical Inspector M. Van Hoode, and individual inspectors. The thrust of their objections was that, although Sohier demanded an "active and engaged" spirit among the inspectors, he, as chief judicial officer of the province, had not given them any real power to remedy industrial problems or to censure the big industrial companies, particularly the Union Minière. Dufour asserted that if his men were remiss in their overall duties it was because of the lack of personnel and adequate means of transportation to scour the entire province regularly and consistently. He minuted that this was especially the case with the far-flung work sites of the Union Minière. In closing his written response to Sohier's admonishments Dufour quipped, "We have a good spirit, but in order to be active we must know precisely what our role is in the scheme of things."[75]

The Union Minière also attempted to get around legal barriers impeding its acquisition of more labor by increasing its control over the BTK. Through a complex set of maneuvers in the local committees, it could appoint or dismiss an executive director of the agency at will if his views on the labor problem diverged too radically from its own.[76] As its tax burden grew, the mining company's control over the BTK became very nearly absolute — so much so that it compelled the agency to rename itself the Office central du Travail du Katanga.[77] But the mining company continued to piece together its own Department of Native Labor (Département du Main-d'Oeuvre indigène) as further insurance against labor shortages.[78] It also remained heavily dependent on African recruits from Northern Rhodesia — a weak point in its labor policy that was not overcome until the middle of the next decade.[79]

The Union Minière was not unaware of the long-range implications of the shift in the legal and social conditions that underscored the growth and changing characteristics of the African workforce. First of all, between 1923 and 1930 the African population of Katanga began to increase at a faster rate than in previous years. Officially the population went from about 900,000 to 1,092,255 people; but as Table 3.2 shows, Katanga's actual number of African inhabitants was at least 1,127,991 — 35,736 more people than the 1930 census counted. According to the census, the ratio among men, women, and children stood at 83 men for every 100 women and 98 children. But the census data were extremely distorted, as local demographic studies of given territories were to prove. The Government Study Group reports of 1931 projected the mean level of distortion in the Haut-Luapula District as 27.27 percent more men, 13.67 percent more women, and 25.27 percent more children; in Lulua District, 5.84 percent more men, 3 percent more women, and 6.6 percent more children; and in Tanganika-Moero there were 3.7 percent more men. What the distortions signified was that a large portion of the African population, particularly men, had already made its way to the towns before the commencement of stabilization. By 1930 the number of Africans working for wages for at least six months reached 90,000 — allowing for a large rate of turnover due to death and flight.[80] In 1930 Lulua, Lomami, and Tanganika-Moero disposed of 24,338 men, almost all of whom had been recruited from administrative centers and towns for long- and medium-distance labor. Most of these men were earmarked for work at the Union Minière.[81]

Between 1924 and 1930, therefore, the collective character of the African workforce at Union Minière, and in Katanga as a whole, began to take shape. By 1928 there were over 16,000 African workers at the Union Minière — 1,000 more men than the previous peak year.[82] Copper production reached an annual average of 80,000 tons, and the extraction of tin, cobalt, radium, and uranium went beyond their earlier experimental levels. The consumption of imported food and manufactured products took a marked leap.[83] Workers living in the African quarter of the various industrial towns took to building their own houses in brick and cement rather than renting stands of wood and straw. In order to keep pace with these developments, the Union Minière began to improve housing in the workers' camps.[84] The mining company abruptly ended its emulation of the South African model of management.[85]

Table 3.2. Official African Populations of Katanga in 1930 and Augmented Total

District	OFFICIAL FIGURES					
	Men	Women	Boys	Girls	Total	Augmented Total
GENERAL POPULATION						
Haut-Katanga[a]	1,531	1,973	1,382	1,318	6,204	–
Haut-Luapula	35,467	45,719	29,250	29,167	139,603	155,773
Lomami	138,946	166,710	74,131	62,601	442,388	448,773
Lulua	63,179	70,734	39,360	35,612	208,885	218,239
Tanganika-Moero	84,329	102,874	56,102	51,870	295,175	305,206
Total	323,452	388,010	200,225	180,568	1,092,255	1,127,991
FLOATING POPULATION[b]						
Haut-Katanga[a]	19,256	2,368	476	499	22,599	
Haut-Luapula	29,333	8,963	2,722	2,516	43,534	
Lomami	3,455	1,307	308	389	5,459	
Tanganika-Moero	8,377	5,408	1,762	1,644	17,191	
Total	60,421	18,046	5,268	5,048	88,783	
UPROOTED POPULATION[b]						
Haut-Katanga[a]	2,896	1,758	890	841	6,385	
Haut-Luapula	766	507	239	244	1,756	
Lomami	282	222	93	86	683	
Tanganika-Moero	2,842	2,662	1,782	17,815	25,101	
Total	6,786	5,149	3,004	18,986	33,925	
Official total minus floating and uprooted populations					969,547	

Sources: *Rapports annuels du Congo Belge*, 1929 and 1930; Engels, "Katanga."
[a]These figures are limited to the city of Elisabethville; they do not pertain to the entire Haut-Katanga District.
[b]No figures for the floating and uprooted populations are available for the Lulua District.

In the main, African workers refused to be transformed into beings whose culture was tailored to the specifications of industrial production and supply and demand. The basic social determinants of the African workers' consciousness remained, to some extent, outside the boundaries of the labor market. Their desire to return to their villages as successful peasants conditioned their acceptance of the new labor policy. Between 1927 and 1929, for example, the most consistent reply by African recruits from Lomami as to why they had come to the mines was: "I have become a worker so that I may do as my father. My father has three or four wives. . . . They grow cotton. He, therefore, holds on to them. But one day I will inherit them all."[86] The agricultural price slumps of 1926 and 1930 closed off the peasant farmer option for most of these workers, however. Combined with the demands of wage labor, the slumps made a triumphant return to the rural world little more than a lingering fantasy.

IN THE SHADOW OF THE CHIEFS: AFRICAN LODGES AND VOLUNTARY ASSOCIATIONS IN THE INDUSTRIAL TOWNS

Among the unskilled and illiterate mass of African workers, the number of ethnically and regionally based lodges and friendly societies grew steadily. Although such tendencies merged with more secular trends of worker organization over the long run of the African workers' experience, they often became powerful defense mechanisms against the negative consequences of short-term economic crises and the prospects of abuse from whites.[87] While some government and business leaders expressed trepidations about the "tribal" nature of the lodges, they disingenuously fostered their survival by making every other form of combination illegal or socially objectionable.[88] This contrasted sharply with the social impulses originating within the labor process and the forces of production themselves.[89]

Voluntary associations and a growing collective consciousness among the African mineworkers were more than mere reactions to miserable working and living conditions. Despite the sharp and widespread character of these conditions in the 1920s, they did not, in themselves, provide sufficient stimuli for town-based organizations concerned to give African workers proper burials and to aid them in conserving and enhancing their meager resources. Inasmuch as they could, African workers attempted to make practical use of their memories of the most notable precolonial sovereigns and chiefs.[90] For it was within the arc of circumstances surrounding the passing of a sovereign or great chief and the emergence of a new one that the precolonial polity was reborn — and, subsequently, all clans and household groupings.[91] Although many aspects of village life accompanied the African worker to the towns and work sites, they simply could not mean what they had meant in precolonial times.[92] For example, the rearguard despatching of a dead notable's enemies was often symptomatic of an underlying current of instability in the same sense that a sudden increase in the number of witches or sorcerors might have been.[93] But the discontinuity experienced by African workers, particularly the mineworkers, was of a different species. Thus, African workers selectively rescued the elements of their rural experience. Those aspects of the precolonial experience that spoke to the need for order and rebirth out of chaos and havoc survived the rupture and became important sources of inspiration for worker combination.

Butwa, a popular voluntary society of the Luapula Valley and the western backlands of Lakes Mweru and Tanganyika, was widespread among the Luba-Shankadi and Bemba recruits for the Union Minière and also among the African townspeople in general during the First World War and the early 1920s. Butwa and another association, Bambudye, which had been brought to the Luapula Valley by the Lunda Kazembe, ultimately became the means through which chiefs and aristocrats spoke to their people on the work sites.[94] These associations offered their members recreation in the form of beer drinks and burlesque dance performances which mocked Christian marriage vows, baptism, and the Eucharist. As early as 1912, only four years after the opening of the Union Minière, public dancing by Africans had become enough of an irritant for the European population of the town to prompt a police ordinance banning it along the main thoroughfares of the town and near the European living quarters after 9:00 P.M. The spread of the dance called *mbeni* or *bena ngoma* into the mining camps of Katanga was carried out through the agency of the voluntary associations.[95] By 1924 *mbeni* was also considered a public menace. Similarly, *kaonge*, a dance which probably found its way to Katanga via travelling Hausa merchants and demobilized African soldiers from Senegal, was seen in the same light.[96]

Care of the sick and injured also became one of Butwa's functions, because Africans at work on the mines encountered a spate of new and unfamiliar diseases. Usually each work day one member of the association would stay home to cook meals, care for the sick, and gather firewood and water. In the mining camps such arrangements must have been fairly common because of the relative ease with which an absent African worker could escape the casual inquiry and notice of camp and mine management up to 1929, when the *ticket du travail*, or work billet, method of accounting for the number of Africans actually at work on a given day was reorganized at the major work sites of the Union Minière.[97] Given the wholesale nature of death at the mining company, Butwa was also obliged to ensure its members decent funerals despite unfamiliar surroundings.

Butwa was an important hedge against the failure of the mining company to provide the necessary amenities for the maintenance and reproduction of the African workforce.[98] But by the mid-1920s it became merely one of several African voluntary associations operating in the industrial towns. As the wages of African mineworkers rose in relation to other African workers between 1926 and 1930, responsibility for entertainment of the notables and for subvention of the subterranean side of town life in the African quarters fell increasingly on their shoulders. Thus Butwa receded into the background with the growth of African friendly societies and lodges.[99]

The African lodges, or *bashikutu*, absorbed many of the functions of the earlier voluntary associations by the middle of the 1920s. They also incorporated women's organizations like *bulindu*; for women figured very prominently in the smuggling networks that brought reminders from home—indigenously prepared beer and spirits, regional foods and spices, and marijuana—onto the work sites. Women were much in the limelight because such activities were very lucrative and gave the lodges a source of funds for bribing African policemen and lower-level European officials. By 1928 several women were listed as officers in a number of the lodges.[100] The lodges quickly assumed responsibility for preparing proper funerals for their members, for death was a pervasive reality for the mineworkers, particularly those at the underground mines at Kipushi and Kamoto. The sudden cracking of a gallery joist, the reticence of a pulley, or a badly placed charge of explosives could send an entire crew of workers to their death. Exactly how many such workers returned to their villages at death is not known for the 1920s. But with the appearance of the lodges and friendly societies, a larger number of men must have made the journey back to the resting places of their ancestors than did during the Spanish influenza epidemic or before; moreover, a larger number of men now chose to be buried where they lived and worked.[101] The intense efforts of some of the lodges such as the Bena Kibeshi and the Shikutu wa Kabinda to buy plots of land near the workers' camps or in Elisabethville for the construction of cemeteries and lodge houses between 1926 and 1928 illustrated this desire.[102] Many of the lodges also absorbed the rituals of extant secret societies like *bukanzanzi*, a Luba cult which protected the dead from witches and vampires; for it was believed that without such rituals the alleged European penchant for human flesh could not be appeased.[103]

In addition to deaths and maimings, there was also the terrible psychological disorientation that came with arduous work — particularly work underground. The workers' consumption of marijuana — almost always under the sponsorship of the lodges — was a temporary means of keeping their anxiety and fears at bay.[104] This was particularly so for men from the territory of Kabongo, which was also the apparent source for the networks of smugglers who brought the marijuana into the workers' camps.[105] Between 1926 and 1930 there were 326 mass arrests for marijuana consumption at Kipushi alone. In one instance in late 1927, 23 workers at Kipushi, including a handful of African clerks, were arrested.[106] The effects of marijuana were only temporary, however. And the acceleration of output under increasingly harsh conditions at Kipushi augured more in favor of better organization, cooperation at the work place, and collective self-discipline rather than the illusory respite of marijuana.

Toward the end of 1923 Henri Segaert, the magistrate–cum–public commissioner, interviewed the "sultan" of the Bena Kibeshi lodge, who was probably Kabongo Kungu, an African clerk at the Prince Léopold Mine. On the basis of this interview, Segaert warned the provincial government and the Union Minière to suppress the lodges or suffer grave consequences:

> Although this might seem like a parody of the judicial and administrative agencies of our colony, this parody is not without a certain amount of danger to the authority of the *Chef de Camp* and the prestige of government magistrates and officials.[107]

Here is the portion of the interview that Segaert took greatest offense at:

Segaert: What measures do you take against one of your members who disrupts a meeting or the speech of a *Chef de Camp* or white magistrate?
Sultan: I punish them.
Segaert: But you do not have any means to punish a native. [Vous ne disposez d'aucun moyen pour punir cet indigène.]
Sultan: Si. Nous il supprimerons tout cadeau au moment de son retour vers le village natal.[108]

No doubt the potential double meaning of the "sultan's" last response was what put Segaert on guard. For the "si" could mean "Yes, you are right. We cannot punish him in any explicit way, but . . ." or "No, you are wrong. We can punish him by impounding the gifts that he would take back to his home village." The whole sense of what was being said turned on what the meaning of punishment was — and, more important, who defined its meaning. It was probably at this point that Segaert began to have ominous second thoughts.[109]

The Union Minière's management became fully aware of the existence of the lodges in late 1925, as recruitment of Africans for work on the mines was stepped up in Kabinda, Kanda Kanda, Tshofa, and the other more densely populated territories of Lomami. By December 1927 the central office at Elisabethville was sufficiently alarmed by the presence of the friendly societies in the workers' camps to issue a circular exhorting all the camp managers to learn all they could about the activity of the "Belges" among the African workers, and to keep updated lists of the leaders and members of the various friendly societies operating in their respective camps. As far as the mining company was concerned, the most pressing questions about the lodges were: (1) How many reengaged workers, divided into categories of one, two, and three years, belonged to "Belges"-type organizations? (2) Do the "Belges" exist in every camp? (3) Who distributed beer and *lutuku* to the African workers? and (4) How did the chiefs use the cash bonuses given them?[110]

In 1927 the most notable lodges operating in the camps of the Union Minière and in the towns of Katanga were Shikutu wa Bruxelles and Bena Malela from Tanganika-Moero District, Shikutu wa Lwango from Lulua District, Bena Bakusu from Lomami, and Bena Kibeshi from Kabongo. Although the lodges were divided along ethnic lines, such divisions were not rigid; and, on occasion, common regional origin took precedence over ethnic affiliation.[111]

Records of members in good standing were kept by a *caissier*, or treasurer. These records consisted of a member's name, his occupation, and where he was employed. Monthly dues varied from 5 to 20 francs. Officers in the lodges often took names or titles that were reminiscent of their homes or a great event or chieftain from the past. Although a number of sources indicate that few officers in the lodges had chiefly lineages, their constituencies expected them to have attributes and personal traits that harked back to the more illustrious notables of precolonial times. In late 1928 the three most important officers in the Shikutu wa Kabinda were "chiefs" Lumpungu, Kasongo, and Kalamba, each of these names referring to famous paramount chieftains of the Songye, Luba, and Lulua of the Kabinda territory. The grand chief of the Bena Malela was "Nduba of Kongolo," called so after a semilegendary hero, Nduba, from Kongolo in northern Tan-

ganika-Moero. The example of the Bena Malela was most illustrative of the selection process for officers in the lodges, because a blood-
line notable, Sefu, was also a member of this particular lodge. While
Sefu happened to be an officer of the lodge, it seems that his position
was mainly honorary, and that real power within the organization
was vested in Nduba and the other two nonnoble officers.[112]

In August 1928 the camp manager for the Union Minière at Lubumbashi interrogated several officers of the lodges operating in the
workers' camp. The lodges wanted to purchase some of the land
owned by the mining company. After several days of inquiry into the
motives of their desire to purchase the land, the camp manager
concluded:

> The stated purpose of the Belges [lodges] is unity and mutual aid. They
> convene periodically to discuss and iron out differences existing among
> members of the society and also among other groups. They pay the funeral
> and interment costs of their members and aid in the cost for those who must
> go back to their villages or are repatriated. They maintain ties with groups
> in the countryside. On different occasions they organize fêtes and dances.
> They claim to promote goodwill and discipline in the camps.[113]

All the leaders of government and business were not of the same mind
about the lodges. Gaston Heenen—secretary of the minister of
colonies' cabinet during the Musafiri case and, by 1926, vice governor-
general of Katanga—thought the lodges were fairly innocuous, since,
from the lists of officers ("governor," "magistrate," "police commissioner"), they appeared to be mere copies of European administration.[114] But in the minds of other officials such "imitations" were
inherently subversive because they implied equality with whites.
Monsignor de Hemptinne, for instance, said that he could not suppress a certain amount of anxiety about the lodges because they did
in fact represent a pole of authority that no European had access to.
Moreover, he maintained that if one were to do a casual census of
Africans in the industrial towns, one would find that they all "talk
incessantly of America"; and if one were to ask an African worker
how he wished to be treated, he would say that he wished to be treated
like the blacks in America who, in his mind, were treated on terms
of equality with the whites. De Hemptinne went on to say that it
was not clear whether such aspirations originated with the lodges,
but if they did, the lodges should be suppressed.[115]

As the economic downturn and the advent of worker stabilization
compelled the mining company to thin the ranks of their African

workers, the lodges became particularly concerned to maintain the jobs held by their members. If a propensity toward collective violence appeared to be emerging within the lodges after late 1929, it was largely because of their inability to keep a number of their members from being laid off and repatriated. Mass returns to the countryside meant a sharp contraction of the cash subscriptions flowing to the lodges. The leadership of the lodges feared this prospect more than anything else.[116]

The Union Minière and the provincial administration launched a combined and multileveled offensive against the lodges at the end of 1928. At first there was the barrage of local ordinances and decrees that derived from the *ordonnance-loi* of 11 February 1926 and the Union Minière's enthusiastic sponsorship of the *tribunaux indigènes*, or native courts, in the workers' camps. The proliferation of the local ordinances and African courts was an attempt by the mining company and the administration to short circuit the African mineworkers' adherence to customary law and the lodges, and to encourage them to look more to the mining company and the colonial administration for solutions to their grievances. Secondly, the Union Minière, with the aid of the Benedictine order and the territorial administration, attempted to kill off the African lodges at their source in the countryside by establishing *ateliers centraux*, or trainee workshops, *écoles professionelles*, and a network of African social assistants, or *moniteurs*, in the territories from which the largest number of recruits for the Union Minière were drawn.[117]

By 1927 it was clear to everyone—particularly the workers themselves—that the lodges represented a way station between the forms of expression that had given life meaning in the agrarian world and those that threatened to tenant the grim industrial future. Behind the rhetorical flourishes about the dangers of the workers' lodges lay the more immediate prospect of social control over the African workforce. But before some form of constraint could be placed on the workers' activities its purpose had to be restated in a way which made it a goal for civil society as well as industry. For this, the methods to be used and the points of cooperation between the state's administrative machinery and the mining company had to be clearly outlined. The need for such elucidation was proved in the breach by the events that led to the labor unrest of 1931.

CHAPTER FOUR

From Stabilization to Labor Unrest, 1927–1931

STABILIZATION VERSUS THE AFRICAN WORKERS

> . . . The brains of the foremen are under the worker's cap.
>
> William "Big Bill" Haywood, testifying before a United States congressional committee investigating working conditions and scientific management, circa 1914[1]

> Here organization has reached an American standard. Every man has a nail and a number on the wall of a big office. Here everyday he brings his little book of work tickets and the half is torn off and stuck on the nail. At the end of the six months the whole book goes on. Then there are a whole series of other labels, a red one when the man is on holiday and a blue one for bad work and so the reduction of pay, a yellow one for absence at hospital, a green one for prison, etc. It is possible by looking at a man's nail to see at a glance his whole industrial history. . . .
>
> Margery Perham on a visit to the Union Minière in April 1930[2]

In the mid- and late 1920s the Union Minière sought to capture a larger portion of the world market by simultaneously increasing output and valorizing its finished product at a higher level.[3] More copper ingots and cathodes were produced than matte or blister copper. As a result, the mining company increased its complement of African factory operatives, foundrymen, and skilled workers in response to the new production requirements. These workers became an indispensable feature of the stabilization and reproduction of the entire industrial workforce.[4]

86

The cutting edge of the new output strategy was formed by changes in productive techniques — many of which had come from the United States rather than from Europe after the First World War, and of which scientific management was not the least.[5] The new developments in investment and technology had a differential impact on mining operations in the advanced industrial world and in the colonial and semicolonial worlds of Africa and Latin America. The only certainty of the period was America's loss of an absolute edge in terms of global copper production.[6] North American–based copper companies attempted to mitigate some of these disadvantages by forming the Copper Exporters Cartel and raising the global price for copper from 13 to 25 British cents a pound.[7] They also closed or scaled down their operations in Latin America, while taking a headlong plunge into the burgeoning copper mining industry of Northern Rhodesia, just across the border from Katanga.

In southern Africa, the interrelated problems of appropriate technology and investment realization expressed themselves in spot and general labor shortages as new industries such as food processing and textiles opened up, and as mining and other primary industries sought to discipline their more experienced and skilled workers with piece rates and other cost-cutting features.[8] At the Union Minière, between 1923 and 1929, the percentages of ore extracted by hand and by machinery were virtually reversed — going from 90 and 10 percent, respectively, to 16 and 84 percent.[9] The amount of copper sulphate ore from the underground Prince Léopold Mine at Kipushi — almost all the ore extracted from the open-pit mines was copper oxide — rose sharply as well. By 1928, although employing less than 8 percent of the total workforce, the underground mine was producing almost 10 percent of all the copper ore extracted at the Union Minière and almost 25 percent of the ore smelted at the Lubumbashi factory complex.[10] In general, the amount of finished copper produced by the company increased almost 600 percent, going from 25,374 tons in 1919 to 151,008 tons in 1929 (see Table 4.1). This increase caused the company's share of global copper production to leap from 2 to 8 percent. Yet the African workforce merely doubled in the same time period — going from a little under 7,500 men to about 16,000.

As the mining company attempted to adjust to greater market opportunities and pressures, the wage bill for the more skilled and experienced African workers rose.[11] The company sought to achieve some control over wage increases by implementing piece rates and redefining the nature of "skill."[12] The latter measure also increased

Table 4.1. Number of African Workers at the Union Minière and Gross Annual
    Copper Production (in tons), 1919–1931

	Number of Workers	Gross Annual Production at Union Minière	Gross Annual Global Production	Union Minière's Production as a Percentage of Global Production
1919	7,435	25,374	1,083,000	2
1920	10,833	20,902	1,000,000	2
1921	9,475	33,581	708,333	5
1922	6,488	47,798	1,000,000	5
1923	8,723	63,808	1,500,000	4
1924	11,495	94,325	1,580,000	6
1925	12,680	99,323	1,670,000	6
1926	11,816	88,890	1,830,000	5
1927	15,184	98,278	2,167,000	5
1928	14,422	123,396	2,000,000	6
1929	16,127	151,008	1,915,000	8
1930	12,029	153,317	1,750,000	9
1931	10,010	132,482	1,083,000	12

Sources: *Rapport sur l'Administration du Congo Belge*, 1918–1933; Kindleberger, *World in Depression*; Orris Herfindal, *Copper Costs and Prices: 1870–1957* (Baltimore: Johns Hopkins University Press, 1959); Perrings, *Black Mineworkers*.

the degree of redundancy among white workers, while compelling a reclassification of all skilled African workers who had not been trained in the company's workshops and apprentice schools, or whose skills were not directly related to mineral extraction and metallurgy.[13] Consequently, many of the African carpenters, bricklayers, and masons, whose labor had been so crucial to the company in its earlier developmental phase, were suddenly declared redundant.[14]

The Union Minière's central workshops and *écoles professionelles* became the social laboratories where a dilution and disaggregation of industrial and manufacturing skills took place.[15] The mining company tried to insinuate Fredrick Winslow Taylor's "mental revolution" into every aspect of its program of worker stabilization.[16] As early as 1925 the company, in conjunction with the Benedictine Fathers, began to deploy hundreds of African "trainees" and apprentices – adolescents as well as work-age males – to rural workshops in the districts of Lomami and Maniema. There were also training installations in many of the recruiting camps and shoemaking factories at Luishia and Kipushi.[17] The latter installations functioned as conveyor belts for the larger, more machine tool–oriented central workshops at Panda and Lubumbashi.[18]

The priests, who served as instructors in the workshops, were seconded by African auxiliaries — *moniteurs* and *instituteurs*, "social assistants" and "schoolmasters." The primary job of these African auxiliaries was to make the apprentices carry out commands with a "sense of awe and passivity in the face of the sublime character of European civilization."[19] The priests, social assistants, and schoolmasters were also obliged to "educate" their wards by their own example. And between 1925 and 1930 the schoolmasters and social assistants were called upon to be leaders in a number of voluntary associations organized by the Benedictine monk Gregoire Coussement. These organizations sought to counter the growing influence of the lodges and friendly societies among prospective workers.[20] Such efforts constituted yet another prong in the mining company's attack on the more resilient forms of African culture in the towns.

In general, the company's "workshops" and related voluntary associations tended to attract only the most assimilated Africans or those who sought European protection — particularly after 1928, when the workshops themselves were moved closer to the towns and work sites.[21] African auxiliaries were attracted to the workshops and Catholic-sponsored voluntary associations, not only because of palpable material incentives such as better education for their children and a more prestigious form of employment for themselves, but also because the levelling of wage rates among the elite strata of African workers in the mid-1920s preempted any kind of leadership role for them in the lodges. However, they could not really turn the workshops and church-sponsored voluntary associations into genuine alternatives to the lodges for African operatives and mineworkers. In many instances the company's workshops and church-sponsored voluntary associations served to alienate the social assistants and schoolmasters further from the urban masses.[22]

Evidence of the mere cosmetic influence of these institutions came in the form of the obsequious and self-serving correspondence between African auxiliaries and the central office of the Union Minière at Elisabethville. One such letter, written by a social assistant named Tshikontshie Gabriel, is illustrative of the kind of indirect dissemination of company propaganda that the social assistants and schoolmasters engaged in on a daily basis. Tshikontshie's letter concluded:

We are pleased to see you in our school because many of us work for you in the mines. You do a lot of good things for the workers such as clothing them and feeding them; and that is why they are wealthy enough to afford bride prices. We ask you on behalf of all of us who are among you to continue to do well. Many of us are attending classes at the workshops. As a result, you have said, "I want to see more in class." Thus we are obliged to thank you for the good that you have done. For that reason we wish you well with your work in this land always. We, the social assistants, hope that we are truly of service to you. We only seek to do well. We salute you with good wishes.[23]

Between 1925 and 1932 the Union Minière received hundreds of such letters from handpicked African auxiliaries. Not one of them, however, was penned by an African recruit or apprentice.

Once an apprentice was moved to one of the larger central workshops at Lubumbashi or Panda, special care was taken to keep him segregated from the main body of factory operatives.[24] Of the two main workshops, Panda was the largest; by 1929 it housed as many as 500 apprentices and machinery in the prisonlike Orenstein dormitories just south of the refining mill and the sulphuric acid plant.[25] A first-degree apprenticeship in woodworking took six months to complete, and one in metalworking took eight months. Second-degree apprentices worked eight hours a day on the work sites — roughly three to five hours less than ordinary unskilled hands — and spent one hour a day at classroom work. In theory the highest-paid apprentices received a wage of 7.50 Congolese francs a day — a third more than a factory operative at Lubumbashi and almost twice as much as an ordinary worker at the open-pit mines or a surface worker at the underground mine at Kipushi. The lowest-paid apprentices received a daily wage of four Congolese francs, or slightly more than the average unskilled African operative. But European operatives earned almost 20 times as much as the highest-paid African apprentices in the same time period.[26] Thus, while the workshops and apprentice schools were vectors of upward mobility within the new world of industry, neither the prestige nor the wage was great enough for prospective skilled workers to cut themselves off completely from the great mass of African workers.

The Union Minière's creation of the apprentice schools and workshops, and an intrusive network of African auxiliaries, reflected its determination to eradicate agrarian mores and reshuffle preindustrial conceptions of work to its advantage. It also sought to tailor the demographic characteristics of the African workforce in a way that would make the company less dependent on large-scale labor recruitment.[27] On the other hand, the company sought to enhance its control further over the productive process and over the more skilled workers by speedily introducing self-timing blast furnaces and ovens into foundries and refining plants. Technology was merely the handmaiden of a more totalitarian vision of company control. Management pursued this vision relentlessly and with an eye toward cutting costs during a period of rapid industrial growth. It also envisioned a smooth and uncomplicated implementation of such objectives. Some of the envisioned ease comes out in this excerpt from a company *mémoire* written in 1952 by Emile Toussaint, one of the chief architects of the worker stabilization program:

> Stabilization was above all an economic necessity for the Union Minière. For the native worker and the native population in general it was a benefit. The native placed in the service of the enterprise ceased to be an anonymous auxiliary; his willingness to work was increased; he was better remunerated; and he lived better. He gave his labor willingly and without undue strain. He was pleased with his new existence. His personality developed and he acquired the dignity and conscientiousness of a true worker.[28]

The implicit goals of the new industrial discipline — punctuality, temperance, and sexual restraint — were not easily won, however. The lurches that accompanied the attempts to recompose the African workforce around an expanded core of factory operatives and skilled workers at Lubumbashi and Panda were a result of the failure of the mining company to make a smooth transition from the migrant labor system. As late as 1930 half of the company's African workforce still came from the neighboring colonies, although not necessarily from the areas of those colonies that had become its customary redoubts. Where it could, the mining company jealously guarded the inherent political and social advantages of the migrant labor system, while seeking to acquire some of the economic advantages held out by a self-reproducing industrial workforce. But the company could neither always predict the forms of class expression nor engineer them. At times the manner in which the workers chose to make their aspirations known clashed sharply with the new and extant forms of social control; at others, they conformed all too well.[29]

Out of the new methods of management emerged a war of attrition. The war was fought on the southernmost mining sites until 1931.[30] The experiences of the African workers at the Lubumbashi foundry between 1928 and 1930, the mass abscondings of African workers from the underground mine at Kipushi between 1927 and 1930, the African attempts to prevent a second razing of the African quarter of Elisabethville between 1928 and 1930, and the labor unrest of 1931 represented the major campaigns of the war.[31] Each of them was sparked by the plight of a particular ethnic enclave among the workers. The sabotage at the Lubumbashi works and the boycotts at Elisabethville in 1931 were primarily the doing of the African workers from the two Rhodesias and Nyasaland. The mass flight and sit-down strikes of underground workers at Kipushi were initiated by Luba from Kabinda territory in Lomami. The antirepatriation riots and faction fights at Mwene Ditu and Kipushi were more or less a Hutu-Luba affair.

What actually happened during the initial phases of stabilization contrasted sharply with the vision of its authors. The replacement of the military metaphor, which had characterized the mining company's management for the previous 20 years, with a bureaucratic and scientific one reflected the imperatives of technical control as perceived by the Union Minière's administration; but at another level the technical and social changes at the point of production generated a palpable weakening of the old chain of authority, which began with the white machinist or steam shovel driver and ended with the camp manager and police commissioner, and which had been anchored more in coercion than technical control.[32] Centralization meant fewer white supervisors in many areas of work, particularly the more skilled ones. But it also meant that the system's response to challenges from the workers was often narrow and parochial rather than dynamic and manifold.[33] Such rigidity meant that worker protest was not easily absorbed as part of the "give and take" of the new production process, and was often met with a degree of force that was out of proportion to the challenge posed by the workers. There were two occasionally contradictory impulses within the new method of worker control—a bureaucratic one and a paternalistic one—and the clash of the two sometimes afforded the African workers some room to manipulate the system for their own ends, but more often provoked imagined and real flashpoints which led to subsequent repression.

The initial worker stabilization plan, which was conceived by Léon Rasson, Emile Toussaint, and Léopold Mottoulle between 1926 and 1928, sought to stratify the work routine and wages along ethnic lines.[34] Unduly optimistic about the success of the plan, largely because of their uninformed view of the basis of ethnic and tribal association among the African workers, Mottoulle and Toussaint floated a series of schemes that appeared patently ridiculous when seen from the vantage point of the post-1931 situation. In general, such schemes called upon African workers to accept the notions that certain ethnic groups were predisposed to particular skills and work tasks and that, although the wage structure was informed by science and technology, it was articulated by criteria that were not directly related to the connection between wages and productivity.[35] For example, the received wisdom among some levels of management had it that Hutu workers did not really need cooling houses after they came from work underground, since the air in their mountain homeland was so thin anyway. Most workers thought otherwise, even if they did not say so. And most recognized that management's attempt to convince them that the Hutu workers did not need cooling houses violated the assumptions of the new methods of work and their own safety to some degree.[36] At the same time the workers were faced with a sixfold increase in copper production, along with an increase in the production of cobalt, tin, and radium, with only a twofold increase in their own numbers (see Table 4.1).

In the early 1920s similar conditions would have simply led to mass flight. But by 1930 absconding seemed an inadequate means of redress to a growing number of African workers. However slight, the improvement in the quality of life in the towns and in the camps had caused the aspirations of some of the African workers to rise on the eve of the Depression. The standard of living also rose; and more than any other group of African workers, those at the Union Minière were affected by its elevation. But the improved standard of living was adumbrated by the wholesale introduction of piece rates and by new kinds of pacesetting machinery at work, particularly at the factories and the underground mine.[37] African workers came to realize that the improved standard of living was not without certain social costs, and that improved living standards did not allay the dangers that work continued to have.

The Union Minière's pleas for austerity and self-restraint therefore seemed all the more unreasonable to the African workers, particularly since the company was demanding more output. Excessive workloads at Kipushi and the Lubumbashi works, a surge of absenteeism, falling attendance at the *palabres indigènes* — the institutionalized grievance sessions set up by the company — and the growing influence of the lodges were all indicative of a widening breach between the mining company and the workers.[38] Finally, a long line of what the workers perceived as spectacular betrayals, beginning with the razing of the workers' cemetery at Ruashi in 1928, provided the fuse for future unrest.[39]

Most of the sources of African discontent were embedded in company policy and practice. After the commencement of stabilization African workers no longer worked from sunup to sundown. Their work day was punctuated by whistles and sirens. Yet they lost a great

deal of control over their time during the more abbreviated periods
of work, while producing almost three times as much as they had
under the old system.[40] African workers occasionally opted to challenge the new arrangement of time and work, but they more often
chose to improve upon the stakes they had acquired in it. A growing
number of them began to feel that the mining industry was a permanent and ineffaceable presence in Katanga. Inasmuch as it was, they
sought to accommodate themselves to it and make some demands
on it as well. With stabilization, the Union Minière sought to position a permanent industrial workforce; the African workers a community.[41] Both got some of what they wanted — but with all the
liabilities generated by the contradictory impulses at the point of production and within the incipient working-class community.

The "Troublesome Rhodesias"

From the outset of worker stabilization the Union Minière sought
to rid itself of the "troublesome Rhodesias" and, at the same time,
increase the number of Luba and Hutu workers from Lomami and
the Belgian protectorate of Ruanda-Urundi. By February 1930 management intended to cut the number of African workers from the two
Rhodesias and Nyasaland by at least 60 percent.[42] But on the eve of
the riot at Ruashi in May 1931, which broke out when municipal
and mining camp police attempted to level the houses of Rhodesian
workers, they were still an important component of the company's
workforce.[43] There were, in fact, two populations of "Rhodesias" in
Katanga: the skilled and semiskilled workers in the building trades
and in the Union Minière's Lubumbashi factory complex, and the new,
and in some cases underaged, recruits who were the village "leavings"
of the fierce competition for manpower between the Union Minière
and the Roan Selection Trust and Anglo-American Mining Corpora-
tion in Northern Rhodesia.[44] The Union Minière was relatively successful in removing the latter population from the Prince Léopold
Mine at Kipushi and the other mining sites, but it fared less well at
getting rid of the more experienced and skilled workers.[45]

Africans from the southern British colonies were a thorn in the side
of the mining camp's administration for a number of reasons: many
of them were literate and were quick to quibble about the absence
of conformity between the written terms of a contract and the actual
conditions of work; they called on industrial inspectors to pursue their
duties and to expose disease-ridden quarters and hazardous working
conditions when the inspectors were most reluctant to challenge pre-

vailing industrial practices; they taught their Congolese workmates the industrial rules of the game by means of the strike and other kinds of work actions, for by 1926 many of them had been working in Katanga for almost a generation.[46] Finally, the Rhodesians and Nyasalanders were British subjects, and the Union Minière was obliged to pay them British pounds rather than hyperinflated Congolese francs. In the 1920s, depending upon the degree of fluctuation between the franc and the pound, this could mean that a Rhodesia might be paid almost three times as much as his fellow Congolese worker. It was not for nothing, then, that the mining company resolved to get rid of them.[47]

Rhodesians and Nyasalanders also acquired the largest portion of brick and cement housing in the African sections of Elisabethville and in the surrounding workers' camp between 1926 and 1931—a factor which, no doubt, exacerbated the scramble for resources within the camps, since brick and cement housing was the best insurance against tick fever and pneumonia.[48] At Ruashi, the African workers' suburb that grew up on the route between Elisabethville and the Star of the Congo, Africans from the two Rhodesias were in firm control of the township's best housing as early as 1926. The majority of them worked for the Union Minière, but indirectly either in the construction gangs of European subcontractors or as supplementary skilled labor. As a result of their access to building materials, the Rhodesias could often build houses in brick and cement themselves if they were not provisioned them. By 1928 Ruashi had become the chief area of settlement for Africans from the neighboring British colonies in Katanga.[49]

The position of the Rhodesias within the production process at the Lubumbashi Refinery paralleled their place in the cultural life of the African quarter of Elisabethville.[50] For example, by September 1928 the factory complexes A and B at Lubumbashi were regularly producing over 5,000 tons of copper ingots a month with an average copper content of 87 percent. This meant that the manufacture of nearly 50 percent of the Union Minière's finished product rested on the efforts of the 1,000 or so workers at the factory complex—5 percent of the total workforce of the mining company, most of whom were from the two Rhodesias. The on-site administration at the Lubumbashi works sought to alter this potentially dangerous arrangement by attempting to increase the number of Congolese in skilled and semiskilled job categories while readjusting the hours of the work day for more experienced workers. Also, prison seemed to have been as much a school in which the workers were to learn the imperatives of the new industrial era as the workshops in this short period (see Table 4.2).

The importance of experienced African workers from the British colonies was signalled by their pervasiveness in all categories of skilled work. Although their numbers declined among the furnacemen at Lubumbashi by almost a third between September 1928 and February 1929, as graduates from the Central Workshop began to show up in the plant works, they remained constant in every other branch of skilled work, except at the electrical power station.[51] Between 1928 and 1930 the factory departments containing the largest number of Rhodesias led the others in overtime work as well. Furnacemen on the waterjacket furnaces, the repairmen for the furnaces, Africans responsible for unloading the ore cars, and the maintenance crews also put in a great deal of overtime (see Table 4.3). These workers were given little time to prepare for the abrupt and cataclysmic changes in factory discipline and the expectations of their supervisors. They did indeed adjust to the new circumstances, but not without great physical hardship and other difficulties.[52]

Whether such changes in the internal structure of the factory complex solved the problem of synchronizing the output of the underground workers at Kipushi with production of a more highly valorized end-product at the foundry might have been the most immediate problem facing the company, but in the long run management came to see the problem of the regularity and quality of the ore supply as merely the obverse side of its attempt to mold a more skilled, pliant, and permanent factory proletariat. In turn, this quest merged with the company's efforts to rid itself of African factory hands and skilled workmen from the British colonies. The dialectical relationship of the two sides of the problem was much appreciated by the Union Minière when the price of copper on the world market went from 12½ to 24 British cents a pound between September 1928 and March 1929.[53] Solving the problem of output and productivity at the foundry was an important step in increasing the general workload and reducing the number of operatives. The switch to hydroelectric power at the end of the 1920s helped this along.

However, a portion of the factory's African workforce felt obliged to make its own statement about the shift in the productive forces. Sabotage therefore was the most immediate reason for cutting the workforce at the factory complex.[54] It was at the power station that management sought to strike out first against potential saboteurs. By the end of January 1929 incidents of sabotage were disrupting the running of the station at regular intervals.[55] The incidents began in

Table 4.2. Number of African Workers at Lubumbashi, by Job Classification or Department and by Worker Status, from August 1928 to February 1929

	Aug.	Sept.	Oct.	Nov.	Dec.	Jan.	Feb.
Furnacemen	827	841	—	655	603	708	626
Furnace repairmen	113	134	—	141	110	—	125
Agglomerators	159	153	—	168	165	164	151
Pulverisers	—	51	—	54	54	51	50
Traffic controllers	58	59	—	68	55	55	55
Power station	25	31	—	50	44	13	10
Workshop	28	15	7	11	9	239	244
Garage	21	21	—	20	21	21	21
Plant maintenance	129	124	—	99	93	6	5
Chaufferies	71	66	—	74	63	69	70
Ill	32	37	—	48	56	42	30
In prison	27	22	—	17	12	16	23
On leave	35	33	—	49	174	189	194
Unaccounted for	10	7	—	11	13	12	11

Source: TC/UM, 98, Usines Lubumbashi, août 1928–février 1929.

the last week of January, reached a peak around the middle of February, and trailed off unexpectedly in the first week of March. Mining operations at Kipushi and at the small ore-concentration plant at Ruashi came to an almost complete standstill during February in the wake of the damages sustained by the power lines. Production at Lubumbashi itself also fell well below the planned reduction projected by the factory's management on 13 November 1928.[56] Although management attempted to feign a normal state of affairs for the first three weeks of February, the evidence pointing to the conscious destruction of company property had, by this point, become overwhelming. Much of it was probably aimed at provoking slowdowns in the factory and at Kipushi and Ruashi as well. By 23 February the entire affair had become too vast to camouflage. A special report on the problems in the power station was included in the factory report for that month. The report ended on a wry, disingenuous note:

. . . production has suffered more than it has in the previous month. It is worth noting that the transport of power to Lubumbashi and Kipushi cannot be done without some degree of danger when the strength of the electrical current conducted by the large pylons is not balanced by a series of smaller ones. This danger has been particularly manifest in the present instance because the conductor heads of the posts are so difficult to repair.[57]

By the second week of February 1929 the incidents of sabotage had increased. European foremen and timekeepers were compelled to

patrol and inspect more frequently the power lines leading from the
electrical station. Such instances were often written up in this
fashion:

On 7 February 1929 the foreman Chausotte visited the installation. He discovered the support post with the conductors half torn off. He had to shut
off the current and replace the conducting head. This operation lasted about
45 minutes.[58]

Sabotage of plant and factory equipment was not limited to the electrical generators and power lines. The furnaces themselves were often
the targets of the saboteurs. The fact that ore was smelted during
"down time," or *temps de campagnes*, made the furnaces at Lubumbashi, especially the high-speed ones, particularly vulnerable to
sabotage.[59] For at this point the electric flues that regulated the flow
of air and water were most exposed. This was not the most frequent
kind of damage sustained by the furnaces, however. Well into the
1930s, small-scale explosions and instances where the wrong proportions of ore, fuel, and reactive or catalytic agents blew holes through
the walls of the furnaces were the most common kinds of "accidents"
on the charge floor. By the end of February 1929 the number of
furnacemen was reduced to between 600 and 700. Table 4.3 shows
the relative impact of this reduction on the distribution of overtime
work. As the number of operatives was reduced, the amount of overtime work in the department rose to 943 hours in October 1928 and
to a devastating 1,710 hours in November 1928. At the end of February
1929, after the saboteurs' season, overtime work for the furnacemen
dropped to 591 hours without much of a reduction in the number
of men tending the furnaces (see Table 4.3).

The furnacemen and African workers in the electrical power station were the obvious source of the sabotage. The rigors of factory
work and the huge amounts of overtime sustained by these two groups
of workers on a monthly basis gave them reason enough to be so.
Although the connection between the sabotage at the Lubumbashi
works and the labor unrest at Elisabethville in 1931 remains circumstantial, workers from the Rhodesias and Nyasaland figured importantly in both. Yet few European foremen or timekeepers cared to
pursue individual instances of sabotage beyond the initial stage; and
for that reason Chausotte, sniffing the trail of anonymous African
saboteurs down the power lines leading from Lubumbashi, was
atypical. Few saboteurs were punished because only a few were discovered. Any European supervisor who had hopes of staying on at
the factory complex understood this from the outset.[60]

Table 4.3. Number of Overtime Hours for African Operatives, by Job Classification
or Department, at Lubumbashi, from August 1928 to February 1929

	Aug.	Sept.	Oct.	Nov.	Dec.	Jan.	Feb.
Furnacemen	495	755	943	1,710	1,706.5	1,482.5	591.5
Furnace repairmen	310	153	217	171	171.5	–	287.5
Agglomerators	64	85	63	258	294	284.5	109.5
Pulverisers	57	81	67	162	183.5	171.5	124
Traffic controllers	331	303	301	410	565.5	470	288.5
Power station	41	80	161	225	197	90.5	35
Workshop	233	183	214	223	246	240.5	a
Garage	449	276	248	331	441	304	323
Plant maintenance (Travaux en cours)	430	191	233	294	341.5	428	67.5
Chaufferies	159	42	110	196	145.5	152	204

Source: TC/UM, 98, Usines de Lubumbashi, août 1928–février 1929.
[a]Overtime for skilled workers was listed according to their craft in February. The
breakdown is as follows: welding and soldering shop, 35 hours; mechanical shop, 743
hours; carpentry shop, 169.5 hours; masonry shop, 221.5 hours; electrical shop, 174
hours; forge shop, 41 hours; brazier's and boilermaker's shop, 494 hours.

With a significant slowing of labor recruitment in Lomami by 1928,
the continued presence of African workers from the southern British
colonies at the Star, Shinkolobwe, Kakontwe, and as a skeleton crew
at the underground mine at Kipushi became relatively more important.[61] Despite its declared intention to thin out their ranks speedily,
the Union Minière continued to make extensive use of these workers,
particularly at the underground mine at Kipushi. This was prompted
by what the company described as the "excellent physical condition"
of the Northern Rhodesians, particularly the Barotse and Baluvale,
and by the frightening decimation of the Hutu recruits from Ruanda-
Urundi by malaria.[62] However, more than 30.47 percent of the African
workers from the British colonies were slotted for *travaux légers*, or
"light work," at the end of 1928 in spite of their "excellent physical
condition." This contrasted sharply with the percentages of Luba and
Hutu workers classified in this way. The percentages for these two
groups of African workers stood at 10 and 3 percent, respectively. Of
course, these low percentages were due in part either to flight or to
bottlenecks in recruitment between 1928 and 1930.[63]

The mining company often used the classification of *travaux légers*
to camouflage lingering illness among its African workers during the
initial phase of worker stabilization. It was not coincidental, therefore, that the highest percentages of *travaux légers* were usually registered at the work sites known to have the worst working conditions
or at the underground excavations. At Kipushi, for instance, workers

were regularly given a day of light work every week. This institu-
tionalization of *travaux légers* at regular intervals for workers in gruelling or irremediably hazardous jobs spread to the tin mine at Busanga
as well. The data in Table 4.4 reflect the relationship between this
approach and the conditions on the work sites themselves. Predictably, the percentages of *travaux légers* were highest where the African
workforce was pressed hardest to increase output. Kipushi was the
only exception, and this was due to the fluctuations in the African
workforce discussed previously and the way that management
adjusted the work routine. Underaged youths composed a growing
proportion of the new recruits coming from Northern Rhodesia. This
too contributed to the number of Northern Rhodesians scheduled for
"light work"; for as I mentioned earlier, the commencement of large-
scale copper mining in Northern Rhodesia greatly aggravated the previous pattern of labor recruitment in many of its rural districts and
in the Haut-Luapula District of Katanga.[64]

Toward the end of 1928 the number of deaths among workers at
Ruashi shot up unexpectedly because of the spread of typhoid. Earlier,
the mining company had cut the amount of money it spent on food
for workers at Ruashi from 2.50 to 1.80 francs per capita. Fruit and
green vegetables—items that were eventually classified as "supplementary rations" for workers from Northern Rhodesia—were replaced
by bread. The mining company saw reduction in the amount of
money spent on food as a means to recoup some of the loss it sustained in wages paid to the Rhodesias. And, no doubt, the withdrawal
of fruit and green vegetables made these workers more vulnerable to

Table 4.4. Number and Percentage of *Travaux Légers* among the African Workers at the
Major Work Sites of the Union Minière du Haut-Katanga as of
31 December 1928

| | | Travaux Légers | |
	Total Number of African Workforce	Number	Percent of Total
Lubumbashi	2,416	295	12.21
Prince Léopold (Kipushi)	1,139	17	1.49
Star of the Congo	1,488	89	5.98
Panda	5,264	550	10.45
Kakontwe	1,453	9	0.62
Kambove	949	45	4.74
Kolwezi	1,041	39	3.75
Kikole	450	18	4.00

Source: AG, C8, Service médicale: Procès-verbal, 31 décembre 1928.

disease. But the destruction of the African cemetery at Ruashi in October 1928, just at the point when the local typhoid epidemic was reaching its peak, elicited the most immediate and bitter complaints from the workers.[65]

The destruction of the cemetery at Ruashi was part of a larger plan to raze and rebuild Elisabethville's much expanded African quarter once again, as the Union Minière attempted to induce, cajole, and compel a greater portion of that third of its workforce who lived there to move into the workers' camps. But it was, by far, the plan's most callous and devastating component, for with the destruction of the cemetery the mining company demonstrated to the foreign African workers that stabilization meant a complete rupture of their ties to the mining community. The cemetery's destruction became the vortex of an escalating spiral of violence which had begun years earlier with clashes between groups of workers from Ruashi and mine and municipal police officers. The workers sought to arrest at least the pace of stabilization. The violence of May 1931 marked the culmination of their efforts.[66]

"When Copper Bracelets Were Traded for Food": The Hutu Workers of Ruanda-Urundi at the Union Minière

In 1926 fewer than 500 Hutu recruits from Ruanda-Urundi – almost all of them with their immediate families – crossed over into Katanga on the way to the Union Minière's work sites. The majority were sent to the Prince Léopold Mine at Kipushi and to Kakontwe. Others were dispersed among various work sites behind Jadotville. By the end of the year the Hutu recruits still constituted less than 3 percent of the Union Minière's workforce. At best, the company considered them a partial hedge against labor shortage.[67] By 1929, however, the Hutu workers were almost 9 percent of the Union Minière's African workforce. Table 4.5 shows that the number of Africans from Ruanda-Urundi working at the Union Minière jumped from 3 to 30 percent in less than five years. The sharpest increase probably took place in late 1928 when the number of Hutu went from 1,300 to 2,500, or from under 9 to over 15 percent of the African workers on the mines.

This dramatic increase of Hutu recruits was hardly coincidental, although it was indeed a windfall for the mining company. Famines and epidemics in central and eastern Ruanda and Urundi, and the determination of the major European companies in Katanga and Kivu provinces to take advantage of the subsequent dearth, provided the context for the sudden increase in recruitment.[68] The weight of taxa-

Table 4.5. Number and Percentage of Africans from Ruanda-Urundi at the
Union Minière, 1926–1930

	Total Number of Workforce	Workers from Ruanda-Urundi	
		Number	Percent of Total
1926	13,200	400	3
1927	15,400	1,300	8
1928	15,900	1,300	8
1929	16,500	2,500	15
1930	15,700	4,700	30

Source: AG, C9, Elément etranger en MOI (R.U.), mars 1931.

tion and famine imposed a huge burden on the village economies of
the Hutu and Hima peasantry of Ruanda-Urundi in the late 1920s
and 1930s. The names given to the famines by the peasantry reflected
the desperate nature of their plight: *rumanura,* or "the exhaustion
of the economy," and *gakwege,* or "when copper bracelets are exchanged for food," readily attested to the gravity of these periods of
extreme dearth in the consciousness of their victims.[69]

The famine of 1928 in Ruanda and northeastern Urundi was probably the most important and most immediate stimulus to increased
recruitment for work at the Union Minière in Ruanda and in the
Muhinga District of Urundi. Although the regions of Shangugu,
Kisenyi, and Ruhengeri had returned to a relatively normal state by
the end of 1928, large portions of the population of the Gatsibu District and Kigali continued to be scourged by famine. Table 4.6 shows
that the regions most affected by the famine of 1928 were also the
ones that paid the most taxes in cash in the same year—the tax having
been skimmed off the top of the prospective wages of new labor
recruits. The only two exceptions to this were the territories of
Kabaya and Kisenyi.[70]

Quite consciously, then, the Union Minière used the famine as a
means to draw more men out of those areas of Ruanda-Urundi where
it had taken its greatest toll. The mining company saw its recruitment campaign in the East African protectorates as a fulcrum for
several short-term objectives at this point. These objectives were: (1)
inducing the more "desirable" or tractable African workers to draw
up three-year contracts with the company; (2) easing the transition
associated with the lessening of the company's dependence on African
labor from Northern Rhodesia; (3) precipitating a decline in African
wage rates; (4) synchronizing the needs of the Union Minière and
those of the colonial state; and (5) gradually slowing the rate of rural
African immigration to the towns of Katanga. Famine in Ruanda-

Table 4.6. Taxes Paid (in Congolese francs) in Ruanda-Urundi, by Territory, 1928

Urundi		Ruanda	
Territory	Tax Payment	Territory	Tax Payment
Kitega	135,000	Astrida	57,000
Ngozi	71,000	Nyanza	50,000
Usumbura	50,000	Kigali	50,000
Ruyiga	42,000	Ruhengeri	46,000
Muhinga	27,000	Gatsibu	39,000
Ruminga	25,000	Shangugu	24,000
Muramivya	24,000	Rukiro	32,000
Rufamu	20,000	Lubengera	22,000
Lake Kyanza	20,000	Kabaya	15,000
		Kisenyi	12,000

Source: AG, C7, Impôt: R.U., 31 décembre 1928.
Note: The regions are listed in descending order of the famine's initial severity.

Urundi as a means of attaining these goals was clearly not an issue of great moral concern for the company.[71] By November 1928 the recruitment of workers from Ruanda-Urundi was seen as an integral component of worker stabilization.[72]

Despite burgeoning protest, the Union Minière continued to squeeze the incoming recruits from Ruanda-Urundi into the labor vacuum created by its failure to meet its recruitment quotas in Lomami. The transfer of Hutu workers to Kipushi continued under a heavy pall of disease and illness. Between December 1928 and 1930 well over a third of the recruits transferred to Kipushi were scheduled for *travaux légers*.[73] Death and illness cut a particularly wide path at the acclimatization camp because of malaria, a disease for which Africans from the mountainous uplands of Ruanda and Urundi seemed to have no defense. Yet the Union Minière ignored the widespread morbidity among the Hutu recruits and chose to press its manpower objectives to a potentially bloody-minded conclusion.[74]

For the Wives of My Father: The Luba Presence on the Mines, 1927–1931

By 1926 the Union Minière was already heavily committed to tapping the huge reservoir of African recruits in Lomami. Consequently, the colonial government extended the provincial rail line to the more populous regions northwest of mining sites. But the initial efforts to extend the rail line northward were considered a partial failure because they opened up the less populated regions of

Lomami. In the words of Chief Justice Sohier, it was "a road which led to nowhere."[75] Later, however, the prospect of employment and a new life in the recently constructed town of Port Francqui drew thousands of Luba and Lulua out of the countryside and away from clientage to Kuba overlords. Eventually contingents of Luba and Lulua moved southward down the rail line to mining camps.[76]

Between 1926 and 1928 the number of Africans from Lomami recruited for work on the mines of the Union Minière rose sharply. At the end of 1926 there were over 8,000 of them on the work sites. Perhaps 4,591 of them had allegedly "volunteered" for work on the mines. The degree of cooperation between territorial administration and the Union Minière with respect to recruitment in the larger territories of Lomami such as Kabinda, Kanda Kanda, Pania Mutombo, and Tshofa could not have been greater if the government personnel of these regions had been paid employees of the mining company.[77] In Kabinda, for example, the district commissioner, M. Wilmin, and the territorial administrator, G. Lanaert, allowed the drawing up of labor contracts to take place in their offices. Territorial administrators de Ziglick at Tshofa, de Marchovette at Pania Mutombo, and Arens at Kanda Kanda acted similarly. Arens, in fact, had to be removed from his post at the end of 1928 because of his recruiting workers for the Union Minière through his offices. Government intervention was the catalyst for the rapid increase of African workers from Lomami at the Union Minière.[78] The increase was all the more remarkable since Kanda Kanda was the only one of these territories traversed by the rail line.

Initially, the rapid increase in the number of African recruits from Lomami was alarming to the Ministry of Colonies. The ministry lodged a protest with the mining company on 9 January 1928, demanding that it drop its quota of recruits from 3,000 to 1,500. The Office central du Travail au Katanga (OCTK), the former Bourse du Travail du Katanga, was also drawn into the fight. By the end of January the government labor agency was fighting for its very life, because the direct ties between the territorial administration and the Union Minière began to make it somewhat redundant.[79] Thus, when the new imperatives of worker stabilization took hold at the Union Minière, the geography of labor recruitment in Lomami was also altered. But unlike large portions of Ruanda-Urundi, the chieftaincies remained relatively unaffected, although there was a noticeable but cosmetic increase in the number of recruitment bans in many of the territories. Most of the recruitment bans were designed to assuage the allegation of the League of Nations that labor recruitment in Katanga was tantamount to slavery. In the main, impressment of Africans from Lomami did not slacken.[80]

Some company and government officials were worried about whether the combined effects of stabilization and international censure would eventually slow down recruitment in the more densely populated areas of Lomami. The Union Minière forged ahead, however, and stepped up private recruitment, while increasing the bonuses given to chiefs and headmen. In 1928, the year of both censure and labor shortage, bonuses went from 50 to 100 Congolese francs.[81] In 1929, in parts of Lulua District close enough to Lomami to absorb some of the cash spin-off of the new recruitment tactics, a number of chiefs exhorted Union Minière workers from their chieftaincies not to return to their home areas, not only because of the spread of sleeping sickness, but also because their presence in the villages would tend to undermine the ability of the chiefs and headmen to profit, in the form of higher bonuses from the labor recruiters, from the labor shortages induced by the disease.[82] Labor recruiters were painfully aware of this ploy, and did everything in their power to regain some of the initiative, including fostering more trips back to the countryside for workers from Lomami. In the heady boom period between 1926 and April 1930 the Union Minière felt that greater contact between workers from Lomami and their relatives in the villages was valuable—so much so, that by the end of the 1920s the mining company began to give workers from the territories of Tshofa and Kanda Kanda cash bonuses in hopes that they would use them as payment for brides, thus reassuring their return. Such a policy was never encouraged among African workers from other regions.[83]

Obviously the OCTK and its director, Raoul Strythagen, were against the new recruiting arrangements, not only because they increased recruitment quotas beyond what was deemed humane, but also because the increased amount of cash in the hands of the chiefs strengthened their ability to bargain for better terms of hire for their clients or, more often than not, for more money and amenities for themselves.[84] Strythagen's public stance, which called much attention to the needs of the mining company, belied this. But in December 1927 he lodged a vigorous protest with the mining company over the volume and poor health of the recruits from Lomami. He maintained that his agency had isolated at least 350 recruits that were, in his estimation, absolutely unfit for work.

Dr. Dedechère, a company doctor, strongly disagreed with Strythagen. In response to Strythagen's allegations he claimed that the 350 recruits in question were not healthy enough to engage in underground work at Kipushi, and that they would be slotted for *travaux légers* at the mines they were assigned to, or, under "exceptional circumstances," *travaux de roulages*, or convoy work, if they were assigned to Kipushi. Dedechère never spelled out what, in fact, constituted "exceptional circumstances."[85] However, the Union Minière was compelled to address itself to several negative trends that accompanied its increased dependency on Lomami. For as the OCTK noted, mortality rates for recruits from Lomami, particularly those from Pania Mutombo, were staggeringly high.[86]

The year 1928 was one of shrunken opportunities for the Union Minière in Lomami. Labor recruitment experienced a significant decline. The original projections for December 1928 and January 1929 — the peak of the rainy season and also the prime period for labor recruitment — had been 1,050 and 1,300 men, respectively. The actual figures were 940 and 1,150. Hundreds of recruits from Lomami fled as soon as they arrived on the work sites. Numerous "volunteers" also fled, as many as 185 in the first few months of the year. Sixty-seven of them had taken out three-year contracts with the company, which meant that they had been employed by the company for at least a year. While the number of abscondings among African workers who had freely contracted with the Union Minière tended to go down at the outset of worker stabilization, some veteran workers from Lomami continued to use flight as a means of stating work preferences, particularly as the prospects of being sent to either Kipushi or the prisonlike tin mine at Kikole increased. In general, veteran African workers also became increasingly reluctant to work on Sundays.[87]

As early as October 1928 the administration of the mining company was advised to introduce Africans from Lomami to the more gruelling occupations on the mines, especially underground work, on a more gradual basis, and to use workers from Northern Rhodesia and Kabongo in these job slots as much as possible. Africans from Lomami were to be used primarily for convoy work. But the relatively high wage associated with underground work was enough of an inducement for some Africans from Lomami to undertake the more difficult work; and one of their principal grievances just before the violence of 1931 — however imaginary it might have been — was that Hutu recruits directly from Ruanda-Urundi were being paid the same wage as experienced underground workers.[88]

The Union Minière projected that it would need between 3,300 and 3,500 Africans from Lomami by the end of the year — 1,500 from Kabinda, 1,000 from Tshofa and Pania Mutombo, and between 800 and 1,000 from Kanda Kanda. Again Strythagen protested the mining company's total and suggested that it be brought down to 2,700. Beyond his own trepidations, Strythagen felt that the mining company's manpower demands might endanger the long-term viability of Lomami as an area of labor recruitment. As a kind of compromise, he consented to an arrangement whereby the *chef de mission* for the OCTK, A. Deluuw, would monitor the recruitment activities of private recruiting agents sent into the area by the Union Minière as well as those of the agency itself.[89] Ostensibly, Deluuw would also oversee the establishment of several *ateliers centraux* and *écoles professionelles* in Kabinda. These workshops would then train Africans from the district as bricklayers, sawyers, carpenters, and masons. The company saw this last part of the compromise as a quick means of replacing privately contracted African artisans in the building trades. As mentioned earlier, many of the skilled workers in the building trades were Rhodesians and Nyasalanders, and they were seen as an unruly and dangerous element within the workforce. However, neither the Union Minière nor Strythagen was aware of the mounting indigenous forces militating against increased recruitment in Lomami by 1929.[90]

The 1926 slump in cotton prices undermined the ability of Africans from Lomami to maintain the initiative in establishing the terms under which they would contract for hire at the Union Minière. Peasant growers earned less than 500 francs a year from the sale of cotton after the slump. Those in the neighboring district of Tanganika-Moero barely earned more than 100 francs, although the sale of food to the Union Minière increased their annual cash income by another 400 or 500 francs. Taxes, however, absorbed more than half the cash earnings of the peasantry in the two districts. Meanwhile the average annual wage for an underground worker at Kipushi had risen to about 500 francs. The village clan structure was simply not flexible enough to prevent thousands of young men from leaving, particularly since wages at the mining company were rising just as cotton prices were beginning to fall.[91]

Even before the extension of the Tenke-Dilolo railroad, cotton had become an important cash crop for the peasantry. By 1929 there were 70,000 peasant growers in Lomami itself and another 190,000 in the adjoining regions of Kasai and Sankuru.[92] With the advent of the rail line, cotton could be sent to closer ocean ports in Angola rather than to the more distant one at Matadi on the river Congo. Both European refineries and African peasant growers saw an opportunity to recoup what they had lost in 1926 by increasing the output of cotton. While this possibility portended an increase in the amount of cash on hand for chiefs and headmen, at least potentially, it also compelled them to buttress the local labor supply for agricultural production by extending the number of pawn households and polygynous relationships under their supervision. Young, nubile women were obviously a more reliable workforce with which to increase the output of the cotton than sons or young nephews.[93]

By 1930 the price of cotton had fallen again. This particular slump was disastrous for most African growers in Lomami. Speculation and hoarding by the private companies and the government alike further exacerbated the peasantry's anger, pushing local selling prices to depths lower than those of the collapsed world market. Since the conditions of cultivation disallowed the use of plows after 1930, the peasant growers' dependence on female labor increased: women were cheaper and more available than either cattle or plows.[94] At Matadi, the only port town of the Congo with access to the Atlantic Ocean, cotton from Lomami and points southeast would be kept for as long as three years depending on global fluctuations. This in turn pushed the peasantry to the breaking point as the sources for cash dried up and taxes fell due.[95]

With the rise of cotton cultivation and the subsequent slump in crop prices in 1926 and 1930, both women and cash became indispensable as factors of production as well as items of social prestige.[96] The countryside of Lomami was closed off as a source of cash and wives for younger men. Conflict between the big men of the villages and their sons, nephews, and cousins mirrored the transformation of customary and even kin relationships by the cash nexus. After 1927 an indispensable part of the Union Minière's recruitment pitch to the men of Lomami was that it could provide them with both women and cash—women from points farther north along the line of rail, although not necessarily from the workers' home region, and cash as wages and bonuses for work on the mines. But after April 1930, when the first signs of economic downturn set in, the Union Minière offered its workers from Lomami less money in the form of annual wages than the pre-1926 fetching price for the average peasant yield of cotton and women who, in the estimation of the workers, were no more than prostitutes.[97] The participation of Luba workers in the protests of April–December 1931 was thus assured.

PRELUDE TO VIOLENCE: APRIL 1930 TO MARCH–APRIL 1931

In April 1930—exactly a year before the collapse of the world copper market—Margery Perham reached Katanga by train from Bechuanaland.[98] Perham, later to become Dame Margery, was struck by what she saw: a degree of mechanization comparable to anything she had seen in South Africa or Europe, although on a much smaller scale;

towns such as Elisabethville and Jadotville literally reverberating from the working of machinery; large (larger than the compound houses in the Union Minière's camps) and well-built houses which the workers had built for themselves in the African quarter of Elisabethville *and* which the colonial government was in the process of tearing down (she did not know that this was the second time in less than a decade that the government had razed large sections of the African quarter); and skilled African workers in virtually every phase of modern industrial life, from motormen on the trains to tool and die makers in the Union Minière's repair and machine tool shops, all with only a bare minimum of white supervision.[99]

Obviously all this was a great shock to the future Dame Margery; but the African workers she was observing experienced a greater shock when the mining company attempted to repatriate them a year later, after the bottom fell out of the global copper and tin markets and the company attempted to effect economies of scale—at the workers' expense.[100] The workers were taken aback as they saw their homes razed, output quotas increased, and their neighbors and relatives herded into the workers' camps or marched back to the countryside under cover of night and with the policeman's gun and whip at their backs. All this the future Dame Margery missed. Nor had she perceived the more subtle side effects of industrial growth—the nagging feeling of exhaustion that made for industrial accidents and a penchant for strong drink; the screams of the injured, which were camouflaged by the din of machinery and the furnaces; the gratuitous badgering of the workers by partly redundant white foremen; the despatching of inexperienced men into the cavernous shafts of the Prince Léopold Mine as more experienced ones stood by and wondered at the point being made by it all. This time the industrial world, as opposed to the rural one from which the workers had come, was being turned upside down—and with it, the more self-serving features of stabilization.

Perhaps the most self-serving of all of the mining company's initial attempts at worker stabilization obtained at the underground mine at Kipushi. For example, recruits from Lomami usually spent several weeks in acclimatization camps before assuming underground duties. Afterwards they were integrated into the underground work gangs in three stages. First, they were placed in maintenance groups, which cleared away the debris left by the initial scouring of the ore. Later, they were shifted to convoy work or hauling ore out of the underground shafts by foot trolley. Finally, after a period of approximately two to three months, the company put them to work digging the ore directly out of the underground shafts.[101] On the other hand, Hutu recruits were put directly to work underground. By 1929 new recruits from Ruanda-Urundi were being taken from the acclimatization camps at Kanzenze and Usumbura or, in some instances, directly from their home areas, and placed in underground work at Kipushi or on the more removed underground work sites like Busanga, where they doubled as miners and construction workers. As a result of living conditions or work—cooling houses for instance were almost completely absent on the underground sites—and the insufferably short time for adjustment to the rigors of mine work, the Hutu died or fell ill by the scores.[102]

Once Hutu workers became relatively entrenched in the scheme of underground work at Kipushi, the mining company dragged its feet even more on the construction of cooling houses at this mine. Change, or cooling, houses were indispensable on underground mining sites because they helped the workers make the transition from the temperature in the mining shafts to cooler surface temperatures.[103]

Workers from the two Rhodesias and Lomami were outdone by this maneuver. While putting a ceiling on the wages of the more experienced workers, it also forced recruits from newly opened regions of Lomami and southern Kasai to enter the industry at lower starting rates of pay. This skewed ethnic totem pole of occupations and wages was a direct result of the connection between the mining company's quest for profits and the destructive impact of that quest on the organization of work.[104] By making the Hutu recruits the bottom of the totem pole the Union Minière hoped to supplant increasingly expensive African labor from Northern Rhodesia before the copper mines there went into full operation. But the mining company was also bent on wringing the last bit of labor out of its Rhodesias before dispatching them across the border, or leaving them to their own devices in the squatters' zones around the industrial towns.[105]

Obviously the Hutu workers were the least prepared of all the workers to challenge the Union Minière. With their backs to an unknown hinterland, over 1,000 miles from their homeland, and accompanied by their women in some instances, it was impossible for them to use flight as a tactic for better working conditions or higher rates of pay. Protest, if it surfaced at all among the Hutu workers, was orchestrated by their women. Usually such protests centered around the size and extent of garden plots allotted to the Hutu recruits.[106] Consequently, the mining company used the low wages and ghastly working conditions of the Hutu workers as an iron rod with which to beat the other groups of African workers into submission. It was acutely aware of the importance of timing in its efforts. For, if any given factor was acted upon a moment too soon or too late, it would lead to the collapse of the work routine in the underground mine at Kipushi and elsewhere—and ultimately to a drastic decline in the company's profits. This is precisely what happened between April 1930 and August 1931. Predictably, the weakest stratum of African workers, the Hutu, were some of the first victims of the repercussions.[107]

All these developments upset a fragile balance between violence and restraint that the African workers and the mining company had only recently arrived at. This balance proved to be as secure as the mining company's commitment to the well-being of African workers from the British colonies.[108] Yet up to the first peak of the Depression in late 1931, the Union Minière was still dependent on the labor power of this small but strategic segment of African workers. Although the official number of workers from the Rhodesias fell from 35 to 5 percent between 1928 and the unrest of 1931, the real figures were somewhat higher. Moreover, the Lubumbashi works, which produced between 83 and 57 percent of the Union Minière's finished product between 1928 and 1941, respectively, would have cooled to an unproductive standstill without them.[109] This was in spite of their reputation for "contumacious, and even outrightly rebellious, behavior."[110] On the eve of the global collapse of the copper industry, therefore, the most important catalyst for worker unrest at the Union Minière was the increasing divergence between the basis of authority in the industry and the changing requirements of production. Underground workers, factory operatives, and skilled workers, within and without the metallurgical departments of the mining company, were hardest hit by the schism.

The forced march toward a more coherent plan of industrialization of the mines compelled the Union Minière to resort to a more sophisticated kind of social engineering to keep the more skilled workers in line—particularly since the Union Minière's share of global copper production doubled between 1926 and 1931, going from barely 5 percent at the earlier date to 12 percent on the eve of the global market's collapse (see Table 4.1). With only threadbare incentives, it attempted to make the African worker a more pliable, if not more willing, accomplice in its efforts. It succeeded better than it knew. For there was indeed a kind of "paper prosperity" in the 1920s—one which translated to the acquisition of stupendous personal fortunes and a large cash flow and stock volume for the mining company. But underneath this very sophisticated generation and manipulation of commercial paper lurked the inevitable problem of transforming paper profits into real ones. This problem came to a head between the fall of the American stock market in October 1929 and the collapse of the world copper market in April 1931. The mining company was compelled to overhaul drastically its initial plan of worker stabilization as a result, but not before the labor unrest of August–December 1931 had demonstrated the extent to which the company's new management methods lagged behind the aspirations of the workers.

CHAPTER FIVE

The Labor Unrest of 1931 and Its Aftermath

CAPITAL AND LABOR AT ODDS: THE STRUGGLE FOR ORGANIZATION

The uprooted natives constitute an anonymous heterogeneous crowd struggling with new desires and needs. These hordes are composed of natives in search of labor, intermittent vagabonds, uprooted independents practicing a trade or working for a salary, and natives who have taken to truck farming on the edge of the city. Disturbing currents abound among them, making them, in turn, difficult to govern.

> Governor Gaston Heenen on the eve of his retirement from the provincial government of Katanga in 1934[1]

Let us return to history. The Belges [the workers' lodges or brotherhoods] of Kasai existed up to 1930. But the crisis which dissolved them in 1931 provoked a return to the countryside of some of their more militant members. With the exodus, they found themselves functioning under duress and profoundly transformed. When the basic conditions of life improved in 1934–35, other elements tried to reconstitute the movement. But the long period of interruption allowed for the formation of smaller tribal and clan based organizations. The efforts of the latter kinds of groupings were not as successful as those of the Belges. Yet despite the disorganization of the Belges, the powerful sense of fraternity that had unified them in the past could not be stamped out. The newer organizations owed their success to the imprint of the past.

> excerpt from a report to the secretariat of the *sûreté* on the activities of the Lulua Brotherhoods at the Union Minière shortly after the Second World War[2]

By 1931 the industrial boom conditions of the previous 10 years had created a sharp rural-to-urban shift in Katanga's population. Officially there were 7,112 African workers from other provinces and 15,103 from neighboring colonies working in the province. The official count of Africans in Elisabethville was over 30,000 — more than a fourth of the entire population of the Haut-Luapula District.[3] In reality the numbers were much higher. The ease with which Africans crossed colonial borders and the rapid dissemination of reports about the improvement of the basic conditions of life in the workers' camps and the towns of Elisabethville and Jadotville facilitated a greater influx of potential workers.[4] As rail lines began to connect work site after work site, and as the workers' own routes to the work sites traversed the home regions of more-removed ethnic groups, the older form of the migrant labor system began to break down. But underlying economic constraints and the Union Minière's use of corporal punishment and other forms of coercion further reinforced the workers' political dependency while limiting their ability to engage in collective action. Flight and sabotage were one set of worker responses to such policies. Mutual aid societies and lodges were another. Rural ideologies such as the various Watchtower sects also began to have a compelling effect on the workers. The workers' response to these stimuli underscored the intrinsic value of organization and the workers' new cultural traditions.[5]

As in South Africa and Southern Rhodesia, periods of economic downturn often saw the locus of worker protest in Katanga shift from the workplace to the urban areas and workers' compounds. For example, the workers' boycotts of the stores in Elisabethville, rather than the strike and subsequent riot at Kipushi, provoked the strongest police repression during the industrial unrest of 1931. Although strikes and work actions did occur during such periods, they were usually defensive in nature. The industrial sabotage at the Lubumbashi works and the strike at Kipushi bore powerful witness to this.[6] Changes in the production process also facilitated greater labor militancy among some African workers, particularly where such changes meant fewer white supervisors and foremen. But militancy and class consciousness did not increase like so many ingots of metal, and the main categories of workers who became more militant — skilled workers outside the metallurgical trades, factory operatives, and underground workers — believed that they were defending recently acquired gains that appeared to be threatened.

Yet the mining industry, despite stabilization, still depended on brutal methods of repression and social control. Work actions and protest could extract a high toll from disaffected workers.[7] For unlike South Africa and Southern Rhodesia, such protest did not have the benefit of a palpable form of trade union combination. By August 1931 the workers at the largest work sites of the Union Minière were drawn into a tug-of-war with the company over whether they would have a voice in determining the nature and extent of the layoffs that followed the global collapse of the copper industry. As the crisis in the mining industry deepened, the preservation of their numbers and their communal and workplace organizations became the workers' most immediate objective.

The crisis of 1931 also enhanced the split between liberals and conservatives within the colonial government and the Union Minière. The origins of the split went back to the economic crisis of 1921 and the debate over whether the Ministry of Colonies or the provincial government should regulate British investment, the flow of African workers from the British colonies, labor recruitment in general, and the network of industrial inspectors. The liberals felt that the Ministry of Colonies should oversee all these matters. Conservatives felt that such tasks should be left with local administration. But since there were no political parties in the Congo, liberals and conservatives were often compelled to submerge their differences in order to carry out the complex demands of administering the province and the mining company.[8] Liberals had it that no serious political repression of the workers could be effected without invading the realm of African culture. But African workers did not respond to the prospect of increased economic exploitation according to a standard set of formulas. The forms of class expression were not always predictable. The changing relations of force and political power, as well as the productive forces, often determined the options of African workers. Moreover, conservatives were not convinced by the liberal strategy. The manipulation of "bush institutions" such as the lodges and friendly societies grated sharply on their sense of propriety. Yet they proffered no solutions and tended to address the problem of the relations between African labor and European capital in the old way — with corporal punishment and state coercion.

The moving spirit behind the conservative, anti-British faction in the early 1920s was Katanga's Attorney-General Martin Rutten. While attorney-general, Rutten had been haunted by the specter of an African rebellion in the Congo, which he believed English-speaking Protestant missionaries would orchestrate. Rutten did not shed this obsession when he was appointed governor-general of the Belgian Congo in July 1925. When the liberal vice governor-general of Katanga Gaston Heenen and the territorial administration of Elisabethville gave tacit official recognition to the lodges later the same year, Rutten drafted an amendment to the Charte coloniale which stated that only those African associations sponsored or supervised by the government or a religious order would be considered legal. Rutten's amendment was promulgated on 11 February 1926.[9]

But Rutten, as head of government, was more removed from the daily workings of Katanga's administration. And since Vice Governor-General Heenen had given recognition of the lodges his explicit support, local officials did not feel very compelled to enforce Rutten's amendment rigorously. Heenen, and those officials who were loyal to him, thought Rutten and the conservatives overly paranoid about the motives of the lodges and their claim of a connection between the lodges and the African Watchtower sects utterly preposterous. Heenen and the other liberals thought it best first to gain access to the way the African thought when he was not answering to his employer or the state before attempting to remold his personality. The conservatives remained unconvinced. Perhaps the least convinced were local conservatives in Katanga itself. After the partial failure of Rutten's legal initiative, they chose a more conspiratorial route for their aims.[10]

Between 1929 and 1931, the conservatives perceived the liberal strategy, along with the Union Minière's plan of worker stabilization, as a mere shirking of duty. Frightened by what they felt would be the results of such a strategy, the conservatives moved quickly to set up a provincial secret police force with the aid of Governor-General Rutten, his handpicked successor, Auguste Tilkens, and the more senior commanding officers of the colonial army. Heenen was aware of the burgeoning conspiracy. Aided by the energetic district commissioner and fellow liberal Auguste Verbeken, he was able to thwart the conservatives' plans for most of this brief period. But between September and December 1931, in the midst of the labor unrest and while Heenen was away in Europe, the conservatives put their plan into action.[11] As a result, the mining company and the provincial government came to see the question of worker organization in a new light.

The mining company's view of the lodges, which was similar to Heenen's, might have remained unchanged had it not been for the failure of the Catholic-sponsored voluntary associations to absorb them. But by the end of 1930, many of the Catholic associations formed by the Benedictine order and its intrusive agent Father Gregoire Coussement had become disaffected with their mentors and eagerly sought affiliation with the independent African lodges.[12] A growing number of managers at the Union Minière, as well as more conservative elements in the government, saw this potential connection and the lodges' weekend bouts of dancing, drinking, and footballing as harbingers of a major threat to public order.[13] Feuds among individual members of different lodges were occasionally resolved with faction fights, but such violence was enacted only in extreme cases. These minor incidents of violence became widespread only when the government, fearing that the lodges were connected to the spread of the Watchtower sects, embarked upon a wholesale suppression of African public dancing in the late 1920s.[14] Consequently, working-class aspirations came to be insinuated deeply into the more general ones of the urban African population when the municipal authorities turned the *cités* and workers' camps into ghettos.[15] They also fostered patterns of consumption among the workers that tended to thwart the Union Minière's efforts to cut back selectively on rations and other amenities. Rivalry among the various lodges may have been a catalyst for the unrest of May–December 1931, particularly since the layoffs tended to hit some ethnic groups harder than others, but it was by no means the only or the most important factor in the violence that followed the initial protest.[16] In the midst of the escalating repression the lodges attempted to point out to their members that cooperation with Africans from other ethnic and tribal groups was indispensable, particularly at work.[17] What, in fact, provoked the violence was the unanticipated intervention of the regular territorial police at the outset of the industrial unrest and the newly formed secret police several months later.[18]

Despite the wrongness of their views, the mining company and the provincial government saw clearly that the question of organization was central to everyone's concerns. The mining company viewed the unrest of 1931 as a logical conclusion to the expansion of the lodges, while the more hardline elements in the government posited a direct connection between the lodges and the Watchtower sects.[19] Both the lodges and the Watchtower sects did play a role on the African side of the conflict; for the mineworkers and other African workers were in a transitional phase in which they were moving rapidly from protest aimed at foremen and labor contractors to protest aimed at the nature of the work itself.[20] But the timing and evolution of protest suggested the African workers took over such ideologies – many of which had been quietist movements of passive resistance among the peasantry – and refashioned them with industrial discipline and organization into compelling visions of distributive justice. Solidarities formed at the workplace affected the course of events as well, although their impact was not a literal transfer of the work gang from the work site to work stoppage and boycott. Rather, the method of organization which derived from the production process at the Union Minière seemed to indicate that certain times of the year and particular forms of protest were more fruitful than others. The timing of the unrest therefore merits some attention.

CAPITAL AND LABOR AT ODDS: THE LABOR UNREST OF AUGUST–DECEMBER 1931

Between April 1931 and July 1932 the global copper industry collapsed. Even though the Union Minière had left the Copper Exporters Cartel a year earlier and also markedly increased its share of the world market, Katanga's mining industry was not spared: Copper production in Katanga went from 139,000 tons in 1930 to 120,000 in 1931 to 54,000 in 1932.[21] The production of cobalt fell just as precipitously, going from 800 to 200 tons between 1929 and 1932.[22] Exploitation of the smaller mines on the periphery of the mining complex, particularly the tin mines, ceased altogether. At Jadotville the ultra-modern refining and concentration plant for copper and cobalt closed at the end of 1932. Laboratory and research facilities closed, as did the company's coal mine at Luena and the sulphuric acid plant. The company's flour mill, Minoteries du Katanga, ground less than 5,000 tons of corn, wheat, and cassava in 1932, whereas in 1931 it had produced more than 8,000 tons. And between May and August 1931, the company laid off almost 4,000 workers, approximately a third of its workforce.[23] Three instances of industrial unrest, each involving several hundred direct participants and a large body of less-active supporters, broke out at Ruashi, Kipushi, and Mwene Ditu partly in consequence of the layoffs and the hard times. Also, a boycott of all the stores in Elisabethville catering to African workers took place between September and 17 December 1931.[24] Of the four locations, the unrest at Kipushi and the workers' boycotts in Elisabethville were perhaps the most significant.

On 16 August 1931 the Luba mineworkers from Lomami refused to carry the cars of ore out of the underground shafts of the Prince Léopold Mine at Kipushi. That the work stoppages occurred on

Sunday only added to their ominous portents, since African workers had refused to work on Sunday at both Kipushi and Kambove earlier in the year.[25] Management's response to the work stoppage quickly dissolved into panic. African mine police were sent into the shafts to force the workers to start the ore cars moving within hours after the initial work stoppage. At that point the Luba workers turned on the Hutu maintenance workers at the entrance of the shaft and those who were actually digging ore in the lower recesses of the mine.[26]

By 20 August 1931 Kipushi had not completely settled down. "Order and discipline" were still painfully absent, as officials of the mining company were to observe during an inspection tour of the mine and workers' camp. Although the initial violence had been quelled, the officials were incredulous at the number of camp detectives and police running around the camp without apparent purpose and those who were simply idle.[27] Emile Toussaint, the assistant director of native personnel, and Father Coussement stopped an African camp detective named Sokoni to question him about the continued restiveness in the camp. Sokoni was transporting Yamba Mulamba, one of the arrested leaders of the workers' action, to a makeshift jail near the work site. But as Toussaint was to discover, jail was not Yamba's final destination. When asked where he was taking the prisoner, Sokoni replied that he was taking him to jail until he could find him a work ticket, so that he could continue working while he awaited trial.[28]

This incident demonstrated the extent of mismanagement before the unrest; for despite the 1928 ban on the work ticket system, it was obviously still in force at Kipushi. Since camp managers chose not to enforce the ban with great rigor, management was uncertain about exactly how many underground workers were at Kipushi between 1928 and 1932.[29] The workers also had some vested interests in the system's maintenance. For after the selective ration cuts in late 1928, manipulation of work tickets was no longer a matter of bilking the system but one of survival.[30] Africans from the British colonies felt particularly exposed to the cuts, since the mining company was anxious to repatriate as many of them as it could.[31] Workers from other areas also manipulated work tickets, but those from the Rhodesias and Nyasaland had to with greater urgency. Since many of them were literate and could alter or forge official documents on their own, there were also fewer risks of being caught.[32] Literacy and more experience with wage labor enabled them to exploit management's weaknesses with greater facility.[33]

The unrest at Kipushi also illuminated the shortcomings of the nonsecular approach to the problem of social control over the workforce. That approach, which had been articulated by the Benedictine order of the Catholic church and Father Coussement, placed as much emphasis on moral coercion as it did on the threat of physical force and material incentives.[34] Coussement had been deeply involved in organizing the church-sponsored voluntary associations that the Union Minière and the colonial administration had hoped would act as a countervailing force to the influence of the lodges and independent Watchtower sects among the urban working population. Thoroughly disillusioned by the unrest of 1931, Coussement, a man of weak character and shallow convictions, drew closer to the conservatives.[35] Consequently the door was opened to a series of conservative initiatives within the ranks of the mining company and the provincial government by late August 1931. But the reasoning behind conservative opinion was cast in negative terms. The conservatives saw the unrest at Kipushi as a result of an overly permissive attitude toward the African workers and an absence of vigilance within the ranks of the police and the army. They believed that fewer legal restraints would have enabled the police to attend to the "strains of subversion" that were allegedly running rampant among the urban African population.[36]

Liberals at the mining company and in the government were shocked at the conservatives' unyielding criticism of their policies and the fact that such criticism was acquiring support in many different quarters in the aftermath of the unrest. As a result, the liberals convened two emergency meetings of government and mining company officials on 21 August and 20 October 1931.[37] At the initial meeting in August the liberal faction was tentative and unfocussed — absorbing conservative code words such as "order" and "discipline" where it could, while focussing on how to administer better rather than improve working conditions. The opening remarks of Leo Pusmans, the recording secretary of the August meeting, are fairly indicative of the amorphous character of the liberal defense:

> The recent events which occurred at the Kipushi mine have placed in full light the new necessities whose implementation becomes more acute each day. The blacks of the larger camps especially need to be better administered; and this administration must address itself to that fact in a direct fashion. The only way to do this is to create a permanent state of coexistence between us and these evolved but uprooted masses, which is bound by order and discipline.[38]

The liberal faction at the Union Minière was able to triumph over its conservative opposition purely on the strength of its command over the major decision-making positions within the mining company's administration, and by co-opting as many of the major points of the conservative critique as was politically possible. Also, the liberals did drastically reduce the size of the African workforce between October 1931 and March 1932. And despite the accompanying violence, the reduction of African personnel demonstrated to the conservatives that the liberals were still capable of making policy decisions quickly and with few blunders.[39] Since the layoffs were effected with only a slight drop in production during the first year of the Depression, a complete scuttling of the worker stabilization program was prevented, but its goals were substantially changed. Instead of untrammelled economic growth, stabilization now sought to maintain a uniform ratio of approximately 10 to 1 between the company's net profits and the wages it paid its African workforce. For given the impact of the Depression, both liberals and conservatives agreed that the maintenance of order had to be based on a lower uniform living standard for African workers (see Table 5.1).[40]

The 10 to 1 ratio obtained even after the company's posted net profits had revived. Of course management would have argued that the total cost of African labor offset the negative implications of the relationship of wages to profits. But if one closely examines the categories that made up "total cost," it is clear that many were irrelevant at best in the context of the 1930s. For example, between 1931 and 1935, the number of mineworkers with immediate dependents fell by at least 10 percent at all the major work sites; the number of childbirths fell by more than 40 percent; and there were no recruitment costs for 1932 and 1933 and virtually none for 1934 and 1935. Between 1932 and 1935, moreover, "total cost" remained fixed at a little more than 2 million American dollars, even though the workforce doubled within the same time period. Consequently, despite the transformation of the African workforce in terms of skills and occupations, management tied African wages to the downward course of output (see Table 5.1).[41] The relatively high cost of white labor, the company's pressing need to increase the market value of its finished product, and falling copper prices composed the other leitmotiv for the company's renewed interest in cost effectiveness. Table 5.1 shows something of the extent to which the company cut back on the living standards of its workers in order to stabilize costs and output.

Neither liberals nor conservatives were content to allow economic gestation alone to govern their response to labor unrest.[42] The conservatives were particularly skeptical of a strategy based on the economic asphyxiation of protest. And although they had lost the first round of political struggle with their liberal opposition by September 1931, they continued to piece together a secret police force by administratively manipulating the police tribunals. The new governor-general in Léopoldville, Auguste Tilkens, gave them his assent by establishing a secret committee devoted to gathering intelligence about African millennial sects and the means to suppress them.[43]

With order contingently reestablished, liberals too began to worry about whether the repression had been extensive enough — and in so doing, drew closer to the conservatives. For example, Léopold Mottoulle, the Union Minière's director of native personnel, insisted that the government take a more active role in the prosecution and punishment of those African workers who were the alleged leaders and instigators of the unrest at Kipushi. But the provincial administration maintained that it did not feel itself obligated to rule on the measures that should be taken against the workers beyond trying and sentencing them for civil crimes. For although the police tribunal of Elisabethville sentenced the spokesman for the Luba workers, Tshimanga André, to six months in prison, it shrank from Mottoulle's suggestion that they prohibit his return to his home chieftaincy of Mutombo Katshi in Lomami. Mottoulle feared that Tshimanga and the other apprehended leaders might play a role in the burgeoning rural unrest in Lomami and the other troubled areas of Katanga's hinterland.[44] Mottoulle first voiced this fear at the special session of government and company officials on 20 October 1931. He concluded that the leaders of the protest like Tshimanga André could not remain in the industrial areas, nor could they be allowed to return to their chieftaincies. Mottoulle's view was all the more striking, since it was customary for an African convicted of a felony to be returned to his home village after serving a prison sentence. Mottoulle, and those who agreed with his conclusions, thought that once in the countryside these men could sustain what the mining administration thought to be a copious network of connections between themselves and other African workers.[45] It was precisely these kinds of ominous projections that made conservative criticism and the liberal response to it sound like one voice between the quelling of unrest at Kipushi in late August and the commencement of the workers' boycott in September.[46]

The boycott began in September 1931, one month after the suppression of the unrest at Kipushi. Initially it attracted only a small number of mineworkers; but after the protests at Ruashi and Kipushi in May and August failed to stem the layoffs and incurred so many violent reprisals, a growing number of workers were drawn into the more pacific boycott by the beginning of October.[47] The boycott reached its peak in late October and November, just when new recruits were being brought to the work sites. The Union Minière's

Table 5.1. Union Minière du Haut-Katanga: Net Profit, Output, and Wages (in U.S. dollars), 1929–1935

	Net Profits	Copper (Cu) and Cobalt (Co) Output (in metric tons)	Wages and Total Costs[a] of African Labor	Number of African Workers[b]	European Wages	Number of European Workers	Ratio of African to European Workers
1929	12,351,495.00	140,000 + (Cu) 800 + (Co)	1,101,600 (w) 6,552,000 (c)	17,000	1,014,503.23	2,261	8:1
1930	12,096,778.20	142,000 + (Cu) 810 + (Co)	1,036,800 (w) 6,318,000 (c)	16,000	2,021,760.00	1,951	8:1
1931	3,638,138.40	120,000 + (Cu) 300 + (Co)	777,600 (w) 4,665,600 (c)	12,000	2,431,369.01	1,388	9:1
1932	—	55,000 + (Cu) 200 + (Co)	324,000 (w) 2,376,000 (c)	5,000	1,995,840.00	644	8:1
1933	—	65,000 + (Cu) 350 + (Co)	388,800 (w) 2,116,800 (c)	6,000	1,587,600.00	487	12:1
1934	—	114,000 + (Cu) 200 + (Co)	583,200 (w) 2,138,400 (c)	9,000	1,463,115.79	550	16:1
1935	5,732,688.00	110,000 + (Cu) 180 + (Co)	648,000 (w) 2,376,000 (c)	10,000	1,669,621.62	596	17:1

Sources: TC/UM, 64, Union Minière: rapports annuels, avril 1932–novembre 1934; *L'Union Minière du Haut-Katanga* (monograph series, Bruxelles, L. Cuypers, 1954), 36 (graphs on copper and cobalt production); Fetter, "L'Union Minière du Haut-Katanga," 13; Gouverneur, *Productivity and Factor Proportions*, 168; Perrings, *Black Mineworkers*, 80 and 250–52.

[a]Most of the categories of "costs" do not apply throughout the Depression. Consequently such figures have to be treated with some caution.

[b]These figures do not include workers at the tin mines or privately contracted auxiliary workers.

company store and the smaller merchants did their greatest amount of business with African workers during this period. It was therefore the most propitious time for the leaders of the boycott to exhort the new recruits and other African workers to join their action. Outside of casual laborers working in the commercial establishments of the town, the greatest source of support for the boycott was among the African construction workers at the Union Minière, particularly those at the Star of the Congo. Bricklayers and carpenters, for example, figured prominently among those Africans who the police claimed were both Watchtower and boycott "leaders" after the police raid of 17 December 1931.[48]

African workers were beginning to follow and comprehend the importance of the market and the business cycle for their employers. But their grasp of the market's importance was infused with a great deal of moral content. Since the market in an abstract sense did not fully determine the African workers' social consciousness at this point, they were largely unaware of its impact on the price structure of imported items such as sardines, belt buckles, felt hats, and so on.[49] Nor were they aware of the fact that the world market for copper, rather than the apparent goodwill of the Union Minière, had been the principal source of the slight increase in their real wages. Consequently, they placed the onus of the blame for the hard times of the first years of the Depression on the mining company. In the workers' view and perhaps in that of all the African inhabitants of Elisabethville, the Union Minière had allowed them to be unjustly exploited by the smaller retail merchants. African workers did not object altogether to the exploitation of their labor power at this point, but "unjust" prices were, in their estimate, insufferable and a legitimate cause for protest.[50] They sought to use their increased buying power to censure local merchants and the mining company for violating what they saw as a customary and socially just relation between wages and prices.[51]

It was perhaps the tailings of the workers' moral indignation that the authorities mistook for membership in one of the several African Watchtower sects. Although many of the workers had been influenced by millennarian beliefs, by October 1931 only a small core of them belonged to any one of the several Watchtower sects. A case in point was that of Vula Aroni, or Vula Jean as he was known to the police.[52] Vula became an organizer of the Elisabethville boycott in September 1931, shortly after dismissal from his job as a shovelman at the Star of the Congo Mine. According to the police, he was linked to African Watchtower through his relationship with Mumbwa Napoleon Jacob.

Apparently Vula and Mumbwa were from the same village in the Haut-Luapula District. However, it seems Vula actually converted to Watchtower only after he had escaped the police in Elisabethville and fled south to Sakania between late November and December 1931.[53]

Although the boycott was organized in part by African Watchtower leadership, African workers at the Union Minière who were not necessarily Watchtower adherents played important roles. A core of workers who were either leaders of the Elisabethville boycott or played an active role in it did eventually join one of the several African Watchtower sects. But this was only after the beginning of the police raids in the *cité indigène* in November 1931, when the Watchtower leader, Piala, or Pearson Musonda, was arrested with some of his followers.[54] Apparently the ability of many of the Watchtower networks to elude the newly formed secret police was one of the major reasons that some workers joined the movement at this point. For example, of the 180 known members of Watchtower sects, only 60 had been arrested by the secret police as of 17 December 1931.[55]

Watchtower did have a compelling influence on many of the workers before the commencement of the boycott, even though the Catholic church was the state church in the Belgian Congo. Translation of the Bible into local languages had only the most limited support from the Catholic clergy, for example, and the church forbade the reading of other religious publications.[56] Watchtower leaders opposed such practices. Many were literate but saw themselves less as teachers and preachers and more as adepts, deacons, "baptists," and cell leaders. Few of them had come to the movement as a result of intellectual or doctrinal disagreement with the Catholic clergy. Rather, they were men who had "wrestled with Satan" in the labor camps and in the homes of Europeans as domestic servants. They believed that the "new heaven and earth" of the Book of Revelation would be set up in the everyday world, and that they could inform others of its advent by open-air baptisms, witch-finding, and spreading the message that all secular governments were creations of the devil. Their outlook and personal aspirations did not differ much from the masses of underpaid and mistreated colonial subjects they sought to convert. However much Watchtower leaders denied a political interpretation of their doctrine — and many did in the face of the police dragnets — the vagaries of colonial rule itself determined the degree of politicization that adventist and millennial beliefs underwent. For in the estimate of many African subjects, colonialism presented itself as an alien claim on their labor which left them little in the way of dignity. Inasmuch as this was true, they secretly wished for its demise.[57]

Who were the leaders of the 1931 protests? Were they in fact harbingers of rural protest as well as insubordinate voices at the workplace, as the secret police claimed? To be sure, some of them might have been, although this cannot be determined from the arrest records of any branch of the police. Some of them did have connections to millennial African religious sects, although such connections were, at this juncture, fleeting and circumstantial. Whether such connections suggested an insurrectionary nature for the protests cannot be easily posited; yet they do suggest that the extreme measures taken by the police compelled some workers to join secretive and underground forms of organization in an attempt to survive.

AFTERMATH

What both conservatives and liberals failed to realize about the post-1931 situation was that Katanga and the contiguous countryside were no longer a series of subsistence redoubts, and that peasants would not easily swallow industry's losses in the form of repatriated workers. Nor would they bear the reproduction costs of a future generation of workers unless coerced. Given the recurrent food shortages of the 1920s, however, the peasants did want to preserve a portion of the land for food crops. And since the 1930 slump in cotton prices caused them to limit their use of plows, the colonial administration and mining company thought that they would willingly limit themselves to food cultivation.[58] But instead of planting less cotton, as they had in response to the 1926 price slump, the peasants planted even more when wage remittances from younger relatives working at the Union Minière disappeared with the layoffs.[59] Thousands of young women fled the land as cotton and sesame placed an even heavier burden on the soil and their hopes for the future.[60] Thousands of mineworkers returned to the rural areas in the wake of the strikes and antirepatriation riots at the Union Minière. The peasants rose but in a more inchoate fashion than the workers; local rebellions flickered throughout much of rural Katanga. The immediate cause of the rural unrest — the contradictory attempt of the cotton refineries and local government to encourage cotton cultivation without allowing the peasant direct access to the market — was fairly easy to discern. Rather than destroy their own fields, peasants burned the refineries and warehouses and smashed the government-issued plows. Military promenades in the rural areas followed closely behind. Land chiefs

Table 5.2. Production of Cash Crops and Food Crops (in hectares) in Tanganika-Moero and Lualaba, 1930

| | Cash Crops | | Food Crops | | |
	Cotton	Peanuts and Sesame	Cassava	Sweet Potatoes	Differential between Cash Crops and Food Crops[a]
			TANGANIKA-MOERO		
Albertville	1,442	1,417	2,417	–	+ 442
Kongolo	5,287	1,877	355	–	+ 6,809
Ankoro	2,184	1,236	1,546	–	+ 1,874
Moba	–	544	2,100	1,004	– 2,560
Mwanza	2,637	1,248	1,119	–	+ 2,766
Total	11,550	6,322	7,537	1,004	+ 9,331
			LUALABA[b]		
Jadotville	–	–	1,324	–	– 1,324
Bukama	1,175	[294]	–	–	+ 1,469
Kabongo	[2,786]	706	–	–	+ 3,492
Kamina	3,056	[6,473]	–	–	+ 9,529
Malonga[c]	4,512	[2,245]	–	–	+ 6,757
Sandoa[c]	4,497	[5,061]	–	–	+ 9,558
Total	16,026	14,779	1,324	–	+29,481

Sources: *Rapport sur l'Administration du Congo Belge*, 1930; *Bulletin agricole du Katanga*, 1932–37; AG, B6, SM/MOI, Statistiques, 1928–32.

Note: No doubt corn and other cereals were in production as well. However, no statistical information is available for them in the official records.

[a]Where the number of hectares planted to cash crops exceed those planted to food crops, a + precedes the figure; where food crop production exceeds cash crops, a – precedes the figure.

[b]Although the official records show no difference between the number of hectares planted to cotton and those planted to peanuts and sesame in Lualaba, differences in production did, in fact, exist between the two categories. The narrative evidence suggests that the territorial agents fudged on these figures, making one entry in their day books but another in their territorial reports. The figures shown in brackets have been adjusted to account for the discrepancies between the official sources and the agents' own records.

[c]A large number of hectares may have been "disguised" cotton lands.

and returning workers regarded each other differently in the midst of the turbulence.[61]

The workers did not return home empty handed. They returned with a powerful sense of organization in the form of a more refined version of the *bashikutu*, or lodges. As precolonial and colonial political conventions wore thin, the workers' lodges moved into the breach and partly recast peasant protest in modern terms of political subversion. But the government remained fixed in its contention that rural unrest was the result of "atavistic native beliefs."[62] Failing to see the practical connection between worker and peasant protest, the provincial secret police suppressed first the one and then the other. The Union Minière saw its interests from a different vantage point, however. The mining company favored the commercial production of foodstuffs over cotton as a means to hold down wages and to facilitate better the reproduction of the workforce. Its view changed somewhat during the first phase of the Depression; but its basic components – peasant cultivators, an internal market for food, casual laborers for development work at the mines, and a relatively skilled, poorly remunerated core of miners and factory operatives – remained the same.[63] Incredulous over the government's actions and hardpressed by soaring freight rates and the cost of imported food, the mining company partly withdrew from provincial politics. Moreover, there was still a long way to go before peasants and workers would be unilaterally receptive to a call for insurrection. The distance narrowed considerably throughout the 1930s.

At the outset of the Depression the Union Minière and the provincial government of Katanga believed that nonindigenous African workers, both foreign and Congolese, could be laid off and repatriated without great difficulty. The instances of labor unrest at Ruashi, Kipushi, and Mwene Ditu and the Elisabethville boycott – which all took place at a time when the mining company was most vulnerable because of its production schedule – proved that this was not so. Hunger and the scale of the layoffs were indeed the workers' main grievances, but they did not compel the workers to act spontaneously or without planning. The judicious nature of the workers' actions was borne out by the fact that management was forced to put many of those who were incarcerated back to work immediately after the violence subsided. Luba workers from Lomami were perhaps the most pivotal group of African workers, having provided much of the leadership for the work stoppages at Kipushi. The bargaining position of the Luba workers was further enhanced once the protest took a violent turn, for the company failed to see that the protest turned into a full-fledged riot only after the intervention of the police. State intervention at this point worked against the interest of the company as well. Nevertheless, the scale of the repression compelled all the workers to seek a broader base of solidarity in order to negotiate survival on the work sites. However, the violent reaction of the police to the workers' protest at Ruashi and Kipushi constrained its positive effect. In September many workers turned to a more effective form of protest – the boycott of Elisabethville's stores. The boycott threatened to shut down the provincial capital and gave the government cause to make use of the newly formed secret police. While not unhappy about this turn of events, the mining company felt it should have had more control over the new police apparatus. As the methods of the secret police became more extreme, the company's view of the situation became less benign.

By December 1931 the Union Minière and the African workers had fought each other to a standstill. The Depression and the secret police broke the spell of the contest and gave a victory by default to the company. The work stoppages and subsequent violence had indeed hurt production. Moreover, they demonstrated that an ethnically stratified work routine was unworkable. But management had retained a large measure of its legitimacy and the power to define the terms of work.[64] Consequently, after 1932, the mining company began to reorganize itself on a new basis. Yet the fruits of its victory over the workers were short lived. Between 1934 and 1937, as the company began to expand its operations to the hinterland of the mining complex, the minimum requirements for agrarian unrest — forced labor, increased taxation, and falling prices for crops — were greatly exacerbated. Industrial unrest resumed as well, but in different forms and with slightly different objectives in some instances. Once again the stage was slowly set for widespread popular unrest.[65]

CHAPTER SIX

The Reconstruction of the Mining Industry, 1932–1939

THE ADMINISTRATIVE REORGANIZATION OF THE UNION MINIÈRE AND THE COLONIAL GOVERNMENT

The Depression and the labor unrest of 1931 compelled the Union Minière to reorganize the profitability basis of the mining industry and, in turn, to redefine its relationship to the colonial government and the world market. These measures pushed the company to the brink of collapse. By 1932 it was operating under a growing political disadvantage as well, for, with profits down, its tax contribution to the colonial government declined just when the colonial government itself was undergoing administrative reorganization.[1]

By 1933 the previous division of the Congo into four provinces under a governor-general and three vice governors-general was replaced. Instead of four provinces, there were six under one governor-general and five provincial commissioners. In effect, any vice governor-general who remained in office, as did Katanga's Gaston Heenen, was demoted.[2] Between 1933 and 1934 the number of territorial agents in Katanga went from 81 to 66, whereas the ranks of the provincial secret police increased markedly under Heenen's successor, Provincial Commissioner Amour Maron.[3] Katanga also lost Lomami, its most populous district, and was renamed the province of Elisabethville. More than half of the province's land area and population was regrouped under the newly created district of Lualaba, which was administered from the highly industrialized town of Jadotville.[4]

The government's reorganization tended to work against those liberal officials who had been closely allied with the mining company during the unrest of 1931. Between September 1933 and 1934 the four most powerful liberals in the provincial government — Vice Governor-General Heenen, Auguste Verbeken, the district commissioner of Elisabethville, Fernand Grevisse, the district commissioner of Luapula-Moero, and Antoine Sohier, Katanga's chief magistrate — resigned. All four left under pressure, in the face of the growing power of the secret police. By 1934 Heenen, Grevisse, and Sohier had returned to Belgium — Heenen eventually to become minister of colonies, Grevisse and Sohier to be remodelled into official watchdogs of metropolitan interests within Katanga itself several years later. Verbeken defected to the cause of the educated mining clerks at the Union Minière.[5]

Between 1932 and 1939, in its efforts to discipline and control its workforce, the mining company was compelled to accept the reorganized provincial governments of Elisabethville, Lusambo, and Kasai (formerly Katanga and the Sankuru and Lomami districts), while assuming more responsibility for the acquisition and reproduction of its workforce. Since the government officials of the 1930s and the Second World War era were thought of as less competent than their predecessors, the company willingly chose such an alternative.[6] Yet the selection of Jadotville as the capital of the largely agrarian district of Lualaba was allegorical evidence of the company's continuing hegemonic influence over the government. Nevertheless, it sought to stabilize the African workforce under conditions of severe economic stringency, using a minimum of material incentives to maintain a uniform complement of workers and output.[7]

Tightening the lid on the social and economic expectations of the workers encompassed both short- and long-term objectives. The short-term objectives were fairly straightforward; for they were designed to facilitate the social reproduction of the workforce and to preempt worker protest through an expanding nexus of social control. This nexus included: (1) the *écoles professionelles* and their array of schoolmasters (*instituteurs*) and social assistants (*moniteurs*); (2) the *tribunaux indigènes*, or native tribunals, the primary means for surveillance of the urban African community; (3) the *centres extracoutumiers* (*CEC*), the all encompassing institutions of African communal government, whose powers had been greatly expanded under Heenen's administration, so much so that they periodically became the government's tax farmers in the African quarters of the industrial towns; (4) the Union Minière's revamped *pointage*, or management, system, which combined wage penalties and compulsory transfers by means of the hated *feuilles disciplinaires*, and which redefined the classification of *main-d'oeuvre indigènes/specialisée* (*MOI/s*), or "skilled" African worker, so that the acquisition of artisanal or industrial metallurgical skills did not in itself guarantee promotion to the skilled category. None of these components was mutually exclusive. Schoolmasters and social assistants often doubled as officers of the CEC, and African foremen and gang bosses were encouraged to sit as judges on the *tribunaux indigènes*, particularly when such courts were charged with hearing work-related grievances.[8]

The more conservative and security-minded officials of the post-1933 governments were unnerved by African participation in such institutions. In their minds, the continued existence of ethnic and communal organizations – even when they assumed the most elementary and innocuous forms – undermined the government's authority; for they were a kind of proving ground upon which urban Africans could test their ability to run their affairs.[9] But the company's lack of trust in the combined abilities of the government's officials, and the government's own confusion about whether the brunt of its police power should be imposed on the urban or rural population, guaranteed the survival of a few of the pre-1931 urban associations. Their survival was predicated, however, on the belief that protest and the existence of an aggrieved state among the workers were not abnormal responses to industrial reorganization, and that both lay just beneath the surface of the workers' everyday routine.[10]

THE CONSTRAINTS ON RECONSTRUCTION

By 1934 work resumed at the larger mines on the western and northern periphery of the mining complex. In the western sector, Kolwezi yielded as much cobalt as copper. Farther north, the tin mines, which had been closed since 1928, reopened. Open-pit and underground sources of radium and uranium were exploited at Shinkolobwe when the facilities for their refinement were expanded at the Union Minière's factories in Oolen, Belgium.[11] Evacuation of the company's raw materials increased markedly once the Tenke-Dilolo rail line, which connected Katanga to the Atlantic Ocean at Lobito Bay, Angola, was completed. By 1936 the recovery was in full swing. The mining company had managed to recoup its fortunes by an extensive plan of mining and development in what had formerly been its hinterland – and by shameless and exhaustive exploitation of African labor. Once the physical infrastructure was restored and expanded, only the workforce itself needed remolding.

In addition to attempting to constrain and disaggregate the working day, the mining company also attempted to curtail the social life of the workers, particularly at the work sites in the areas of expansion in the northern and western parts of the province. Because of the dearth of women and the absence or partial destruction of the lodges at many of these work sites, the company's low-budget Victorian morality often gave a wide berth to prostitution, gambling, and the excessive use of drugs and alcohol. The irony was not that such crimes followed in the footsteps of the arid cultural conditions of the camps, but that the mining company believed it could prevent them from occurring without providing the workers with an alternative to recreation and the spontaneous aspect of sexual love. This unbalanced view of the workers' private lives tilted further as the 1930s wore on and as the number of single men increased on the work sites north and west of Jadotville.[12]

By 1935 prostitution and similar crimes were the bane of effective administration at work sites such as Kolwezi, Busanga, and Kikole. On 29 June 1936 two African workers at Kikole, Asani Sumaili and Saulu Auguste, were arrested and imprisoned for being purveyors of illicit activities at that camp. Both these men had engaged in regular work at Kikole for almost two years, even though they had both been classified *travailleurs indésirables* in April 1935. Sumaili was accused of being a "bully, troublemaker, thief, con man and pimp."[13] He allegedly brought a number of "femmes publiques" into the camp who, in addition to plying their trade, were used systematically by Sumaili to burglarize the homes of other workers. According to the camp administration, the women that had been brought into the camp by Sumaili were the source of a mild epidemic of venereal disease there from April to June of 1935.[14]

Of Sumaili's "accomplice and fellow tribesman," Saulu Auguste, the administration said:

This man virulently denounced Senga Albert and several other police of the camp for having struck his "wife" and also for attempting to woo her away from him. He made these complaints to the Inspector of Industry, then residing at Kikole, while in the presence of the chief colonial officer in the area. An inquiry revealed that the "wife" of this native is named Daye Jeanne, the daughter of the chief of Mutombo Katshi, who fled from her husband several months ago. He is now hospitalized at Kabinda. She has lived with several natives of the camp and even a European. She is allegedly the woman who contaminated the *instituteur* Gabriel. This woman has been chased from the camp and subsequently barred from its surroundings by me and the chief colonial officer at Luena.

Saulu Auguste drove his real wife away in order to replace her with this woman as his concubine. Senga Albert, who had been charged with the surveillance of Saulu Auguste, found this woman in the latter man's house. Saulu then — in order to avenge himself — made these false allegations against Senga Albert. We lodged a complaint against him with the chief colonial officer at Luena and called for his arrest.[15]

Needless to say, the imprisonment of Saulu and Sumaili did not
bring an end to crime in the workers' camp at Kikole. Despite frequent arrests in the camps, crimes against property and those of a
social nature persisted.[16] Implicit in the African resort to crime was
a belief that the inequities of the social system were not going to disappear. Ironically, between 1932 and 1939, the frequency and widespread nature of African crimes against property widened the breach
between African mineworkers and the Union Minière, and also between the African working class as a whole and colonial authority.[17]
African criminal behavior at the mines and in the industrial towns
became, in an indirect way, the harbinger of a much broader but
roughly articulated challenge to authority.

The mining company vociferously championed the proliferation
of the native tribunals on the work sites as a means of limiting crime,
stanching African Watchtower, and limiting the influence of the
lodges.[18] It was agreed that the African members of the courts should
be chosen from the gang foremen and older workers. The first examples of such institutions were set up at Lubumbashi, Kipushi, and
Jadotville.[19] Within three years the tribunals expanded throughout
the entire mining complex. In the wake of such rapid growth, the
Union Minière and the colonial government were compelled to admit
that the workers' enthusiastic adherence to such institutions resulted
from the fact that almost nowhere else in colonial Africa, with the
exception of South Africa, had the indigenous population been forced
to adapt to industrial life as rapidly, and on so large a scale, as in
Katanga.[20]

The mining company and the 1933 provincial government believed
that the tribunals were a necessary step in levelling the influence of
"bush institutions" like the lodges, even though they disagreed about
the amount of magisterial power the tribunals should have.[21] None
of their conceptions of how the courts should function and which
groups of Africans would activate those functions was very democratic. The provincial secret police, for example, were not always in
need of actual evidence of worker unrest to cast aspersion on the way
the courts functioned. Allowing the workers and the urban population even a pretense of governing themselves was dangerous from
their point of view.[22] The mining company maintained that while
it agreed with the idea of the tribunals in general, it would be "dangerous for such institutions to leave a modern framework"—in short,
to develop to a point where Africans on the tribunals had real authority and power.[23] But in view of workers' mounting enthusiasm over
the prospects of more African participation in the tribunals, the company thought it best to risk the potential dangers. As early as 1932

Auguste Verbeken, the former district commissioner of Elisabethville, put his finger on the company's likely position on the tribunals:

> What is incumbent upon us and what we are obliged to do is to direct this movement, canalize it, and control its growth. We can only do this through trusted intermediaries, men who have proven themselves to be worthy of our confidence.[24]

Far from trusting the African workers serving on the courts to keep their own counsel and arrive at their own decisions about each instance or complaint that came before them, the Union Minière and the colonial government attempted to intervene at every turn. In 1932 the report to the Belgian Parliament started off with an apology for instituting the tribunals in certain districts of Katanga "too soon" or, in some instances, before the territorial administration could sound out the indigenous chain of authority and effectively integrate the courts into it.[25] Consequently, the mineworkers desperately clung to the tribunals. With only a few other legal means to protect their slender body of rights, particularly after the dismantling of the Office for the Inspection of Industry and Commerce in 1935, the mineworkers made use of the courts for essentially negative reasons.[26]

Between 1932 and 1936 African workers maximized their participation on the native tribunals and in the other agencies that sought to regulate African life in the industrial towns. By 1935 their increased participation was alarming to both the Union Minière and the provincial government.[27] By 1936 both thought that the African courts might become spurs of insurrection if control over them fell into what they considered the wrong hands. As a result, all the tribunals throughout Katanga were required to record their proceedings in French. This built-in means of surveillance was an important factor in the rapid decline of the courts. By 1939 they had virtually disappeared on all of the company's work sites except those at Lubumbashi, Kipushi, and Jadotville.[28]

The Union Minière also sought to standardize the payment of taxes by its African workers during the reconstruction period. Prior to the 1931 unrest, African mineworkers had paid their taxes through their chief or headman or through an officer of the CEC. Under the mining company's new scheme, workers were exhorted and, more often than not, coerced into paying their taxes directly to the territorial administrator in the vicinity of a given work site. At Kipushi, for instance, the local territorial administrator made special periodic visits to the workers' camp to collect installments on tax payment. Upon his arrival, the workers were to queue up in the middle of the camp to pay their tax installments.[29] Workers who lived on the out-skirts of the towns, however, continued to pay their taxes grudgingly to the local chiefs. In some instances, many refused to pay at all. Those who were fined or imprisoned for refusal to pay taxes often received a sympathetic audience from workmates, who occasionally aided them in escaping the authorities. For example, between 1933 and 1934, Mufunga Kanimbo concealed Mulunga Katoto in his house for over a year after Mulunga had escaped from the territorial prison following his conviction for tax evasion. These men had been work-mates at the Shituru works in Jadotville. Mufunga's action demon-strated the workers' willingness to protect each other from what they considered unjust demands.[30]

European managers and foremen attempted to disguise their mis-givings about the new management system by pitting the African mining clerks against the African schoolmasters and social assistants. As mentioned earlier, by the late 1920s the Union Minière began moving many of the social assistants out of the company's recruiting posts in the countryside and into the workers' camps.[31] Almost none of the social assistants and schoolmasters had any special skills beyond a desire to be the eyes of the mining company on the work sites. This distinguished them from the clerks, who, as the animators of the new management system, had to be moderately proficient in French and mathematics, and who were rather more useful to the workers as a source of forged release papers, passes, and other work-related documents. As watchers rather than reporters, the social assistants and schoolmasters underwrote management's authoritarian character outside the workplace, particularly at the newer work sites and in Jadotville's factories. For this, they were despised by the generality of workers.

At Busanga, Kikole, and Kolwezi, however, when management's control over the workforce appeared to falter, schoolmasters joined work actions and even engaged in crimes against property. For example, Motokaa Alphonse, a schoolmaster at Kikole from 1938 to 1940, was a consummate thief and black marketeer. Between 1938 and 1939 he waylaid several truckloads of food scheduled for the exca-vation sites at Busanga and sold or bartered them away between Kabongo and Kamina. Yet he presented himself as the very soul of dutiful obedience. The camp manager at Kikole even commended him at one point for his level-headedness and the fact that he had not asked for a raise. No doubt, Motokaa's other activities must have more than compensated for the fact that he was the second lowest-paid school-master at Kikole.[32] At Kolwezi, Muhemili Abeli, a schoolmaster and former chauffeur of Marcelin Devaux, Kolwezi's camp manager, was arrested on 6 March 1939 for theft. Between October 1938 and March 1939 Muhemili had stolen a bed, trunk, mattress, two tables, seven chairs, a wash basin, and sundry other items from Devaux and other whites at Kolwezi. He, in turn, sold these items to African workers at the mine. At the time of Muhemili's arrest, Devaux was so incensed that he attempted to have the workers who had purchased the stolen items arrested and imprisoned as well.[33]

Crimes bent on relieving hunger and material want—from poaching to petty theft—were widespread during the latter part of the Depression. They were perhaps the most commonplace form of indiscipline. Although it could hardly be said that crime was "organized," except on the most parochial level, the schoolmasters and social assistants were obviously not a deterrent to it. They, along with the upper strata of production workers, were not immune to hard times.

Since the most important mines that went into operation after 1932 —Shinkolobwe, Kolwezi, Busanga, and Kikole—had both open-face and underground operations, the new work routine was modelled on the one in force at the underground Prince Léopold Mine at Kipushi. Under the new system, management attempted to reduce the number of men working on a task basis or at their own pace at the open-face mines and in maintenance, while increasing the complement of those who dug uranium, cobalt, copper, and tin directly out of the underground galleries.[34] In order to widen the gap between surface and underground wages and to encourage the more intransigent workers to take on underground work, both surface and underground workers were subjected to piece rates. Surface workers also became more subject to wage penalties and general harassment. Underground workers withstood a greater amount of corporal punishment, however, and were more directly threatened by mining accidents; for underground veins beyond the mining company's central sectors were worked by cutting irregular tunnels directly into the richest veins of ore, since timber and other construction materials were scarce at the more removed work sites. Consequently, underground workers at these mines carried the ore to the surface on their backs rather than in hauling cars or with the aid of winches. A momentary loss of footing or artificial light was often fatal.[35] European supervisors derived a double advantage, therefore, from their control over the distribution of equipment, particularly lamps. It was to their immediate advantage to have African workers know that supervisors could determine whether workers lived or died. This understanding, if one can call it that, meant that the workers were less inclined to attack foremen. Moreover, underground workers were not much inclined to risk the destruction of lamps and other life-saving equipment by responding in kind to their supervisors' assaults, even though gratuitous corporal punishment was widespread.

The new management system was also thwarted at the more removed mines by European foremen and camp managers' flagrant abuse of African clerks and timekeepers. As a result of such abuse, African clerks and gang foremen often refused to act as rate-keepers and makeshift motion-time study men.[36] Despite wage penalties and piece rates, the new work routine was much less effective at the work sites where the workers had not felt the full weight of company and state repression. An exemplary case was that of Dombe Mathieu. On 27 August 1935 Dombe Mathieu sent a letter of complaint to the central office at Elisabethville regarding his mistreatment by the *chef de camp* at Busanga:

> Monsieur, presently I have the honor to bring to your attention that I have just been fired by the camp manager of Busanga where I had previously worked. Allow me to explain the latter decision. M. Arnould, the office manager, gave me a defective typewriter. It did not have a letter "I." You must understand that I had no other choice but to attempt to rectify this matter. Consequently, M. Arnould heaped the grossest kinds of verbal abuse on me in public. Also, he docked me for 15 days. At the time I had given more than two months of service at Busanga. I leave a review of the situation in your hands. . . .[37]

Dombe Mathieu had been one of the founders and most important contributors to the magazine *Ngonga.* Most of his contributions were short stories written in Swahili about the personal tragedies that took place in the mining camps. No doubt, Dombe's connection to a magazine that was seen by the mining company's administration as a voice of African opposition to its policies strongly influenced the timing of his transfer from Elisabethville to Busanga and his subsequent harrassment at the latter camp. He was eventually replaced as chief clerk at Busanga by one Bawa Jules who, after two years of protracted embroilments with white employees in the front office, was imprisoned on 8 December 1937.[38]

At Kolwezi, Kikole, and Kengere, clerks were readily dismissed and imprisoned. A number of them had been transferred to these work sites from Kipushi, allegedly because they could not keep pace with the quickened demands of local management or make the workers "respect them." However, their workloads at the above-mentioned mines were far from enviable.[39] For example, by December 1938 absenteeism had become so chronic at these mines that clerks had to check the number of work tickets and reset the rate for each worker at least four times a day. Moreover, Kengere was less than 15 kilometers from the notorious territorial prison at Sakabinda. And although no European foremen would have dared to write down that the mine was using convict labor alongside freely contracted workers or, worse, that management was having the more recalcitrant workers prosecuted by civil magistrates and then returned to the mine as work-released prisoners, it appeared that foremen often chose to chasten workers with the threat of imprisonment.[40]

Hunger and dearth were the primary reasons for absenteeism. Some workers would be away from the work sites for as long as three weeks in search of either wild game or fish to supplement their meager rations. Poaching, which some workers found to be commercially lucrative as well, often strained the relations between the mining company and the local chiefs. For example, the chief of the Lubende region, Kibanda, complained bitterly to the mining company about the workers from Kolwezi and Kikole encroaching on his fisheries. Kibanda maintained that the workers set dynamite charges in the lake, and that this method of fishing depleted the spawning beds and schools of fish too rapidly. The chief indicated that he and his constituency wanted 500 francs from the mining company for the damage done by its employees. The mining company maintained that the poaching was a matter for the territorial police and that under no circumstances would it pay Kibanda an indemnity.[41]

The effectiveness of the new low-cost form of corporatism lasted only as long as the demand for output remained at the drastically low levels of the first years of the Depression.[42] Also, until 1940, the mining company attempted to threaten the main body of workers with a virtual army of *travailleurs non immatriculés*, or unregistered workers, whose number never fell below 2,000. The unregistered workers cost a little over a fourth of what the company paid for the regular body of African workers. They also served to drive down the wages of the African workers while the company attempted to reconstruct the industry. The most effective means of achieving this objective, however, rested with the company's efforts to refashion the demographic characteristics of the peasant squatters and the factory proletariat.[43]

AFRICAN SQUATTERS AGAINST THE MINING COMPANY

The long-term objectives of the mining company's new strategy were not as straightforward as the short-term ones. The former objectives were motivated by the prospects of compelling the peasantry of the newly created Lualaba District to produce food for the company's workers, thereby enabling the company to exploit the northern and western mines — particularly the tin, cobalt, and uranium mines — at a commercially feasible level, and to increase the factory proletariat and skilled workers in the metallurgical and engineering trades at the expense of other skilled occupations.[44] The company saw the new management policy as a means to make peasant squatters, factory operatives, and skilled workers conform more to its image of them. This quest evoked three interrelated problems: (1) reasserting the ultimate authority of the company's administration on the work sites and in the camps; (2) bringing the growing number of squatters on the edge of the work sites — a good number of whom were former employees of the Union Minière — under the tacit control of the camp manager at the nearest work site (the CSK would, of course, continue to lease and distribute land); (3) stimulating regular and relatively high levels of food production among the squatters in order to offset the increasing cost of food for workers and their families.[45] Taxation figured importantly in such efforts. In 1932 the company projected that the squatters' communities around Elisabethville, Kipushi, and Jadotville would produce enough food to reduce the cost of feeding the workers and their families substantially by 1934. The company also saw the imposition of a special tax on the squatters as an indispensable means of tying their expectations to cash and the market.[46]

As early as 1929 the Union Minière felt that the peasant squatters should be compelled to produce for a commercial market. Food prices had begun to rise rapidly and continued to do so well after 1931, as a result of the drastic decline in food production in Lomami and Kasai. Increasing freight rates for grain, vegetables, and canned food coming from the British colonies and Angola also contributed to escalating food prices. By 1932, for example, a standard 200-pound bag of maize, which sold at a median price of 10–12 shillings at its place of origin in the Kafue or Luapula Valley in Northern Rhodesia, rose to 75 shillings once it was transported more than 30 kilometers by rail.[47] Peasantization of squatters through taxation and cash incentives became both a reasonable and relatively inexpensive way to get around increasing food costs. After the unrest of 1931 the company quickly set such a plan of action in motion.[48]

The mining company wanted to restore food production to approximately what it had been in 1918, before the rapid despoilation of the countryside.[49] In 1918 the Union Minière's African workers consumed 2,160 tons of maize, 144 tons of beans, 144 tons of peanuts, and 280 tons of unspecified green vegetables. African growers produced perhaps as much as 300 tons of the maize and almost all the cassava and sweet potatoes the workers consumed. But in 1918 the Union Minière was just beginning to enclose large tracts of land beyond the mining sites. The displacement of the peasantry was, therefore, at its most elementary stages. Consequently, neither the mining company nor the provincial government could directly control local food costs.[50]

By 1932–33, however, the mining company was the province's second largest landowner.[51] Between 1931 and 1937, by manipulating the special convention which gave the Comité special du Katanga the right to stake claim on any land in Katanga that could be mined profitably or "in the interests of science," the company circumvented the provincial ordinances which banned free prospecting. This loophole indirectly netted the Union Minière over 50 new land concessions, thus increasing the land area under the company's control by over 270,000 hectares, or 28 percent of the mining company's total land area at the time. Table 6.1 indicates the ostensible use the Union Minière made of its land acquisitions between 1935 and 1937.[52] Although radium, uranium, and lead were allegedly being mined on the 10 percent of the Union Minière land designated as "other," most of these minerals, with the exception of lead, were in the cupriferous zone of the mining complex. What was being mined by the company on this land was the peasantry's independence. The mining company was finally in a position to control the local selling price of food.[53]

After the massive layoffs at the Union Minière, the squatters' areas and unincorporated zones were transformed from an ungainly collection of subsistence redoubts to vital communities in their own right. This was due as much to African efforts as to those of the provincial government and the mining company.[54] But under Heenen's governorship the provincial government attempted to create an administrative and legal environment whereby the squatters' com-

Table 6.1. Proportional Land Uses of the Union Minière, 1937

	Number of Hectares	Percentage of Total Land Use
Copper	439,000	46.3
Tin	167,000	17.6
Iron	103,000	10.9
Gold	91,400	9.6
Coal	53,600	5.7
Salt	1,250	0.1
Other	92,000	9.7
Total	947,250	99.9

Source: *Le Matériel colonial* 27ème année, no. 126 (mars 1937), 113.

munities could be regularly assessed for taxation, first by declaring them *communes indigènes*, and then *centres extra-coutumiers* by virtue of the decree of 23 November 1931. After 1933 such communities were composed almost entirely of former employees of the company and their families. For the provincial administration, they were reminiscent of the *villages des licenciés* that had so bedevilled territorial administrators in the 1920s. Like the latter communities, the squatter settlements often refused to attach themselves to local chieftaincies.[55]

The incorporation of the squatters' areas was a rough and uneven process which fell far short of a solution to the problems generated by mass unemployment. Moreover, because the decree of 5 December 1933 stripped local chiefs of some of their executive powers and created a nebulous administrative category called the *circonscription indigène*, which applied to the entire range of agricultural settlements, the squatters' settlements enjoyed some measure of protection under the law in spite of the designs of the mining company.[56] In many instances the incorporation of the squatters' areas merely served to spread the problems of the industrial towns to the edge of the countryside. By 1933, for instance, semirural communities such as Karavia and Kiswishi were regularly absorbing Elisabethville's excess population from the Kenia quarter and the area that was incorporated later under the name Katuba. After the passing of the provincial decree of 13 July 1935, Elisabethville's rural quarters took in 7,000 hectares and were divided into four specific areas—Karavia, Kiswishi, Kilobelobe, and Luano. Still the African population of the squatters' areas of greater Elisabethville remained largely unaccounted for, a fact the provincial government freely acknowledged. As late as 1935, the official census for the African population of all four of the rural zones was set at a ridiculously low figure of 2,000 people.[57] The existence of the rural quarters, therefore, relieved Elisabethville's administration and the Union Minière of any responsibility for stabilizing the housing situation for these four parcels of the town's African quarter.[58]

By 1931 the *communes agricoles* of Buluo, Luambo, Lufira, and Kambove near Jadotville were also absorbing an increasing number of unemployed workers, but in a manner somewhat different from Elisabethville's rural quarters. The Africans who came to reside in Jadotville's squatters' areas deliberately attempted to resist government and mining company intervention. The territorial government was bent on incorporating them. By 1932 Buluo's peasant squatters were forced to move twice before they finally settled on the upper banks of the Buluo and Kaponono rivers, just beyond the northwestern limits of the city. Between 1933 and 1934 pollution and acid rain from the Union Minière's factories forced squatters on the southern banks of the rivers to move upstream. At the end of 1934 the territorial administrator of Jadotville finally forced them to move closer to the town itself.[59] Between 1934 and 1936 the squatters of Luambo, Lufira, and Kambove were forced to move closer to the mines at Kakontwe and Shangulowe, where there were more unemployed mineworkers.[60] Yet the colonial government refused to recognize the relative autonomy of Jadotville's squatter communities, as it had done in the instance of Elisabethville. For the mining company and the CSK wanted to absorb these areas and levy taxes and production quotas on their inhabitants. By 1936 the mining company and the CSK had drawn up new leases on all the land settled by African squatters after the territorial government had neatly divided it into arable parcels and distributed them to the squatters' households.[61]

As early as 1931 the mining company was parcelling out tons of imported maize seed to squatters in Jadotville's vicinity. By 1934 the company, backed up in part by the coercive power of the territorial government, compelled the squatters to use nonorganic fertilizer, raise goats, and sell almost all of the maize they produced to its subsidiary Minoteries du Katanga. The squatters continued to sell greens and sweet potatoes directly to the workers, but the sale of maize came under the same regulations as the sale of cotton. Also, the CSK, at the prompting of the Union Minière, imposed a special tax on the squatters.[62]

The mining company believed that peasant squatters could supply most of the food consumed by its workforce. The company attempted to compel them to grow only the crops it demanded. It also convinced the colonial government to allow it to create cash incentives for the squatters and to assume direct control over the price of sale for cultivated food products. Squatters who were forced to accept the joint protection of the CSK and the mining company received only the slightest cash return for their produce. But between 1935 and 1937, as crop diseases and measles raged through Jadotville's hinterland, such protection did little to improve the living conditions of the squatters.[63]

Both the mining company and the provincial government were anxious to control the expansion of the squatters' communities near the industrial towns. For rather than oscillating between the agrarian and industrial economy, squatters in fact aided in shoring up the industrial one.[64] On the other hand, the provincial government wanted to preserve public order in the midst of the worsening Depression.[65] But the squatters' communities were neither failsafes for public order nor a means to hinder the burgeoning social awareness of the company's workers, particularly the factory operatives and skilled workers, for whom food shortages and low wages remained unacceptable.[66] Bracketing the aspirations of the squatters was not easy; the attempt to hem in those of the workers even less so.

SKILLED WORKERS AND FACTORY OPERATIVES
AT UNION MINIÈRE

Gaps in the evidence make it difficult to discern the characteristics of the early factory proletariat beyond the Lubumbashi works. In 1921, the fledgling concentrator at Panda in Jadotville was built. As late as 1928, however, the factory operatives merited only the briefest mention in the monthly reports of the mining company. Statistics on the actual size of the factory proletariat at Jadotville were extremely impressionistic up to 1932. The actual number of African hands at the refinery and concentrator works had to be inferred from the number of recorded man-days, or *journées de boy*.[67] No doubt the company used this method of accounting to conceal high rates of turnover.[68]

Before 1929 the output of Jadotville's factories was unimpressive. Despite the newness of their machinery and technology and the construction of a gigantic ore-crushing machine at Kakontwe in 1928, the factories remained partly dormant. By 1928 Panda had so betrayed the company's initial expectations that some of its concentrator equipment was dismantled and moved to Lubumbashi and Ruashi by rail.[69] Between 1931 and 1933 the switch from thermo- to hydro-electric power solved a large portion of the factories' technical problems. But the problem of sufficiently trained and abundant manpower persisted. In 1932 there were 72 fatal or near-fatal accidents at Jadotville alone, or an average of six a month.[70] By 1933 there were still perhaps no more than 220 men for each 12-hour shift at the Panda and Shituru factories.

Before 1933 the work week at Jadotville's factories usually extended into Saturday; and, more often than not, men and machines were kept at work on Sunday at least twice a month. The number of hands at Panda was anywhere from 86 to 100 every 12 hours. The first eight hours of Saturday and all of Sunday were taken up with shaving the excess flakes of metal from the copper and cobalt ingots. Eye injuries and maimings of the hands and feet were most frequent; for the company demanded that 35–40 loads of ingots, the total production for the week, be shaved before the casting of new ingots and cathodes of metal on Monday.[71]

After 1933, the number of operatives per shift leaped to almost 1,000.[72] The widespread use of hydroelectric power had precipitated an increase in the number of factory workers; but as the number of operatives increased—with the greater concentration of machinery under one roof—so did the number of fatal or near-fatal accidents. The lack of affordable and durable clothing among Jadotville's factory workers, particularly metal-plated shoes, militated strongly in favor of higher accident rates. African workers at the Panda works were also hard hit by malaria and bronchitis. Between October 1936 and April 1937 African operatives were struck by a short but formidable epidemic of influenza and bronchitis.[73] Three years before, in November 1933, the activity of the plant had been interrupted by an outbreak of malaria. Large numbers of recruits fled the factory at Panda in both instances. Even though the context of flight from the workplace changed rapidly after 1931—when workers began to use it more as a means to bargain with their employers over working conditions—the Union Minière tended to ignore such signs of worker dissatisfaction.[74]

The increasing number of African factory operatives and skilled workers during the Depression was quite in line with the Union Minière's desire to effect economies of scale, since the increase in African workers acted as a countervailing force to the increasing cost of white labor.[75] Before the Depression, as we have seen, the division between skilled and unskilled African workers was rather ambiguous except at Lubumbashi. The mining company had to recruit 196 workers in order to keep 100 at work for a 9–12-month period.[76] This haphazard deployment of workers ceased in part between 1932 and 1935, when the global copper industry experienced a recomposition of markets, output, and capital. By 1935, as a result of British rearmament and preparations for the Second World War, global production of copper increased. Actual production went from 1,250,000 tons in 1934 to 1,500,000 tons in 1935, despite the two major producers of copper, Chile and the United States, having drastically reduced their output during the first five years of the Depression. However, by the end of 1935, world consumption of copper exceeded 1,600,000 tons.[77]

After 1935 Belgium was able to pay off a considerable portion of its external debt, once output in Katanga's mining industry began to exceed the highest points of the pre–Depression era, even though selling prices for raw materials had fallen drastically. Similarly, the Union Minière, in spite of a reduced net profit, was once again able to purchase new machinery and technology.[78] The mining company also decided to invest more money in the construction of brick houses for its factory hands. Meanwhile the older segment of factory workers at Lubumbashi bore up under a steadily falling wage rate and a sharp increase in overtime.[79]

Table 6.2 shows just how drastic the decline in African wage rates at Lubumbashi was between 1935 and 1939. In addition to a general decline in wage rates, there were equally dramatic decreases in pay scales within the various grades of proficiency and skill at the factory. Only 46 workers (4.3 percent) with a *cote*, or grade of nine or above, made less than four francs a day in 1935. By 1939 at least 183 of the workers (18.7) percent who were paid the four-franc rate or less had a proficiency level of above nine. Moreover, after 1935, the posted wage rates at Lubumbashi did not allow for the debilitating effect of wage penalties.[80] Wage penalties increased to the point that African workers at Lubumbashi believed that the company was bent on driving conditions back to what they had been at the end of the 1920s.[81]

The factory operatives and skilled workers of Lubumbashi and Jadotville formed the apex of a new occupational pyramid at the Union Minière. By late 1934, however, the mining company began an assault on the wages and working conditions of factory operatives and skilled African workers. Meanwhile the output of the underground workers at Kipushi—and later that of the workers at the Kamoto underground section of Kolwezi—quickly became the chief sources of metal ore for the company's refining operations. Kolwezi and Ruashi also became the company's principal sources of cobalt. Hence, at the very moment that the need for more skilled African workers increased, it was also necessary to increase the ranks of the underground workers at Kipushi and the smaller underground sites.[82] Securing the top and the bottom of the pyramid became the mining company's chief priority.[83]

Table 6.2. Percentage Distribution of Wage Rates for African Factory Workers at Lubumbashi in 1935 and 1939

Daily Wage Rate (in francs)	1935[a] (%)	1939[b] (%)
2.50	38.7	63.0
4.00	12.5	10.8
4.50	16.8	11.4
5.50	12.5	5.5
6.00	19.5	9.2

Sources: AG, A9, no. 508/D-40 de MOI, Barème de salaires, juin 1935, Lubumbashi; AG, B5, dossier d 15, MOI: Taux salaire, 16 avril 1929.

[a]The average daily wage rate for the 1,080 African factory operatives at Lubumbashi in 1935 was between 3.20 and 4.00 francs.

[b]The average daily wage rage for the 981 African factory operatives at Lubumbashi in 1939 was between 2.40 and 2.90 francs.

The increase in the number of factory operatives at Jadotville in the first half of the 1930s also owed something to the voluntary in-migration of Africans from the smaller industrial towns of the province. Between 1930 and 1934, for example, the number of workers in Elisabethville and Jadotville who originated from company towns such as Mwanza and Manono increased more than threefold (see Table 6.3). By 1935 well over a third of Jadotville's African population had come from Elisabethville. By the latter 1930s their voluntary association, La Société Elisabethville-Katanga, dominated the social life of the town's African population.[84] However, the standard of living of Jadotville's factory operatives did not differ markedly from those of the African mineworkers at nearby Kakontwe or Shangulowe, or from those of the squatter peasants among whom many of them lived.[85]

Most of the available housing in Jadotville was in miserable condition, even by company standards. By the end of 1938, 150 of the

Table 6.3. Number of African Workers at the Union Minière du Haut-Katanga, by Origin and Seniority (10 or More Years), 1944

Area of Origin	Number of Workers by Seniority					
	More Than 30 Years	25–29 Years	20–24 Years	15–19 Years	10–14 Years	Total
Viable agrarian regions (Kasenga, Sampwe, Kamina, Kabongo, Malonga, Sandoa, etc.)	5	41	273	572	924	1,815
Rural areas that had ceased to be productive from a commercial vantage point (Katako-Kombe, Luebo, Mweka, Tshikapa, Lodja, Sakania, etc.)	3	12	26	32	98	171
Older industrial towns (Elisabethville, Jadotville, Bukama)	0	1	12	29	109	151
Industrial boomtowns of the 1930s (Kolwezi, Manono, Mwanza, etc.)	1	1	20	55	171	248
Other colonies (including Ruanda-Urundi)	11	35	62	130	308	546

Sources: AG, A9, SM/MOI, Instruction de reference no. 8; Conseil de province du Katanga, 1944, "Annexe à l'instruction No. 77/MOI," 126.

Note: Workers from provinces other than Katanga and Kasai are not accounted for in the table. Their total number in 1944 was about 70.

250 dwellings at Shituru were scheduled to be razed. And as late as 1938 most of the factory operatives at Shituru had to pay a sum of 30 francs per month, or perhaps as much as four-fifths of their monthly wages, for lodging. As long as rent absorbed most of the monthly salary of the average factory hand, conditions of overcrowding and ill-health were reasonable certainties for those African workers who lived in either the workers' camps or the town proper.[86]

Wages at both Lubumbashi and the Jadotville works were a far cry from the pay scale projected by the Union Minière. After September 1933, when the Union Minière redefined the classification *main-d'oeuvre indigène/specialisée*, or skilled native worker, "skilled" workers made between 2.40 and 6.00 francs a day. Yet Table 6.4 shows that, as of 1935, more than a third of the most experienced African operatives at Lubumbashi made a wage close to the minimum. Moreover, wages at Jadotville were far below the alleged minimum. The average hand at both Shituru and Panda made between 39.56 and 40.45 francs a month. The mean daily wage for a 30-day month was, therefore, around 1.35 francs a day.[87]

At Jadotville the 2.50-franc minimum prevailed only when overtime was averaged in with straight time for the unskilled African workers. That factory workers had to work overtime consistently in order to make their scheduled wage at Jadotville was a major factor in the African work actions at the factories between May 1936 and June 1939.[88] The overall significance of these work actions will be discussed within the total framework of pre-1941 African worker protest at the Union Minière in the subsequent chapter.

The cost of the mining industry's reconstruction was particularly heavy for skilled workers who had not been trained in the Union Minière's *écoles professionelles* or whose craft lay outside the metallurgical or engineering trades. Consider the situation of Kaumba Kalubatini, a carpenter who had been transferred from Jadotville to the Kikole tin mine in early 1935. After he pointedly refused to work in the underground galleries, Jean Schroeven, the work-site manager, had Kaumba arrested and sent his personnel file to Elisabethville for further instructions:

We are sending you the dossier of worker number 47/5236, Kaumba Kalubatini. This worker has been working at Jadotville but was recently transferred to Shienzi (Kikole). He maintains that he is a carpenter, and that he has always been employed as such. He disregards the fact that this specialty is not mentioned in his contract. I have deposited a complaint with *Chef de Poste* of Luena about his refusal to work.[89]

Table 6.4. Number of Factory Workers and Daily Wage Rates before Penalties at Lubumbashi in 1935, by Grade and Seniority

Grade	Seniority, by Year of Hire					Total
	1933–35	1930–32	1927–29	1924–26	pre-1924	
4	140	17	18	14	15	204
	(2.46F)	(3.88F)	(4.31F)	(4.76F)	(5.00F)	
5	84	38	46	19	29	216
	(2.52F)	(3.86F)	(4.15F)	(4.65F)	(4.64F)	
6	61	28	52	23	31	195
	(2.85F)	(3.96F)	(4.59F)	(5.04F)	(5.12F)	
7	89	24	38	35	43	229
	(2.50F)	(3.88F)	(4.42F)	(5.17F)	(5.35F)	
8	6	1	1	2	1	11
	(2.50F)	(3.50F)	(4.50F)	(6.55F)	(14.80F)	
9	4	2	5	7	12	30
	(2.40F)	(3.25F)	(5.10F)	(5.50F)	(6.82F)	
10	22	14	13	13	35	97
	(2.60F)	(3.90F)	(5.50F)	(5.00F)	(6.62F)	
11				1	2	3
				(8.00F)	(6.00F)	
12	6	9	8	16	38	77
	(2.50F)	(6.00F)	(6.12F)	(7.06F)	(8.78F)	
13		2		1	1	4
		(3.75F)		(10.50F)	(12.50F)	
14				4	1	5
				(12.50F)	(12.50F)	
15					3	3
					(15.50F)	
Number of workers	412	135	181	135	211	1,074
Mean salary	2.55F	4.02F	4.57F	5.65F	6.33F	4.20F

Source: AG, A9, no. 508/D-40, Barème du salaires, juin 1935, Lubumbashi.

The *chef de poste* upheld Kaumba's claim over the livid protest of Jean Schroeven. He maintained that since Kaumba had indeed been employed as a carpenter, Schroeven had no grounds to punish him for his refusal to work. Kaumba was eventually fired, but his example caused Schroeven and his European subordinates a good deal of consternation. The following year, in 1936, when it was rumored that the number of African carpenters at Kikole (i.e., at the Shienzi tin mine) would be reduced, Schroeven drew up an unsolicited report on the state of skilled African workers at Kikole. He closed his report to the central office in Elisabethville with these remarks: ". . . From what we have heard, the central office intends to reduce the number of carpenters here by a dozen. We would like to know if there is another work site where they can be employed."[90] It was not surprising therefore that the wage issue and that of job control were inseparable for such workers during the latter 1930s.

The sudden upshot of worker militancy among skilled and semi-skilled workers, and management's excessive dispensation of wage penalties, did not occur in a vacuum. Although the factories at Shituru, Panda, and Lubumbashi were the focal point of the mining company's review of the stress points in the upper strata of its African workforce, its conclusions came to be levelled more at skilled workers at the newer work sites. Wage penalties and fines for failure to make one's rate were particularly severe at the tin mines, where many of the tools used by the workers were made and machined on the spot.[91]

The clamor over fines was so great by June 1938 that Léopold Mottoulle himself felt obliged to make a special inspection tour of Kikole and Busanga. After leaving Kikole, Mottoulle maintained that he thought most of the complaints by African workers were ill-founded, but that several of the European gang foremen should be severely reprimanded for "overzealous" conduct. In closing his report Mottoulle concluded: "It is necessary to demand production, but not to discourage the men by a shower of penalties that are distributed arbitrarily for nebulous reasons."[92]

THE REEMERGENCE OF WORKER PROTEST

The opposite side of much of the unnecessary cruelty wielded by the company's officials at the more removed mines was the relative ease with which some African workers managed to get around such exactions. Very often African workers worked for months at a time, coming and going as they pleased. For example, Lukingama Kabila and Kasongo Pisa, two masons attached to the construction gang at Busanga, left their posts at that mine and hired on at Kikole in April 1938. Manda Enea, an African clerk, forged visas and work papers for the two men. When they were finally discovered, the mining company's response to the incident was as arbitrary as its more gratuitous displays of force. Although accused of the same infraction, Kasongo was sent back to Busanga after being "severely reprimanded," while Lukingama Kabila was sent to prison.[93]

By 1936, "discipline," as the company had envisioned it in 1932, was slowly deteriorating on all the work sites north of the partly abandoned Star of the Congo Mine. The company's methods of isolating and punishing dissidents became more sophisticated, however; and between 1936 and 1941, factory operatives and skilled workers were compelled to seek more organized and combative forms of protest. This collapse of strategic areas of control over the workforce — which began less than a decade after the labor unrest of 1931 — was less the result of a going conspiracy than the uncertain and often irrational way the Union Minière chose to combine the workers' aspirations with the prospect of greater output and productivity. Nevertheless, output did increase between 1934 and the close of the Second World War.[94]

Was there a core of contented workers upon whose backs the burden of increased output was hoisted? Or were the "disciplined" African worker and the truculent rebel merely two of several faces of the emerging mining proletariat during the era of general business recovery? The evidence seems to point more toward the latter. By the end of the 1930s African workers of the Union Minière were able to draw on a rich storehouse of accumulated information about the attitudes of their employer during different phases of the business cycle. This was largely a result of the relative success of some African workers at getting what and where they wanted within the world of the Union Minière. As daring as the action of the two workers who used forged papers to hire on at Kikole must have seemed to the mining administration, for instance, it was motivated nonetheless by a belief that working conditions were better at Kikole than at Busanga. Between the 1930s and the 1941 general strike, worker protest was geared more toward coping with sudden — and seemingly arbitrary — shifts in company policies.[95]

Initially the company's efforts to impose a new kind of industrial work discipline on its workers without opening the pandora's box of higher wages and living standards experienced some measure of success.[96] But by 1935–36 the factory operatives at Shituru and Panda and the mineworkers on the other work sites within the vicinity of Jadotville had become active purveyors of a culture and set of ideas which were partly antithetical to the new work discipline, and which eventually stretched all the way to Kolwezi in the western sector of the mining complex and to Busanga and Kikole in the northern sector.[97] Because the new measures did not engender protests on the model of those of 1931, and because of the size of its new profit margins, the company chose to ignore the subtle change in the workers' expectations.

Much of the change in the sensibilities and outlook of the workers was forwarded by the partial transformation of the production process, which, in turn, altered the relations of production. The most palpable manifestation of this transformation was the reduction of white supervision in making the finished product.[98] Despite the apparent subtlety of the workers' outlook, they were compelled by rapid industrialization to seek leaders who could speak not only to their God or the ancestors but also to their employers—and if need be, lead them in strikes and work actions. Many of the adepts and millennarian bush prophets, who had found a ready constituency among the workers during the late 1920s and in the troubled first years of the Depression, were replaced by men from the workers' own ranks. As the numerous work actions and strikes during the latter 1930s and the 1940s attested to, the more skilled and experienced workers often assumed the leadership in such protest. Their intuitive grasp of how to turn the work routine and workplace organization to the advantage of the workers convinced thousands to follow their lead and their new conceptions of organization.

Lubumbashi Works circa 1920. Courtesy of the National Archives

Busanga circa 1935. Courtesy of the National Archives

153

Kipushi circa 1939. Courtesy of the National Archives

Furnacemen and supervisor at Lubumbashi circa 1922. UMHK brochure

154

Working a handjig at Busanga circa 1935. Courtesy of the National Archives

Machinists at Atelier Centrale in Jadotville circa 1935. Courtesy of the National Archives

European workers and their families at the company mess in Elizabethville circa 1948. Courtesy of the National Archives

Wives and children of African workers in line for rations circa 1948. Courtesy of the National Archives

Forty- and fifty-year men receiving company medals and commendations. Courtesy of the Munger Collection, California Institute of Technology

Forty- and fifty-year men pose for a group picture. Courtesy of the Munger Collection, California Institute of Technology

Fifty-year men. Courtesy of the Munger Collection, California Institute of Technology

PART THREE

Mineworkers against the Company and the State

CHAPTER SEVEN

The Political Experiences of the African Mineworkers, 1937–1941

THE MORPHOLOGY OF PROTEST

Many whites are astonished when they hear us ask for better housing and to be treated better on the work sites. They maintain that we are stretching their goodwill and asking for too much, or, more often, that we desire to live like them. . . .

Allow me to draw attention to the fact that while a small hut might have been suitable for our needs in the past, it is altogether unsuitable now. In the past we used our dwelling for sleeping primarily, living most of the time in the open air or under the shade of a large tree or hangar. But now, given the new mores and customs that have been introduced into our country, we can no longer live as we did in the past; we are obliged to live in houses that are fit for receiving our relatives and friends.

> A. J. Beia, a clerk and former factory operative at the Union Minière, November 1934[1]

My dear D'Orjo: The increased number of desertions and work stoppages is as astonishing to me as it is to you. . . . Can I ask you to seek out these deserters and return them to Kikole as soon as possible, and if possible, to provide them with police escort? *It is only by relentless and energetic repression that we can stop these interruptions definitively.* Send the deserters back in small contingents. I will send you six white foremen to accompany them.

> Emile Rolus, director of native personnel at the Union Minière, during the course of an instance of worker unrest at the tin mines, July 1937[2]

Although the Depression was far from over by 1938, Anglo-American and German rearmament began to push the global economy out of the terrible depths it had reached between 1932 and 1937. By the end of the year, copper and tin prices shot well past their 1928 peak. And by the commencement of the Second World War in 1939 the Union Minière was taking full advantage of the new surge of activity. Its copper and tin exports to the United States alone increased 1,000 percent.[3] Cobalt and uranium were also mined extensively.[4] Yet as we have seen earlier, the rapid increase in output was achieved by extracting a particularly heavy toll from the African workers. At the more removed mines the scale of operations and, to a lesser extent, the workforce expanded, although productivity increased but slightly. At the older mines and factories of the central and southern sectors both the total output and the productivity of each worker increased because managerial innovations and transfers of technology from Belgium and the United States were effected. The transfer of technology was especially crucial to the company's operations after the onset of the German occupation of Belgium between May and December 1940.[5]

Between 1936 and 1944, as a result of increased output and productivity, virtually all of the mining company's work sites came under the sway of a new, more protracted wave of protest. This new wave of protest was, in part, a reaction to the mining industry's reconstruction and subsequent wartime increases in output and the sharp decline in the living standards of the mineworkers and their families. Workers at the tin mines, the railway camps, and the copper and cobalt mine at Kolwezi in the western sector provided the initial impetus for the protest. Within 1½ years those of the central and southern sectors of the mining complex were also restive. The Union Minière thought that it had quashed the new unrest by the middle of 1938, when it declared a general wage increase, relegated several hundred factory operatives and skilled workers from Panda and Kipushi to rural penal colonies for Watchtower activities, and closed the troublesome work site at Kengere.[6] But by the end of 1938 instances of arson and sabotage broke out in Kipushi, Kambove, Shinkolobwe, and Luishia.[7]

There were obvious differences in the way the workers and management perceived the consequences of increased production and not so obvious ones among various groups of workers, particularly in terms of how one made use of one's time after work. For example, some work sites operated on a rather widely skewed system in which cash payments, rations "in kind," and ration tickets were given to workers who provided part or all of their own food.[8] In the hard-bitten two years before the inadequate general wage increase of 1938, carcasses of stolen cattle were regularly found in the bush just beyond the workers' camps at Kolwezi, Ruwe, and Kambove. Poaching by African workers and their women occurred frequently at the more removed work sites and made the maintenance of order a difficult proposition indeed. The food issue — which was usually a rather straightforward though inequitable one — became exceedingly nuanced and complex.[9]

The frequent use of pilfered explosives by the African workers for large-scale trap fishing, for instance, was clearly something that caused the mining administration a great deal of consternation. For behind the more immediate problems of the theft of detonating caps and explosives lurked the grim prospect of the use of such equipment in protracted class warfare. Consequently, reprisals taken against African workers who were caught stealing explosives could be quite severe. For example, Kulu Samson, who was wounded severely after stealing 8 detonators, 15 blasting caps, and 2 boxes of dynamite, was sentenced to 7–10 years in prison after his release from the hospital.[10] A similar incident took place on 27 and 28 April of the same year at Musonoi, just outside Kolwezi. Because the mine police failed to come up with a culprit, a sense of dread pervaded the memorandum that was written to the *chef de poste* for the area in the wake of the incident. Cremion, the camp manager, maintained:

> We are obliged to lodge a complaint against an unknown who, on the night of the twenty-seventh and twenty-eighth, broke into two powder houses. This morning at 7:30 A.M., Toussaint, desiring some dynamite, found blasting caps and detonators scattered about. Twenty-five rolls or 1,250 meters of safety wire and several boxes of dynamite had been taken. The detonators were not taken, although the boxes had been broken into. We hope this matter receives your urgent attention because it could very well compromise the security of the entire region as well as the mining camp.[11]

By October 1938 poaching and pilfering from company stocks were especially acute at the central-sector work sites of Panda, Shinkolobwe, and Kakontwe. Between 1936 and 1938 the number of workers at these three work sites went from 2,489 to well over 3,000 men, and the general population, including women and children, came close to 6,000.[12]

Flight and absconding by African workers increased at all the Union Minière work sites as well. In fact at Kolwezi, Musonoi, Kengere, Busanga, and Kikole, workers began to abscond as a means to bargain for better working conditions. Consequently, absconding had a more organized character in the late 1930s than it had in the 1920s; for in the latter period workers had been merely fleeing a terrible combination of misfortunes.[13] During the period in question, however, flight reflected the African mineworkers' growing awareness of the value of their labor in marketplace terms.

Workers often timed their flight in a way that resulted in financial loss for the company rather than for themselves.[14] Table 7.1 shows that the workers who came from the territories farthest removed from the mining sites, such as Malonga and Sampwe, and those from territories at the very hub of mining activity, such as Bukama and Mwanza, were equally disposed to absconding with wages "in kind" — items that they considered roughly equivalent to the value of their labor.

The fact that workers with respectable stakes in the industrial system in the form of households and four or five years of seniority began to flee as frequently as less seasoned workers illustrates just how commonplace flight had become by the middle and late 1930s. Two fairly representative cases were those of Buyu Behuka and Kamandande André. Both of these men were married and, by 1935, had been employed at Kikole for at least three years. In September 1935 Buyu Behuka had his wife repatriated to their home region at the company's expense after feigning a fight with her. Two weeks later he himself fled.[15] Between 12 and 29 December 1935 Kamandande André and his wife, Munyembe Josephine, carried out a similar ruse.

Table 7.1. Instances of Flight at the Tin Mines[a] of the Union Minière, 1934

Number of Absconding Workers	Territory of Origin	Total of Outstanding Salaries (in francs)	Value of Equipment Taken (in francs)
163	Sampwe	1891.95	2403.70
143	Bukama	2268.20	3903.75
191	Mwanza	3061.20	3959.05
43	Kamina	850.00	816.40
3	Kasenga	27.00	61.45
16	Jadotville	163.40	455.35
9	Ankoro	232.00	325.50
4	Kabongo	55.00	142.45
102	Malonga	926.25	2147.45
40	Sandoa	332.35	903.85

Source: AG, D6, Mottoulle, Compte salaires dûs à déserteurs des mines groupe Kikole, 18 octobre 1934, Elisabethville.

[a]Kikole, Wuto, Shienzi, Mwanza, and Kayumbo.

In 1935 the Kikole camp experienced seven similarly planned abscondings, a fact which did little to endear the local management to the central administration at Elisabethville.

At Kengere, shortly after the June 1938 flight of 44 workers, a list of demands and conditions under which the workers would return to work was presented to the territorial administrator. The administrator maintained that the demands and list of grievances had been drafted by skilled workers. Upon receiving the report of the territorial administrator, the camp manager at Kengere sent a disposition of the incident to the Elisabethville office along with a list showing the length of service, village, chieftaincy, marital status, and job classification of each of the fleeing workers. The first part of the camp manager's cover letter read thus:

We have initiated a secret inquiry, as you have asked and besides the motives that you are already aware of, it so happens that a number of these workers had contracted with us in order not to be pressed on to the cotton plantations, and that they are now in their village attempting to organize the population to forcibly occupy the plantations that the latter are forced to work on. (This has been confirmed by the Territorial Administrator at Musonoi.) Also, we have sought to discover just how much influence their spokesman, who was transferred from Jadotville, has over them. His name is Malambi Tshokonie, category R/L.[16]

In addition to making common cause with their rural kinsmen against well-to-do African peasant farmers and the cotton refineries in Lulua and upper Lualaba, the workers who fled from Kengere also demanded hoes for their women as well as rations and wages comparable to those paid at the larger work sites. Becoming rural rebels was therefore a card that the workers sought to play only after their other options had proved unsuccessful.[17] Although it did not surface in the list sent to Elisabethville, more than half of the fleeing workers had spent a portion of their length of service in one of the factories at Jadotville. At least seven had spent three years or more at work on one of the mines of the southern sector and must have been sent to Kengere because of their involvement in work actions at either Kipushi or one of the other mines of the south between 1932 and 1937. All of them, while not artisans, were either semiskilled or in the possession of a relatively high proficiency rating. In short, they were far from the dregs of the workforce.[18]

We still know very little about why unsatisfactory working and living conditions compelled some workers to abscond and others to strike. And although there was perhaps a greater number of strikes at the more centrally located work sites, they were also much more frequent than usual on the outlying mines during this compressed period of labor unrest. In March 1936, for example, a major strike broke out at the tin mine at Busanga. The immediate cause of the strike was the death of an underground worker, Kapolo Katshelewa, on 16 March 1936. Kapolo's death provided the catalyst for the airing of long-standing grievances. The initial work action began with nine workers from the underground gang. By midafternoon virtually the entire corps of 300 underground workers had gone out on strike. The camp manager at Busanga, Schroeven, described the events surrounding the strike in the following manner:

> We are informing you about the events subsequent to the death of worker no. 71, Kapolo Katshelewa, in the underground works on the 16th of this month. While the body was being transported to the hospital, several demonstrations broke out. Given the shroud of secrecy surrounding their organization we have been unable to discover the leaders. They are, in all likelihood, underground workers.
>
> Yesterday at two o'clock 9 out of 31 workers, who had previously agreed to new 3 year contracts with .25 franc increase for both surface and underground workers, have now shown a great deal of discontent on the subject of salaries paid for underground work and have refused to enter the mine. By three o'clock they had convinced the entire crew of underground workers to leave their equipment on the front steps of the camp office. We have lodged a complaint with the *Chef de Poste*, and called for the immediate arrest of the ringleaders.[19]

Wages at Busanga and other work sites had been severely reduced by a shower of penalties during the previous year. Forced overtime and corporal punishment were also part of a long list of grievances.[20]

The relative calm of the southernmost mines at the outset of this period may be only an illusion created by a dearth of written sources. Much "abnormality," except for routine absenteeism and drunkenness, was either suppressed or camouflaged in the company's written records for the work sites closest to Elisabethville. There is also the distinct possibility that after the defeat of the workers' actions of 1931 and the rapid change in the characteristics of the African workforce on the southernmost mines, the workers there deliberately chose to wait for a new breach in company power to arise elsewhere and for a new means to articulate lingering grievances.[21] Yet despite the apparent calm in 1936, instances of mass flight, small departmental strikes, arson, and sabotage began to break out more frequently in the south and west and along the rail line two years later.[22]

Because of the industrial but nonurban physical context of a major portion of the mining complex, the rural areas of Katanga were automatically caught up in the new current of worker protest.[23] Moreover, the burden of the peasantry was an especially heavy one. Between 1938 and 1944 forced and *corvée* labor went from 38 to 78 percent. Taxes and starvation increased rapidly with obligatory cultivation of sesame and cotton. Diseases such as beriberi and yaws swept over a wide portion of the province between the Biano Plateau in north-central Katanga and Jadotville.[24] Large segments of Katanga's peasantry became an army of rural laborers in all but name. The flight of thousands of rural inhabitants to the towns and the devolution of the territorial administration further exacerbated the highly contingent state of law and order.[25] Entire territories were virtually cut off from the major towns because of the collapse or disappearance of many of the road systems. Imported items such as manufactured clothing, sardines, cigarettes, and matches disappeared from the rural areas altogether. African peddlers moved marijuana, *lutuku*, dried fish, and protective *"dawa,"* or medicine, in their stead.[26] Rural cult movements such as Ukanga, Kamutshapa, and Confirmash were all symptomatic of a cycle of agrarian "abnormality." In the countryside behind Jadotville and at the work sites in its vicinity these local sects converged with various African Watchtower sects and gave unrest an apocalyptic context at many of the mines on the perimeter of the mining complex and in the central sector.[27]

So great was the influence of incipient proletarian unrest on the rural population of the Lualaba District during the Second World War that the provincial government created a censor and hired a translator, one Djapao Arthur, to seize and read routinely the correspondence sent by workers and other African townspeople to their rural kin. Ostensibly the censor was to check for evidence of alleged mulatto Axis agents sifting into the district through Angola.[28] But by the end of 1940 the censor's efforts were directed almost exclusively at the local population. Letters were randomly selected, so the censor had no previous knowledge of their contents. This, of course, made the implications of suspect correspondence all the more ominous; for local officials wondered about how many incriminating letters might have gotten past the censor given the rather inefficient method of selection.

Only a few of the letters seized yielded anything remotely seditious. But on 23 November 1940 the censor seized a letter from Mutuka Burton Fabian, a telephone and telegraph clerk at the Union Minière Kolwezi site, which—in the mind of the censor—bristled with disloyal utterances. Mutuka addressed the letter to his kinsman Florentin Chemise in the village of Saluiji in Malonga territory, even though he had written it for the benefit of several of his younger relatives.[29] It caught the censor's eye because Mutuka forged the cancellation date of the postage. The letter's contents appeared to justify the worst fears of the provincial commissioner and secret police:

> Many of the workers here say they will go to Kenya to be soldiers, and to make war with our brothers there. [This was roughly 1½ months before the vice governor-general and head of the Force Publique, Paul Ermens, visited Kenya's governor to discuss the integration of some Force Publique units into the king's African Rifles.] In many towns, in Jadotville and E'ville, men have already been drafted, particularly clerks, hospital boys, cooks and students. All the unemployed have been conscripted. Here at Kolwezi all the unemployed will be drafted.
>
> Listen Florentin, Romain and Jugi, if you are going to flee, flee now and go far away. Go far into the bush, where no one can find you. If someone does find you, give him a sound beating because he has come to take you to the war, and the war might kill you. For that reason alone you should try to prevent such a situation.
>
> Listen well now, the soldiers who used to steal our chickens are now going to die. They have not called me up yet, but when they do I will go. Once there [in Kenya presumably], however, I will flee with the others. Many of us here at Kolwezi will be compelled to go, but you down there, flee as soon as you can; for everybody who reaches the front is going to die. Those young men who hide themselves quickly and well will not die so soon. But of those who are conscripted, both black and white, many will die. This information will not be disseminated everywhere because of the palavers. You get what I mean?[30]

There was indeed disloyalty here and some measure of disaffection toward the policies of the regime. An undertone of revindication pervaded the note: old scores would soon be settled; moreover, despite the adversity of a cataclysmic war, there were gains to be made if one was aware of the war's significance; the most important thing was staying alive, so that one might fight in more meaningful battles of the future.

WATCHTOWER'S INTERLUDE

> Judge not, that ye be not judged. For with what judgement ye judge, ye shall be judged: and with what measure ye mete, it shall be measured to you again.
>
> (Matthew 7: 1-2)

> Tuna niama ya Bazungu. Lakini tuna bantu kama basunga. Kweli mbalo ya Baba yenu. (We are oppressed by the whites. Yet we are men just as they are. Truly, you [the whites] have strayed far from your God.)
>
> Amonzi Miselo, a Watchtower "baptist" and worker at the Géomines tin mine, testifying before a police tribunal several days after the 19–20 November 1941 strike at Géomines[31]

Why hadn't this wave of unrest, which had been conceived in the relative isolation of the northern tin mines and Kolwezi, moved farther north and east instead of south toward Jadotville and Elisabethville? One possible reason was the protracted resurgence of various African Watchtower sects in the vicinity of Jadotville and their spread to the western regions of the province.[32] Gradually, throughout the 1930s, Jadotville had replaced Elisabethville as the chief stronghold of the Watchtower movement. With its stronghold in the most heavily industrialized town of the province, Watchtower reached new heights of proselytization and recruitment. The economic misery of the Depression decade killed off much of its former fundamentalism and orthodoxy. Also, a strong commingling with other, more parochial, millennarian sects made it more palatable to the mineworkers and the African masses in general.[33] The precipitous decline of the living standards of factory operatives and skilled workers opened up a new front of proselytization as well, although these workers were less susceptible to the more utopian expectations of the various sects, and attempted to mold Watchtower doctrine to their more secular ambitions. The key to Watchtower's resurgence was the concomitant expansion of the mining industry and the towns. For example, with a growth rate of 18 percent and a population of over 46,000 people at the end of 1941, Elisabethville became a small industrial city rather than a large town.[34] Jadotville and Kolwezi followed suit. Between 1939 and 1944 the number of people migrating to these two towns doubled, going from 34,267 to 72,862.[35] Expansion brought areas that were formerly on the periphery of the industrial world into the very center of its operations. Many of the Watchtower sects, which had been incubating in the rural areas and in the more remote camps of agricultural and railway workers since the crisis of 1931, burst forth with an urgency and vitality that startled the authorities.[36]

While the Watchtower movement in southern Africa was never a proletarian movement in the same sense as the Chartist movement in England in the 1830s and 1840s, it did bear a strong resemblance to the Primitive Methodist churches that emerged during the turbulent second phase of the Industrial Revolution. Just as early Methodism inadvertently became a dramatic instance of popular reaction to the spread of factory production, so Watchtower doctrine came to reflect the African reaction to the drastic change in the modalities of capitalism in southern Africa in the 1920s and 1930s.[37] The centerpiece of Watchtower theology—the belief that the "new heaven and earth" of the Book of Revelation would be established here on earth—was particularly appealing to hard-pressed African colonial subjects. One did not need a very vivid imagination to see where such a theological doctrine must have led people who were underpaid, mistreated, forced to pay absurd taxes, and arbitrarily imprisoned—however much the original bearers of the theology protested a political interpretation of their doctrine. Moreover, the absence of any specific ritual in the original American-based Church of the Watch Tower gave breakaway African sects room to improvise. As a result, some local traditions were integrated into African Watchtower. Those which were at odds with the prerogatives of local government often made a better fit.[38]

Initially Watchtower had appealed primarily to rural people in Katanga. But after the unrest of 1931 the colonial police began to see the movement as a dangerous disturber of the peace in the industrial areas as well. The paradox of the official view was that while Watchtower sects did play a role in the urban unrest of 1931, particularly in the Elisabethville boycotts, they did so to preserve their shrinking urban constituencies and to protect their prophets and adepts as they fled from the newly formed secret police.[39] For a brief time—from 1927 to 1931 and again from 1936 to 1944—Watchtower was indeed a catalyst for revindicating working-class ideologies. But in the long run—given the extent of police repression and the movement's subsequent periods of fragmentation and containment in the countryside—it was an insufficient foil for the industrial workers.[40] Yet during the 1930s its catalytic role was of great importance in articulating the common thread of grievances among diverse strata of miners and industrial workers at the Union Minière and in Katanga generally.

By the end of 1936 many of the Watchtower sects and portions of their constituencies had begun to coalesce in the vicinity of the Géomines tin mine at Manono and the Union Minière tin mines at Mwanza and Kikole. Prophets, adepts, and preachers of the *banapoleoni* sect, which had lost its base in Elisabethville during the unrest of 1931, and those of the Djoni sect, a sect which grew up in reaction to the repression of 1931 and the tactical mistakes of pre-1931 Watchtower leaders, jointly proselytized the mineworkers.[41] Less than 124 miles from the mines, Watchtower made important inroads among the African railway workers of the Chemin de Fer du Grand Lacs (CFL) who lived in company compounds between Niemba and Kabalo. Virtually all of these workers had been baptized by pastors, preachers, and deacons belonging to the *banapoleoni* network organized by the adept Kulu Mupenda, also known as Sendwe Kandeke. Kulu Mupenda had been brought into the *banapoleoni* sect of Watchtower in 1930 by Lobati Kima, an adept from Nyasaland. After the police repression of December 1931, Lobati and Kulu fled south to Sakania along with other Watchtower adherents. Lobati's place in the Elisabethville organization, which had been second only to that of the sect's founder, Mumbwa Napoleon Jacob, was taken over by an African clerk in the municipal courts, Mutombo Stephane.[42]

Still under the supervision of Lobati Kima, Kulu left the border town of Sakania and went north to Albertville in 1935. Lobati was finally arrested in 1936 after almost a decade of narrowly escaping the Belgian authorities. Following these events, the *banapoleoni* tendency of Watchtower shifted its emphasis from the southern end of Katanga to the northeastern and north-central regions of the province under the leadership of Kulu Mupenda in Albertville, Musipi Mwanza in Bukama, Tambwe Janvier in Kongolo, and Bilato Lazaro at the Union Minière tin mine at Mwanza.[43] Shortly after Lobati's arrest, Kulu Mupenda assumed responsibility for the entire network, which stretched from the northernmost tin mines to the port town of Bukama.

Under Kulu's expansionist leadership the *banapoleoni* experienced a large degree of internal reorganization. Sensitive to the frequent arrests and relegations of Watchtower members, Kulu created the office of *portier*, or "doorkeeper." The primary duty of the *portier* was to give shelter and anonymity to Watchtower adepts and preachers passing through a given region. The *portier* also arranged the circumstances and time of mass baptisms. He was also constantly in touch with the most physically mobile rung of Watchtower leadership, the baptists. In fact, the doorkeeper acted as a more clandestine kind of baptist who coordinated the movement of the sect's leadership rather than its followers. The implications of this new office were vast. For now the fragmentation that the movement sustained previously as a result of police repression could be turned into a tactical advantage. The creation of a kind of mobile general staff prevented the sundering of the movement's basic organization by the colonial government and the police. The protection of adepts and preachers on one hand and the expansion of the movement at the local level on the other fell largely into the hands of this vertical file of leadership.[44]

On 26 September 1936 Kulu Mupenda himself was arrested in Albertville and sent to the rural chieftaincy of Benze along with his deacon, Muhanguka Fungatumbu. By 27 April 1937 Kulu, Muhanguka, and another Watchtower adept, Mwamba Mangaiko, had forged a network of adherents that extended from the Catholic mission at Niemba near Nyunzu to the tin mines at Manono. This network seriously undermined the authority of the nearby chieftaincies. According to the territorial agent in the area, Marcel Etienne, the chief at Benze had been forced to flee the village by the end of February 1937. His authority had been completely undermined by Kulu's "dini ya haki," or true religion. Yet despite the movement's rapid erosion of the chieftains' political authority in Benze and villages in the vicinity, its most important dispersal points were the workers' camps of the CFL near Nyunzu and the rail line going from Albertville to Kabalo.[45]

Kulu Mupenda was aware of the close surveillance of his activities by the police investigators and the government-appointed chief at Benze. Consequently, instead of resuming his preaching and evangelization in the rural areas, he and the other Watchtower leaders in the region turned first to the agricultural laborers at the parastatal cotton refineries and farms and to the African railwaymen, who eventually carried Mupenda's message south to the tin mines of Manono between 1937 and the time of the great strike and Watchtower protest of November 1941. Watchtower was therefore a catalyst for worker unrest at the camps of the CFL, the cotton mill at Niemba-Lukombe, and the tin mines at Mwanza, Manono, and Kikole.[46]

The manner in which the colonial government attempted to stamp out Watchtower reflected the growing importance of African workers in the spread of the sect. During the wave of repression that followed Mupenda's second arrest at Benze, the chief police investigator, Louis Wauthion, borrowed a locomotive from the chief engineer of the CFL, Paul Bruart, and swept through the workers' camps from Nyunzu to Kabalo. Wauthion travelled up and down the rail line in his borrowed locomotive arresting alleged Watchtower adherents among the African workers from 24 April to 8 May 1937. All of the men arrested during this period were held in the military prison at Albertville rather than rusticated.[47]

Wauthion maintained that the African Watchtower movement in the area had been finally decapitated once the suspected African railway workers were arrested. But on the occasion of his trial Kulu vigorously denied this. He also eschewed the police allegation that he and the other adepts of his persuasion had received assistance from whites in spreading the movement, given the size of the area from which they had drawn adherents. Rather, Kulu said that the reason the movement had inspired so much fear among the colonial authorities and among the whites in general was that the authorities doubted the Africans' ability to accomplish all this without help.[48]

After the unrest at Benze and Nyunzu it appeared that the Watchtower network on the province's work sites began to acquire definite shape.[49] It was at this point that Watchtower became a political means to indict the colonial regime, not just a mere psychological redoubt for its adherents on the work sites and in the military camps. Members began to see reality as an animated version of biblical prophecy; they expressed their grievances against the colonial order—and in some instances their desire to overthrow it—in its idiom.[50] The strike of the mineworkers at the Géomines works at Manono in November 1941 and subsequent incidents of worker unrest on the nearby work sites of the Union Minière are the best examples we have of Watchtower as a formidable incipient ideology among the mineworkers.[51] The strike at Manono collapsed the wall of differences between the Djoni and *banapoleoni* sects, the two major Watchtower sects in Katanga. Some of the apparent leaders of the Manono strike such as Mupenda Kumwimba and Goy Samuel had been associated with both the *banapoleoni* and Djoni tendencies of the movement before the strike. Goy and Mupenda were accused of having been adepts in both sects between 1937 and 1941 by the prosecution at their trial before the district tribunal of Tanganika-Moero at Manono on 6 January 1942.[52]

The strike at Manono began on 18 November 1941. Shortly after the work stoppage, a group of Watchtower adherents, whose spokesman for the occasion was Amonzi Kiluba Miselo, marched to the territorial administrator's office to air their grievances against the company. Amonzi read a list of misdeeds that the workers attributed to the Géomines company and the government. By midday a crowd of over 2,000 people had gathered at the territorial administrator's office. According to the prosecution's report, many of them were singing the Watchtower anthems "Mataifa" ("All Nations") and "Kuliana" ("Stick Together"), and some were chanting antigovernment slogans.[53] The official report went on to say that by late afternoon the African demonstrators had broken the outer barricades of the territorial administrator's office. The soldiers who were guarding the Europeans "panicked." Fourteen African demonstrators were killed, and another 30 were wounded. Despite eyewitness reports that said the troops had fired on the miners and their wives without provocation and that the miners were unarmed, the government held to the opposite view. The report of the prosecution maintained that "all would have been lost had it not been for the steadfastness of the European officers."[54]

On 19 November 1941, a contingent of workers returned to the vicinity of the territorial administrator's office. A European witness described the events of the second day of the strike in this manner:

> They did not try to hide their purpose. It was to drive the whites from the country and replace the blue flag of Belgium with the black flag of *kitawala* in order to signal a change in the regime. On the other hand, some of the defendants had come to the demonstration without arms and without hostile intentions.[55]

Although the prosecution's account of the strike mentioned that the African demonstrators had been unarmed, it maintained that the *kitawala* adepts had told the demonstrators that "divine intervention would vanquish their enemies." Assuming that the government's allegation against the sect's leaders was true and that the government and the military knew beforehand that the demonstrators were going to be unarmed, the soldiers and their officers simply took their common expedient of firing on unarmed civilians. The tribunals chose to ignore this logical inconsistency in the prosecution's case, while adopting the position that the African mineworkers "simply could not resist these skillfully advanced doctrines because their primitive minds had been so disheveled by modern industry."[56]

Women also played a role in the strike and in the witness-bearing and prophesying that accompanied it. On the second day of the strike several groups of African workers and their wives ran through the workers' camps of Manono announcing the "second coming" and the end of the colonial government. Two women leaders, Ilunga Eva and Kabangi Alikoya, emerged. Little is known about the nature of their leadership in the strike and demonstration except that the police tribunal thought it crucial enough to give them both two-year prison sentences. Thus the tribunals abetted the not uncommon method of deadly force against the unarmed, and also the uncommon approach of taking women demonstrators seriously enough to punish them with prison sentences. Doubtless, the court resorted to such severity so that others would not choose to emulate the example of these two women.[57]

By 20 November 1941 the impact of the African strike at Manono had spread to the nearby Union Minière work sites through the efforts of the adept Goy Samuel. Goy himself was not a mineworker, but an itinerant African peddler who had been a pivotal figure in bringing the Watchtower message from the rural areas onto the mines in the 1937–41 period. In addition to the Watchtower network, Goy must have made use of his kin group to spread the news of the strike, since he had been born in the nearby village of Kisungu. Kisungu was midway between the Union Minière work sites at Mwanza and Busanga.[58]

In addition to making use of word-of-mouth forms of communication in the vicinity of the tin mines, Goy Samuel had written letters to Watchtower adherents at Mwanza and Kikole. Some of Goy's letters to Watchtower members at Mwanza were intercepted by the police. According to the police, the letters had been written "in such a fashion that they struck the natives with fear and anxiety."[59] Whether Goy Samuel's letters had stricken the African mineworkers at Mwanza with "fear and anxiety" was, of course, debatable. By the end of November, however, both Mwanza and Kikole had also been shaken by African worker protest. The protest that broke out at Mwanza was very much like that at Manono. Flags, Watchtower songs, and instances where European officials were "threatened" by crowds were very much in evidence. A strike, however, did not emerge.[60]

On the other hand, a strike did break out at Kikole a week before the unrest at Manono. Like the strike at Manono, the strike at Kikole revolved around a rumor of an American occupation of the Congo and a subsequent seizure of the mines. Moreover, the workers at the Kayumbo site of the Kikole complex had gone on strike the month before in October; and this departmental strike was also an important turning point in the decision of all the workers at Kikole to strike shortly before November.[61] Worker unrest moved steadily southward toward the copper mines and the rail line. Its chief aim was a general improvement in the living standards of all the miners. The precipitous decline of living standards for the tin miners and the factory operatives at Jadotville sped it along.[62]

The beginning of the German occupation of Belgium the year before was also of some importance in spreading worker protest, for it shattered the notion of Belgian invulnerability. At Kikole, for instance, African mineworkers talked of commandeering jeeps and joining forces with "Africans" from America and Kenya in the wake of the occupation. At Kikole one strike leader exhorted his fellow workers in the following manner:

The whites have been defeated in Europe by blacks from Kenya and America. Why can't we defeat them here as well? . . . We have the right to eat eggs and own automobiles just like the whites. Let us break into the store and divide up the stock. It belongs to us anyway since the Union Minière has bought these goods with our labor. We will cut down the trees and bridges and thereby keep the boss from sending us to Kayumbo. Let them send us to Kenya instead, so that we may kill whites.[63]

The theme of "American liberators" was as old as the first instances of millennarian popular unrest in southern Africa. The rumor of an American seizure of the mines was not. And insofar as the rumor was based on an actual American presence at the Union Minière during the Second World War, it was an important factor in the spread of the 1941 strike movement.[64] By July 1941 the Union Minière's quotas for cobalt, uranium, copper, and tin were set by the American government through the office of the assistant secretary of state for economic affairs, Herbert Feis. The subsequent increase in output fell hardest on those African workers at the outlying mines, for it was there that the largest deposits of strategic minerals were found. The new rates of output seemed very nearly impossible in relation to previous ones. By 1940 the mining company was supplying the United States with virtually all of the uranium, cobalt, tin, and manganese used for military purposes. It also supplied the United States with over 13 percent of the copper used for wartime purposes and Great Britain with 60 percent of its copper needs. The "American takeover" of the mines had, in fact, already taken place by the time of the strike at Kikole in November 1941.[65]

An inchoate but insurrectionary language and vocabulary was injected into worker protest by Watchtower adherents. Perhaps only a minority of workers took it literally. Years of deference to the colonial masters and political repression had made them cautious — even in the face of incipient popular protest. But African Watchtower generated a political vocabulary in Swahili and other indigenous languages that was shared by both the credulous and the skeptical. Once Watchtower's chief strongholds of proselytization came to be situated at a point equidistant from Jadotville, the most heavily industrialized town in the province, and the removed work sites of the north and west, it was in a better position to do this.[66] This vocabulary could, in some ways, elucidate the nature of colonial oppression and economic exploitation, even though it could not say how freedom from both would look. This task fell increasingly to the workers themselves. Like Caliban they were obliged to seize upon the magical powers of language, but for their own purposes and behind the back of the Belgian Prospero. As a result, strikes and other forms of protest became more prevalent.[67]

The workers' movement's period of gestation at work sites so near the rural areas gave it access to the world out of which many of the workers had come a generation before. Peasant support was, in fact, crucial to the strike movement. And the peasantry did not hesitate to give it in view of its own bleak circumstances. For a brief time proletarian and peasant leaders moved easily among each other's constituencies. The initial impetus for the general strike, therefore, had come from the outlying mines as a call for a collective test of strength against the mining company — from the tin mines of the north to the factories of Elisabethville and Jadotville.[68]

BACK TOWARD THE ABYSS

The purchasing power of the natives decreased by 25 to 35% in the second third of 1940 following the outset of wartime conditions. Wages have not been increased, although food and imported items such as clothes, cigarettes, etc., . . . have undergone increases of anywhere between 20 and 50% since the beginning of the year.

an anonymous territorial administrator in Katanga, circa December 1940[69]

There has been a considerable amount of propaganda literature issued during this war by the Belgian Government, depicting the work that has been done in the Congo, and while we do not wish to minimize the considerable contribution to the war effort made by the Colony, nor withhold praise where praise is due, yet [sic] these propaganda efforts tell but one side of the story. In spite of what has been accomplished in providing war material or advancing a few natives out of the great population towards civilization, the vast majority of the natives have not benefited by the white man's rule to the extent that would be implied by a Governor's statement that "to dominate is to serve. . . ."

opening statement of the deposition of James Morrison, director of the American Presbyterian Congo Mission, to the Office of Strategic Services (OSS), July 1945[70]

While not as terrible as it had been just before the First World War or in the early 1920s, the plight of the African mineworker, by 1940, was beginning to curve back toward what it had been in the terrible five-year period between 1931 and 1936 (see Table 7.2).[71] Wages for both African and European workers did not keep pace with prices. Working conditions deteriorated. And by the end of 1940 all the major political and economic forces in Katanga—the Union Minière, the hierarchy of the Catholic church, the provincial administration, the colonial army, the newly arrived American military and business presence, and the industrial proletariat—were convinced that some kind of social crisis was imminent. What was uncertain was its scale and potential impact.[72]

Although the situation of the workers was not as desperate as that of the peasantry, it was certainly as exploitative—more so in fact. By 1925 the mining company had drawn off a large portion of the male population of the Luapula Valley and Zambezi floodplain for wage labor. It had done this either by disrupting the precolonial pattern of trade between these two areas or through the use of armed force and coercive short-term labor contracts. By 1928 the mining company and the state had cut the Luba redoubt of southern Kasai into two parts. As a result, a major portion of both its male and female population was forced down the rail line to Katanga; an equally large portion was propelled westward toward Léopoldville. Finally, between 1928 and 1941, the mining company transformed the once semi-deserted pedicle of Katanga—from Sakania to Jadotville—into one of the largest industrial African populations outside of South Africa. By the outset of the Second World War the Union Minière had drastically altered the social and economic context of a major portion of South-Central Africa.

Very little of this had been done with an eye toward expanding the human potential of the African workers. By December 1940, for example, the company's African workforce took in at least 20,000 men, perhaps as many as 25,000 if African workers in construction and the building trades are taken into account. In 1940 alone, the amount of leisure time given to the African workers was cut from 16 to 12 percent. The mineworkers amassed 500,000 hours of overtime. From one end of the mining complex to the other, the African workers were simply overworked.[73]

Despite political liabilities occasioned by American intervention in the determination of output and production relations, the expansion of the mining company's market and subsequent profits had never been greater. Between 1940 and 1944 the company's net profits averaged between 3 million and 5 million contemporary American dollars a year, or roughly six times that amount in present-day American currency.[74] Yet there were no guarantees that such a buoyant situation would outlast the war. At the end of 1940 the Union Minière's chief executive officer, Edgar Sengier, who was then residing in New York, summed up the mining company's relationship to the wartime market and at the same time extended a note of caution:

> From a strictly current viewpoint, the American business situation is most satisfactory. Looking at it with a longer view, however, the position is not so satisfactory, since both America and Britain are spending money which is yet to be gleaned from the work of the average man. The spectre of inflation hovers ever nearer.[75]

In an attempt to hedge against this "spectre" in Africa, the Union Minière and the colonial government formulated an even more stringent wage policy for the mineworkers, which envisioned raises only for those African workers who seemed more prone to insurgency or whose work was considered "très intense" or "important." By November 1941 such a policy had done little to curb the growing dissatisfaction of African and European employees of the mining company. For even with three rather cosmetic wage increases between 1938 and 1941, and a more selective fourth one in November 1941 for underground workers and factory operatives at Lubumbashi, wages continued to lag behind the phenomenal wartime price increases.[76] Although wages were no longer tied directly to the price of food, the rapid increase in prices made it virtually impossible for African workers to purchase anything but the bare necessities of life. For example, bicycles and sewing machines may have been more accessible and less often thought of as luxury goods than they had been a decade before, but the 50–70 percent inflation on such items and wartime shortages cancelled out their otherwise greater accessibility.[77] As Table 7.2 shows, the purchasing of food for African mineworkers was an important expenditure for the mining company from 1938 to

Table 7.2. Mean Daily Salary of an African Mineworker and Daily Food Costs for the UMHK, 1938–1943 (in Congolese francs)

	1938	1939	1940	1941	1942	1943
Salary	4.92	5.30	5.42	5.36	6.73	7.25
Food costs	3.14	3.04	3.49	3.38	3.87	4.05

Source: AG, B4, MOI "1941 + ," Barème des salaires.

1943. Yet, by 1940, the cost of food absorbed a large portion of the African mineworker's household budget. It dropped slightly in 1941, only to double in its rate of increase the following year. Of course, the Union Minière continued to provide a portion of the alimentary needs of the workers and their families through rationing. However, the method of distribution, as well as the quantity and quality of the rations, failed to keep pace with the actual needs of the workers' households. This was particularly so at the more removed work sites. Even at Kipushi, however, at the close of the strike of early November 1941, the Union Minière was compelled to admit that it had allowed the workers at the underground mine to be victimized by local European merchants. These merchants placed usurious rates of interest on loans made to the workers and sold them shoddy, overpriced food and household staples. The mining company freely admitted that it had underestimated the gravity of the rationing problem in an *aide-memoire* drawn up in February 1942.[78]

Between May 1940 and December 1943 the general cost of living in Katanga increased 63 percent. Wages, however, rose only by 10 percent. The overall price index at Elisabethville and Jadotville rose by almost 200 percent between 1935 and 1943.[79] Staples of the African mineworkers' diet such as coffee, sugar, tea, and bread were strongly affected by the steep price increase. The increase in the price of bread hit the African workers' households especially hard.[80] Table 7.3, for instance, indicates that the cost of the constituent elements of bread—imported grain and the cost of labor—rose rather rapidly between 1941 and 1944. Labor costs went from under two francs to nearly three francs in a three-year period. The cost of imported grain rose in complementary fashion going from 5.00 francs to 7.60 francs between 1941 and September 1943, or almost six times the rate of increase for domestic grain. Domestic grain was rarely used in the making of bread because of its propensity to spoil, given the fact that it came from the humid lowlands of Kasai and was usually hand threshed. Imported grain, however, was almost always threshed by machine and shipped in refrigerated cars to Katanga from Northern Rhodesia.[81] Consequently, the consumption of bread by the general populace—and also its price—increased rapidly until 1944. Consumption of bread in 1941–42 alone went from 405 tons to 840 tons.[82] Bread had become the principal staple of working-class African households.

While the retail price for bread went from 6.35 francs in 1941 to 10.00 francs in September 1943, it did not rise as fast as the costs of the factors of production suggested. The sum of the cost of making

Table 7.3. Annual Consumption and Retail Cost of Bread (in Congolese francs) in Katanga, 1939–1944

	Retail Cost of Bread	Cost of Imported Grain	Cost of Domestic Grain	Cost of Making Bread	Consumption (in tons)
1939	5.75	4.30	3.30	1.79	304
1940	5.85	4.30	3.30	1.89	247
1941	6.35	5.00	3.90	1.73	405
1942	8.00	6.40	4.10	2.12	840
1943					
January–August	9.20	7.60	4.25	2.18	820
September	10.00	7.60	4.25	2.98	–
1944	10.00	7.80	5.10	2.80	104

Source: "Vie chère," *L'Essor du Congo* 5454 (4 avril 1944).

bread and the retail cost of imported grain was consistently higher than the retail price for bread from 1941 to the end of the war. No doubt, this was due to the fact that the Union Minière would often purchase the largest portion of the retail supply of bread and then sell it to its African workers below the market price. The mining company, therefore, was not unaware of the importance of bread in the diets of its African workers. However, its action demonstrated its unwillingness to improve the dietary profile of its African workforce during the war unless it was coerced or threatened by the workers themselves. The company's response to the wildcat strike at Kipushi on 10 November 1941 proved this succinctly.[83]

At 4:00 in the afternoon on 10 November 1941, the underground workers from the day shift at Kipushi went on a wildcat strike. Shortly after they stopped work, the surface workers joined them. A body composed of both underground and surface workers along with their African *capitas*, or foremen, gathered in front of the camp manager's office and began to chant, "The prices are too high, the prices must come down."[84]

In one sense the strike and subsequent boycott of the African workers at Kipushi in November 1941 was a last resort. The failure or unwillingness of the Union Minière to protect the African workers from what they interpreted simply as the greed of the smaller white merchants influenced their decision to strike as much as the company's stagnant wage policy.[85] African peddlers and Watchtower members also helped to articulate this phase of the protest. Paternalism, therefore, in the form of the company's stabilization policy, had its liabilities as well as obvious advantages. From the workers' vantage point, the mining company should have assumed a greater responsibility for their well-being, since it had relieved them of their mobility within the labor market. The astronomical price increases that followed the German invasion of Belgium aided in disabusing the workers of any sense of obligation to the company in this regard. The workers' decision to strike was animated largely by the company's failure to keep prices from rising.[86]

Although the workers resumed work on 12 November 1941, they organized a boycott of the local stores and the company store that lasted for a week. The workers also demanded that a wider range of merchandise be stocked at the company store. At one point during the boycott the African workers even threatened not to pay their outstanding debts to the stores in the mine's vicinity. Violent reprisals were taken against workers who did not join the boycott.[87]

Finally, at the end of the week-long boycott, the company promised to lower the prices in the company store and to exert pressure on the smaller merchants to follow its example. Predictably, the company's spokesman said that he had given in to the workers' demands in order to stem the influence of "an incipient cabal of subversives," thus avoiding any discussion of the company's culpability in provoking the unrest.[88]

Clothing and fish were also important factors in the relationship between escalating prices and the company's hegemony over the workers. African control over the distribution of fish, as well as blankets that could be turned into protective work clothing, tended to undermine the notion of total company control over the workers' lives. This was doubly so with respect to dried and smoked fish. As Table 7.4 indicates, from 1937 to 1940, the workers consumed more dried than fresh fish. Also, with the absence of coarser cuts of meat on the market or their prohibitive price, a growing number of workers' households consumed dried fish almost exclusively. By 1940 African workers were consuming six times as much dried fish as they had in 1936. Although meat was ostensibly still available, a large number of workers' households were doing without it altogether. By July 1941 thousands of African workers and their families lived almost entirely on a diet of bread, rancid fish, and what few vegetables they could forage from their truck gardens or purchase from African hawkers and peddlers. As a result, the tie between the organization of the workers' households and the specific demands of industrial production was cut and respliced in a way that undermined company paternalism.

Table 7.4. Proportions of Fresh Fish, Smoked Fish, and Meat (in kilograms) in the African Mineworkers' Diets, 1936–1940

	Fresh Fish	Smoked Fish	Meat	Percentage of All-Fish Diets
1 January– 1 August 1936	–	28,836	53,205	45.47
1 January– 31 August 1937	38,972	47,720	611,550	14.74
1 January– 31 August 1938	45,847	92,496	629,362	26.36
1 January– 31 August 1939	163,975	114,710	511,426	38.83
1 January– 30 September 1940	96,138	195,813	476,424	43.73

Source: AG, A6, D1510 b13 and b14, Dept. MOI, août 1940.

Since African peddlers controlled a large number of the lines of distribution for dried fish, its increased prominence in the diets of many of the workers during hard times was pretty much assured. Even the mining company was dependent on the peddlers for its source of dried fish, and for that reason the mining company was unable to control its price or monopolize its distribution.[89] Peddlers also figured importantly in providing the workers with some items of clothing. On the eve of the general strike the lack of durable clothing among the African workers had reached crisis proportions.[90] For example, from the outset of wartime, production factory operatives at Lubumbashi and Shituru-Panda and underground workers at Kipushi and Busanga complained bitterly that the lack of sturdy shoes, heavy jackets, and outershirts caused them to sustain a larger number of injuries at work. Heavy woolen shirts were especially favored by furnacemen and workers in the foundry because they acted as a safeguard against burns received from flying ash and slag. The presence of the African peddlers in the workers' camps was especially favored, therefore, since they sold not only brightly colored and well-made "Kitenge" cloth but also woolen blankets that either the workers or their women sewed into heavy shirts and capes to protect them from drastic temperature changes and injury.[91] In late November 1941 one company official observed that peddlers literally "invaded" the workers' camps at Kipushi and Panda on payday.[92] As the ideological facade of philanthropic partnership between the company and the workers came undone, the connection between the workers and the peddlers became that much faster.

Despite its weakened political position and the partial paralysis of the government machinery after the German occupation of Belgium, the Union Minière endeavored to stretch the African workers to the limits of their physical endurance and capacity. To some degree, however, the company tried to guard against severely taxing the African mining proletariat's ability to reproduce itself. For with African labor recruitment possibilities as slim as they were between 1934 and 1945, the mining company did not dare tamper with its potential to meet the demands of the wartime market. Nevertheless, the volume of interwar profits was enough to make the company occasionally forget its abstract commitment to a future generation of African miners. Edgar Sengier's trepidations about the "average man" were apparently not shared by the company's on-site administration in Katanga—at least insofar as they pertained to the company's African workers.

The demand for increased individual productivity also added a new twist to the situation on the work sites.[93] Strikes and work actions increased. The Union Minière factories at Lubumbashi, Shituru, and Panda, and also the underground mine at Kipushi quickly became the strongholds of strike activity. African workers in other phases of the mining industry and other industries followed their lead.[94] The colonial government's appeal to patriotism as a means to increase wartime production was not only ill-conceived in terms of the African workers but also misdirected in view of the initial African enthusiasm over Germany's military occupation of Belgium. With the head of the colonial Leviathan decapitated, the African masses, particularly the industrial working class, prepared to strike a blow at what remained.

By the onset of the war, the outlook of many of the African mineworkers changed markedly. Although they believed that the Union Minière could accommodate their expectations given the dramatic increases in production and profits, these workers felt their interests to be largely incompatible with those of the mining company. While such workers did not possess a revolutionary consciousness, the war and the German occupation of Belgium had destroyed the illusions and social conventions—in short, the culture of deference—associated with the old order. Also, these workers discovered agrarian allies who seconded their views. War and military defeat set out in bold relief the dual crisis of capital accumulation and the social reproduction of the next generation of the industrial workforce.

CHAPTER EIGHT

The Leviathan Collapsed and Rebuilt

THE GENERAL STRIKE

At the bottom of much of the differences of opinion is the "King" question. There is no doubt but that most of the Belgians are royalists at heart, and while the surrender of King Léopold III in May 1940 caused consternation, shame and despair, some of the high officials expressed the view that he must have known what was best for the country. At first all pictures of the King were removed from the Government offices and the bitter criticism of the King in the local press and the remarks of Churchill and Reynaud over the radio went unanswered. After the withdrawal of the British Army from the continent and the subsequent surrender of France, a spirit of defeatism coupled with anti-British and anti-French sentiment seemed to be growing.

> excerpt from the report of Patrick Mallon, American consul at Léopoldville, Belgian Congo, to the American secretary of state, January 31, 1941[1]

> The strike spread like a fire driven by the wind.
> a retired Union Minière worker reminiscing about the 1941 general strike[2]

The Union Minière lost much of the apparent allegiance of the African workers after the initial failure of its wartime policies and its failure to stem the price increases on the basic necessities of life.[3] Other groups and forms of organization leaped into the ideological vacuum created by the explosion of the myth of philanthropic paternalism.[4] Watchtower or *kitawala* briefly assumed such a role. Networks of African peddlers living on the perimeter of the work sites and in the squatters' areas also began to fill the gap in communication between the mineworkers and the company. Officers of the near moribund *tribunaux indigènes*—some of whom were skilled or semiskilled workers on the mines—were prodded into action as well.[5] All of them provided the organization and leadership of the moment at given work sites and during specific phases of the general strike. It was from the great masses of African workers, however, particularly the underground workers and factory operatives, that many of the strike's leaders and initial shock troops came.

The ultimate significance of the general strike of the African workers was not its success or failure, but that it reestablished the boundaries of what was possible in the relations between the workers and the company in a way which gave the workers greater room to maneuver. Even if the African workers were caught in a web of subordination and deference, which was reinforced by the colonial legal codes, they were also indispensable. It was their indispensability, placed against a background of deteriorating working conditions and rising prices, that made the implications of the strike so threatening for the long-term interests of the company and the colonial government. Relegation of worker militants to the more peripheral work sites, for example, often expanded the field of insurgency rather than defused it. In some instances, where the communication links between the particular work site and Elisabethville or Jadotville were weak, these measures brought the adjacent rural areas into the ambit of insurgency. Underground workers and factory operatives figured importantly in spreading a nexus of protest traditions throughout the mining complex. Their networks of communications, which had been forged by frequent instances of exile, carried the call for a general strike back to the smaller and more removed work sites by the end of November 1941.

After the first week of December 1941, these lines of communication, which were articulated by footpaths and village rumor mills rather than rail lines, propelled the news of the strike as far west as the Angolan border. Bands of African peddlers originating in Kasenga, the Dikulwe Valley, Bunkeya, and the Biano Plateau intersected these proletarian lines of communication at strategic work sites such as Luishia and Kikole.[6] Millennial and adventist sects like Watchtower acted as political checkpoints along the lines of communication that carried the strike message to the work sites of the far western sector of the mining complex. In fact, some workers at Kolwezi, Kamoto, and Kamatanda transformed the call for a general strike into a millennial wake.[7] Others saw events from a more activist viewpoint, however, and attempted to convince the land chiefs of their home villages to support the strike. As we shall see, their efforts were not altogether unsuccessful.[8]

For all intents and purposes the general strike at the Union Minière had been in the offing since at least November 1941. At Jadotville, Kipushi, Likasi, Luishia, and perhaps among the foundrymen at Lubumbashi, plans for the strike proceeded slowly and with meticulous attention to the likely impact of the strike on African workers in other industries and among the rural population in the surrounding villages; for at least some of the workers had it in mind to involve the entire African community in the strike effort.[9] As early as April 1940 the Union Minière's administration was becoming mildly alarmed by the number of Lubumbashi's factory workers who were fleeing the older industrial neighborhoods in the commune Kenia and the workers' camps of the Union Minière for squatters' areas like Katuba. As a result, many of the factory operatives' households were brought into closer proximity with the teeming world of squatters, peddlers, and railway construction workers that existed just on the edge of the city. The workers' wives and other women of their households cleared new garden plots on the unclaimed land in Katuba and settled into a familiarity with their surroundings and new neighbors that was born more out of the contraction of their living standards than their own volition. Although conspiracy was not the immediate objective of this exodus from the cramped and dilapidated conditions of metropolitan Elisabethville, by 1941 it became the most important consequence of the exodus.[10]

The mining company's Department of Native Personnel turned its attention elsewhere after noting the initial trickle of migrants. It had not seen the connection between this out-migration of workers and the rapid expansion of the general strike's field of activity in Elisabethville. In March 1946 a special committee was formed within the Department of Native Labor to review the causes of the general strike. Given the advantage of hindsight, the conclusions the committee came to were rather startling, for it completely missed the mood of the African population of Elisabethville on the eve of the general strike. Its recording secretary wrote: "There was no indication of discontent among the African workers to signal the crisis. The population of the camps was morally healthy; it was industrious, disciplined and happy."[11] Yet five years earlier, between September and November 1941, officials of the mining company and the colonial government in Elisabethville were writing about the "air of premeditation" that had swept over the African workers. Something was afoot that neither the mining company nor colonial government could comprehend.[12]

Sometime between 20 November and 1 December 1941 the African

workers decided that there was no way to solve their particular grievances against the mining company short of a general strike. Individual
strike attempts at Kikole, Kipushi, and by the company's European
workers in October 1941 preceded the general strike and met with
only limited success. Like the strikes at Kipushi and Kikole, the white
strike effort did indeed hurt wartime production; but it was certainly
no organizational model for the African workers, given the hostile
relationship between black and white workers.[13] Moreover, the Union
Minière had successfully isolated much of the white workers' leadership by branding it "communist," or worse, "fascist" and Nazi
inspired. To be sure, some white workers, particularly those of
Flemish and Boer origin, did express some sympathy for the Nazis,
but whether this was an organizing principle of the white workers
was quite another matter. Nevertheless, by virtue of an edict from
the governor-general, under the pretext of ferreting out traitors and
protecting the colony from "pernicious ideologies," the provincial
government placed the majority of the white workers' leadership in
preventive detention or exiled them to Léopoldville for the duration
of the war. If the African workers had any hopes of joining with or
attaching themselves to the strike effort of the European workers,
they were, no doubt, preempted by the initiatives of the mining company and the colonial government. Bolstered by the tactical advantage
of their numbers and the weakened position of the mining company
after the previously mentioned strikes, however, the African workers
struck the company on 3 December 1941.[14]

On the night of 3 December 1941, the workers at the Shituru and
Panda factories in Jadotville decided to go out on strike the following morning. Shortly afterwards, the leadership of the strike movement sent representatives to the surrounding work sites at Likasi,
Luishia, and Kambove to inform the workers there of their decision
to strike.[15] Within a week workers at all the mining company's major
work sites joined the strike movement. African workers from Kipushi
to Kolwezi rose in solidarity with their fellow workers, and also rose
to express their own particular grievances against the company.

The first eight hours of the strike revealed that the most important vector of leadership for the African workers was between the
factory workers at Lubumbashi and Jadotville and the underground
workers at Kipushi.[16] In the early morning hours of 4 December 1941,
500 factory workers from Panda set out on the road to Jadotville in
order to make a show of strength with the factory workers at Shituru.
Unfortunately, on the very same night that the factory workers
decided to strike, one of their leaders, Mutamba Léon, betrayed the

plan of action to the police tribunal at Jadotville. As a result, Mutamba was arrested, and troops from the Thirteenth Battalion of the Force Publique under a European officer, Edouard Cardoen, were dispatched to halt the march of the workers from Panda and to contain the extent of the strike at Jadotville.[17] Between 4:30 A.M. and 7:30 P.M. the African troops under Cardoen's command attempted to turn back the demonstrators. Eventually the government decided to sequester them at the workers' camp at Shituru. In the midst of their efforts to corral the workers from Panda, however, some 700–800 workers struck the factory at Panda. Another 800 workers struck the Shituru works shortly afterward.[18]

By 10:00 A.M. on 4 December, 1,400 African workers in all had joined the strike. Another 700 workers from the night shift remained in the plant at Panda but refused to work. Only 400 highly skilled African workers and new recruits remained at work in the two plants. Some incidents of sabotage occurred, but eyewitnesses of the strike pointed to the "incredible discipline" displayed by the strikers, even after their number swelled to over 1,000.[19]

Shortly after 10:00 the African strikers were joined by their wives, who later surrounded the camp manager's office. In addition to supporting the workers' demand for an unequivocal wage increase of 1.50 francs, the women also demanded that the company restore the practice of giving them *primes en rebours,* or material incentives, in the form of sewing machines and cloth to remain in the camps. They also demanded that the customary distribution of ration tickets to them as well as their men be restored.[20]

The participation of women in the strike was perhaps a more important feature at Jadotville than Lubumbashi. Their special grievances against the company reflected the relative parity between the living standards of the mine and factory workers' households and those of the Africans in the nearby squatters' areas. In addition to sewing machines and ration tickets, the women also demanded that the mining company stop its attempts to get them to use green, or nonorganic, fertilizer instead of ashes in their garden plots.[21] Like the squatters on Union Minière land, the wives of the factory workers saw the company's attempt to force them to use green fertilizer as no less than an imposition on their time and, therefore, on the work rhythm of their households. At the heart of the women's protest over green fertilizer lay the larger issue of producing to meet the food needs of the broader market over those of the individual African household. Protest over the issue of green fertilizer surfaced at other Union Minière work sites during and after the general strike. But it was at those work sites where the living standards of worker and squatter households were in close economic proximity that this particular protest acquired some prominence in its own right.[22]

Between 10:00 A.M. and 12:00 noon on 4 December the strike and demonstration at Jadotville took a violent turn. Predictably, much of the violence at Jadotville was provoked by the police and the military. Those incidents of violence that originated with the workers were of a rearguard nature and took the form of sabotage or the instrumental destruction of public property, once it became clear that the military had been given a free hand to suppress the strikers. The workers from the Panda works, who had been in the forefront of worker protest against the company since at least 1936, held out the longest against the attacks of the police and the soldiers.[23] A week later, just as the general strike was reaching its peak at Lubumbashi, an article in *L'Essor du Congo*, the weekly newspaper of Katanga, maintained that the strike at Jadotville had been a veritable "orgy of violence," and that the civil authorities and company officials had done everything in their power to prevent violence and to quell it once it had broken out. Yet on 5 December 1941, the paper's coverage of the strike had drawn attention to the "calm and disciplined" disposition of the strikers. The rapid spread of the strike to the mines surrounding Elisabethville and the Lubumbashi works clearly had a negative impact on the paper's reportage of the strike.[24]

After over 2,000 people had massed on the playground of the primary school at Panda, the European officers abandoned their African troops, thus compelling them to fend for themselves against the strikers. Meanwhile the camp manager's office had been surrounded by the women of the African workers' households. The women demanded to see both the factory officials and the territorial administrator, simply for the opportunity to air their grievances. Cardoen, the commander of the battalion, panicked and attempted to seek refuge in the camp manager's office. A group of workers began to throw stones at him as he tried to escape the action on the playground. At that point, Cardoen emptied his revolver into a group of African workers.[25] In the violence that ensued an untold number of workers were wounded. Fifteen men and several women were killed; six of them were buried in unmarked graves.[26]

After the massacre at Jadotville the strike movement spread rapidly to the other work sites. On 5 December the nightsoilers and watchmen at Likasi, the mining site that was wedged between the two factories at Shituru and Panda, joined the strike movement. A large number of the nightsoilers were Chokwe. Many of them were also peddlers of food and other staples used by the African workers. Some of them carried the news of the strike south to Luishia and north to Kambove. By 6 December, following their example, all the workers at Luishia, Likasi, and Kambove came out on strike. The railway workers at Likasi also struck in solidarity with the mineworkers. Doubtless, kinship and strong associational ties of the Chokwe railway workers and miners prompted the sympathy strike.[27]

The spread of the strike movement by "marginal" members of the Union Minière's African workforce at this juncture was extremely important. The range of support from outside the mining community showed just how valuable the Chokwe and Luba worker-peddler networks were for the execution of the general strike. Although few Chokwe workers emerged as leaders of the strike movement in the central and southern sectors of the mining complex, it became obvious by the third day that whether the strike movement stopped at Likasi or spread south to Lubumbashi and to the mines of the north and west depended largely on the strength of the Chokwe and worker-peddler communications networks.[28] According to several eye-witnesses, the first African workers to join the strike at Lubumbashi and also to be killed in the subsequent massacre of 9 December 1941 were Chokwe. G. Montenez, a territorial administrator at Elisabeth-ville at the time, maintained that the Chokwe had been engaged in sabotage at the foundry. He also maintained they had tried to foment a riot inside one of Lubumbashi's factories a week before. Immediately after the commencement of the protest at Jadotville, the backland routes, over which *lutuku* and marijuana had been transported in the 1920s and 1930s, began to carry the call to strike.[29]

The worker-peddler networks were strikingly effective at Luishia and Kambove because many of the workers at these two mines were former peddlers. A large number of African peddlers were forced to hire on with the Union Minière after the fees for peddlers' licenses went from 50 to 250 francs in January 1940. While this increase in licensing fees had little or no effect on African peddlers who trafficked in food or "illicit" items, its impact was devastating for those African traders who sold manufactured goods and were registered with the provincial government.[30] When African commerce in Katanga was reconstituted exclusively on the basis of foodstuffs and the "illegal commerce" at the end of 1940, many of the former peddlers left the work sites near Jadotville to take up trading once again. African merchants and peddlers profited from the uncertain character of the two years before the general strike by filtering more into the interstices of wartime economic organization. They became more enterprising in eluding legal and administrative impediments, although they encountered opposition from government-appointed chiefs and their headmen and retainers.[31]

Between 7 and 9 December 1941 the strike movement finally reached the factory at Lubumbashi and the mines on the outskirts of Elisabethville. The strike began at Lubumbashi and Ruashi when a large number of workers either stopped work in the middle of the day shift or simply refused to pick up their ration tickets at the beginning of the work day on 7 December. On 8 December, however, the situation at Lubumbashi was described as "normal" by the provincial newspaper *L'Essor du Congo* and by the company officials, although minor skirmishes between mine police and maintenance workers did take place at Ruashi and the Star of the Congo. Also, one Chokwe worker was shot and killed by the authorities in the workers' camp near Lubumbashi.[32]

On 9 December 1941 during the first two hours of the day shift, virtually all the African workers at the Lubumbashi works and the surrounding mines stopped work.[33] Between 10:00 and 11:00 A.M., 500 African workers surrounded the camp manager's office at Lubumbashi. However, the main body of workers, which increased to over 1,500 workers by the afternoon, massed on the company soccer field where they remained until the night of 9 December. Troops were moved in subsequently. According to company sources, the government forces, including the governor of Katanga, A. Maron, and the territorial administration of Elisabethville lost control of the situation at this point. Shaken by the news of the continued work stoppages and departmental strikes at Luishia, Kambove, and Likasi in spite of the presence of the army battalions at Jadotville and a promise of a unilateral wage increase of 30 percent, Maron first sent in the troops at Lubumbashi and then appealed to the strikers to return to work.[34] The general strike had begun in earnest.

Maron addressed the African strikers on the afternoon of 9 December. By that time, however, the troops that he had called in as soon as the workers had gathered on the soccer field were being placed into battle formation by their European officers. Machine gun turrets were set up in each corner of the playing field.[35] According to Emile Toussaint, the associate director of the Union Minière operations in Katanga in 1941, Maron delivered his appeal to the strikers in "kitchen," or "*kisettla*," Swahili. Toussaint maintained that he had tried to get Maron to deliver his appeal in French, but Maron insisted on speaking in Swahili, maintaining that "he knew the mentality of the blacks." After his appeal failed to make any impact on the mood of the strikers, Maron quickly withdrew, leaving the situation at an impasse.[36]

After Maron's exit, L. Marchal, the territorial administrator for Elisabethville, harangued and threatened the workers, exhorting them to disperse and return home. Sensing that neither the government nor the mining company had a clear plan of action, the strikers became even more restive by early evening. A few of the workers began to throw stones at the troops in battle formation. When the police attempted to arrest the more recalcitrant workers, the soldiers plunged into the crowd. At that point the soldiers manning the machine gun to the extreme left of the soccer field began to fire into the crowd. G. Montenez, another territorial administrator, described the situation on the evening of 9 December in this way:

The strikers held an all night vigil at the football field. More troops were called out under my command. They had strict orders not to shoot. The crowd began throwing. One soldier's ear was cut off by a rock. The soldiers grew angry. To warn the crowd, an order was given to load the rifles. The crowd still did not disperse. The soldiers became even angrier (perhaps when the soldier lost his ear). They opened fire and 70 plus were killed.[37]

According to Georges Lievens, a white trade-union leader, the soldiers' attack on the African strikers was not as prudent as Montenez's account suggests. Lievens claimed that the soldiers had been called in to surround the workers' camp as early as the evening of 8 December and that they were charged with ensuring that those workers who had joined the strike did not receive rations at 8:00 that evening. He also claimed that the African machine gunners had not fired into the crowd of strikers on impulse, as Montenez implied, but that they had been ordered to fire on the workers by the captain of the artillery, Demilde. In turn, Demilde had received his orders directly from Governor Maron. This part of Lievens' account was corroborated by the testimony of an African *instituteur* who acted as a spy for the mining company during the strike, and whose testimony was entered into the force report drawn up by the company on the general strike in January 1942.[38] Forty-eight African strikers were killed initially and another 150 were wounded, according to Lievens' account of the strike. About 50 of the wounded died the following day. Many of the demonstrators who died from their wounds were women.[39]

Lievens also said that the massacre of the African strikers did not occur on the night of 9 December but shortly after 12:00 noon. The mining company simply waited until nightfall to remove the dead and the dying with dump trucks.[40] Emile Rolus, the director of native personnel, oversaw the removal of the bodies. Lievens described Rolus' role in concealing the exact number of workers who were killed on 9 December:

> Rolus had just returned rather hastily from Jadotville. Apparently, a telegraph had been sent to him there concerning the events at Lubumbashi, and he returned in the late afternoon or early evening. As soon as he had surveyed the playing field, he rushed into the central store at Elisabethville and ordered a large number of blue canvas cloths to wrap the dying in so that they could be carried to mass graves—in a respectable number of instances while they were still alive. After he had purchased the wraps, he turned to the proprietor and said, "We have a lot of work to do before morning."[41]

On 10 December, the day after the massacre, virtually all of the Union Minière's 3,000 African workers in the vicinity of Elisabethville returned to work. A week later the mining company gave in to the African workers' minimum demand for a unilateral wage increase of 1.50 francs.[42] Shortly after the massacre the mining company built several wings of camp housing over the soccer field in order to blot out any signs of what had happened.[43]

By the end of the strike the death toll for African workers at Elisabethville alone was close to 100. And although the white workers and their organization, Association des Agents de l'Union Minière et Filiales (AGUFI), had remained aloof from the African general strike, partly because of coercion and intimidation by both the government and the mining company, many of them came forth to testify about the atrocities they had witnessed during the sessions of the commissions of inquiry that convened after the strike. In several instances white workers paid dearly for their testimony. George Lievens, for instance, was imprisoned under a wartime preventive detention act, blacklisted for employment, and then deported to Belgium on 31 May 1945.[44]

The front line of leadership in the strike movement had been composed of the factory workers at Jadotville and Lubumbashi and the underground workers at Kipushi. It was broken by the police action at Jadotville and Lubumbashi between 3 and 10 December 1941. The assumption of the strike's leadership by these two groups of African workers was not coincidental. As early as 1937 an area of maneuver had been opened up for these two strata of workers as a result of the drastic reduction of European supervision at the Prince Léopold Mine and at the two factory complexes. Between 1929 and 1940, for example, the number of Europeans for every 1,000 Africans went from 162 to 109 in the Union Minière's factories and from 104 to 62 at the Kipushi underground mine. Other work sites experienced a decrease in the number of European supervisors, but it was in the factories and at the underground mine that withdrawal of supervisory personnel was most pronounced.[45]

A slight increase in the real wages of African factory operatives and underground workers accompanied the reduction of European supervisors. As previously indicated, this wage increase, which took place in incremental stages between 1938 and 1940, did not keep pace with the cost of living. The tremendous lag between the wage increases and soaring prices, combined with the more self-sufficient role of the underground miners and factory workers within the production process, created the preconditions for their leadership role in the strike wave at the end of 1941. But it was precisely because they had no footing in any other economic activity except for wage labor, and thus no social space beyond the mines and the factories in which to challenge the power of the mining company, that the leadership of the factory workers and underground miners was crushed shortly after the massacres at Panda and Lubumbashi.[46]

Other forms of leadership such as the worker-peddler networks carried the strike farther afield. Toward the end of the strike the purpose of worker protest at Kikole and Kolwezi was enveloped by either millennarian beliefs or the aspirations of an increasingly disgruntled rural population in the home villages of many of the mineworkers. But unlike the factory operatives and underground workers, the new leadership lacked the political will to forge a unified program for all the workers in the mining industry. Their influence over the workers at the outlying mining sites was short-lived. It was essentially a peasant program of rural reform, for instance, rather than an outright proletarian one that prolonged the unrest at the outlying mines.

The ultimate purpose of the African strike movement varied from work site to work site. This was, at least in part, because of the different forms of organization that communicated the intent to strike to the African workers. Even though the participation of the African mineworkers in the strike was general, its purpose and objectives were not. Several years after the strike, some of the African workers saw what had happened as an instance where their compatriots had "died for their wages."[47] But a large number of them saw the strike as the beginning of the end for Belgian rule in Katanga, much like the spokesman for the November 1941 strike at Kikole, who claimed that "the whites had been driven out of Kenya" and that the African mineworkers should do no less with their own white foremen and supervisors.[48] The secret police, by 1947, saw the strike as a smoke screen for the resurgence of more politicized versions of the lodges and ethnic brotherhoods.[49] In its last phases, therefore, the African general strike began to look like the "festivals of the oppressed" of the failed Russian revolution of 1905, when the workers and common people took the institutions at hand and molded them to new, more insurrectionary purposes.[50]

THE UNMADE INSURRECTION: THE PROVINCIAL RISING OF 1944

There are two theories prevalent as to the cause of the trouble. One is that it came from subversive elements among the native mineworkers of Northern Rhodesia, the other that it came from Axis agents operating across the border in Angola. I am inclined to reject the latter theory since during the last four years no acts of sabotage have been committed in the Congo, and even unskilled saboteurs could easily have caused great damage to railway lines at many points and to the oil bulk installations at Léopoldville and Matadi, the latter less than two miles from the Angola border. . . .

The worst effect of the whole affair is the loss of face sustained by the *Force Publique* and the feeling of shame among the white population that such a thing could have occurred.

> Patrick Mallon to the American secretary of state after having read the intelligence report of Major Kenyon Bolton, an American military advisor attached to the provincial secret police of Katanga, 6 March 1944[51]

Several attempts were made to reason with the soldiers, and it seems they asked for more pay, less work and less discipline [corporal punishment?], which makes me think it was a strike and not a revolt.

> the Reverend John Morrison, legal representative of the American Presbyterian Congo Mission, 17 March 1944[52]

Despite the unilateral wage settlement and the defeat of the general strike, strikes and other forms of worker protest persisted. Until 1947 departmental strikes and other rearguard job actions were commonplace at Union Minière installations. Kolwezi and Kikole were especially affected by worker protest.[53] From 1942 to 1946, in fact, "unrest and indiscipline" spread to other industries. African transport and building-trades workers attempted to organize industry wide strikes in 1946, for example. Their efforts failed in large part.[54]

Despite its breadth, the current of restiveness did not signal a new surge of worker militancy.[55] For the main body of African workers was either too politically exhausted or too disorganized to carry the cause of the workers forward after the defeat of the strike movement in the mining industry. But the persistence of industrial unrest, even after the massacres at Jadotville and Lubumbashi, created a platform for alarmists in high places. Predictably, the conservative and ultramontane Roman Catholic Monsignor de Hemptinne was the most outspoken of them. On 15 December 1943, a month after the official visit of Paul Tschoffen, counselor of state for the Belgian government-in-exile, de Hemptinne aired his trepidations about the future in an official letter addressed to the prime minister, the minister of colonies, and the governor-general:

As a result of the rural population's discontent, one encounters a thousand different variations of the demand for reparations in the bush. These demands are made with indefatigable logic — and with bitterness. A spirit of antipathy and defiance is spreading everywhere. The native is detaching himself from our authority. More and more, he seeks refuge from our influence and prestige. The face of the Congo is changing. Belgium is on the way to losing its crowning achievement in Africa.[56]

The peasantry had indeed experienced some of the repression associated with the general strike, but they had not been initially involved in the strike. Yet on the eve of de Hemptinne's letter a portion of the peasantry felt aggrieved enough to become directly engaged in popular protest. So did a number of the African soldiers who, on order from their European officers, had shot down relatives and former neighbors at Jadotville and Lubumbashi. The paradox of their actions was not lost on the soldiers. The peasants and workers had been fiercely savaged and exploited from the outset of the war. The soldiers had often been the agency of the savaging and exploitation. Yet their commanding officers continued to call them "apes" and "monkeys" on the parade ground and in the barracks and to exact discipline and obedience with corporal punishment. Given the extraordinary context of the Second World War and the repression that had already been heaped on the industrial workers, the grievances of the soldiers could not be easily addressed by either the colonial authorities or the soldiers themselves. Moreover, the active role of the soldiers in the massacres during the general strike, combined with the strike's defeat, made a long-term political alliance between soldiers and mineworkers unlikely.[57] But by the end of 1943, despite an undercurrent of disunity, a portion of the peasantry of Lualaba District and the province of Lusambo, several battalions of the colonial army, and a portion of the mine and factory workers at the Union Minière resolved to rise against the colonial government in what began as an army mutiny but was quickly transformed into an ill-starred provincial insurrection.[58]

The aborted rising of February–May 1944 was the closest thing to a genuine insurrection that the Belgian colonial government had experienced up to that point. All of the right ingredients were there — but in the wrong proportions. Soldiers, workers, and peasants all took part in their turn, but not in concert or for the same reasons. Yet there was a minimum program of reform that all the protagonists agreed upon: (1) an end to hunger and starvation; (2) the abolition of the forced cultivation of cotton and of the abusive power of the government-appointed chiefs and rural social assistants; (3) reduction of the head tax, which, given African wages, was higher than similar taxes levied in South Africa; (4) better treatment by European officers and the abolition of racial epithets such as *"macaque"* and *"singe"*; (5) the abolition of corporal punishment in the prisons; (6) the abolition of the economic privilege of white skin.[59]

Initially the rising had been planned to take place over a large and strategic portion of the Belgian Congo. Southern Kasai, western and northeastern Katanga, and the towns of Léopoldville, Luluaburg, and Elisabethville were to be seized and held until the government consented to negotiate with the African insurgents. In Katanga and its contiguous regions the strategy of the rebels was to secure the rail line and occupy those areas that had been in the immediate path of the Union Minière's attempts at expansion for the previous decade.[60] If the rebels had been successful, negotiation with them would have been the least of the colonial administration's problems. For at that point, in Katanga at least, the administration would have ceased to exist.[61]

But in addition to the undersized constituency of the rebellion, its ill-timed armed phase so weakened the insurgent forces that they were unable to implement any portion of their political program in the areas that joined the rebellion. The rebels did manage to usurp some of the chiefs and headmen in the more removed chieftaincies for a brief time; but it was more difficult to unseat the existing chiefs in the areas where they were paid handsomely for their cooperation in exploiting the peasantry.[62] Thus the insurgents found it less easy to win over the more economically vital portions of Lusambo and Lualaba than to win over the regions where annual incomes of the chiefs were often less than those of African mineworkers.[63]

The plan for the rising began to take shape in May 1943. It was to begin on Christmas Day. However, the preemptive actions of the territorial police in northeastern Katanga in July 1943 and those of the civilian conspirators in Elisabethville forced the core leadership to postpone the major thrust of the rebellion until the beginning of the following year.[64] By the time the armed action did occur, the colonial authorities had been aware of the conspiracy for several months, although they did not know its extent. Thus, in addition to their failure to give the rebellion a secure social basis by attempting to draw a broader segment of the African mineworkers and peasantry into its ambit, the more immediate problem of the rebellion's timing was to haunt its leadership until their capture.[65]

The initial core of the conspirators included a large number of African soldiers and noncommissioned officers at Luluaburg, Kamina, and Bukama. The majority of them had come from Lusambo Province and the villages that dotted the countryside between the Union Minière work sites at Kikole and Mwanza. The latter region was just north of the port town of Bukama. Moreover, it was at Kikole that the strike movement had taken its most insurrectionary turn two years earlier.[66]

As plans for the rebellion progressed, the seizure of Bukama began to figure importantly in the plans of the rebels. The town's port played a role similar to that of the north-south rail line in the plans of the detachments of rebel soldiers at Luluaburg. For with the port securely in their hands, the conspirators could hold up shipments of food and machinery going downstream to the northernmost mines as well as delay shipments of cassiterite ore and tin coming upstream.[67] If the armed phase of the rebellion had taken place at the appointed time in December and lasted for no more than a month, the rebels would have acquired an immense tactical advantage over the government forces. The Union Minière would have been forced to negotiate with the rebels because of its desperate need to meet production and shipping schedules, whereas food supplies for the African miners would have already been shipped downstream.[68] If the seizure of the port took more than a month, or worse, dragged on to the dry season, its political liabilities would have begun to outweigh its strategic value. A potential social base of support in the form of the tin miners would have been literally starved out of existence.[69]

In July 1943, when the police swept the rail town of Kongolo in search of Watchtower adherents, they also arrested a number of the leaders of the planned insurrection. It is not clear whether this leadership cluster was among the noncommissioned African officers who were eventually acquitted of conspiracy charges or among the lower ranks of the soldiers arrested with the Watchtower leader Kianza Djoni. Circumstantial evidence pointed to the acquitted African officers, although these two groups of soldiers were aware of each other's existence.[70] At the beginning of 1943, for example, one of the arrested noncommissioned officers, Sergeant Poyo Booma, appeared to have consciously developed a friendship with a Madame Huart, a missionary who arranged for the transport of large amounts of medical supplies to the military camp near Kongolo. Sergeant Poyo was also in touch with the Watchtower adept Kianza Djoni. The implications of Poyo's network of acquaintances continued to weigh on the authorities long after he was acquitted of conspiracy charges.[71]

The mass arrest of July 1943 must have caused some reshuffling of the leadership of the rising. Whether the reconstituted leadership came upon the idea of stopping the flow of commercial traffic out of Bukama's port independently of the pre-July strategy is rather unclear.[72] But certainly they must have made their decision to continue with the plan while being fully cognizant of its potentially negative effect on the mineworkers after January. The two wings of the army conspirators — the one in Luluaburg and the one in northern Katanga — began to feel that they could bring the insurrection off with only minor assistance from the industrial workers and the educated Africans in the towns. They were to learn differently during their painful and protracted defeat in the countryside of western Katanga between mid-March and the first week of May 1944.[73]

Almost all the army conspirators at Luluaburg were Luba-Kasai. They conveyed their plans to revolt to other Luba who were employed at Elisabethville as clerks for the Union Minière and for other European enterprises through their kin networks. This was the only direct connection that the soldier conspirators had with any African employees of the mining company. Those that they eventually formed with workers at the outlying mines and at Luishia were developed after the insurrection had gone fully on the defensive, and when the last contingents of army rebels were running for their lives toward the Angolan border.[74]

Working-class leadership of the kind that led the strike movement was therefore conspicuously absent in the planning stages of the conspiracy, even though the soldiers were obviously influenced by the mineworkers' tactics and the new idiom of industrial protest. The few mining clerks and skilled workers involved in the planning of the insurrection came from the ranks of those workers who had not supported the general strike. All of them, in fact, had been hastily upgraded during the 1941 strikes and assigned to jobs usually designated for Europeans. Once the strike movement was suppressed, however, most of these workers were forced back to their former positions. More than the seizure of political power, they were concerned with regaining the benefits that they had rather effortlessly acquired during this sharp period of class warfare. It was only after collaboration with their employers and colonial masters had failed that they took seriously the prospects of an insurrection. What little evidence we have about their role in the actual planning of the initial rising suggests that their co-conspirators might have been better off without their lukewarm assistance.[75]

After having been postponed or preempted by government dragnets in Léopoldville, northeastern Katanga, and Elisabethville between July and December 1943, the initial armed thrust of the rebellion took the form of a mutiny at the Luluaburg garrison on Sunday, 20 February 1944.[76] At around 3:00 in the afternoon, upon hearing that 60 or 70 of their comrades had died in Elisabethville after receiving a yellow fever innoculation, 700 African soldiers—minus their European officers—seized the town's armory, capturing millions of rounds of ammunition and large quantities of weapons, including heavy artillery. Despite their seizure of the armory, the soldiers exerted no force against their officers or any other whites. Instead they picketed the streets and refused to perform any of their regular duties. They kept strict order in the town, and in a number of cases prevented African domestic servants from looting the houses and stores of their employers.[77] By early evening all of the white officers had fled the military camp. The white civilian population convened in the town's largest hotel and then moved quickly to the Roman Catholic cathedral on the outskirts of town. With the exception of a handful of white civilians who fled by automobile in the first several hours of the mutiny, the entire white population of the town remained barricaded in the cathedral for eight days. There were only two initial casualties:

a white lieutenant who, after plying himself with liquor, attempted to disarm a mutinous soldier and was shot in the stomach; and an African soldier who stumbled while walking behind a senior European officer and was shot by a European cadet who thought he was attacking the senior officer.[78]

By 22 February unrest broke out at Kamina and Jadotville, 265 and 465 miles away from Luluaburg, respectively. At Kamina a detachment of soldiers mutinied and deserted, while at Jadotville the mutiny of some of the soldiers in the town's garrison was accompanied by sporadic sabotage of machinery and rail lines at the Union Minière's factories.[79] In some areas of the countryside between Luluaburg and Jadotville the intervention of the mutinous soldiers was not accompanied with the same order that characterized their occupation of Luluaburg. Many peasants took the occasion to burn the local cotton warehouses and to sack and destroy the homes of territorial administrators and their African agents. Telegraph, telephone, and postal communications were disrupted. Traffic on the rail line was interrupted until the second week in March. And between 22 and 27 February columns of rebel soldiers moved into the territories of Kanda Kanda, Tshofa, and Kabinda, advancing right up to the banks of the Bushimaie River, 55 miles due west of the Lubilash River, without experiencing any opposition from the government's ground units or air force.[80] Many of the rural areas north of the garrison town of Kamina along the Lubondai River also received the rebels with some measure of enthusiasm.[81] As late as April 1944 many of the villagers in these two areas continued to support the rebels. This was well after loyal government troops had retaken Luluaburg and the most important northern routes leading from Lusambo and Kasai into Angola — in short, after it had become painfully obvious that the rebels were surrounded by the government's forces.[82]

A decisive show of force within three days of the initial mutiny might have preempted civilian participation in the unrest. But by the end of February it was clear that the unrest had become more than a mere mutiny and that a significant portion of the African population had cast its lot with the mutinous soldiers. It was at this point in the rebellion that Major Kenyon Bolton, an American military officer attached to the Office of Strategic Services (OSS), was seconded to the colonial army and the secret police in Katanga.[83] Bolton's assessment of the unrest must have shocked his Belgian colleagues; for in his view it was the result of long-standing grievances which partly mirrored those of the African workers and peasants. The massacre of the mineworkers two years before had been the catalyst

for the emergence of the specific grievances of the soldiers. Consequently the paradoxical role played by the African soldiers in the
massacre became the solvent which loosened their loyalties to their
European officers and the colonial government.[84]

After 29 February 1944 the insurgents had to relinquish Luluaburg.
But after a rumor spread that the whites intended to poison the
remaining detachments and feed them to the civilian population as
emergency rations, other soldiers joined the rebels. After Luluaburg
was retaken in the first week of March, the insurgents retreated
toward central and western Katanga and Angola.[85] The most heavily
armed rebel detachments fought government troops along a western
perimeter, which included Malawoie and Lueta in Kasai and the territory of Sandoa in Katanga, while the rebellion's military leaders and
the bulk of their followers fled deeper into the Lualaba District —
away from their first primary objective, the rail line. By the second
week in March, as they moved closer to Kapanga, the ancestral capital
of the Lunda *mwaant yavs*, or paramount chieftains, the insurgents
were more concerned with staying alive than defeating the government troops. By the third week in March they were militarily defeated
by the government's forces and by mobile bands of white reservists
and irregulars who had organized themselves into armed detachments
on 10 March at Elisabethville. Many of the white irregulars were trade
unionists and skilled workers who had escaped incarceration at the
outset of the war and who vowed to aid the government in "restoring
all necessary authority for the sake of our country vis-à-vis the natives
and the world abroad."[86]

As the government troops retook the northern border regions, the
grim shadow of defeat settled over the main rebel force. After March
the insurgents fought to maintain their access to the southern escape
routes into Angola rather than to defeat the government forces.[87] Once
the main force of the rebellion was defeated in the second week of
March, rebel columns under the command of Tshanza Elias and
Mafuta Kapanga began to seek the support of many of the very chiefs
they had tried to overthrow the month before. The most notable of
these, of course, was the Lunda *mwaant yav* Kaumba.[88] Mineworkers
from Kolwezi, Luishia, and the outlying mines, as well as sections
of the peasantry, guided them along the backland routes which led
to the Lunda paramount's capital and surrounding villages. It was here
in the Lunda heartland just south of the Nkalaany Valley and the
ancestral burial site of the Lunda sovereigns that the rebels made their
last stand before attempting to escape en masse into Angola.[89] Undoubtedly the irony of the rebels' situation was not wasted on

Kaumba. The name of the rebel second in command, for example, meant literally "we are stuck in Kapanga."[90]

The advent of the rebel soldiers and returned mineworkers came on the heels of a succession crisis in the Lunda paramount's chieftaincy. Starvation had caused the peasantry to chafe under Kaumba's paramountcy. A steady erosion of his power had been occurring ever since 1932, when a millennarian uprising led by disaffected Chokwe youth had first threatened to drive him from power. Despite the defeat of the 1932 rebellion, many of Kaumba's subjects came to see him as no more than a figurehead;[91] for shortly after the rebellion, the colonial government reduced the number of chieftaincies in the west from 205 to 105 by means of the 1933 Land Act. With Kaumba's tacit consent, therefore, the colonial government initiated what amounted to a government-sponsored enclosure movement. This policy drove even more Lunda and Chokwe peasants off their ancestral land and onto the vacant land and outlying mines of the Union Minière. Much of the land they left behind fell into the hands of Lunda aristocrats in Kaumba's court.[92] The disgruntled peasants who remained on these holdings as clients of the paramount and his officials probably saw the rebels as the means through which some of their land might be restored. It was perhaps for this reason that their kinsmen working on the outlying work sites led the armed group of rebels into Mwaat Yav Kaumba's capital.[93] With the defeat of the general strike and the steady worsening of working conditions during the war, a return to the countryside was as reasonable as any other alternative for the less seasoned mineworkers, particularly if they returned with armed allies who could aid them in settling old scores.[94]

The administration of the Union Minière followed the rebellion closely and with some trepidation once it appeared to be transforming itself into a peasant uprising: Lusambo's territories of Kabinda, Kanda Kanda, and Tshofa provided the mining company with thousands of its workers; Lualaba's northern and western territories contained the mines that provided the catalyst for the company's wartime expansion. Consequently, at the close of the rebellion the mining company was one of the strongest supporters of *dégorgement*, a land reform policy which sought to win over the peasantry in the western regions by giving them more land at the expense of white farmers, cotton speculators, conservative Lunda aristocrats, and commercially minded Luba clan leaders.[95] With its mines stretching almost to the Angolan border and thousands of workers to maintain, food loomed much larger than cotton in the company's plan for the western regions.[96] But like most land reform policies that are unaccompanied by some political empowerment of the prospective recipients of land, *dégorgement* turned into its opposite; and the peasantry was forced to fend off the predations of the Union Minière as well as those of its older enemies.

THE AFRICAN MINEWORKERS AND THE COLONIAL ORDER

By 1945 the affairs of rural administration in Katanga had festered for too long. The aftermath of the 1941 strikes and the failed provincial insurrection made rural reconstruction very difficult indeed without supervision and funds from the metropolitan government in Belgium. But with a postwar government barely in place, Belgium was in no position to give the provincial government of Katanga the funds it needed to rebuild the physical infrastructure of administration in the rural areas. In June 1945, for example,the provincial government had to lay aside even those reconstruction projects whose need could be clearly demonstrated, like the paved highway from Elisabethville to Jadotville.[97]

The only source that the government could turn to for funds for its rural reconstruction program was the Union Minière. However, the mining company's help came too late and with too many reservations. The company's major concern was to synchronize the expansion of the western mines, from Kolwezi to Kisenge, with the spread of law and order in the Lualaba District. Predictably, the landless and extensively proletarianized Chokwe people and ambulant African peddlers were singled out as especially worrisome fomenters of lawlessness and disorder.[98] Older adolescents in the workers' camps of the western mines were also targeted.[99] The fate of the rural areas in the rest of the province did not greatly concern the mining company. As far as it was concerned, the Haut-Luapula District, Tanganika-Moero District, and the extreme north could be left to their own devices.[100]

Large-scale abandonment of ancestral lands was the order of the day after the failed insurrection. For example, at Befale, a chieftaincy on the border between Kasai and Katanga, the number of inhabitants dropped from 53,000 to 43,000 by 1945. Most of those Africans who abandoned the rural areas went toward the towns or else deep into the forest lands. Tens of thousands of young men and women as well as adolescents fled to the industrial towns and the workers' camps, thus further unhinging rural life.[101] Despite the mining company's burgeoning influence, the western portion of Katanga also experienced a rural outpouring. After 1944 the number of Africans in the western region who left their home villages increased by almost 10 percent. But they did not leave the western region entirely. Rather, they were shepherded in ever-increasing numbers to the newly opened cobalt, uranium, and manganese mines.[102]

The persistence of unrest on the western mines, even after the defeat of the 1944 insurrection and the accession of the colonial government's candidate, Mwaant Yav Ditende, to the Lunda paramountcy, compelled the Union Minière to bypass the colonial government in bringing the region to heel.[103] Increasingly, the mining company entered into relationships with rural strong men—many of whom were petty entrepreneurs or, in some cases, black marketeers— to garner support for its edicts and policies. Perhaps the most notable of these strong men in the late 1940s and early 1950s were Tshombe Kapenda Joseph and his two sons, Moise and Daniel.[104] These relationships with a nascent African lumpen bourgeoisie, along with the company's efforts to introduce corporatist industrial councils in lieu of trade unions, served to blunt the newly acquired class consciousness of many of the mineworkers while giving their aspirations a more populist character.[105]

Since wages had increased so rapidly after the general strike and failed insurrection, even though they continued to lag pitifully behind inflation, the appointment of African representatives to the industrial councils was neither a hurried nor completely token gesture.[106] Most of the Africans selected to sit on the industrial councils by the companies were those who had benefitted from the rapid wage increases—foremen and social assistants; yet a respectable number of decidedly more militant workers were selected to sit on the councils by the workers themselves. Initially the councils were seen as a means to implement the new "color bar," or graduated wage policy. But by 1948–49, as the more militant workers gained the upper hand in the councils, the industrial companies—particularly the Union Minière—began to have second thoughts about their efficacy.[107]

Katanga's mineworkers, as well as millions of other Africans throughout the Belgian Congo, realized that their accession to political power would entail the administration of a vast and complex political organism. Consequently, the miners and other segments of the industrial working class were prompted to give their contingent support to what seemed to be a more parochial version of political independence—a version that did not envision the dismantling of the Union Minière. Into the political impasse created by the mineworkers' reservations stepped men like Moise Tshombe.[108]

While both he and his father, Joseph, served on the Provincial Council of Katanga from 1947 to 1956, Moise Tshombe shrewdly avoided any association with the industrial councils and with an economic and social policy that sanctioned racial discrimination.[109] Tshombe, then, was less a leader of the mineworkers than a spokesman who appeared to be against the implementation of a wage policy based on the South African "color bar."[110] Because of his mother's blood ties to two of the lines of the Lunda royal family and his father's entrepreneurial skills, he was able to wear simultaneously the face of an aristocrat and an *évolué* in his forays among the workers. Until 1957, he kept his connections to the Union Minière's administration loose and ambiguous.[111] As far as the miners could see, Tshombe's position in the unfolding political drama in Katanga was one of opposition to the mining company's wage policy.

Fully cognizant of this, Tshombe formed his base of operations among the workers at Kolwezi and the outlying mines instead of at Elisabethville and Jadotville.[112] Exercising extreme caution, he entrenched himself at those points of the mining complex where the African workers had been defeated early on by the Union Minière's counteroffensive against the 1941 strikes, or where labor radicalism had been transformed into millennial expectation. However, with the defeat of the 1944 insurrection, millennial beliefs began to wear thin among the African mineworkers. The connection between the mining company's quest for a greater portion of the workers' labor power and its intrusive presence in their lives after work became painfully obvious. The workers came to understand these two different manifestations of power as obverse sides of the same phenomenon. Consequently, a transformation of the mineworkers' consciousness did take place. The impact of the local setting, however, continued to remain important in determining its forms of expression.

The 1941 strike movement and the failed 1944 provincial insurrection, therefore, were not "disturbances," for it could not be said that social peace had been effectively established in Katanga at any point prior to their occurrences. Nor can it be said that the strikes and insurrection "erupted," for it was fairly obvious that in previous times the mineworkers and the other African protagonists simply bowed to the combined superior force of the mining company and the state in order to prevent more bloodshed—not because they had come to share either's sense of justice. Both the strike movement and the insurrection had been seething for a long time.

The scale of the workplace and its proximity to the company and provincial government's administrative center greatly influenced how readily workers sought to intervene in redressing what they deemed intolerable or unjust living and working conditions. At work sites where large concentrations of skilled African workers modified the existing chain of authority, workers quickly learned how to test the validity of the company's demands against their own frustrated and misunderstood expectations. It was on these work sites—often peripheral in location but strategic in terms of the company's wartime production—that workers made the sharpest break with existing authority. The regime was found wanting. The mining company's attempt to blur the distinction between its desire for profits and the needs of society was fully exposed. As the ground rules of industrial production shifted, those workers who were skilled and conversant with but unencumbered by custom and tradition played a key role in transforming the various groups of African mineworkers into a conscious mining proletariat. By the close of the Second World War their struggle against the mining company had made an impact on the entire population of Katanga.

CHAPTER NINE

Conclusion

THE MATURATION OF THE WORKING CLASS

The wealth of the Congo is incalculable. During these war years what tremendous riches have been sent to the white man's countries. How much of this has been used for the benefit of the natives? Does the government really need the pitiful tax that the native often has to sell his chickens and his goats to pay? Look at the exports: Diamonds, gold, copper, tin, iron, manganese, raw silver, platinum, cobalt, uranium, coal and other minerals; cotton, rubber, cocoa, coffee, castor oil, tobacco, corn, manioc, palm oil and nuts, sesame, copal, pepper, sugar, peanuts, raphia, etc. . . . What a howl this would occasion were the shoe placed on the other foot!

> excerpt from a deposition taken from John Morrison for the OSS, 20 July 1945[1]

The present rate of pay is 2, 3, or 4 francs per day. What can be said of those who make speeches proclaiming the progress of the natives, but who pay them ten times less than Europeans they replaced. . . .

> excerpt from an editorial by Emile Dehoux in *L'Informateur*, 23 November 1949[2]

The experiences of Katanga's mineworkers demonstrate that the economic exploitation of the African continent was a much more subtle proposition than many historians of colonial Africa have made it out to be. Despite official explanation, Belgian rule in the Congo was never philanthropic. In Katanga especially, it was more a creature of an increasing scale of economic exploitation than philanthropy.[3] If the process took a protracted form, it was not out of concern for the African's welfare. Rather, the weakness of Katanga's provincial government in relation to the power and influence of the Union

Minière compelled it to go slowly in its attempt to expand its authority. Only when the mining company was being encroached upon by foreign capital or when it was in a phase of reconstruction could the state really assert itself and give form to the nascent working class.

Contrary to the received wisdom, the overwhelming influence of the mining company over the colonial government was neither fortuitous nor a "historical accident."[4] After 1926 its control over the state was the logical culmination of its social and economic policies. Yet the state remained, in some ways, autonomous. Rather than Plato's trim, efficient state machinery, it resembled Hobbes's bustling and organically contentious Leviathan.[5] Where the state adopted an authoritarian stance with the African workers, it did so less out of reason than fear and an inability to see its alternatives clearly. The formation of Katanga's provincial secret police was the quintessential expression of this hit-and-miss policy.

The mining company did not come suddenly to this more hegemonic view of its control over the state. For example, between 1927 and 1931, the state and the mining company appeared to exchange places. The results of the attempted switch were disastrous. The provincial government was left almost powerless to mediate disputes between the mining company and its workers. This was especially so in the smaller boomtowns such as Ruashi and Kipushi, where the company's European foremen and camp managers, along with the native tribunals, often undermined the authority of the colonial army and the police tribunals. The persistence of corporal punishment on the work sites, the introduction of piece rates, and the subsequent decline in the wage rate for skilled and semiskilled African workers threw the state's authority further into question. The collapse of world copper prices in 1931 created a general atmosphere of uncertainty in Katanga. Having undermined both the police powers of the state and the most experienced and skilled strata of African workers just before the collapse, the mining company unwittingly provoked the labor unrest of 1931.

The repression of the 1931 unrest was the catalyst for the creation of the provincial secret police and the emergence of white opposition to the corporate policies of the Union Minière. It also presaged a new working relationship between the mining company and the state. For although the small European farmers and retail merchants disagreed violently with the company about how the state's institutions were to be refashioned in order to police the African population better, all quarters of European opinion agreed that the African workers' heightened awareness of the class and racial basis of colonial rule had to be stanched. Yet the short-lived efforts of usurping the mining company's influence over the state forced the Union Minière into a speedy consummation of its new relationship with the provincial administration, a relationship in which the state became the mining company's junior partner in the attempt to reconstruct the industry's profitability. The collapse of the global economy reinforced the urgency of the new phase of limited collaboration. And after the quelling of the unrest, the provincial government became more deliberate in its attempts to arrest the burgeoning social consciousness of the urban and rural African population.

Despite the Union Minière's and the provincial government's new priorities, labor unrest continued. Arson and sabotage were frequent at the new and more mechanized work sites such as Luishia, Musonoi, and Kakontwe. Absconding not only persisted but also took on a more instrumental character. Flight often became a means to bargain with the company for specific concessions for some workers. Neither the mining company nor the provincial government was prepared for this new dimension of worker protest. Consequently, the spiral of worker protest continued to grow throughout the Second World War. Moreover, the anticlimactic rebellion of 1944 showed further that the provincial government was in fact drenched in the blood of the workers and its other African subjects. Yet the workers were not always victims of a grinding repression. Nor were they always the recipients of the benefits of a sophisticated system of rewards, protection, and control.[6] By the middle of the 1930s, when the mining company was just beginning to acquire something more than formal control over its African workers, the reality of the workers' condition lay somewhere between these two extremes.

THE SETTLING OF TRADITIONS

Despite the brutal nature of colonial rule and the overtly coercive features of the wage labor system, Katanga's mineworkers managed to form a rich and useful set of traditions. The growth of the lodges and friendly societies among the workers was a case in point. During the 1920s the lodges proved the intrinsic value of cooperation among workers from different ethnic backgrounds at the workplace. The lodges of Luba-speaking and Chokwe workers from Lomami, Kasai, and central Katanga were perhaps more successful than others. They were closed forms of association, however, which selected their

members on the basis of a given worker's ethnic or regional ante-
cedents. African Watchtower, on the other hand, was an open form
of association whose two points of entry into Katanga—one via the
Lamba, Aushi, and Lala in the Luapula Valley and the other by way
of the Luba-Hemba on the western banks of Lake Tanganyika—were
initially too removed from the birthplaces of the lodges to allow for
cross-fertilization.[7] Yet by the mid-1930s many mineworkers had
become adherents of Watchtower, and had even produced some of
the sect's most powerful adepts and proselytizers. But this occurred
only after the lodges had been uprooted by the police and the military
or had collapsed under their own weight.

Workers who arrived at the work sites between the repression of
the 1931 unrest and the emergence of a new wave of worker protest
at the end of 1936 were to discover that a broader base of solidarity
than what the lodges provided was needed to negotiate wage labor
and life in the workers' camps. Moreover, toward the end of the 1930s,
an increasing number of the more skilled and literate African miners
and industrial workers began to believe that they at least deserved
economic equality with the white workers of the province. Liberals
like Auguste Verbeken convinced many of them that most government officials above the provincial level thought similarly.[8] Unable
to comprehend fully the source of the change in the attitudes and
disposition of the African workers, European foremen and supervisors
were content to believe that the new methods of repression and social
control—particularly the relegation of factory operatives and skilled
workers to the more removed work sites—would deflate such aspirations. But the conjuncture achieved by the suspension of recruitment
for the outlying mines and the relegation of factory operatives and
skilled workers to these very same mines deepened and embellished
the new current of protest; for despite the deliberate nature of the
transfers, many of the more militant workers were not broken by this
relegation. Moreover, many of their comrades managed to slip
through the company's dragnet.[9] The widespread receptiveness of the
factory operatives at Shituru, Panda, and Lubumbashi to the goals
of the general strike proved this conclusively. The rapid growth of
a factory proletariat, which included skilled workers in the machin-
ing and engineering trades, powerfully underscored the articulation
of class feeling among the African workers.

Despite the burgeoning character of urban and proletarian traditions, the African mineworkers did not break cleanly with their rural
past. The retention of rural mores and connections with their former
villages continued to be an important component of survival on the

work sites and in the workers' camps. By the end of the 1930s these connections to the rural African world became a source of leadership in the form of the worker-peddler networks as well as marijuana, food, and home-brewed liquor. The workers' continued attachment to the rural world acquired a new significance in the 1930s because of the changing social context of colonial society and wage labor. The legal and social restraints imposed on the African workers by colonial rule reinforced their refusal to dispense totally with rural habits of thinking. Moreover, despite its claims, the mining company fell very much short of total control over the African workforce. By the onset of the Second World War the gap between the significance of individual and collective African responses to company policy and the perception of these responses by European foremen and company officers had grown very wide indeed — so wide that the mining company's African workers felt obliged to challenge the company's control over the pace of industrial expansion and community life.

With the defeat of the 1941 strike movement and the 1944 rebellion, the Union Minière and the provincial government beat back the two most formidable African challenges to Belgian rule in the Congo up to that point. But unlike the labor unrest of the previous decade, the strikes and the rebellion three years later were not simply spasmodic responses to worsening economic conditions. Preparations for the period of war production had given labor organization and the work routine an increasingly industrialized character. The new emphasis on the individual productivity of each African worker as well as total output marked an important change in the outlook of both workers and management. Consequently, as events and circumstances moved toward the wartime strikes, even the African mutual aid societies and lodges took a more combative stance with respect to company policy. The African workers' quest for power and better organization, at least on a local level, merged with African discontent over rising prices. Organization had become as important as the more immediate issues of productivity and escalating prices. Progress, in the form of the basic preconditions of industrial class formation, had become imminent.

The problem of organization presented itself in two different forms, however. The most proletarianized sectors of the company's workers at the central and southern work sites became the men of the hour once the strike commenced. But the leadership of the factory operatives, industrial artisans, and underground workers was short-lived. The entrance of the military and the show of force that ensued crushed them underfoot. Their greatest advantage was their ability to occupy and hold the workplace. Once the mining company retook Panda and Lubumbashi in the wake of the massacres perpetrated by the military, the African strikers' basis of support fell away rapidly. What they needed after the intervention of the troops was a broader base of support among the Africans in the villages and squatters' areas surrounding the work sites. Support from rural communities in their home regions was also necessary. The factory and underground workers could not marshal such support. Thus, after the second week of the strike, the baton of leadership passed to other hands.

By this point in the strike new leadership emerged at the outlying mines. Instead of striking exclusively for higher wages and recognition for African-initiated forms of local organization, this wing of the strike's leadership called for an end to Belgian rule over the Congo and for the forcible expulsion of their colonial masters. Former peddlers and ambulant traders who were forced into the ranks of Union Minière's African workforce at the outset of the war composed a large portion of this stratum of leadership. The increase in both retail and wholesale prices squeezed most of the African traders into the colonial workforce. This group of semiproletarians began to acquire its latent sense of nationalism in the marketplace for its labor power. Yet its constituency on the work sites such as Kikole, Kolwezi, and Busanga was unable to muster the necessary armed support to overthrow the regime. Religious millennarianism grew where armed force should have been brought to bear. But because the workers on the outlying mines had been relatively removed from the massacres at Panda and Lubumbashi, it was not difficult for some of them to join with soldiers of the Force Publique in the attempt to foment a provincial insurrection three years later.

The strike wave at the Union Minière and the failed provincial rebellion were virtual models of combined but uneven development.[10] Both illustrated the degree to which the uneven character of industrialization had been inscribed in the political views of the African mineworkers. Rural and "modern" values were not mutually exclusive for the African miners. However, the social lag between workers on the more centrally located work sites and those on the outlying mines was real. It was perhaps the single most important factor in the defeat of a general strike. The political and social restrictions imposed on the workers underscored their economic compartmentalization. Without the right to express their political and social opinions freely, the African workers had no means for adequately counterposing their own power to the economic might and political access of the Union Minière. One cannot overestimate the importance of this factor in bringing about the defeat of the mineworkers in 1941 and that of the insurgent microcosm of workers, soldiers, and peasants in 1944.

Despite the failure of the general strike and provincial insurrection, the African mineworkers moved from the "singular vocabulary of motives" of village life to something akin to class consciousness.[11] This new awareness of the fundamental nature of colonial society in Katanga was fixed within the framework of a set of new urban traditions that had crystallized in the middle and late 1930s. Even though this new awareness came initially in the utopian dress of African Watchtower and was inadequately orchestrated by armed and political force, it helped to clarify the differences between the new proletarian way of thinking and the thought processes that had governed the African workers' behavior on the eve of the 1931 unrest. The African workers had been defeated, but they had resisted the mining company's efforts at socially engineering their personalities.

CONCLUSION

Many of the weaknesses of recent studies of industrial workers in southern Africa derive from an overly narrow conceptualization of the problem of worker consciousness.[12] Much has been written about how employers in southern Africa sought either to "stabilize" African workers or to keep them oscillating between town and countryside in order to gain control of the wage bill; to splice the social ties between African workers and peasants along "tribal" lines; and to marshal the combined forces of the state, capital, white settlers, and an infinitesimal white working class to keep African workers safely within the urban locations and workers' compounds.[13] As recent work suggests, the evidence can be read in more than one way.[14]

The tension between southern Africa's old and new labor history is a result of the confusion between a heuristic and a purely descriptive use of the term "worker stabilization." Along with terms such as "desertion" and "deserter," "stabilization" contributes to a vocabulary which, in many instances, trivializes the experiences of working people in southern Africa.[15] Like the concept of social control, stabilization is a subjective entity, which is generalizable to the point of meaninglessness.[16] No one thus far, for example, has ever recorded the thoughts of any individual African worker or any group of African workers who felt themselves to be "stabilized."

"Stabilization" does have some value as a descriptive term, however—as a historical artifact by means of which industrial firms in

southern Africa chose to obfuscate a drastic reduction in the rate of
what they were willing to pay in order to maintain and reproduce
subsequent generations of African workers.[17] Coming in the
mid-1920s — and borrowed from the arcane language of European
statesmen who were attempting an explanation of the soaring monetary inflation of the early and mid-1920s — stabilization was designed
to legitimate a culture of deference based upon physical coercion and
racial superiority at the workplace and in the society at large.[18] As
such, it was an ideological means by which industry's owners skewed
the political calculus of increased production in their favor.

By focussing too much on management's justification of these policies and too little on the worker's response to them, many historians
of the region have passed over some of the most important features of
its history.[19] Consequently, when contemporary labor historians
of southern Africa combine stabilization's terminology with what one
might call a "volcanic vocabulary" — of which a phrase like "a disturb-
ance erupted" is characteristic — the results often obscure more than
they reveal.[20] For in its original intellectual context, stabilization
assumed a set of preconceived results as it went about describing the
nature of wage labor and the way in which it impinged upon the consciousness of African workers. Its power to apprehend the actual
condition of the workforce was therefore metaphorical at best.[21]

Although Katanga's mineworkers rarely saw themselves as agents
of their own political empowerment before the end of the Second
World War, the yearning for mastery over the local circumstances of
work and town life was pervasive. Moreover, the workers came to
see that ethnic particularism could be as much an obstacle as a
shelter. Protest often rushed out of the turbulent pools of everyday
life under colonial rule and was exacerbated by the contradictory
demands of the productive process. All of these developments bore
importantly on the African workers' assessment of the ultimate meaning and objectives of colonial rule.[22]

The failed general strike and provincial insurrection marked the
beginning of the end of the colonial order in Katanga. They provided
the essential choreography for the force and violence that compelled
the Belgian administration to relinquish its hold on the Congo less
than a generation later. Many of the African miners who were alive
during this period did not live to see independence. But the events
of their own time — particularly the strike movement and failed provincial insurrection — had at least given them a glimmer of power.

Epilogue

New Battles, Old Terrain: A Note on the Conseils indigènes d'Entreprise

Perhaps the most concrete expression of the workers' new vision of power came out of their participation in the *conseils indigènes d'entreprise* (CIE), or industrial councils. All enterprises having at least 100 employees were obliged to form such councils. Many firms which had between 75 and 100 workers set up councils as well. From their inception in 1946, the councils grew rapidly. Their growth was especially marked between the middle of 1948 and the end of 1949, when their number increased from 94 to 147.[1]

Within this brief period, a point of conjuncture was achieved between the aspirations of the workers and the declining political fortunes of one of their archenemies, Governor Henri-Léon Keyser. In September 1948 Keyser was forced to step down as governor because the provincial court of appeals threw out a libel suit in which he claimed that the newspaper *Echo du Katanga* had falsely accused him of misappropriating government funds. The court proceedings, which dragged on from April to September 1948, demonstrated that Keyser had, in fact, stolen money and materials from the provincial government to build himself a palatial private residence. African court recorders unofficially circulated portions of the trial's transcripts; and for six full months *Echo du Katanga* reported the details of the case on its front page.[2] The workers and the rest of the African population of Elisabethville followed the proceedings closely, since this was no ordinary *muzungu* (white person or European) who was being disgraced and made to account for himself, but the representative of the king and the ally of the industrial firms such as the Union Minière. The myth of Belgium's absolute power, which had begun to dissipate during the war, was now very nearly exhausted. For Keyser had also been the former head of the provincial secret police. He directed the suppression of Watchtower adherents and striking workers between 1942 and 1946, sequestering hundreds of them in the military prison at Albertville. Now his own name was on the docket. To the workers, justice appeared to be literally reverberating through the corridors of power, shaking them to their very foundations. Old scores appeared on the verge of being settled.

By 1950, however, the workers' representatives on the industrial councils were forced to go on the defensive. In Elisabethville 45 of the councils were disbanded. The authorities claimed that the "instability" of African labor in the smaller companies had compelled them to dissolve some of the councils. One official claimed that the bannings were necessary "because one can find no trace of a spirit of mutual interest or concern for the company among the workers." What the official meant was that the councils had indeed fostered a group spirit among the workers, but one that was inimical to the interest of their employers. The workers continued to be enthusiastic about the councils, but their enthusiasm centered around issues and expectations that the industrial companies and the state viewed as antithetical to industrial expansion at best and subversive at worst.[3]

Initially the industrial councils met every three months, but by the end of 1950 the government decided that they should meet every six instead. From the outset of Keyser's trial a core of the same demands were made by the workers' representatives in every industrial council from Elisabethville to Albertville — to the point that the government's representatives and those of the private firms claimed that such demands had become a general slogan:

Apart from several specific questions, the same demands are made everywhere — so much so, that they are beginning to sound like a slogan. . . .

The exchange of views in the councils does allow for a line of discussion which might, with time, improve some situations and thus prevent them from becoming serious problems; but they, on the other hand, have not fostered a sense of professionalism among the workers or a desire to be more attentive to the needs of their employers.[4]

The most immediate reason for the reduction of the number of meetings was that issues were taken up spontaneously from the floor by the workers' representatives before the European advisers to the various African syndicates and workers' committees could render them innocuous. Consequently, the ordinance of 1 August 1949 on the compensation of workers for injuries sustained at work, that of 1 July 1950 on compensation for work-related illnesses, and that of 16 March 1950, which reinstated the Inspectorate of Labor, were promulgated before the state and the employers could really assess what had happened. What lay behind the demands of the workers' representatives? Most of them, on the face of it, seemed innocent enough. But when examined more closely, even the more innocuous ones reveal that complaints of a more political nature, or at least ones that raised the prospect of social equality between Europeans and Africans, were concealed within the routinized and choreographed grievance procedure. For example, the workers at the Tenke-Tshilongo camp of the BCK asked that a new camp be built and also that, while the company was building the new camp, a search be made for a new camp manager. Doubtless the dismissal of the camp manager was what the workers really wanted, but they had to approach the prospect of getting rid of him disingenuously, so as not to ruffle the sensibilities of the more powerful whites. After some deliberation and jockeying, the new camp was built. But given the circumstances, the BCK thought it prudent to retain the old camp manager.[5]

As mentioned earlier, there were other grievances that were striking, not only because they persisted over time, but also because they were very nearly universal among the African workers. As a result of the employers' alleged willingness to increase wages in relation to proficiency, output, and skill, factory workers at the Union Minière's Jadotville plants and at the company's subsidiary Sogechim asked that any honorific awards bestowed upon them become the equivalent of a *carte de mérit civique* — the card given to *évolués*, or Africans whose civil rights were the same as Europeans. Skilled workers at Bozzone Frères, Pileri, and Public Works, all in Katanga, made similar demands.[6] The demand for night schools was tangential to the one for more civil rights. Workers at virtually all the companies wanted night schools for themselves and their children. They also wanted a course in French taught at such schools. The majority of these requests were denied.[7]

There were also grievances and demands which had the workers' desire for a higher standard of living inscribed in them. Hence the demand for higher wages was merely the tip of the iceberg. Workers at UMHK-Jadotville, UMHK-Shinkolobwe, Sogechim, and BCK-Lubudi wanted individual toilets as opposed to latrines; those at UMHK-Kolwezi, Pileri, Safricas, UMHK-Shituru, and Vielvoie wanted to be able to buy or improve their houses. Almost all the workers wanted better lighting in their homes and neighborhoods, better roads and streets, larger and more accessible stores, motorized hearses for funerals, and better-maintained cemeteries. They also wanted canteens and bars in the workers' camps, the camp policemen disarmed, some insurance that camp managers and foremen would be compelled to listen to their complaints by virtue of institutional constraints, and permission to purchase firearms.[8] None of these requests received a positive judgment.

The workers were also concerned about those of their comrades who had been grossly victimized by the arbitrary judgment of an employer or foreman. Numerous instances came before the councils where workers with 20 years or more of seniority had been dismissed for minor offenses. In such cases, in the columns alongside the written transcripts of the meetings, one often finds the brusque and insensitive conclusion *"procédure irregulière"* or *"recidiviste"* — or, when the arbitrators felt a greater need to justify the short shrift they had given such cases and to protect themselves from future recrimination, *"soumis à l'avis de l'Administration"* or *"se fait à l'intervention de l'Administration."*[9]

Perhaps the most banal and self-serving demands came from the European foremen at the Union Minière's uranium mine at Shinkolobwe — they asked that the workers' representatives on the council wind up their demands quickly and without verbal remonstration. The minutes noted that the undercurrent of rage among the workers' representatives was almost visible at that point in the session. On the following day the workers' representatives from the nearby Pacquay Construction Company asked to be allowed to set up their own tribunals without the intervention of the foremen or the European counselors.[10]

That Africans could now bring forth the same demands and grievances that they had been voicing for a long time under the shadow of dismissal or imprisonment in a government-sponsored forum must have been both exasperating and ominous for their employers and government officials. For one must keep in mind that this sharp, albeit choreographed, form of class struggle was taking place less than 10 years after the 1941 strike wave at the Union Minière and less than 5 years after the failed provincial insurrection. The industrial councils were dismantled shortly after 1951, for as the proceedings of the council demonstrated, widespread repression had not fundamentally changed the workers' aspirations.

Notes
Bibliography
Index

Notes

Introduction

1 Quoted in Richard Mahoney, *JFK: Ordeal in Africa* (New York: Oxford University Press, 1984), 43.

2 Bwelenge and I encountered each other on a bus going to the towns of Mulungwishi and Kasumbalesa.

3 Rich descriptions of how this objective was to be realized take up much of the space in the official colonial journals from the 1920s on; see Felix Varbeke, "Du régime de la main-d'oeuvre," *Congo. Revue générale de la colonie* 2, no. 2 (juillet 1921): 176–80. For a good description of the cumulative effect of such policies, see T. O. Ranger, *Dance and Society in Eastern Africa* (Berkeley: University of California Press, 1975), 1.

4 See Pierre Ryckmans, *Dominer pour servir* (Bruxelles: Editions universelle, 1948).

5 Some recent works on industrial workers elsewhere in southern Africa have touched on these problems. Perhaps the best overall piece of work on the subject has been Charles van Onselen's *Chibaro*, which is concerned with the plight of African mineworkers in Southern Rhodesia. However, van Onselen and another historian of the region, Ian Phimister, have recently begun to rework some of the more ambiguous points of *Chibaro*. They have done this through a series of recent essays in the *Journal of Southern African Studies* and in a two-volume study entitled *New Nineveh* and *New Babylon*. See I. R. Phimister and C. van Onselen, eds., *Studies in the History of African Mine Labour in Colonial Zimbabwe* (Gwelo: Mambo Press, 1978); see also I. R. Phimister and C. van Onselen, "The Political Economy of Tribal Animosity: A Case Study of the 1929 Bulawayo Location Faction Fight," *Journal of Southern African Studies* 6, 1 (October 1979): 1–44; Charles van Onselen, *New Nineveh* and *New Babylon*, Vols. 1 and 2 of *Studies in the Social and Economic History of the Witwatersrand* (London: Longman, 1982); and Charles van Onselen, *Chibaro* (London: Pluto Press, 1976).

6 Jean Stengers, "Léopold II et la rivalité franco-anglaise en Afrique, 1882–1884," *Revue belge de philologie et d'histoire* 47 (1969): 425–79; Robert Lemoine, "La Concentration des énterprises dans la mise en valeur du Congo," *Annales d'histoire economique et sociale* 29 (30 septembre 1934): 437. Such attempts at redrafting the society's demographic features to fit more explicit forms of repression have been much

223

appreciated by subsequent regimes; see: Conseil de province du Katanga (Comptes-rendus des séances), 1951, Annexe I, Question No. 1: Recensement et identification des indigènes, 58; John Vinocur, "Zaire's Capital Puts on a Sunday Look for Visitors," *New York Times* (11 October 1982): 4; also see Lemarchand Collection, Hoover Institution on War, Revolution, and Peace (henceforth LCHI), Congo Belge, Administration de la Sûreté, Notice relative à l'Association Lulua-Frères, 1947, Elisabethville; Conseil de province du Katanga (Comptes-rendus des séances), 1946, Etat d'espirit des populations indigènes, 11 octobre 1946.

7	See Anatole Romaniuk, *La Fécondité des populations congolaises* (Paris: Mouton, 1967); Léopold Mottoulle, "L'Aspect social de l'attraction exercée par les centres urbains et industriels sur les populations Baluba du Congo Belge: Populations rurales de province de Lusambo," *INCIDI* (1952): 304–9; Johannes Fabian, "Popular Culture in Africa: Findings and Conjectures," *Africa* 48, 4 (1978): 317.

8	Léopold Mottoulle, "Contribution à l'étude de déterminisme fonctionnel de l'industrie dans l'education de l'indigène Congolaise," *Bulletin de l'Institut royal colonial belge* (1934): 210–15; J. Gouverneur, *Productivity and Factor Proportions in Less Developed Countries* (Oxford: Oxford University Press, 1971), 80–92; Charles Perrings, *Black Mineworkers in Central Africa* (London: Holmes and Meier, 1979), 250–60.

9	See Marie-Claire Lambert-Culot, "Les Premières Années en Afrique du Comité special du Katanga," *Etudes d'histoire africaine* 3 (1972): 304–17; Lemoine, "La Concentration des énterprises," 437; Jerome Sternstein, "The Strange Beginnings of American Economic Penetration of the Congo," *African Historical Studies* 3, 2 (1969): 190.

10	J. Wilmet, *La Repartition de la population dans la depression des rivières Mufuvya et Lufira (Haut-Katanga)* (Liege: Fonds nationale de recherche scientifique, 1961), 5–13.

11	During the colonial period these settlements shifted to the northern upcountry regions and the southern plateaus. The mining and rail industries periodically drew a migrant labor force from them to supplement the levies of workers coming from the neighboring colonies. See Wilmet, *La Repartition,* 5–14; Fernand Grevisse, "Salines et saliniers indigènes du Haut-Katanga," *Bulletin du CEPSI* 11 (1950); see also: Jean-Luc Vellut, "Rural Poverty in Western Shaba," in *The Roots of Rural Poverty in Central and Southern Africa,* ed. Robin Palmer and Neil Parsons (Berkeley: University of California Press, 1977), 301–5; Jan Vansina, *Introduction à l'ethnographie du Congo* (Bruxelles: Editions CRISP, 1966), 7–12; Edmond Leplae, "Histoire et développement des cultures obligatoires de coton et de riz au Congo Belge de 1917 à 1933," *Congo. Revue générale de la colonie* 5, no. 5 (mai 1933): 646; and William Hance, *The Geography of Modern Africa* (New York: Columbia University Press, 1964), 313.

12 Of this time in Katanga's history, a former provincial commissioner of Katanga and amateur historian Fernand Grevisse said this:

> While insuring relative tranquility and security in the country, and by simultaneously establishing economic ties between the most removed peoples of the Luapula, Lualaba, Lulua, Zambezi and so on, the Lunda created a major commercial current in Central Africa by conquest. They gave a wider currency to the value of local products – copper and salt in particular. (Grevisse, "Salines et saliniers indigènes," 19)

If one ignores the politics of Grevisse's time – the Belgian colonial government, holding the Lunda paramount chieftain firmly in its grip by 1950, was concerned to make his ancestors greater conquerors than they were – and replaces Lunda with Luba and Lunda Kazembe, one has a fairly accurate picture of the events of the day. See also Andrew Roberts, "Pre-Colonial Trade in Zambia," *African Social Research* (10 December 1970): 728; Christopher St. John, "Kazembe and the Tanganyika-Nyasa Corridor, 1800–1900," in *Pre-Colonial African Trade*, ed. Richard Gray and David Birmingham (London: Cambridge University Press, 1970), 212; for a broader, regional examination of these developments, see: D. N. Beach, *The Shona and Zimbabwe, 900–1850* (London: Heinemann, 1980); Andrew D. Roberts, *A History of the Bemba* (Madison: University of Wisconsin Press, 1973); Luc de Heusch, *Le Roi ivre ou l'origine de l'etat* (Paris: Gallimard, 1972); Jan Vansina, *The Children of Woot* (Madison: University of Wisconsin Press, 1978); John K. Thornton, *The Kingdom of Kongo* (Madison: University of Wisconsin Press, 1983).

13 See, for example, Joseph Miller, "Chokwe Trade and Conquest in the Nineteenth Century," in *Pre-Colonial African Trade*, ed. Richard Gray and David Birmingham (London: Cambridge University Press, 1970), 189–90; see also Jacques Jean-Marie François Depelchin, "From Pre-Capitalism to Imperialism: Social and Economic Formations in Eastern Zaire, 1880–1960 (Uvira Zone)" (Ph.D. dissertation, Stanford University, 1974); Mugeya Mukome, "Kalemie: Des origines à 1935," *Likundoli* 2 (1974): 10–14.

14 Consider the Kambove-Ruwe region, for example: this region is a 4,000-square-kilometer natural depression bounded by the Lualaba and Lufira rivers and intersected by the Biano Plateau and Dipompa Mountains. A century ago the majority of the people in the area lived north of the mountains. Today they have been squeezed into the relatively inarable hinterland of Likasi, the most industrialized city of Shaba, whose land area is a little more than one-twentieth the size of the northern agricultural redoubt. See Wilmet, *La Repartition*, 13; Romaniuk, *La Fécondité*, 157–69; Wa Nsanga Mukendi, "Le Gisment de manganese de Kisenge: Source de croissance de pauperisation," *Bulletin de Gécamines* (Maadini) 8, 4 trimestre (1975); Hance, *The Geography*, 332.

15 Conseil de province du Katanga, 1951, Question No. 1: Recensement

et identification des indigènes; see also James Scott, *The Moral Economy of the Peasant* (New Haven: Yale University Press, 1976), 13–34.

16 Lambert-Culot, "Les Premières Années," passim; Lemoine, "La Concentration des éntreprises," passim.

17 See Lemoine, "La Concentration des éntreprises," 437; recent years have seen a marked upshot of such problems as research topics in the social history of Europe and America. The recent work of John Foster and Gareth Stedman Jones, working in the middle and late nineteenth-century England, respectively, Herbert Gutman and David Montgomery in the nineteenth-century America, and Joan Scott in the late nineteenth-century France are some of the most representative examples. See: John Foster, *Class Struggle and the Industrial Revolution* (London: St. Martin's Press, 1974); Herbert Gutman, "Le Phénomène invisible: La Composition de la famille et du foyers noirs après la Guerre de Secession," *Annales: economies, sociétés et civilisations* 27e année, no. 45 (juillet-octobre 1972); Joan Scott, *The Glassworkers of Carmaux* (Cambridge: Harvard University Press, 1974); Catherine Coquery-Vidrovitch, *Le Congo au temps des grandes compagnies concessionaires: 1898–1930* (Paris: Mouton, 1972); Gareth Stedman Jones, *Languages of Class* (New York: Cambridge University Press, 1982); David Montgomery, *Workers' Control in America* (London: Cambridge University Press, 1979).

18 Perrings, *Black Mineworkers*, 8–9.

19 Pierre Paul Leroy-Beaulieu, *De la colonisation chez peuples modernes*, cinquième édition, Vol. 1 (Paris: Editions Guillaumin, 1902), 324.

20 Ibid., 331; "La Situation industrielle en Belgique," *L'Economiste française* (1 avril 1888); J. L. de Lanessan, "La Crise coloniale," *Revue économique internationale* 4ème année, 3, no. 4 (avril 1907), 7; British Public Record Office (henceforth BPRO), file FB/FO-10-757, fiche 228, no. 32, Correspondence of Constantine Phipps [1897].

21 *Documents parlementaires*, no. 59, Annexe I, no. 129, "Chambre des representants project de loi approuvant l'acte additionel en traite de cession de l'Etat independant du Congo à Belgique," séance du 5 mars 1908 (Bruxelles, 1908), 2; BPRO, file FO-84/1203, fiche 148, Letters on Public Opinion in Belgium from Sir E. Monson to the Earl of Rosebery, 19 November 1892; Maxime Steinberg, "La Crise congolaise dans le parti ouvrier belge," in *La Deuxième internationale et l'Orient*, ed. G. Haupt and Madeline Reberioux (Paris: Editions Cujas, 1967), 114–17.

22 Industrialization commenced in 1907 with the founding of the Union Minière du Haut-Katanga and the large-scale exploitation of Katanga's copper mines. The Union Minière was unique, however, for although a model of twentieth-century capitalist organization, it maintained direct ties to the royal house of Belgium. These ties were particularly ironic given the inept and bloodstained rule of Léopold II. The participation of the Belgian royal house in the affairs of the mining company

was often mediated, however, by institutions such as the Comité special du Katanga and Societé générale de Belgique. B. S. Chelepner, *Cent ans d'histoire sociale en Belgique* (Bruxelles: Editions de l'Institut de Sociologie Solvay, 1956), 198–99; S. N. Katzenellenbogen, *Railways and the Copper Mines of Katanga* (London: Oxford University Press, 1973), 64–66; Lambert-Culot, "Les Premières Années"; Sternstein, "The Strange Beginnings."

23 Katzenellenbogen, *Railways*, 66–84; see also Archives africaines (henceforth AA), MOI no. 48 (3553), Correspondance de Wangermée, 31 avril 1913; see also Tanganyika Concessions/Union Minière (henceforth TC/UM), 54, Annexe C, Wheeler Report and Recommendations to the Board of UMHK, 16, 31 December 1918.

24 Fernand Lekime, *Katanga: Pays du cuivre* (Bruxelles: Editions Verviers, 1921), 47–56; F. George et J. Gouverneur, "Les Transformations Techniques et l'evolution des coefficients de fabrication à l'Union Minière du Haut-Katanga de 1910 à 1965," *Cultures et développement* 2, no. 1 (1969–70): 53–87.

25 AA, MOI no. 48 (3553), Transmission d'un procès verbal de la comité de direction de la BTK, 19 août 1913, Elisabethville.

26 See "Circonscription indigène," *Revue juridique du Congo Belge* (28 août 1935); see also the archives of the Musée royal de l'Afrique centrale (henceforth MRAC), no. 20 ATA, Lacanne, Enquête politique sur la région du Luapula-Moero, 1935.

27 The original passage reads: "Comme le singe, le noir est imitateur. Il l'est étonnamment. On voit ici, dans les travaux entrepris par les envahisseurs européens, des escouades de maçons, de forgerons, de mécaniciens devenus promptement habiles. . . . C'est cette dexterité indeniable qui, sans doute, à fait naitre l'illusion d'une assimilation complète, par ceux qui n'aperçoivent pas l'abîme qui separe le simple imitateur dès createur. Là, en vérité, semble posée."

28 BPRO, file FB/FO-10-757, encl. 10 in no. 1, fiche 3, Debate in the Belgian Chamber of Deputies on Reprisals after the Buja Rebellion, 24 April 1900, 4.

29 Emile Vandervelde, "Contre la politique coloniale," *Le Peuple* (18 novembre 1908): 2.

30 LCHI, Emile Rolus, A propos du rendement de la main-d'oeuvre indigène (unpublished report), 7, 1950.

31 In a brilliant six pages Poupart discusses this problem under the heading "L'Impulsion Brousse-Ville"; see Robert Poupart, *Facteurs de productivité de la main-d'oeuvre autochtone à Elisabethville* (Bruxelles: Editions de l'Institut de Sociologie Solvay, 1960), 17–23. See also: "Rapport de la commission pour l'étude du problème de la main-d'oeuvre au Congo Belge," *Congo. Revue générale de la colonie* (juin 1925): 1–12 (annexe); Bogumil Jewsiewicki, "La Contestation sociale et la naissance du proletariat au Zaire au cours de la première moitié du xxᵉ siècle," *Revue canadienne des études africaines* 10, 1 (1976): 47–70.

32 The study of popular dances and dance associations as prisms through which the historian can gauge the pulse of the popular classes has just begun in a systematic way for Central Africa. Sparse but incisive passages on the spread of *kalela* and *mbeni* in the industrial areas of Katanga have recently been written by T. O. Ranger. An impressive analysis of the transmission of *kaonge* from Senegal to Katanga is contained in the unpublished memoir of Malira Kubuya-Namulemba. See Ranger, *Dance and Society*, 116–38; Malira Kubuya-Namulemba, "Les Associations féminines de Lubumbashi: 1920–1950" (mémoire de licence, UNAZA, 1972); see also "Crimes et superstitions indigènes: vol et magie (Kimageni)," *Revue juridique du Congo Belge* 4ᵉ année, no. 9 (septembre 1928).

33 AA, MOI no. 4 (3553), Bourse du Travail, Correspondances de Malfeyt, 29 septembre 1913, Bruxelles; AA, MOI no. 59 (3558), Dr. Amar, Examen psycho-physiologique, 17 février 1922.

34 Fernand Dellicour, *Les Premières Années de la cour d'appel d'Elisabethville, 1910-1920* (Bruxelles: Editions Aurore, 1938), 70–81; see also Bruce Fetter, "African Associations in Elisabethville, 1910-1935: Their Origins and Development," *Etudes d'histoire africaine* 2 (1976): 205–20.

35 Archives gécamines (henceforth AG), D6, MOI no. 488 (Annexe I), "Kengere," 1938.

36 For example, see Malira Kubuya-Namulemba, "Regard sur la situation sociale de la citoyenne lushoise d'avant 1950," *Likundoli* 2 (1974): 63–71; see also Tshibangu Kabet Musas, "La Situation sociale dans le ressort administratif de Likasi (ex-territoire de Jadotville) pendant la guerre 1940-45," *Etudes d'histoire africaine* 3 (1974): 282–313.

37 Hardly any of the scholary work pursued in the late 1960s and 1970s on the former Belgian Congo focusses on the mineworkers of Katanga or the Congolese working class in general. Yet the workers' actions on the eve of independence and during subsequent crises explain how the impulse for independence came about in ways that focussing on the *évolués*, or elite Africans, and the peasantry cannot. (For a large portion of the documentary evidence surrounding the rise of Congolese political parties, see Benoit Verhaegen, ed., *Rebellions au Congo*, 2 vols. [Bruxelles: Editions CRISP, 1969].) Of those studies that do focus on the workers, Jacques Kazadi wa Dile's *Politiques et techniques de remuneration dans l'enterprise au Congo* (Kinshasa: Editions Lovanium, 1970), Michel de Schrevel's *Les Forces politiques de la decolonisation congolais jusqu'à la veille de l'independance* (Louvain: Imprimerie M & L Symons, 1970), Johannes Fabian's *Jamaa* (Evanston: Northwestern University Press, 1971), and Charles Perrings' *Black Mineworkers in Central Africa* are the least scathed by indifference to the political capacity of the African workers.

38 See Fabian, *Jamaa*, 14–21; see also Jewsiewicki, "La Contestation sociale," 47–70.

39 Rik Ceyssens, "Mutumbula. Mythe de l'Opprime," *Cultures et développement* 7, 3-4 (1975): 485–550; Fabian, *Jamaa*, 193–97. For an incisive comparative example from Latin America, see Michael T. Taussig, *The Devil and Commodity Fetishism in South America* (Chapel Hill: University of North Carolina Press, 1980).

40 *Jamaa*'s founder and prophet, the Belgian priest Placide Tempels, was not unaware of the secular implications of the sect. The basic ideas of the *jamaa*—at least as far as its founder was concerned—were conceived in Tempels' book *Bantu Philosophy*. Tempels began his book several months after the suppression of the 1944 provincial rebellion in Katanga. He saw the ideas expressed in it as the first step toward a more comprehensive form of counterinsurgency. "Family" was more than a social metaphor; it was a wedge for the interventionist policies of the Union Minière and the colonial state within the African worker household. In fact, Tempels was the author of the anonymous article in *L'Essor du Congo*, "La Philosophie de la rébellion," August 1944. The Flemish edition of *Bantu Philosophy* appeared five months after the suppression of the revolt; see Placide Tempels, *La Philosophie bantoue* (Paris: Editions presence africaine, 1959).

Fabian's most recent book more than makes up for what remained unsaid in *Jamaa* and is a happy exception to the general run of works on popular culture in modern Africa. See Johannes Fabian, *Language and Colonial Power* (London: Cambridge University Press, 1986); Fabian, *Jamaa*, 192–93; Gerald Althabe, ed., *Les Fleurs du Congo* (Paris: Editions Maspero, 1972), 116.

41 After the 1944 provincial rebellion, the colonial administration realized that it could not simply allow the rural areas to drift, but most of its prescriptive policies took a rather desultory approach to a solution to rural problems. See "La Philosophie de la rébellion," *L'Essor du Congo* (31 août 1944); "La Grande Pitié du paysan indigène," *L'Essor du Congo* (23 septembre 1944); Conseil de province du Katanga (Comptes-rendus des séances), 1945, Réunion du Commission des Travaux publiques, 20–23, 14 mai 1945.

42 A rather interesting discussion of the political implications of "ethnicity" in Katanga appears in Connor Cruise O'Brien's account of his brief career there as the senior United Nations officer; see Connor Cruise O'Brien, *To Katanga and Back* (New York: Pantheon, 1964), 238.

43 For example, Perrings gives the impression that the increases in production during the First World War were achieved without much difficulty. The actual situation contrasted sharply with this view. Instead of focussing on the horrific conditions in the foundry at Lubumbashi and at the Star of the Congo, the largest mine in production at the time, Perrings is content simply to show how misleading labor-recruitment statistics were for this period. He concludes a section pregnant with important social implications by arguing that the state and the private

recruiters were fairly effective in maintaining labor supplies. If this were so, there would have been no need to juggle the recruitment figures. See Perrings, *Black Mineworkers*, 34.

44   Ibid., 201–2; see AG, B12, dossier no. 72, UMHK/Département MOI-Elisabethville, Proteste de surménage (confidentielle), 19 mars 1936, Busanga; Conseil de province du Katanga (Comptes-rendus des séances), 1947, Séance du 16 juin 1947, 255–57; for a different view see Mwabila Malela, *Proletariat et conscience de classe au Zaire: Essai d'explication de la proletariasation incomplète des salaires; L'Exemple des travailleurs de la ville industriel de Lubumbashi* (Bruxelles: Editions Université libre de Bruxelles, 1973).

45   Perrings, *Black Mineworkers*, 17; AG, Proteste de surménage.

46   Edouard Bustin, *The Lunda under Belgian Rule* (Cambridge: Harvard University Press, 1975), 138; Conseil de province du Katanga (Compte-rendus des séances), 1951, Annexe I, Rapport sur le fonctionnement de l'organisation professionelle indigène — exercice 1950, 168; AG, A5, UMHK/Département MOI, Rapport sur la grève des travailleurs de l'Union Minière, 6 mars 1946.

Chapter One. Getting on the Ground

1   Lemoine, "La Concentration des éntreprises," 443.

2   National Archives of Zimbabwe (henceforth Na Zim), RO 1/2/1F 501-818, H. G. Robins Papers, Dixon to Robins at Fwelijanya's Village, 1 August 1911.

3   Na Zim, RO 1/1/11, H. G. Robins Papers, RE: My Alleged Atrocities, 27 May 1907 — 4 September 1908.

4   Ibid.

5   BPRO, file FO-403/425, encl. 1 in no. 17, Star of the Congo Trading Company to Vice Consul Beak, 25 November 1910; Bruce Fetter, *The Creation of Elisabethville* (Stanford: Hoover Institution Press, 1976), 42–44; Thomas Reefe Collection: Luba Documents (henceforth TRCLD), reel 1, Archives sous-region Lomami, Maroyez, Rapports mensuels: CSK, novembre 1907–décembre 1908.

6   BPRO, encl. 1 in no. 19, Vice Consul Campbell to Acting Consul Lyons, 30 August 1912, Katanga, 32–50.

7   BPRO, Star of the Congo; Na Zim, Robins, Atrocities.

8   Lambert-Culot, "Les Premières Années," 275–78; Bogumil Jewsiewicki, "Notes sur l'histoire socio-economique du Congo," *Etudes d'histoire africaine* 3 (1972): 320; Na Zim, Robins, Atrocities.

9   See TRCLD, Maroyez, Rapports mensuels: CSK, octobre 1908–janvier 1909; see also MRAC, no. 20 ATA, Lacanne, Enquête politique sur la région du Luapula-Moero, 1935.

10   *Rapport sur l'administration du Congo Belge*, 1918, 119; AA, MOI no. 46 (3551), Correspondance de l'office du vice gouvernement général du

Katanga," 7 avril 1914, no. 955; and Katzenellenbogen, *Railways*, 8–15 and 47–59.

11 TRCLD, Maroyez, Rapports mensuels: CSK, juillet-septembre 1908.
12 TRCLD, Maroyez, Rapports mensuels: CSK, décembre 1908.
13 TRCLD, Maroyez, Rapports mensuels: CSK, mars-décembre 1908.
14 Ibid.
15 Na Zim, RO 1/2/1, H. G. Robins Papers, Robins to Dixon (private and confidential: Zaziga's village), 22 June 1911, 1–500.
16 *Rapport sur l'administration du Congo Belge*, 1918, 119.
17 Na Zim, RO 1/2/1, H. G. Robins Papers, Robins to Robert Williams from Snodland, December 1910.
18 AA, MOI no. 48 (3553), Transmission d'un procès verbal de la comité de direction de la BTK, 19 août 1913, Elisabethville.
19 AA, MOI no. 56 (3558), no. 11723/561B, Mesures à prendre pour amener les noirs à travailler, 14 septembre 1922, Elisabethville; AA, MOI no. 48 (3553), Nauwalaes, Rapport de Pweto, 7 juillet 1913.
20 AA, Nauwalaes, Rapport de Pweto; see also Table 1 in Bruce Fetter, "The Union Minière and Its Hinterland: A Demographic Reconstruction," *African Economic History* 12 (1983): 78.
21 Na Zim, Robins to Robert Williams.
22 In 1914 one Congolese franc was worth about five or six cents of United States currency; see Grevisse, "Salines et saliniers indigènes," 75–76. See also MRAC, Enquête concernant le rattachement de la chefferie Katete, procès verbal administratif, Congo Belge, province d'Elisabethville, district du Haut-Katanga, rapport no. 3, Van Malderen et Marchal, 1938.
23 Na Zim, Robins, Atrocities.
24 AA, Transmission d'un procès verbal; TC/UM, 64, Annexe D, Horner Report on Native Labor, 29, 1919; Katzenellenbogen, *Railways*, 72; see *Journal officiel du Katanga*, 1911–12, Ordonnance no. 126, "Réglementant l'exercice de la prostitution," n.d.; Ordonnance no. 147, "Sur l'Interdiction de la circulation des noirs pendant la nuit dans les agglomerations Européens," 15 avril 1912; and Ordonnance d'Administration générale (Malfeyt), no. 169, "Relative à la creation d'une cité indigène à Elisabethville," 10 juillet 1912.
25 AA, MOI no. 39 (3554), no. 1161, DeBauw, Organisation nouvelle des recrutements, 4 juin 1914, Elisabethville; and AA, MOI no. 39 (3554), no. 806, Déplacement du siège de la BTK, 11 mars 1914, Elisabethville.
26 AA, MOI no. 48 (3552), no. 1726, Correspondance de Harfeld, 14 avril 1911, Elisabethville; TC/UM, 64, Annexe D, UMHK, London, 15 January 1915, 31; and TC/UM, 64, Annexes A, B, and C, Reports and Correspondence during the Great War 1914–1918, Figures I and II.
27 BPRO, file 801-FO 403/435, encl. 2 in no. 19, Campbell, Report on a Tour in the Northeastern and Western Districts of Katanga, [1905–06?], 53.
28 AA, MOI no. 57 (3558), Dossier Lomami, 1921.

29 "Politique indigène," *Rapport sur l'administration du Congo Belge*, 1918, 74.
30 Henri Segaert, *Un Terme au Congo Belge, 1916–1918* (Sydney, 1918), 116.
31 Ibid., 115.
32 *Rapport sur l'administration du Congo Belge*, 1918, 68.
33 Ibid., 75.
34 Ibid., 74–77.
35 For example, the acquisition of porters for police and military expeditions was equally important as the recruitment of labor for the mines in this period. AA, MOI no. 48 (3553), Correspondance de Wangermée, 18 avril 1913; and AA, Transmission d'un procès verbal.
37 AA, Correspondance de Wangermée, 1911–17; Fetter, *The Creation*, 49–50.
38 TC/UM, 64, Annexe H, Scheme for Future Extension, 1919.
39 AA, MOI no. 57 (3558), Dossier Lomami, 1921.
40 AA, Transmission d'un procès verbal; AA, MOI no. 52 (3555), A. DeBauw, La Main-d'Oeuvre indigène, 11 juin 1921, Etoile du Congo.
41 TC/UM, Horner Report; AA, Correspondance de Harfeld, 1913–17; AA, MOI no. 52 (3555), BTK no. 2201, Note pour monsieur le directeur de la 4ème direction, 22 septembre 1920, Kikondja.
42 AA, MOI no. 50 (3559), Service de l'Inspection de l'Industrie, 26 septembre 1916, Elisabethville; AA, MOI no. 193 (3607), no. 477e, Industrie minière: exploitation souterraine, 15 janvier 1913, Elisabethville.
43 AA, Correspondance de Harfeld (see especially the correspondence between Harfeld and Wangermée and Harfeld and Jules Cousin); BPRO, Campbell to Lyons, 52.
44 BPRO, Campbell to Lyons, 52.
45 AA, MOI no. 39 (3554), no. 806 E, BTK Kikondja, 21 mars 1914.
46 Ibid.
47 Ibid.
48 Na Zim, Robins to Robert Williams.
49 Robert Poupart, *Facteurs de productivité de la main-d'oeuvre autochtone à Elisabethville* (Bruxelles: Editions de l'Institut de Sociologie Solvay, 1960), 3–4; Katzenellenbogen, *Railways*, 34–40.
49 AA, Nauwalaes, Rapport de Pweto.
50 AA, Mesures à prendre.
51 AA, Nauwalaes, Rapport de Pweto.
52 TC/UM, Horner Report. For example, as early as 1909 the railroad was competing for a portion of African casual labor from Northern Rhodesia and Katanga. Listen to H. G. Robins on this point: "I expect the railroad will take a lot of boys and am afraid that this will make carriers between Broken Hill and Kanshanshi almost as scarce as they are now *in the wet season.*" Na Zim, RO 1/1/13, H. G. Robins Papers, Robins to Watson from his camp on the Lufupa River, 14 April 1909.
53 TC/UM, Horner Report.
54 Varbeke, "Du régime de la main-d'oeuvre," 76.

55 TC/UM, 64, Annexe E, Chemin de Fer du Katanga (Report on Negotiations).

56 Ibid.

57 TC/UM, Scheme for Future Extension.

58 Jean-Luc Vellut Collection (henceforth JLVC), fiche 1417B-1418G, Commissaire du district de Kambove, Circulaire au fonctionnaires, 22 décembre 1916, Elisabethville.

59 TC/UM, Chemin de Fer du Katanga.

60 TC/UM, Scheme for Future Extension.

61 In 1917, for instance, the mining company kept 5,000 men at work by drawing on a pool of 52,000 recruits furnished by Tanganyika Concessions. Smaller private labor recruiters, the BTK, and the rail line got by on a recruitment pool of a little over 9,000 men provided by the BTK. When one allows for turnover (contracts were rarely for more than six months), mortality, and flight, the standing workforce for the rail line was probably around 1,300 men. See TC/UM, Chemin de Fer du Katanga.

62 See Table 1.1. The railroad's share of unskilled African labor fell sharply between 1916 and 1918, although the rail line's percentage of new hands exceeded its 1914 level by about 2,000 men at the end of 1918. On the other hand, by the close of the war, the Union Minière could draw on a recruitment pool that was almost six times larger than the railroad's.

63 The negative features of the company's dependence on foreign marketing agents were further exacerbated by its problems with electrification and refinement. There was no lack of water for electric power. The headwaters of the Lufira River and the Lufuba, Lofoi, and Lualaba all bore great promise as sources of hydroelectric power once the natural courses of the rivers had been changed and dams and generators constructed. The problems then encountered were in establishing a proper engineering framework and acquiring enough labor to harness the energy of the waters. Given the phase of capitalization and the manner in which the Union Minière's assets were deployed, both aspects of the problem would remain largely unsolved until the end of the war. The underground operations in and around the Star and Kambove West were partly electrified by 1914; but the restiveness of the work crews there made it virtually impossible to electrify all aspects of production. The situation had not changed appreciably by 1919. The quantity of copper at issue in Katanga was small, however, in relation to other sources. See TC/UM, Horner Report.

64 TC/UM, Chemin de Fer du Katanga. Despite the reduction of speculative foreign capital, the labor policy of the Union Minière was no less rapacious than it had been before the war. The mining company's corporate leadership saw the future of its operations under three broad headings after the war: (1) maximization of the finds of both high- and low-grade ore in view of the cheapness of African labor; (2) extension of the number of options with respect to fuel and sulphur supplies; (3) maintenance of low transport costs, since the transport problem was

a disguised dimension of the refining process. These objectives remained unchanged until the end of the decade. Each of them, separately and collectively, contained practical problems that could not possibly have been comprehended from the lofty vantage point of the boardrooms of the Union Minière in Brussels and London. TC/UM, 64, Annexe C, Wheeler Report and Recommendations to the Board of UMHK, 31 December 1918, 16; TC/UM, Horner Report.

65 AA, MOI no. 51 (3554), A/13, Polidori, Rapport sur la situation sanitaire et hygiénique des travailleurs de l'Union Minière à l'Etoile du Congo, 28 novembre 1916.

66 JLVC, fiche 1419, Rapport sur une visite à l'Etoile du Congo, 5 mai 1917.

67 Ibid.

68 JLVC, fiche 1389-92, S. Claessens, Désertions des travailleurs de la Bourse du Travail du Katanga aux mines de Kambove, Likasi et Chituru: Enquête faite les 23 et 24 octobre 1916; see also Charles Perrings, "Good Lawyers but Poor Workers: Recruited Angolan Labor in the Copper Mines of Katanga, 1917–1921," *Journal of African History* 18, 2 (1977): 237–59.

69 TC/UM, Horner Report.

70 JLVC, fiche 1400, Congo Belge province du Katanga, Service des Affaires économiques, no. 743; JLVC, fiche 1401, De Sloovere, Communications: rapport inspector provincial de l'industrie sur Kambove, 28 février 1918, Elisabethville; JLVC, fiche 1402, Rapport relatif à l'enquête à la mine de Kambove prescrits par la lettre no. 499 du 7 février 1918.

71 TC/UM, Horner Report; Andre Boigelot, *Rapport sur l'hygiene des travailleurs noirs de mai 1918 à mai 1919* (Bruxelles: Presses de Vramant, 1920), 66; see Tables 1.2 and 1.3.

72 See JLVC, Claessens, Désertions des travailleurs.

73 AA, Polidori, Rapport sur la situation sanitaire.

74 JLVC, Claessens, Désertions des travailleurs.

75 Ibid.

76 Ibid.

77 See Tables 1.2 and 1.3. At its peak of operations in June 1916, there were over 1,400 workers at the mine. But by August, after successive waves of pneumonia, influenza, tick fever, and enteritis, fewer than 800 workers remained. About a third were Lozi from Northern Rhodesia, while the rest were Congolese from either Katanga or Maniema. This, in fact, represented a sharp demographic turnabout from the prewar period; for as late as 1913 the preponderant majority of African workers at the Star were from Nyasaland and the two Rhodesias. But between 1913 and 21 March 1914, shortly after Great Britain finally recognized the Belgian claim to Katanga and less than six months before the commencement of the First World War, the number of African workers from the British colonies declined sharply. By early 1915 a large number of workers from Nyasaland, boss boys and clerks excepted, were repatriated because of high mortality rates. Shortly thereafter, the British inspectors were temporarily recalled.

Following these events the workers' living standards deteriorated sharply. Consequently Congolese workers were as anxious about the withdrawal of the British inspectors as their Rhodesian and Nyasalander workmates.

78 AA, BTK Kikondja; AA, MOI no. 173 (3604), Rapport economique, 1er semestre 1918, "Mauvais traitements."

79 Exhaustion of all of the ore above water level at the Star compelled the company to mine a lower grade of copper ore in greater quantities there and at Kambove. Disease and overwork severely crippled the productive capacity of the workforce. Typhoid, pneumonia, and dysentery carried off thousands of workers. The company's response to such conditions was a combination of incompetence, lack of foresight, and callousness. The fact that the African workforce was expanding faster than medical personnel could handle served only to aggravate the situation further. See JLVC, Rapport relatif à l'enquête.

80 On 25 September 1918, 200 contract workers struck at the nearby work site of Likasi in protest over the scheduled destruction of the workers' cemetery. Local officials were at a loss. Inspector Claessens wrote to his superiors at the end of the month, telling them of his frustrations, but carefully eschewing any possible blame for the unrest:

> I would like to know therefore what could be done if an analogous state of affairs (something verging on a general strike) were to break out in the camps at Likasi; could I make a mass arrest for 24 hours and stop work on the new office? Even if it were legal, such a punishment would not make much of an impression on the blacks. And then there is the problem of where one would put them after they were arrested. The chill at night might give rise to more cases of pneumonia if they were held in the open air. Consequently, neither I nor the commissioner would like to assume this responsibility. (JLVC, Claessens, Désertions des travailleurs)

81 AA, Polidori, Rapport sur la situation sanitaire; Boigelot, *Rapport sur l'hygiene*, 84.

82 AA, Polidori, Rapport sur la situation sanitaire.

83 Ibid. Lozi workers might also have been reluctant to return home because many of them were slaves and dependents of Lozi aristocrats; see Fetter, *The Creation*, 61.

84 The frequency of deaths in the camp's hospital, along with the spread of tick fever, caused the workers to believe that they were living in the shadow of a malevolent intelligence. Workers at Kambove attributed the numerous deaths there to an evil spirit who, according to them, lived on top of Mount Kituru. JLVC, fiche 1418, S. Claessens, Inspection de l'Industrie No. 152, Etat sanitaire de Likasi, 14 octobre 1918, Kambove; AA, "Mauvais traitements."

85 JLVC, Claessens, Désertions des travailleurs.

86 TC/UM, Horner Report.

87 AA, MOI no. 50 (3554), Service des affaires économiques, 14 mars 1922, Elisabethville; AG, D13, no. 3437, Sps A/1, Mortalité: Recrues

Lomami, 12 septembre 1928, Elisabethville; see also Badye Kayamba, "Capitalisme et déstructuration de sociétés lignagères dans l'ancien territoire de Sakania au Zaire (1870–1940), Vol. 2 (thèse de doctorat, UNAZA, Lubumbashi, 1986), 271–75.

Chapter Two. Obstacles to Growth

1   J. Vanhove, *Histoire du Ministère des Colonies* (Bruxelles: Académie royale des sciences d'outre-mer, 1968), 51; and Jean Stengers, *Combien le Congo a-t-il coûté à la Belgique?* (Bruxelles: Académie royal des Sciences coloniales, 1957), 80–83.

2   Chelepner, *Cent ans d'histoire sociale*, 324; see also Charles Kindelberger, *The World in Depression, 1929–1939* (Los Angeles: University of California Press, 1975), 77–84.

3   Stengers, *Combien le Congo*, 232.

4   Ibid., 233–34; Vanhove, *Histoire du Ministère*, 70.

5   Fetter, *The Creation*, 78–79.

6   TC/UM, 96–98, Usines de Lubumbashi, rapports mensuels, 1923–27; TC/UM, 112, Usines de Panda, rapports mensuels, 1923–37; *L'Union Minière du Haut-Katanga* (monograph series, Bruxelles: L. Cuypers, 1954), 36.

7   TC/UM, 64, Annexes A, B, and C, Reports and Correspondence during the Great War 1914–1918, 8 and 10; Perrings, "Good Lawyers," 245.

8   AA, MOI no. 59 (3558), Dr. Amar, Examen psycho-physiologique, 17 février 1922.

9   TC/UM, 96–98, Usines de Lubumbashi, 1923–27.

10   The negative effect which the skewed growth rate might have had on the company's profits was mitigated by the Union Minière's construction of a refining complex at Hoboken, Belgium, and the successful vertical integration of its activities in Katanga. By the mid-1920s, for example, the mining company's local executive had formed Charbonnages de la Luena, a coal mining company in northeastern Katanga that reduced the Union Minière's dependence on coal from Southern Rhodesia; Minoteries du Katanga, a milling company that ground the corn meal given to the mineworkers as part of their ration; Sogefor, a company that generated and distributed hydroelectric power; Sogechim, a chemical company that produced sulphuric acid for chemical leaching from the tailings of copper sulfate ore; and Cofoka, a construction company that reduced the Union Minière's dependence on private contractors at the more centrally located mines (TC/UM, 112, Usines de Panda, 1923–37; Fetter, *The Creation*, 70–80).

11   *L'Union Minière du Haut-Katanga*, 1954, 51; TC/UM, Reports and Correspondence during the Great War.

12   AA, MOI no. 49 (3554), no. 4217, Emploi main-d'oeuvre, Correspondance générale, 5 septembre 1924, Elisabethville; Gouverneur, *Produc-*

tivity and Factor Proportions, 27–30; Pierre Daye, *L'Empire colonial belge* (Bruxelles: Editions du Soir, 1923), 1–123.

13 Comité régional du Katanga (Comptes-rendus des séances), Annexe 20, 2ᵉ séance, 19 avril 1921, 20; AA, Dr. Amar, Examen psycho-physiologique; Bruce Fetter, "L'Union Minière du Haut-Katanga: La Naissance du sous-culture totalitaire," *Cahiers du CEDAF* 9–10 (1973): 1–27.

14 AA, Amar, Examen psycho-physiologique.

15 Ibid.

16 Perrings, *Black Mineworkers,* 78–79.

17 Fetter, *The Creation,* 86.

18 AA, MOI no. 173 (3604), no. 279, UMHK, Mortalité en 1924, 16 février 1926; Fetter, *The Creation,* 110.

19 AA, UMHK, Mortalité en 1924.

20 Perrings, *Black Mineworkers,* 50–54. For example, the strike of the white workers at the Union Minière in 1919, comedy of errors that it was, contained some of the same grievances as the larger protest on the Rand three years later. The number of English-speaking white workers at the Union Minière was greatly reduced as a result of the strike.

21 AA, Amar, Examen psycho-physiologique; AA, MOI no. 49 (3554), BTK no. 1941/K, Assistance insuffisante accordée à la BTK (concurrence étrangère), 9 avril 1924.

22 "L'Impôt indigène et développement économique," *Notre Colonie* 21ᵉ année (15 novembre 1919).

23 JLVC, fiche 1663, Lettres et correspondance de Monsignor Jean Felix Jules de Hemptinne.

24 Comité régional du Katanga (Comptes-rendus des séances), 1926, Indisciplines des travailleurs noirs: est-elles réelles? Quelles en sont les causes principales? Quels seraient les remèdes? 163.

25 Comité régional du Katanga (Comptes-rendus des séances), 1927, Personne ne contestera l'immoralité de l'exploitation par des femmes blanches de debits de bière aux indigènes, 85–96.

26 See Charles van Onselen, "The Witches of Suburbia: Domestic Service on the Witwatersrand, 1890–1914," in *Studies in the Social and Economic History of the Witwatersrand 1886–1914,* Vol. 2 (London: Longman, 1982), 50–59.

27 Comité régional du Katanga (Comptes-rendus des séances), Annexe 1, 3ᵉ Session, 1921, Parquet d'Elisabethville no. 273/I.G., 60–61, 10 février 1921; AA, MOI no. 134 (3598), no. 1317, Antoine Sohier, Note de monsieur le procureur général, 26 novembre 1925, Elisabethville.

28 Comité régional du Katanga (Comptes-rendus des séances), Annexe 8, 1923, La Situation politique générale, 45.

29 See cases in *Journaux administratifs du Katanga* from 1920 to 1923. Almost all of the *extraits des jugements* have to do with white mineworkers from British colonies who have reneged on debts in Katanga

and returned to South Africa; see TC/UM, 64, Annexe D, Horner Report on Native Labor, 1919; Perrings, *Black Mineworkers*, 54.

30 TC/UM, Horner Report.

31 See TC/UM, 94–97, Usines de Lubumbashi, 1924–27.

32 TC/UM, Reports and Correspondence during the Great War.

33 See Table 4.1.

34 TC/UM, Reports and Correspondence during the Great War; Perrings, "Good Lawyers," 253–54.

35 AA, Amar, Examen psycho-physiologique; TC/UM, 101, no. 1186, Furnace Work, 28 December 1918.

36 Vanhove, *Histoire du Ministère*, 49–51; Fetter, "L'Union Minière du Haut-Katanga," 1–27; and Stengers, *Combien le Congo*, 76–83.

37 F. Engels, "La Province du Katanga," *Rapport de la Commission du Travail*, 1 juin 1931, Bruxelles, 13.

38 Comité régional du Katanga (Comptes-rendus des séances), 3e Session, 1923, "Situation politique générale," 2–3. After 1919, for example, Tanganyika Concessions Limited, through its own agencies or those of its subsidiary, the Zambesia Exploring Company, drafted over 6,000 Africans in the eastern provinces of Northern Rhodesia alone for work at the Union Minière. The table below indicates that TCL increased the number of African recruits it sent to the mining company by 41 percent the following year.

Union Minière Recruits from Tanganyika Concessions Limited, 1917–1922

	Northern Rhodesia		Angola	Total
	Northeast	Northwest	Angola	Total
1917	600	22 (24?)	966	1,588
1918	1,224	154 (155?)	1,746	3,124
1919	6,239	167	723	7,129
1920	8,845	203	50	9,098
1921	8,334	424	1	8,759
1922	3,901	236	–	4,137

Source: AA, MOI no. 46 (3551), Ministère des Colonies, août 1926.

39 Perrings, "Good Lawyers," 253; Bustin, *The Lunda*, 84; *Rapport sur l'administration du Congo Belge*, 1924–25, 86.

40 The most glaring source of contradiction between the law and its application was the pattern of labor recruitment itself. What, in fact, took place in Katanga was an attempt at internment of the African population directly north and west of the provincial rail line. The districts of Lomami and Lulua were particularly affected by these measures. See: AA, MOI no. 1028 (3604), Rapport du inspection du travail, 17 novembre 1919; AA, MOI no. 59 (3555), annexes 1er–22ème, 20 août 1924; see also TC/UM, 151, Technical Meeting (Messrs. Francqui, Velge, Smith, Deschat, Sengier), 3 June 1921; TC/UM, Reports and Correspondence during the Great War; AA, MOI no. 173 (3604), Rapport economique 1er semestre 1918, "Mauvais traitements."

41   AA, MOI no. 50 (3554), Service des affaires économiques, 14 mars 1922, Elisabethville.

42   Perrings, "Good Lawyers," 242–45; AA, MOI no. 46 (3555), no. 718, annexe 22ème, Impôts, 20 août 1924.

43   AA, MOI no. 51 (3554), A/13, Polidori, Rapport sur la situation sanitaire et hygiénique des travailleurs de l'Union Minière à l'Etoile du Congo, 28 novembre 1916; Léopold Mottoulle, "Mortalité Infantile, Mortinatalité et Natalité," *Bulletin médical du Katanga* 7ème année, no. 1 (1920): 9–10; Annual Report, Northern Rhodesia, 1924–25, 4.

44   Annual Report, Northern Rhodesia, 1924–25, 14; Perrings, "Good Lawyers," 242–45; AA, Impôts; "L'Impôt indigène," *Notre Colonie.*

45   AA, MOI no. 57 (3558), dossier 2424, Rapport du comité local pour juin 1919 au 31 décembre 1923; AA, Ministère des Colonies; see Table 2.2.

46   See n. 43; see also AA, MOI no. 52 (3555), BTK no. 2201, Note pour monsieur le directeur de la 4ème direction, 22 septembre 1920, Kikondja.

47   See n. 43; see also AA, Note pour monsieur le directeur.

48   "L'Impôt indigène," *Notre Colonie,* 22.

49   AA, MOI no. 193 (3604), no. 1028, Rapport du inspection du travail, 17 novembre 1919, Boma.

50   See Table 5.2; see also TC/UM, 101, Weekly factory reports from 28 December 1918 to 3 June 1919; TC/UM, Reports and Correspondence during the Great War, 17; Perrings, "Good Lawyers," 256–58; Bustin, *The Lunda,* 85.

51   See n. 43; AA, Note pour monsieur le directeur; see also Table 2.1.

52   AA, MOI no. 56 (3558), no. 1448/522b, s.2, BTK concurrence, 14 septembre 1921; AA, Note pour monsieur le directeur.

53   See "L'Impôt indigène," *Notre Colonie,* 22.

54   AA, MOI no. 50 (3554), no. 1002, annexe 3e, Lettre à monsieur le ministre, 25 octobre 1920.

55   AA, BTK concurrence; see also n. 50.

56   The BTK's efforts in Lulua were stanched further by the protests of the American Methodist Mission at Kapanga, which, by February 1921, had enough influence at the Lunda *mwaat yav*'s court and among local Lunda notables to recall many of the Africans who had already contracted for work. Agents for the Compagnie du Kasai and Forminière also began to rummage for porters in the same area in early 1921. The columns of BTK recruiters under the nominal leadership of Auguste Thibaut were consequently driven toward Sandoa and the southwestern part of the district by the beginning of the rainy season. See AA, Assistance insuffisante accordée; see Table 2.1.

57   AA, Assistance insuffisante; AA, BTK concurrence.

58   AA, Lettre à monsieur le ministre.

59   AA, BTK concurrence; see also n. 50.

60   AA, Assistance insuffisante.

61   Ibid.

62   AA, MOI no. 57 (3558), no. 2417/238b, Recrutements (Lulua), 7

décembre 1922. There is no direct evidence that the BTK attempted to squeeze out African agents, but it can certainly be inferred from the lists of persons holding valid recruiting permits.

63 AA, MOI no. 59 (3555), no. 718, annexes 22ème, Désertions, 20 août 1924.

64 Some African recruiters were, in fact, notables of the major ethnic groups in the region. They attempted to monitor the terms of hire and physical treatment their subjects received at dispersal centers such as Bukama, Elisabethville, and Sandoa. To be sure, they received no encouragement for their efforts from the recruiting companies. See "Assignation à prévenu (Sale André), *Journal administratif du Katanga*, 26 avril 1927, Elisabethville; and "Jugement à prévenu (Kimputu Mutombo)," *Journal administratif du Katanga*, 6 octobre 1925, Elisabethville; AA, Rapport du comité local, juin 1919–décembre 1923; AA, Service des affaires économiques, 14 mars 1922.

65 AA, MOI no. 57 (3558), Delforge, Rapport du BTK.

66 Ibid.

67 Ibid.; Audrey Richards, *Land, Labour and Diet in Northern Rhodesia* (London: Oxford University Press, 1934), 51.

68 AA, Delforge, Rapport; see Jean-Luc Vellut, "Mining in the Belgian Congo," in *History of Central Africa*, Vol. 2, ed. David Birmingham and Phyllis Martin (New York: Longman, 1983), 148–49.

69 See rosters of "Permis de main d'oeuvre indigène délivres" in *Revue administratif du Congo Belge* from 1914 to 1923 and *Journal administratif du Katanga* from 1924 to 1928.

70 AA, Assistance insuffisante.

71 AA, MOI no. 52 (3555), A. DeBauw, La Main d'oeuvre indigène, 11 juin 1921, Etoile du Congo.

72 AA, MOI no. 58 (3558), no. 1424, 4e Direction, 2e annexe, Recruteurs BTK, 24 juillet 1924.

73 AA, MOI no. 58 (3558), no. 1168, 1e section, 4e Direction, BTK recruteurs, 8 février 1923.

74 AA, MOI no. 58 (3558), no. D/23, 1e section, 4e Direction, Recruteurs, 10 janvier 1922.

75 AA, MOI no. 58 (3558), annexe 2e, "Delforge," 10 novembre 1921, Bruxelles.

76 Ibid.

77 Ibid.

78 AA, MOI no. 39 (3554), no. 1161, DeBauw, Organisation nouvelle des recrutements, 4 juin 1914, Elisabethville.

79 AA, MOI no. 134 (3598), Commissions régionales par districts: district de la Lulua; sous Commission de la Main d'Oeuvre Réunion du 4 janvier 1922 (Sandoa).

80 AA, MOI no. 52 (3555), no. 234, BTK Services des Affaires economiques, 14 mars 1922.

81 AA, Delforge, Rapport.

82 AA, Recrutements (Lulua).

83 AA, Commissions régionales; AG, B12, "Busanga," 18 décembre 1924.
84 AA, Recrutements (Lulua); Rapport sur l'Administration du Congo Belge, 1923–24, 95.
85 While the mortality rate for Angolans at the Union Minière in 1922 was an improvement over those of 1919 and 1920, it was still high. Moreover, the improvement in the rate was largely the result of the reduction of Angolans in the workforce. Congolese mortality, even by the jerry-built figures of the Ministry of Colonies and the Union Minière, showed a steady increase up to 1922 and almost to the end of the decade (see table below):

Number of Deaths per 1,000 Men at the Union Minière, 1919–22

	1919	1920	1921	1922
Northern Rhodesians and Barotse	45.91	26.21	31.76	22.65
Angolans	176.47	170.03	23.15	48.38
Congolese	27.64	18.50	29.70	46.06
Kasai (Baluba)	13.96	95.44	14.25	—
Nyasalanders	21.79	34.70	12.62	7.51

Note: Average rate of death for all African workers at the Union Minière for all four years was 22.67 men per 1,000.

Sources: AA, UMHK, Mortalité en 1924; TC/UM, Reports and Correspondence during the Great War; AA, MOI no. 50 (3554), no. 1939, Correspondances de Heenen, 28 novembre 1922.

86 Among the Luvale of Angola, for example, night drumming was used to cover their escape from the deathly conditions at the Lubumbashi works. But what of the Bena Ngoma Lamba, who had no developed tradition of drumming? The answers to such questions must await more specific research into the cultural traditions of the first set of African recruits of the Union Minière.

Disease and mortality did figure importantly in shaping the context of work, however. The diseases that claimed the greatest number of Africans at the Union Minière in the order of their contribution to mortality and morbidity were pneumonia, typhoid, tuberculosis, dysentery, meningitis, and smallpox. Until 1928, when the general demographic profile of the African workforce at the Union Minière began to change, the conjuncture between death, disease, and flight seemed strongest at Panda, the Star, and Luishia. The mining company surmised that deaths due to illness claimed 18.32 percent of the total workforce in 1920, 26 percent in 1921, and 31.11 percent in 1922. Mortality rates at the Union Minière exceeded those of the gold mines of the Rand in all three of these years. AA, MOI no. 56 (3558), no. 989/9b, BTK fermiers, 19 mai 1921; Perrings, "Good Lawyers," 225.
87 AA, MOI no. 52 (3555), Rapport du comité local pour l'exercice du 1er juin 1922 au 31 décembre 1923; AA, MOI no. 57 (3558), Thibaut et Delforge, Rapport du BTK.
88 Ibid.

89 AA, MOI no. 50 (3554), no. 9634/355B, Indiscipline dans les camps, 5 janvier 1921.

90 AA, Thibaut et Delforge, Rapport.

91 AA, MOI no. 50 (3554), no. 58, Cousin, à la lettre du Katanga BTK, 13 avril 1924.

92 AA, Rapport du comité local, juin 1919–31 décembre 1923.

93 AA, MOI no. 59 (3555), no. 872, Désertion remèdes, 27 octobre 1922, Elisabethville.

94 Engels, "Katanga."

95 AA, MOI no. 57 (3558), Rapport de Tanganika-Moero, 28 octobre 1922.

96 M. Robert, "La Question minière," in *Politique economique du Congo: Rapport au Comité du Congres colonial* (Bruxelles: Editions Gromaere, 1924), 265.

Chapter Three. African Workers in the Industrial Towns, 1919–1930

1 Varbeke, "Du régime de la main-d'oeuvre," 76.

2 "L'Impôt indigène," *Notre Colonie*, 22.

3 See, for example, "Katanga: Politique indigène," in Rapports sur l'Administration du Congo Belge, 1927–39; see also Dellicour, *Les Premières Années*, 70–81.

4 See the testimonies of labor recruiters and territorial administrators in AA, MOI (3557); see also Bustin, *The Lunda*, 89; Fetter, "L'Union Minière du Haut-Katanga."

5 Fernand Grevisse, *Le Centre extra-coutumier d'Elisabethville* (Bruxelles: Institut royal Colonial Belge, 1954), 5–7; Guy Baumer, *Les Centres indigènes extra-coutumier au Congo Belge* (Paris: Editions Montesforet, 1934), 46; "Considerations sur la main d'oeuvre indigène," *Notre Colonie* 10e année (décembre 1928): 239.

6 As late as 1926 most of the African population of Elisabethville, Jadotville, and the other towns of Katanga, whether they were workers or not, were seen as no more than "stabilized vagabonds" by many officials. The European authorities thought the outer edges of the *cités indigènes*—the *faubourgs* and squatters' areas—to be the "refuge of prostitutes, libertines and roughly articulated ideas of rebellion against the colonial order." Yet, after 1924, the colonial administration in Katanga began to abandon a monolithic conception of the urban African population of Katanga in favor of one that divided it into three social categories—*main d'oeuvre indigène*, or native wage labor, *flottants*, or semi-proletarianized casual laborers who moved back and forth between the towns and the rural areas, and *déracinés*, those Africans who had no moorings in either town or country. See Ordonnance-loi no. 3 of 6 February 1922 restricting African residence in the towns of Katanga to the *cités indigènes* and the workers' camps; see also Ordonnance-loi no. 14 of 12 May 1926 on the restriction of recruitment in several

chieftaincies in the Elisabethville and Likasi vicinities; *Journal administratif du Katanga* 15ᵉ année, no. 9 (1926); "Déracinés autour des grandes centres," *Congo. Revue générale de la colonie*, annexe II (juin 1924): 5.

7   Grevisse, *Le Centre extra-coutumier*, 7; Paul Minon, "Quelques aspects de l'evolution recente du centre extra-coutumier d'Elisabethville," *Bulletin du CEPSI* 10, no. 3 (1951): 3.

8   Grevisse, *Le Centre extra-coutumier*, 5; "Considerations," *Notre Colonie*, 239. For a succinct analysis of the problem of social engineerng and "social control" with respect to the laboring classes of late-Victorian England and the possible means of approaching the problem in other societies, see Gareth Stedman Jones, "Class Expression versus Social Control?" *History Workshop* 4 (Autumn 1977): 163–71.

9   The poor health and sanitary conditions at the UMHK camps at the Star of the Congo, Lubumbashi, and the *cité indigène* of Elisabethville were a major preoccupation of the colonial administration from 1913 to 1922. The mortality rate at all three was running well over 4 percent in this period. Dr. Polidori maintained, for instance, that the part of the Lubumbashi River that the Africans used for washing as well as drinking water had become "a major source of contagion" by 1916; see AA, MOI no. 51 (3554), A/13, Polidori, Rapport sur la situation sanitaire et hygienique des travailleurs de l'Union Minière, 28 novembre 1916; Grevisse, *Le Centre extra-coutumier*, 5.

10 AA, MOI no. 173 (3604), Rapports économiques: main d'oeuvre UMHK, 2 février 1922.

11 Ibid.

12 See the cases that came before the police tribunal of Elisabethville from 1926 to 1941. Of particular interest are those of Jali Johan, a domestic servant employed by Gustave Van Rampelbergh, and Kalamba Joseph, an employee of the Chemin de Fer du Katanga. Both Jali and Kalamba regularly stole large quantities of bread and butter from their employers. Both were also part of two relatively large networks of smugglers, and after filching the food from their employers would send it back to Elisabethville and the smaller towns in the vicinity by circuitous hinterland routes. See "Assignation à prévenu (Jali Johan)" and "Assignation à prévenu (Kalamba Joseph)," *Journal administratif du Katanga*, 8 septembre 1925 and 6 octobre 1925, respectively.

13 See "Assignation aux prévenus (Moke Kongolo et Mangili François)," *Journal administratif du Katanga*, 6 novembre 1926, 1136.

14 JLVC, fiche 1705, Cabinets, gouverneur, no. 569, 1–3, 15 septembre 1922, Elisabethville.

15 Ibid., 2; see also Andre Yav, *Vocabulaire de ville de Elisabethville*, Edité par les agents anciennes domestiques aux communes de Elisabethville (Elisabethville, 1965), 13.

16 JLVC, Cabinets, 2.

17 Eventually a department store for Europeans was built on the square

where the hanging took place on avenue limité du sud; see Yav, *Vocabulaire*, 13.

18 JLVC, Cabinets, 1.

19 Ibid.

20 Ibid.

21 See the Monsignor Jules Jean Felix de Hemptinne's commentary: JLVC, fiches 1680–1691, Sous-commission pour la Protection des Indigènes, l'Annexe, 10 décembre 1923, Congo Belge.

22 JLVC, Cabinets, 3.

23 Ibid., 2–3.

24 After July 1923 the power and access of the police tribunals increased markedly. Afterward police commissioners frequently convened tribunals without the presence of a civil magistrate, although paragraph three of the 92nd amendment of the Charte coloniale, which was promulgated on 9 July 1923, strictly forbade such convenings. However, article 93 stipulated that the illegal nature of the police tribunals was of some consequence only when property was at issue; and in such cases the police tribunals were to pass on the responsibility for a judgment, although not the actual proceedings, to a civil magistrate in order to prevent the unlikely situation of an African benefitting twice from a court ruling. For most Africans passing through the courtrooms — whether they were guilty of infractions of the law or not — benefitting just once would have seemed like a godsend. See *Revue juridique du Congo Belge* 4ème année, no. 9 (septembre 1928), i, 253.

25 Yav, *Vocabulaire*, 1–33.

26 JLVC, Sous-commission de la Protection des Indigènes.

27 Ibid.; see also I. K. Sundiata, "The Mores of Expansion, 1837–1914," *Presence africaine* 70, 2e trimestre (1969): 60–65.

28 "Jugement (Fournier)," *Journal administratif du Katanga*, repris sub numeris Parquet 466/475, 4 avril 1927, 311.

29 See "Ivresse publique (Hippolyte)," *Journal administratif du Katanga*, RMP 24864/RG 8979, Tribunal de district du Elisabethville, 9 janvier 1926.

30 For a good character sketch of the monsignor, see Fetter, *The Creation*, 103–8.

31 JLVC, fiche 1680, Congo Belge, Parquet général no. 985, 23 août 1923, Elisabethville; Raymond L. Buell, "Labor in the Congo," *The Nation* 127, no. 8287 (4 July 1928): 24–26; and JLVC, Sous-commission de la Protection des Indigènes (testimonies of de Hemptinne, Heenen, Sohier, Parisse).

32 JLVC, Sous-commission pour la Protection des Indigènes.

33 See Jewsiewicki, "La Contestation sociale."

34 Ibid., 47–50.

35 Léopold Mottoulle, "Contribution à l'etude du determinisme fonctionnel de l'industrie dans l'education de indigène congolais," *Bulletin de l'Institut royal colonial Belge* (1934): 210–15.

36 Ibid., 210; Louis Lotar, "L'Immatriculation et l'ordre économique," *Congo. Revue générale de la Colonie* (juin 1924): 364-71.

37 See n. 24.

38 The Katangese *sûreté*, or secret police, was formed in December 1931, some 13 years before the colonywide secret service was created, as a result of the African labor unrest of that year. See Fetter, *The Creation*, 136; F. Vandewalle and Jacques Brassinne, *Les Rapports secretes de la sûreté congolaise*, 2 vols. (Bruxelles: Editions Arts et Voyages, 1973), 2: 13-14.

39 AA, MOI no. 173 (3604), UMHK, Mortalité en 1924; AG, C8, MOI no. 102/b17, Rapport trimesteriel: Direction générale, 12 janvier 1927, Elisabethville; AG, 08, Procès-verbal 36, 20 novembre 1938; "Considerations," *Notre Colonie*, 239.

40 AG, D6, d6/no. 1479, B.P. 407, Administration, 14 juillet 1937.

41 AG, A1, Administration générale, MOI 673/D-900, Rapport sur la culture par les travailleurs indigènes, 9 septembre 1940.

42 AG, D8, d6/no. 461, Administration générale, Correspondances, 26 mai 1939.

43 Ibid.

44 AA, MOI no. 57 (3558), dossier 2424/b242, Rapports économiques, 8 décembre 1922; see Bogumil Jewsiewicki, "Political Consciousness among the African Peasantry in the Belgian Congo," *Review of African Political Economy* 19 (September–December 1980): 23-33.

45 AG, B6, MOI no. 8253, Contrat du travail, 9 juin 1937, Elisabethville; Léopold Mottoulle, "Aspect sociale de l'attraction exercée par les centres urbains et industriels sur les populations Balubas du Congo Belge: Populations rurales de la province de Lusambo," *Institut international des Civilisations differentes* (1952): 306; Kubuya-Namulemba, "Regard sur la situation sociale," 59.

46 "Crimes et superstitions indigènes," *Revue juridique du Congo Belge* 8ème année, no. 1 (janvier 1932): 102-5.

47 Ibid., 102.

48 Ibid., 103.

49 Jewsiewicki, "La Contestation sociale," 60-61.

50 Mottoulle, "Aspect sociale," 304.

51 AG, A9, SM/MOI, Instruction de reference no. 8; see Table 6.4.

52 For example, maize flour, or cornmeal — *tukutuku* for the people in question — was very expensive and rather useless for the Union Minière's African workers. The workers found it coarser and less palatable than their cassava or sorghum flour. Moreover, because of tariffs and postwar inflation, the price of cornmeal in Elisabethville was three times higher than in Léopoldville; see interview done by Mary Smith of her maternal grandfather, Fernand Mignon, former territorial administrator in Maniema and *restaurateur* at Matadi from 1933 to 1966, conducted 15 July 1975 in Namur, Belgium (audio cassette of interview is in my possession); see also Bruce Fetter, "Elisabethville and Lubumbashi: The

Segmentary Growth of a Colonial City" (Ph.D. dissertation, University of Wisconsin, Madison, 1968), 24–47.

53 AA, MOI no. 46 (3551), Service des Affaires économiques, no. 1973, Désertions, 2 janvier 1923.

54 AG, B12, no. 752 memo/BS-6, Désertions, 16 septembre 1938, Elisabethville; AG, C8, annexe D12, no. 84, Demande d'enseignements, 12 décembre 1927, Elisabethville; Buell, "Labor in the Congo," 26.

55 AA, MOI no. 133 (3598), Observations presentées par l'Association des Intérêts coloniaux belges à propos du dépôt de project de décret sur le contrat de louage de service entre indigènes et nonindigènes, 29 octobre 1926; Buell, "Labor in the Congo," 26.

56 AA, MOI no. 34 (3598), A. Sohier, Note sur le régime du recrutement, 19 octobre 1928; and AA, MOI no. 50 (3554), Service des affaires économiques, 14 mars 1922; AA, MOI no. 46 (3551), Section E.C./B no. 374/719/935, 1er annexe, Ministère des Affaires etrangères: Direction B, 3 août 1926.

57 AG, Demande d'enseignements; AA, MOI no. 59 (3555), annexes 22ème, 20 août 1924. The table below illustrates just how devastating the fluctuation of the unskilled African hands was at the more important work sites of the Union Minière in the prestabilization era. Flight accounted for most of the reduction in the numerical strength of the African workforce, but mortality from disease and industrial accidents was also an important factor, as the previous chapters have indicated. While the subsequent fluctuations of the African workforce at the Union Minière were perhaps not as dramatic as those of 1921 and 1922, they adhered to a trend established by the latter reduction of the workforce. From 1921 to 1922 the Panda works and the mine at Likasi lost close to 2,000 workers. The African workforce was also drastically reduced at the other major work sites — Kambove, Star of the Congo, and Luishia. Even the remote tin mines, with the exception of Busanga, lost significant portions of their African workforce during this recessionary period.

Number of African Workers and European Personnel at the Main Work Sites of the Union Minière du Haut-Katanga as of 31 July 1921 and 31 July 1922

	31 July 1921		31 July 1922	
Work Site	Africans	Europeans	Africans	Europeans
Bureaux générales	–	93	–	87
Lubumbashi	2,249	230	2,314	227
Panda-Likasi	4,187	386	2,301	293
Kambove	1,323	92	864	50
Star of the Congo	723	41	454	24
Luishia	735	38	195	16
Ruashi	113	18	–	21
Busanga	598	11	674	15
Shienzi	300	33	38	1
Kakontwe	400	5	320	4
Shinkolobwe	400	5	350	4

Source: AA, UMHK, Mortalité.

58 AA, Ministère des Affaires etrangères; Grevisse, *Le Centre extra-coutumier*, 13–24.

59 AG, C8, Procès-verbal, 15 mai 1928; AG, B22, no. 104/D6, Situation des logements pour indigènes à Jadotville (Panda et Shituru), 27 août 1937.

60 AA, MOI no. 46 (3551), no. 254, Service des Affaires économiques: Ministère des Colonies, 14 mars 1922.

61 AA, MOI no. 46 (3551), no. 5421/398/B, Natalité, 10 janvier 1924, Elisabethville.

62 Consequently the Salesians focussed most of their attention on their agricultural and trades mission at Kiniama on the right bank of the Kafubu River. It was through this mission and the Africans it attracted that the Salesians were able to give a brace to the sagging fortunes of labor recruiters in Haut-Luapula by providing a constant pool of unskilled and semiskilled African labor for work on a handful of white settler farms. AG, C8, Réunion SM/MOI 1931, Procès-verbal de la séance tenue le 20 octobre 1931 par la Commission Gouvernement-UM.

63 Monsignor Felix de Hemptinne, "La Politique indigène du gouvernement belge," *Congo. Revue générale de la colonie*, annexe II (juin 1928): 359–74; Fetter, *The Creation*, 156; G. Valkeneer, "Centre d'Essais de Cultures Maraichères et Vivrières à Kiniama en territoire de Sakania," *Bulletin du CEPSI* 13 (1950): 336–37.

64 Mottoulle, "Contribution à l'étude du determinisme," 210.

65 AG, Procès-verbal 36, 15 mai 1928; AG, Situation des logements; Fetter, *The Creation*, 100.

66 AG, Instruction de reference.

67 Mottoulle, "Contribution à l'étude du determinisme; and AG, Procès-verbal 36, 15 mai 1928.

68 This side of the process was, of course, absent in the smaller company towns, where the Union Minière often stood in the place of the civil administration and the courts. The manifold response of African workers to the ills of urban life – burial and dancing societies, marijuana and alcohol consumption, vendetta, and occasional protests – could be found in the smaller towns in the 1920s, but without the tension and intricate weave that it acquired in the larger industrial towns. AA, MOI no. 134 (3598), no. 1317, Antoine Sohier, Note de monsieur le procureur général, 26 novembre 1925, Elisabethville; and AG, C8, no. 262, A monsieur le commissaire de police Kipushi," 21 août 1931, Mine Prince Léopold.

69 Malira, "Regard sur la situation sociale," 65–66; Fernand Engels, "Rapport du Katanga," *Rapport de la Commission du Travail*, 1 juin 1931, Bruxelles, 85.

70 A great deal of indirect evidence on absconding up to the middle 1930s tends to support Engels' estimation of the juncture that the African mineworkers' social consciousness had come to at the outset of stabilization. It seems that a large number of African workers who fled from Busanga, Musadys, and, to a lesser extent, Jadotville from 1927 to 1936 would often flee to the *cité indigène* of Elisabethville or to camps

closer to urban areas as opposed to the countryside. On the other hand, women fleeing the camps during the Depression years often attempted to return to their villages. See Léopold Mottoulle, "Mortalité infantile, mortinatalité et natalité: Mortinatalité et natalité chez les enfants des travailleurs Union Minière (camps industriels)," *Bulletin médical du Katanga* 7ème année, no. 1 (1930): 14; Engels, "Katanga," 61 and 92.

71 Lotar, "L'Immatriculation," 364–71.

72 Ibid., 371.

73 AG, C8, MOI D13, Discipline des travailleurs noirs, 1928; Theodore Heyse, *Le Régime du travail au Congo Belge* (Bruxelles: Goemaere, 1924), 5–10.

74 AA, Sohier, Note de monsieur le procureur général.

75 Ibid.

76 Fetter, "L'Union Minière du Haut-Katanga," 34.

77 "L'Impôt indigène," *Notre Colonie*, 22.

78 Fetter, *The Creation*, 102–3 and 110–12.

79 AA, Sohier, Note sur le régime du recrutement.

80 According to several sources the number of work-age men in the floating population of Katanga in general was between 50,000 and 60,000 and among the uprooted it was between 2,000 and 3,000. But these figures did not reveal what state of health these men were in or how many of them were from neighboring colonies. After 1924 the colonial administration felt that corporal punishment had to take precedence over minimum jail sentences with respect to the legal infractions committed by these two segments of the urban population, or else the jails would be filled with them. Forced labor, military conscription in the areas where they could be found, and *depots de mendicité*, or public workhouses, were all seen as aspects of a broad policy of stabilizing this segment of the African population between 1924 and 1930. Also, some sources of evidence indicate that a respectable portion of the floating population, along with prisoners from the territorial prison at Sakabinda, was perhaps used to open up the mines at Kengere and Kamoto between 1927 and 1937. See "Déracinés," *Congo. Revue générale de la colonie*, 7; AG, MOI/1197, B5, Pointage à Ruwe, 12 mars 1937.

81 AG, A monsieur le commissaire de police; Engels, "Katanga," 32; *Rapport sur l'Administration du Congo Belge*, 1932, 143–56.

82 *Rapport sur l'Administration du Congo Belge*, 1932, 143.

83 "L'Impôt indigène," *Notre Colonie*, 22.

84 By the middle of 1928, the management of the Union Minière felt that the most imminently reasonable means of stemming unexpected reductions in the strength of the African workforce as a result of flight and morbidity was to improve camp housing. At Lubumbashi the company built 100 cement Trabeka houses; 550 Kimberly brick huts were constructed at Shituru, and another 250 were built at Kipushi. Four entire villages of 50 brick houses each were built at Kakontwe by the end of

May 1928, and at the same time 85 new straw huts were built at Musonoi. European observers who had no affiliation with the Union Minière maintained that the workers' camps built during and after 1928 and those preexisting ones that had been landscaped again gave the African mineworkers a feeling of being at "home," because they were provisioned with garden plots or, as the company called them, "plantations." See AG, Procès-verbal 36, 15 mai 1928.

85 Fetter, *The Creation*, 112.

86 AG, Demande d'enseignements.

87 AA, Observations presentées par l'Association des Intérêts coloniaux belges, 7 janvier 1926 (draft); see JLVC, fiches 1693–1699, Sous-commission pour la Protection des Indigènes, séance du 14 janvier 1924.

88 LCHI, Administration de la Sûreté du Congo Belge, Rapport du secretariat sur l'activité de l'Association Lulua Frères, exercice du 1 janvier au 31 décembre 1946, Elisabethville; Fetter, "L'Union Minière du Haut-Katanga," 62–63.

89 An important feature of what one might call the practical philosophy of the lodges was their exhortation to their members to get along with people from other ethnic groups, particularly if the nonlodge member was a workmate. The unique feature of this kind of appeal was that it was always cast in terms of the dangers of the workplace. See AG, C8, MOI no. 122, Mutualité indigènes, 20 août 1928, Camp Lubumbashi.

90 See D'Orjo de Marchovette, "Notes sur les funerailles des Chefs Ilunga Kabale et Kabongo Kumwinda," *Bulletin des jurisdictions indigènes du droit coutumier congolais* 3ème année (avril 1935).

91 See MRAC, no. 19 ATA, M. Stoffelen, Etude sur le régime foncier du Bakwa Beya de Demba et sur le régime foncier Congolais en général, 1949; and Vansina, *Introduction à l'ethnographie*, 14.

92 Diambomba MuKanda Maila, "L'Impact de l'industrie minière sur la structure dualiste de l'economie du Zaire," *Bulletin de Gécamines. Industrie minière et développement au Zaire* (1974): 79–83; de Marchovette, "Notes sur les funerailles," 357.

93 De Marchovette, "Notes sur les funerailles," 353; cf. E. P. Thompson, "Le Charivari anglais," *Annales: economies, sociétés, et civilisations* 27e année, no. 2 (mars–avril 1972): 294–97.

94 Yet the Simba, or lion cult, a secret society of Tanganika-Moero which was associated with political opposition to both the Lunda Kazembe and the Nyamwezi warlord of the nineteenth century, Msiri, never appeared in the urban colonial administration's index of "dangerous native institutions." In 1925, however, Simba was conveniently linked to rural unrest at Lubondoie. See MRAC, no. 27 ATA, Investiture de Kashiobwe Mulondera, 13 février 1928; MRAC, no. 20 ATA, Lacanne, Enquête politique sur la région du Luapula-Moero, 1935; "Assignation à prevenu (Lamazani), *Journal administratif du Katanga*, 17 août 1925, Tribunal de Police (Albertville).

95 The majority of African soldiers and porters sent into Tanganyika, where modern *mbeni* societies with cash subscriptions for their members took shape, were Songye. *Rapport sur l'Administration du Congo Belge*, 1918, 18–19; AG, Demande d'enseignements.

96 See Ordonnance-loi no. 129 of 14 December 1912, "Modifant l'ordonnance no. 93 du 7 octobre 1912 sur les danses indigènes." The modification of the Ordonnance-loi no. 93 read, "In an area of five kilometers around this circumference, they cannot, except by special authorization of the Police Commission, dance after nine o'clock in the evening or places where they would tend to hinder movement or disturb the inhabitants"; *Journal administratif du Katanga*, 31 octobre 1921; see also AG, B12, MOI no. 121, Ventes aux indigènes (commerçants senegalais), 12 décembre 1938.

97 Bruce Fetter, "African Associations in Elisabethville, 1910–1935: Their Origins and Development," *Etudes d'histoire africaine* 2 (1976): 209–10; see also AG, B5, MOI-d776, Pointage à Ruwe, 1934.

98 Fetter, "African Associations," 210–11.

99 AG, Demande d'enseignements; Fetter, "African Associations," 206.

100 By the end of the 1920s African women had created their own closed voluntary associations. Perhaps the most important series of them were the infamous *kufunga* bars. These institutions were a crucial facet of urban African life until independence. They served as a means by which women could make money and initiate younger women from the hinterland into the mysteries of town life. They were an important way station in the attempt to construct a stable form of conjugal life and to give male migrants some idea of the assets women of different ages and from different locations might bring with them in the making of urban households. The frequent arrests of African women in both the towns and the rural areas for the illegal sale of beer and *lutuku*, a spirit made from either corn or cassava, suggest that there was more organization among the female population of the industrial towns of Katanga than met the eye of the average colonial administrator. See: Kubuya-Namulemba, "Regard sur la situation sociale," 56; AA, MOI no. 46 (3551), no. 542/398/B, Service des Affaires économiques, 10 janvier 1924, Elisabethville; Engels, "Katanga," 81–85.

101 AG, Demande d'enseignements.

102 Ibid.

103 According to the police at Elisabethville, the adherence to *bukanzanzi* and *batumbula* was dangerously widespread among the African population of the town in the 1940s and 1950s. In the instance of *batumbula*, a cult which was ostensibly controlled by white foremen of the Union Minière, the authorities maintained that the cult assassinated strangers and left their bodies out in the open in the belief that in this way they could appease the alleged European appetite for human flesh. Most of the "cult murders" of the late 1940s and 1950s occurred near the Lubumbashi factory works of the Union Minière. See: "Renaissance de la rumeur sur les Batumbula," *L'Essor du Congo* (10 mars 1956); Fetter,

"African Associations," 206; AG, Demande d'enseignement; see also Ceyssens, "Mutumbula."

104 "Etendue de la compétence des juges de police," *Revue juridique du Congo Belge* 11ᵉᵐᵉ année, no. 3 (mai–juin 1935); "Tribunal de police de Kipushi," *Journal administratif du Katanga*, 7 mars 1934.

105 Apparently the first stop on one of the routes that brought marijuana out of Kabongo was the mining town of Luishia. During the rainy season the traffic was especially heavy. At least seven Africans were arrested for the transportation of hemp in the town during this period, the two most notable traffickers being two Africans who were known to the court simply as Mulenga and Litombe. At the start of 1927, as a result of the marijuana trade, the colonial authorities imposed a revamped curfew on the nocturnal movements of Africans between 8:30 P.M. and 4:00 A.M.; see "Assignation à prevenu (Mulenga)," *Journal administratif du Katanga*, 6 septembre 1926.

106 "Tribunal de police de Kipushi," *Journal administratif du Katanga.*

107 JLVC, Sous-commission pour la Protection des Indigènes, 14 janvier 1924.

108 Ibid.

109 Ibid.

110 AG, Demande d'enseignements.

111 AG, C8, MOI no. 121, Organisation: Les Belges, 20 août 1928, Camp L'ishi.

112 Ibid.

113 AG, Mutalité indigènes.

114 JLVC, Sous-commission pour la Protection des Indigènes, 14 janvier 1924; for the origins of official views on African organization, see Daye, *L'Empire colonial Belge;* see also Bogumil Jewsiewicki, "Zaire Enters the World System: Its Colonial Incorporation as the Belgian Congo, 1885–1960," in *Zaire: The Political Economy of Underdevelopment,* ed. Guy Gran (New York: Praeger Publishers, 1979), 42–43.

115 JLVC, Sous-commission pour la Protection des Indigènes, 14 janvier 1924.

116 LCHI, Rapport du secretariat.

117 AG, Demande d'enseignements; *Rapport sur l'Administration du Congo Belge*, 1932, 65–68.

Chapter Four. From Stabilization to Labor Unrest, 1927–1931

1 For the context of this statement, see William D. Haywood, *The Autobiography of Big Bill Haywood* (New York: International Publishers, 1966); William D. Haywood and Frank Bohn, *Industrial Socialism* (Chicago: Charles H. Kerr, 1911), 25.

2 Margery Perham, *African Apprenticeship* (New York: Africana Publishing Company [Holmes and Meier], 1974), 217–18.

3   AG, C8, MOI D13, Discipline des travailleurs noirs, 1928; see Kindle-berger, *World in Depression*, 144; Alfred D. Chandler, *The Visible Hand* (Cambridge: Belknap Press, 1977), 362.

4   Copper Ore (in tons) Mined at the Union Minière du Haut-Katanga, 1918–1921

	1918	1919	1920	1921
Kambove				
smelter ore	950	450	400	366
concentrator ore	–	1,966	1,723	1,723
Kambove West				
smelter ore	80	40	40	40
concentrator ore	–	100	100	100
Likasi				
smelter ore	184	40	–	–
concentrator ore	–	600	500	–
Shituru				
smelter ore	133	–	–	–
concentrator ore	–	1,216	1,216	916
Msesa				
concentrator ore only	–	366	366	366
Fungurume				
smelter ore	–	–	50	–
concentrator ore	–	–	250	1,823
Kakanda				
smelter ore	–	33	50	50
concentrator ore	–	250	500	750
Others				
smelter ore	83	–	–	83
concentrator ore	–	616	616	616

Source: TC/UM, 64, Annexe D, Horner Report on Native Labor, 1919.

Elements of the new production strategy were in place by the end of the recession of 1921–22. The table above shows that part of the decision to switch to ingot and cathode production had to do with the company's available supplies of ore, since ore that could be directly smelted began to decline as early as 1919 in favor of ore that had to be concentrated by electrolytic or chemical means. Between 1922 and 1925 as well a similar ratio opened up between the two kinds of ore obtained at the mines. See also AG, A9, no. 508/D-40, Barème du salaires, juin 1935, Lubumbashi; AA, MOI no. 49 (3554), no. 518 annexe 4ᵉ D, Heenen, "Liberté du travail," 13 juin 1924, Elisabethville.

5   AA, MOI no. 59 (3558), Dr. Amar, Examen psycho-physiologique, 17 février 1922.

6   Kindleberger, *World in Depression*, 144 and 279; Richard Price, "Theories of Labour Process Formation," *Journal of Social History* (Fall 1984): 98.

7   Fetter, *The Creation*, 123; Jane L. Parpart, *Labor and Capital on the African Copperbelt* (Philadelphia: Temple University Press, 1983), 20.

8   John Higginson, "The Formation of an Industrial Proletariat in Southern Africa—the Second Phase, 1921–1949," in *Labor in the World Social Structure*, ed. Immanuel Wallerstein (Beverly Hills: Sage Publications, 1983), 122–24.

9   Another striking aspect of these developments was the consumption of electrical power at the Union Minière, which went from a mere 17,000 kilowatts in 1920 to 140,000 kilowatts by 1930. Productivity per worker went from 2.5 tons of ore in 1920 to 817 tons in 1930. See Conseil de province du Katanga (Comptes-rendus des séances), 1951, Annexe I, Rapport sur le fonctionnement de l'organisation professionelle indigène — exercice 1950, 193; see also Gouverneur, *Productivity and Factor Proportions*, 58.

10 TC/UM, 98, Usines de Lubumbashi, rapport mensuel, Fourniture d'energie aux sièges de Ruashi et Prince Léopold, février 1929.

11 Gouverneur, *Productivity and Factor Proportions*, 54–80; TC/UM, 96–98, Usines de Lubumbashi, rapport mensuels, 1927–29.

12 TC/UM, 98, Usines de Lubumbashi, rapport mensuel, Procès-verbal de la 48ème réunion mensuelle fonderie tenue à Lubumbashi le 13 novembre 1928, octobre-novembre 1928, 1–5.

13 Ibid.; see Table 5.1.

14 TC/UM, 98, Usines de Lubumbashi, rapport mensuel, décembre 1928, 3.

15 Gouverneur, *Productivity and Factor Proportions*, 56–61.

16 Looking back on the beginnings of worker stabilization, one observer said, "Ce n'est pas par esprit de philanthropie que les gros organismes s'intéressent à l'organisation et à la rationisation de travail en s'inspirant des theories de Taylor et en recourant aux procèdes Bedaux, Gombert et autres similaires. . . ." See Conseil de province du Katanga (Comptes-rendus des séances), 1946, Adaptation de la réglementation en matière de recrutement, 177.

17 AG, C8, annexe D12, no. 84, Demande d'enseignements, 12 décembre 1927, Elisabethville.

18 TC/UM, 96–98, Usines de Lubumbashi, rapports mensuels, 1923–27.

19 AG, C8, no. 4213, MOI D13, Recrutement: Lomami, 23 décembre 1927, Elisabethville; AG, Demande d'enseignements.

20 AG, C8, Procès-verbal 36, 20 novembre 1928, Elisabethville; AG, C8, MOI no. 262, A monsieur le commissaire de police Kipushi, 21 août 1931, Mine Prince Léopold.

21 AG, Procès-verbal 36, 20 novembre 1928.

22 AG, A monsieur le commissaire de police.

23 AG, Demande d'enseignements.

24 Ibid.

25 Perham, *African Apprenticeship*, 221–23.

26 AG, Demande d'enseignements; AG, C8, Procès-verbal (statistiques, septembre), 16 octobre 1928, Elisabethville.

27 AG, Procès-verbal (statistiques, septembre).

28 E. Toussaint, "Le Personnel congolais: Les Besoins de main-d'oeuvre; les moyens employés pour y fair face," in *UMHK* (monograph, Bruxelles, 1952): 237.

29 A case in point was that of Moke Kongolo. Kongolo, a mineworker at the Prince Léopold Mine at Kipushi, and two hospital attendants at

that mine, Mangili François and Mukunda André, were indicted for mutilating the corpse of the wife of another African worker at Kipushi, Mandefu Jacob, on 6 November 1926. Mukunda André was also charged separately with having assaulted Mandefu Jacob as well. Mukunda André was from Arumwimi District in Orientale Province; Moke Kongolo and Mangili François were from the same village of Katombwe in the Kongolo territory of Tanganika-Moero. Both Mangili François and Moke Kongolo were reputed to be powerful sorcerers who were in possession of an extremely powerful kind of *dawa*, or medicine. It was for the concoction of this *dawa* and also a possible exorcism that the two men allegedly severed the head from the corpse of Mandefu's wife. The fact that Mangili François was literate added to his reputation as a sorcerer in the workers' camp. In fact, the basis of association between Moke Kongolo and Mangili François was doubly affirmed by the fact that Kongolo had attempted to bribe Mangili into drawing up an illness report for him so that he could get out of work.

Although the charge of mutilation of the corpse could not be substantiated, all three men were charged with having gravely compromised work discipline at Kipushi. Kongolo and Mangili were cited especially for promoting indiscipline in the camp and given much stiffer sentences than Mukunda André in spite of his additional assault charge. Despite the fact that the local management of the mine works at Kipushi held up this particular case as an example for the African workforce there, the sale of *dawa* and the practice of *bwanga*, or magic, continued unabated on most of the mining sites. See "Crimes et superstitions indigènes: La Secte des Bagabo," *Bulletin des jurisdictions indigènes et du droit coutumier congolais*, 2ᵉ année, no. 11 (septembre 1934): 246–48; "Assignation aux prevenus (Moke Kongolo et Mangili François)," *Journal administratif du Katanga*, 6 novembre 1926.

30 Fetter, "L'Union Minière du Haut-Katanga," 34; AG, C8, Réunion DG, Tanganika-Moero MOI 1928, Procès-verbal, 12 décembre 1928; AG, C8, Réunion MOI, Situation des effectifs au premier mars 1932, 9 mars 1932, Elisabethville; Fetter, "L'Union Minière du Haut-Katanga," 1–28.

31 AG, Discipline des travailleurs noirs; AG, A monsieur le commissaire de police.

32 Gouverneur, *Productivity and Factor Proportions*, 80–92.

33 Perham, *African Apprenticeship*, 229.

34 AG, C8, Réunion SM/MOI 1931, Procès Verbal de la séance tenue le 20 octobre 1931 par la Commission Gouvernement–UM.

35 Ibid.

36 AG, Procès-verbal (statistiques, septembre); AG, C9, Stabilisation du MOI/RU, 15 août 1928.

37 AG, A monsieur le commissaire de police; AG, C8, MOI no. 121, Organisation: Les Belges, 20 août 1928, Camp Lubumbashi; AG, C8, Réunion DG/TM MOI 1928, Procès-verbal 20, 12 décembre 1928.

38 AG, Procès-verbal 20.

39 AG, A monsieur le commissaire de police.
40 AG, Discipline des travailleurs noirs.
41 On 1 May 1926, for example, Kambafweri from the Mulungwe chief-taincy in Northern Rhodesia was arrested for pilfering cement from his employer, Leo Wittacker, a subcontractor for the Union Minière at the Star of the Congo. Apparently, many of the African leaders of the unrest at Ruashi in May 1931 were Northern Rhodesians employed as construction workers at the Star. See *Journal administratif du Katanga*, 26 octobre 1926.
42 AG, Séance tenue le 20 octobre 1931 par la Commission Gouverne-ment–UM.
43 AG, Discipline des travailleurs noirs; AG, A monsieur le commissaire de police.
44 Parpart, *Labor and Capital*, 34.
45 AG, Barème du salaires.
46 AG, Procès-verbal 20.
47 AG, Barème du salaires; Fetter, *The Creation*, 86.
48 AG, Procès-verbal 20.
49 AG, Séance tenue le 20 octobre 1931 par la Commission Gouverne-ment–UM.
50 AG, C8, MOI no. 9-1-28, Note pour Monsieur de Mulder.
51 See TC/UM, 98, Usines de Lubumbashi, rapport mensuel, août 1933, 4–12.
52 TC/UM, Usines de Lubumbashi, rapport mensuel, 48ème réunion mensuelle fonderie tenue à Lubumbashi, 1–5.
53 Orris Herfindal, *Copper Costs and Prices: 1870–1957* (Baltimore: Johns Hopkins University Press, 1959), 277.
54 TC/UM, 98, Usines de Lubumbashi, rapports mensuels, septembre 1928–mars 1929.
55 TC/UM, Usines de Lubumbashi, rapport mensuel, Fourniture d'energie, 1.
56 TC/UM, 48ème réunion mensuelle fonderie tenue à Lubumbashi, 5.
57 TC/UM, Usines de Lubumbashi, rapport mensuel, Fourniture d'energie, 1.
58 Ibid., 2.
59 The self-timing blast furnaces cooled down in phases. New ore was often smelted during the initial phases. See TC/UM, Usines de Lubumbashi, rapports mensuels, septembre 1928, 8, and janvier 1929, 6.
60 AG, Procès-verbal 36, 20 novembre 1928; AG, Discipline des travail-leurs noirs.
61 AG, Note pour Monsieur de Mulder.
62 AG, C8, 37ème Réunion MOI–Service médicale, Procès-verbal, 12 décembre 1928, Elisabethville.
63 Ibid.
64 AG, Discipline des travailleurs noirs; Fetter, *The Creation*, 170.
65 AG, Procès-verbal (Service médicale).

66 "Assignation aux prevenus (Kambafweri, Kasemba, Semakweri)," *Journal administratif du Katanga*, 1926, RMP 23071/R1435, *Etoile du Congo*, 26 octobre 1926; AG, Discipline des travailleurs noirs.

67 AG, Stabilisation du MOI/RU.

68 AG, Discipline des travailleurs noirs.

69 *Rapport annuel sur le Ruanda-Urundi*, 1929, 64–79.

70 AG, C9, Territoire de la province R.U. impôt 1928, 8 mars 1930; Roger Botte, "Processus de formation d'une classe sociale africaine precapitaliste," *Cahier d'études africaines* 14, no. 50, 4ème cahier (1974): 608.

71 AG, C9, C7/20, Syndicat d'étude pour aider et protéger les indigènes: RU, 10 février 1930.

72 AG, Stabilisation du MOI/RU.

73 AG, Séance tenue le 20 octobre 1931 par la Commission Gouvernement–UM.

74 Ibid.

75 AA, MOI no. 134 (3598), no. 1317, Antoine Sohier, Note de monsieur le procureur général, 26 novembre 1925, Elisabethville.

76 Mottoulle, "Aspect social."

77 AG, Note pour Monsieur de Mulder; AG, Procès-verbal (statistiques, septembre).

78 AG, Recrutement: Lomami.

79 Ibid.

80 AG, Procès-verbal 20, 12 décembre 1928.

81 AG, Note pour Monsieur de Mulder.

82 AG, Recrutement: Lomami.

83 AG, Situation des effectifs.

84 AG, Note pour Monsieur de Mulder.

85 AG, D13, no. 3437, Sps A/1, Mortalité: Recrues Lomami, 12 septembre 1928, Elisabethville.

86 AG, Procès-verbal (Service médicale).

87 AG, Procès-verbal 36, 20 novembre 1928; AG, Mortalité: Recrues Lomami.

88 AG, A monsieur le commissaire de police.

89 AG, Mortalité: Recrues Lomami.

90 Ibid.

91 AG, B22, Division A: Service d'Inspection et de Contrôle, Salaires, 27 septembre 1937; AA, MOI no. 52 (3555), Barème des salaires, 25 février 1921, Elisabethville.

92 AG, B6, MOI no. 8253, Contrat du travail, 9 juin 1937, Elisabethville.

93 Ibid; Mottoulle, "Aspect social," 306.

94 AG, Demande d'enseignements.

95 Ibid.

96 Mottoulle, "Aspect social," 308; Leplae, "Histoire et développement des cultures," 233.

97 AG, Situation des effectifs.

98 Perham, *African Apprenticeship*, 212.

99 Ibid., 225 and 227–29.
100 "Province d'Elisabethville: Situation économique," *Rapport sur l'Administration du Congo Belge*, 1932, 233.
101 AG, Procès-verbal (statistiques, septembre).
102 AG, Stabilisation du MOI/RU.
103 Ibid.
104 AG, Situation des effectifs.
105 AA, MOI no. 46 (3551), Section E.C./B no. 374/719/935, 1ᵉʳ annexe, Ministère des Affaires etrangères: Direction B, 3 août 1926.
106 AG, Situation des effectifs.
107 AG, Séance tenue le 20 octobre 1931 par la Commission Gouvernement–UM.
108 AG, Procès-verbal 20.
109 Fetter, *The Creation*, 100; and AG, Barème du salaires.
110 AG, Situation des effectifs.

Chapter Five. The Labor Unrest of 1931 and Its Aftermath

1 Fernand Grevisse, *Quelques aspects de l'organisation des indigènes déracinés résidant en territoire de Jadotville* (Anvers: Editions Institut colonial et maritime, 1936), 11.
2 LCHI, Administration de la Sûreté du Congo Belge, Rapport du secretariat sur l'Activité de l'Association Lulua Freres, exercice du 1 janvier au 31 décembre 1946, Elisabethville.
3 AG, C8, MOI no. 262, A monsieur le commissaire de police Kipushi, 21 août 1931, Mine Prince Léopold.
4 *Rapport sur l'Administration du Congo Belge*, 1932, 65–68 and 143–56.
5 AG, Mutualité indigènes; and Jewsiewicki, "La Contestation sociale."
6 A. J. Beia, "Correspondance," *Ngonga* (3 novembre 1934): 2; and AG, C8, Réunion MOI, Situation des effectifs au premier mars 1932, 9 mars 1932, Elisabethville; see also Phimister and van Onselen, "Political Economy of Tribal Animosity."
7 Although it took place some three years later, the case of Kaumba Kalubatini is illustrative of the plight of such workers. In 1935 Kaumba was a carpenter at the Shituru plant in Jadotville. He was classified as MOI/s, or "skilled native labor." At the end of the year, however, he was transferred to the tin mine at Shienzi and stripped of his former classification. When he protested to the local *chef de poste*, Kaumba was fired by the camp manager, Jean Schroeven, even though the civil official upheld his claim. See AG, D6, no. 1, I dossier MOI, Schroeven, Correspondances, 7 mai 1936, Camp de Kikole.
8 AA, MOI no. 133 (3598), 4ᵉ direction, 1ᵉ section, Recrutement de main d'oeuvre pour le Haut-Katanga, 4 février 1926; AA, MOI no. 175 (3605), Sur le contrat du travail entre indigènes et maîtres civilisés, 12 avril 1926, Elisabethville.

9   AA, Sur le contrat du travail; and Fetter, *The Creation*, 119.

10 Fetter, *The Creation*, 119–21.

11 Ibid., 137–39; and "Prohibition illimitée du permit du travail," *Le Matériel colonial* 22ème année, no. 106 (mars 1939): 110.

12 AG, C8, annexe D12, no. 84, Demande d'enseignements, 12 décembre 1927, Elisabethville.

13 AA, MOI no. 134 (3598), no. 1317, Antoine Sohier, Note de monsieur le procureur général, 26 novembre 1925, Elisabethville; and AG, C8, Procès-verbal 36, 20 novembre 1928, Elisabethville.

14 AG, Demande d'enseignements; and AG, C8, MOI no. 121, Organisation: Les Belges, 20 août 1928, Camp Lubumbashi.

15 AG, Situation des effectifs.

16 AG, Organisation: Les Belges.

17 Japanese and American manufacturers began to replace German ones in supplying the industrial areas of Katanga with manufactured goods after the First World War. The articles that seemed to have the greatest demand among African workers were: buckles, money clips, felt hats, khaki and white pants, gym shoes, coats with gold buttons, naptha, clothes brushes, hatchets, hammers, hoes, hand towels, Flag brand cigarettes, corned beef, sardines, musical instruments—especially harmonicas—and miniature British flags. "Articles par le commerce du Congo," *Notre Colonie* 1e année, no. 6 (20 mars 1920): 39; AG, B6, MOI no. 8253, Contrat du travail, 9 juin 1937, Elisabethville; and Kubuya-Namulemba, "Regard sur la situation sociale," 59.

18 Fetter, *The Creation*, 136–39; AG, Situation des effectifs.

19 AG, C8, SM/MOI 1931, Pusmans, Dossier sur la necessité d'etablir auprès des centres industriels une administration directe et competente, 21 août 1931; Martin de Rycke Papers, Congo Collection (henceforth MRPCC), Secte Kitawala (renseignements généraux), Dossier du police au Katanga, territoire du Kongolo, Extrait du dossier administratif du nommé Kianza Djoni, 1937.

20 MRPCC, Secte Kitawala, handwritten notes; and AG, Pusmans, Dossier sur la necessité.

21 Fetter, "L'Union Minière du Haut-Katanga," 13; and *L'Union Minière du Haut-Katanga* (monograph series, Bruxelles: L. Cuypers, 1954), 36 (graphs of copper and cobalt production).

22 *L'Union Minière du Haut-Katanga* (1954), 36.

23 *UMHK: 1906–1956*, 2d ed. (Bruxelles: L. Cuypers, 1957), 172–73.

24 AG, C8, Réunion SM/MOI 1931, Procès Verbal de la séance tenue le 20 octobre 1931 par la Commission Gouvernement–UM.

25 AG, Procès-verbal 36, 20 novembre 1928; and AG, Séance tenue le 20 octobre 1931 par la Commission Gouvernement–UM.

26 AG, Séance tenue le 20 octobre 1931 par la Commission Gouvernement–UM.

27 AG, A monsieur le commissaire de police.

28 Ibid.

29 Perrings, *Black Mineworkers*, 254 (Appendix iii).
30 AG, C9, Stabilisation du MOI/RU, 15 août 1928; and AG, C8, D13, Discipline des travailleurs noirs, 1928.
31 AG, Discipline des travailleurs noirs.
32 Ibid.
33 AG, Situation des effectifs.
34 AG, Pusmans, Dossier sur la necessité.
35 Ibid.; Fetter, *The Creation*, 165.
36 AG, Pusmans, Dossier sur la necessité.
37 Ibid.; AG, Séance tenue le 20 octobre 1931 par la Commission Gouvernement-UM.
38 AG, Pusmans, Dossier sur la necessité.
39 AG, C8, SM/MOI 1931, Notes pour Monsieur le Docteur Mottoulle, Kipushi; and AG, Séance tenue le 20 octobre 1931 par la Commission Gouvernement-UM.
40 AG, Procès-verbal 36, 20 novembre 1928; and AG, Séance tenue le 20 octobre 1931 par la Commission Gouvernement-UM.
41 AG, Séance tenue le 20 octobre 1931 par la Commission Gouvernement-UM; "Situation économique," *Rapport sur l'Administration du Congo Belge*, 1932, 234; and Perrings, *Black Mineworkers*, 258.
42 AG, Séance tenue le 20 octobre 1931 par la Commission Gouvernement-UM.
43 Fetter, *The Creation*, 139–40.
44 AG, Notes pour Monsieur le Docteur Mottoulle.
45 Ibid.
46 AG, Situation des effectifs.
47 MRPCC, Secte Kitawala, handwritten notes, Origines du Kitawala.
48 AG, C8, Réunion MOI, Rapport du Comité regional du UMHK sur les vivres des camps, 9 mars 1932; AG, B12, MOI no. 121, Ventes aux indigènes — ventes à credit, 21 décembre 1938; see also Bruce Fetter, "Zambian Watchtower at Elisabethville, 1931–1934: An Analysis of Personal and Aggregate Data" (paper presented at the African Studies Association Meeting, 1975), 7 and Appendix I.
49 "Articles demandes," *Notre Colonie*, 20 mars 1920.
50 AG, Discipline des travailleurs noirs; "Province d'Elisabethville: Situation économique," *Rapport sur l'Administration du Congo Belge*, 1932, 233.
51 "Province d'Elisabethville: Situation économique," *Rapport sur l'Administration du Congo Belge*, 1932, 233.
52 MRPCC, Extrait du dossier administratif du nommé Kianza Djoni.
53 Ibid.
54 Fetter, *The Creation*, 128–29.
55 MRPCC, Extrait du dossier administratif du nommé Kianza Djoni; Fetter, *The Creation*, 136–39.
56 Archives of the Watch Tower Bible and Tract Society of Pennsylvania, Brooklyn, New York, A/A, "Histoire du développement de l'oeuvre des

temoins de Jehovah au Congo," 16 décembre 1964, 1-5. I wish to thank the Watch Tower Bible and Tract Society for photocopying and sending me this and other important documents from their archives in Brooklyn. I also want to thank Citoyen Nzazi Kinkobo, the chief administrator of the American Watch Tower Bible and Tract Society in Zaire. Citoyen Nzazi was most concerned to show me the crucial differences between witnesses and the adherents of *kitawala*. He was generous with his time and shared his knowledge and insight with me without imposing stipulations or conditions. For a different view of the problem of language and religious instruction, see Fabian, *Language and Colonial Power*, 59-60.

57 Some portents of this transformation were evident as early as 1915 during the Chilembwe uprising in Nyasaland. While Chilembwe's movement was not a Watchtower movement, many of the agricultural laborers at the base of the movement found Watchtower slogans and themes attractive. "Kairos," the watchword of the poorly remunerated laborers during the rebellion, meant "the due season is here," for example. The advent of Watchtower at Isoka, Northern Rhodesia, in 1922 was heralded by a cessation of crop cultivation. Chiefs were insulted and physically assaulted in some instances. According to a subsequent report by the Belgian colonial administration in neighboring Katanga, ". . . brawls and riots broke out, and the authorities were obliged to call out the military police to quell the delinquents. . . ." See George Shepperson and Thomas Price, *Independent African*, 2d ed. (Edinburgh: University Press, 1958), 409; see also Karen E. Fields, *Revival and Rebellion in Colonial Central Africa* (Princeton: Princeton University Press, 1985); MRPCC, Secte Kitawala (handwritten notes), Tomo Nyirenda alias Mwana Lesa, c.a.d. fils du Dieu.

58 *Rapport sur l'Administration du Congo Belge*, 1932, 234.

59 AG, Contrat du travail; AG, Situation des effectifs.

60 In 1928-29 cotton took more hectares than food crops in Bukama, Kabongo, Kongolo, Ankoro, and Mwanza—five of the most densely populated territories of Katanga. If one considers that much of the land was also planted in sesame—a cash rather than subsistence crop for the population of Katanga at the time—large portions of rural central Katanga must have been on the edge of starvation at this point. See Table 5.2.

61 AG, Contrat du travail; *Rapport sur l'Administration du Congo Belge*, 1932, 234-37.

62 LCHI, Rapport du secretariat; *Rapport sur l'Administration du Congo Belge*, 1932, 234.

63 AG, B22, Division A: Service d'Inspection et de Contrôle, Salaires, 27 septembre 1937.

64 AG, Procès-verbal 36, 20 novembre 1928; AG, Séance tenue le 20 octobre 1931 par la Commission Gouvernement-UM.

65 AG, D6, no. 193, Réquisitoires pour répatriement des travailleurs, 24 septembre 1935, Kikole.

Chapter Six. *The Reconstruction of the Mining Industry, 1932–1939*

1   AG, C8, Réunion SM/MOI 1931, Procès Verbal de la Séance tenue le 20 octobre 1931 par la Commission Gouvernement–UM.
2   Bustin, *The Lunda*, 123.
3   Fetter, *The Creation*, 139.
4   Bustin, *The Lunda*, 124.
5   Fetter, *The Creation*, 74.
6   Ibid., 75–77; Bustin, *The Lunda*, 24–26.
7   "Les Emplois pour indigènes dans l'administration," *Ngonga* 1ère année, no. 20 (13 octobre 1934): 1.
8   AG, Séance tenue le 20 octobre 1931 par la Commission Gouverne-ment–UM; "Province d'Elisabethville: Situation économique," *Rapport sur l'Administration du Congo Belge*, 1936, 14–17 and 64.
9   AG, Séance tenue le 20 octobre 1931 par la Commission Gouverne-ment–UM; *Rapport sur l'Administration du Congo Belge*, 1936, 245.
10 AG, C8, Réunion MOI, Situation des effectifs au premier mars 1932, 9 mars 1932, Elisabethville.
11 *L'Union Minière du Haut-Katanga* (Bruxelles: 1957), 175.
12 TC/UM, 60, Union Minière, rapport mensuel, juin 1937, 17; AG, D6, Département MOI no. 1173, Demande de femme: Kikole, 9 septembre 1937, Elisabethville.
13 AG, D6, MOI dossier no. 90, Travailleurs indésirables, Kikole.
14 Ibid.
15 Ibid.
16 AG, D6, Note pour Mottoulle: Compte salaires du déserteurs du Mine Groupe Kikole (confidentielle), 18 octobre 1934, Elisabethville.
17 Ibid.
18 AG, Situation des effectifs.
19 AG, C8, SM/MOI 1931, Pusmans, Dossier sur la necessité d'etablir auprès des centres industriels une administration directe et competente, 21 août 1931.
20 Baumer, *Les Centres indigènes*, 34–51.
21 AG, C8, SM/MOI 1931, Notes pour Monsieur le Docteur Mottoulle, Kipushi; "Province d'Elisabethville," *Rapport sur l'administration du Congo Belge*, 1934, 65–78.
22 AG, Notes pour Monsieur le Docteur Mottoulle.
23 AG, Séance tenue le 20 octobre 1931 par la Commission Gouverne-ment–UM; *Rapport sur l'administration du Congo Belge*, 1936, 64; AG, Notes pour Monsieur le Docteur Mottoulle.
24 AG, Séance tenue le 20 octobre 1931 par la Commission Gouverne-ment–UM.
25 *Rapport sur l'administration du Congo Belge*, 1934, 70–78.
26 For example, in 1936, the new provincial government decided not to record any industrial accident that did not result in death or at least three days' convalescence; see *Rapport sur l'administration du Congo Belge*, 1936, 21.

27 AG, Séance tenue le 20 octobre 1931 par la Commission Gouverne-ment–UM; AG, D6, no. 609, Mottoulle, Pêcheries du chef Kibanda (Lubende), 15 juillet 1936, Elisabethville.

28 *Rapport sur l'administration du Congo Belge*, 1936, 241.

29 AG, Séance tenue le 20 octobre 1931 par la Commission Gouverne-ment–UM.

30 "Circonscription indigènes," *Revue juridique du Congo Belge* (28 août 1935); "Assignation aux prevenus (Mulunga Katoto et Mufunga Kanimbo)," *Revue juridique du Congo Belge* (22 mai 1934).

31 Bustin, *The Lunda*, 99; AG, A9, MOI 644/39D, Remuneration insti-teurs Kikole, 26 septembre 1939, Elisabethville.

32 AG, Remuneration.

33 AG, D6, MOI no. 463, Procès-verbal de remise des objets, 6 mars 1939, Kolwezi.

34 "Main-d'oeuvre indigène," *Rapport sur l'administration du Congo Belge*, 1936, 19–20.

35 TC/UM, 64, Union Minière, rapport mensuel, septembre 1933, 17; "Prohibition illimitée," *Le Matériel colonial*, 110.

36 AG, D6, dossier no. 75, Clerc Bawa Jules, 8 décembre 1937, Busanga.

37 AG, D6, no. 43, Lettre du Gustave Dombe Mathieu, 27 août 1935, Elisabethville.

38 Ibid.; AG, Bawa Jules.

39 AG, D6, Kw-6/C166-c, MOI, Kolwezi–AME Church, 8 avril 1939, Kolwezi.

40 AG, D6, MOI no. 942, Toussaint, Le Pointage n'était plus effectue depuis le 7 mai, 10 juillet 1937, Kolwezi; AG, D6, Kw-6/C166-c, dossier no. 26, Châtiments: Mwamba Benion et Munthali Joseph, 29 décembre 1938, Kolwezi.

41 AG, Mottoulle, Pêcheries du Chef Kibanda.

42 Ibid.; AG, Notes pour Monsieur le Docteur Mottoulle.

43 AG, Kipushi; AG, Pusmans, Dossier sur la necessité.

44 AG, Situation des effectifs; AG, Pusmans, Dossier sur la necessité; AG, D6, MOI dossier no. 5, Travailleurs du souterrain, 23 octobre 1938, Kolwezi.

45 TC/UM, 64, Union Minière, rapport mensuel, août 1933, 17.

46 AG, C8, fiche 27, Rapport du Comité regional du UMHK sur les vivres des camps, 1 novembre 1932.

47 See: Robert Bates, *Rural Responses to Industrialization* (New Haven: Yale University Press, 1978), 11; Bogumil Jewsiewicki, "Unequal De-velopment: Capitalism and the Katanga Economy, 1919–40," in *The Roots of Rural Poverty in Central and Southern Africa*, ed. R. Palmer and N. Parsons (Berkeley: University of California Press, 1978), 335.

48 AG, Rapport du Comité regional du UMHK sur les vivres des camps, 1 novembre 1932.

49 AG, Situation des effectifs.

50 "Situation économique," *Rapport sur l'administration du Congo Belge*, 1918, 148.

51 "Prohibition illimitée," *Le Matériel colonial*, 110.

52 *Le Matériel colonial* 27ème année, no. 126 (mars 1937), 113.

53 AG, Mottoulle, Pêcheries du Chef Kibanda.

54 Grevisse, *Quelques aspects*, 38–44; "Origine des centres indigènes," *Ngonga* 1ère année, no. 15 (8 septembre 1934); "Les Emplois pour indigènes," *Ngonga*.

55 "Déracinés," *Revue générale de la colonie*, 5.

56 After six months in Katanga's towns, Guy Baumer concluded:

> The modern tendency, moreover, is to surround the African city such as we have just described it with rural neighborhoods established on cultivable land. In this way, it is hoped that a remedy for unemployment will be created, and a means to integrate at least some of the uprooted natives into a healthier social life. (Baumer, *Les Centres indigènes*, 59)

57 "Main-d'oeuvre indigène," *Rapport sur l'administration du Congo Belge*, 1936, 19–20; Minon, "Quelques aspects de l'evolution recente."

58 "Main-d'oeuvre indigène," *Rapport sur l'administration du Congo Belge*, 1936.

59 Grevisse, *Quelques aspects*, 40.

60 TC/UM, Union Minière, rapport mensuel, septembre 1933, 17; Grevisse, *Quelques aspects*, 17.

61 Grevisse, *Quelques aspects*, 34; "Prohibition illimitée," *Le Matériel colonial*, 113.

62 As the Union Minière closed in on the squatters' communities closest to its factories at Jadotville with a much more rigid set of economic and social constraints, many of the former African miners and factory operatives fled to the rural settlements of Jadotville's southwestern hinterland in an effort to escape the mining company's agricultural production quotas. After 1934–35, the African squatters were forced to leave even these settlements for the villages of the western Lunda country such as Nguba and Dena Mitumba. Some went as far as the *musumb*, or capital, of the Lunda *mwaant yav* at Kapanga, as the Union Minière's field of encroachment on the backlands behind Jadotville grew wider. No doubt, many of the African squatters, even those who were not Lunda, thought that the *mwaant yav*, or paramount chief, might protect them against the economic demands of the mining company. AG, B22, no. 2024, DG/1936, Location à la BCK du Camp Atelier Central Jadotville; Grevisse, *Quelques aspects*, 42; see also Bogumil Jewsiewicki, "The Great Depression and the Making of the Colonial Economic System in the Belgian Congo," *African Economic History* 4 (Fall 1977): 153–76.

63 TC/UM, 160, Union Minière, rapport mensuel, janvier 1937, 15; Dr. Reyntjen, "La Rougeole dans les camps de l'Union Minière du Haut-Katanga," *Bulletin médical du Katanga* 12ème année, no. 2 (1935): 70–88.

64 TC/UM, 64, Union Minière, rapport mensuel, 1 novembre 1933, 35.

65 AG, Pusmans, Dossier sur la necessité.

66 AG, Mottoulle, Pêcheries du Chef Kibanda; AG, D6, Kw-6/C116-c, dossier no. 26, La Question alimentaire, 29 décembre 1938, Kolwezi.

67 TC/UM, 99–100, Usines de la Panda, rapports mensuels, juin 1927–novembre 1929.

68 AG, Situation des effectifs.

69 TC/UM, 100, Usines de la Panda, rapport mensuel, mai 1928, 1–3.

70 TC/UM, 64, Union Minière, rapport mensuel, novembre 1933, 3–14.

71 TC/UM, 100, Usines de la Panda, rapport mensuel, septembre 1928, 1–3.

72 AG, Situation des effectifs.

73 TC/UM, 60, Union Minière, rapport mensuel, octobre 1936, 15.

74 Listen to an excerpt from the October 1936 factory report from Panda: "The number of desertions is abnormally high for Panda this month. These desertions have as their principal cause the repression of Watchtower adherents among the native workers" (ibid.).

75 Gouverneur, *Productivity and Factor Proportions*, 54–69; see Table 5.1.

76 Toussaint, "Le Personnel congolais, 237; AG, Travailleurs du souterrain.

77 Herfindahl, *Copper Costs*, 108.

78 Malela, *Proletariat et conscience*, 115–121; Bustin, *The Lunda*, 99; see Table 5.1.

79 AG, B22, no. 2024 dg/no. 1104/D6 (duplicate), Situation des logements pour indigènes à Jadotville (Panda et Shituru), 27 août 1937; AG, D6, MOI dossier no. 5, Toussaint, Le Pointage n'était plus effectue depuis le 7 mai, 23 octobre 1938, Kolwezi.

80 AG, B22, Division A: Service d'Inspection, Feuille de paie, 6 juillet 1939, Jadotville (Panda).

81 AG, Situation des logements; TC/UM, 64, Union Minière, rapports mensuels, août 1933–novembre 1936; TC/UM, 113, E. Sengier to G. C. Hutchinson, 5 September–19 November 1941.

82 TC/UM, 96–98, Usines de Lubumbashi, rapports mensuels, 1927–29; AG, Notes pour Monsieur le Docteur Mottoulle.

83 AG, B22, Division A: Service d'Inspection et de Contrôle, Salaires, 27 septembre 1937; AG, B22, no. 1167/d6, Transfert des travailleurs de Shinkolobwe à Panda, 8 septembre 1937.

84 Grevisse, *Quelques aspects*, 54.

85 AG, B22, Camp de Jadotville (Panda), "Division A: Inspection," 6 juillet 1939; TC/UM, 60, Union Minière, rapport mensuel, juin 1937, 14–17; Grevisse, *Quelques aspects*, 136.

86 AG, Situation des logements.

87 AG, B22, no. 473a, Feuille de paie (Jadotville), 9 juin 1939.

88 AG, Note pour Mottoulle: Compte salaires.

89 AG, D6, no. 1, I dossier MOI, Schroeven, Correspondance, 7 mai 1936, Camp de Kikole.

90 Ibid., date of correspondence unknown.

91 AG, B12, memo b6, Pointage Busanga, 28 novembre 1939.

92 AG, Kipushi.

93 AG, D6, no. 2.549c, Travailleur no. K659 et Travailleur no. K658, 8 juin 1938, Kikole.
94 AG, Pointage Busanga; TC/UM, Sengier to G. C. Hutchinson, 19 November 1941.
95 AG, B22, Division A, no. 136, Salaires de MOI/s, 9 novembre 1935, Jadotville; AG, D6, no. 555 MOI, Transfert de travailleurs de Kengere, 13 juillet 1938, Elisabethville.
96 TC/UM, 64, Union Minière, rapports mensuels, septembre-novembre 1933.
97 AG, Transfert des travailleurs de Shinkolobwe à Panda.
98 See Table 5.1.

Chapter Seven. The Political Experiences of the
African Mineworkers, 1937–1941

1 Beia, "Correspondance."
2 AG, D6, d6/no. 1479, B.P. 407, Administration, 14 juillet 1937.
3 National Archives of the United States (henceforth NAUS), 855A.00/741, Patrick Mallon, Friction between British and Belgians over the War Effort of the Congo (confidential), 31 January 1941, American Consulate, Léopoldville.
4 The highly mechanized Musonoi work site at Kolwezi was an important exception to this general rule; see NAUS, 855A.50/7-2045, CS/D No. 144, American Consulate General, Report to the Secretary of State (unrestricted), 1–3, 20 July 1945, Léopoldville.
5 Ibid.; AG, B22ème, Division A, Inspection: Camp de Jadotville, 6 juillet 1939, Panda; AG, D6, no. 874/kw-6, Feuille de suppression de la prime de regularité, 14 octobre 1938, Elisabethville; AG, B22, Division A, no. 136, Salaires de MOI/s, 9 novembre 1935, Jadotville.
6 AG, B22, Division A: Service d'Inspection et de Contrôle, Salaires, 27 septembre 1937; AG, B22, no. 1167/d6, Transfert de travailleurs de Shinkolobwe à Panda, 8 septembre 1937; MRPCC, Province de Coquilhatville, Secretariat Provincial, no. 33 (sec./A.1/Elv.), ordonnance-loi le 10 juillet 1937, Attendu que des idées subversives ont été propagées dans le district de l'Ubangi par certains relégués, anciens meneurs de la Secte Kitawala; MRPCC, Province de Coquilhatville, Territoire de Bosobolo, Note sur les agissements des relégues adeptes du Kitawala à Bosobolo, 18 janvier 1938; see also Perrings, *Black Mineworkers*, 215.
7 *Rapport sur l'administration du Congo Belge,* 1936, 9; AG, D6, Kw-6/C166-c, MOI, Kolwezi-AME Church, 8 avril 1939, Kolwezi; AG, B12, memo b6, Pointage Busanga, 28 novembre 1939.
8 AG, Service d'Inspection et de Contrôle, Salaires.
9 Since the central administration was largely unaware of the fact that African workers were often compensated monetarily for supplying their own food, its position on the matter was predictably inflexible. When

an instance of the use of ration cards as wages at Kipushi came to the attention of the Elisabethville office in 1937, it issued the following warning to the camp manager there:

> You have been using ration cards for payment of salaries for recruits. We refer you to paragraph 87 in order to remind you that male and female ration cards must remain in the camps after being used. Also, they must be classified every month so that the flow of food can be controlled.
>
> It is clear that if these cards are used to pay salaries, they cannot remain in the camps. The control of the food supply becomes therefore impossible. (Ibid.)

10 AG, D6, no. 1063, Accident (confidentielle), 28 juin 1938, Ruwe.

11 AG, D6, no. 1033, Lettre à M. le chef de poste de Musonoi: Plainte pour vol de mèches de sûreté, 28 avril 1936.

12 Ibid.

13 AG, D6, no. 2.549c, Direction générale, Cimetière à Kengere, 14 février 1938; Musas, "La Situation sociale," 282–313.

14 AG, D6, MOI no. 488, Cremion, Désertions, 23 juin 1938, Kolwezi-Elisabethville; AG, B12, no. 1883/AE, MOI, Déserteurs de Busanga, 8 décembre 1937; AG, D6, no. 429, Note pour Monsieur le Docteur Mottoulle (confidentielle), Kikole.

15 AG, D6, no. 92, Retenues compensatoires: sommes dues par des déserteurs, 1 janvier 1936, Elisabethville.

16 The classification "R/L" was an indication that a given worker was "*recividiste*," or a chronic "troublemaker"; see AG, D6, no. 123/488/Annexe, Désertions Kengere, 9 juin 1938.

17 Ibid.

18 Ibid.

19 AG, B12, dossier no. 72, UMHK/Département MOI-Elisabethville, Proteste de surménage (confidentielle), 19 mars 1936, Busanga.

20 Ibid.

21 AG, D6, MOI dossier no. 5, Travailleurs du souterrain, 23 octobre 1938, Kolwezi; "Reparation judiciaire," *L'Essor du Congo* (12 février 1937): 1.

22 AG, Service d'Inspection et de Contrôle, Salaires; AG, B12, MOI no. 121, Ventes aux indigènes—ventes à credit, 21 décembre 1938, Elisabethville.

23 "Situation économique," *Rapport sur l'administration du Congo Belge,* 1936, 8; Edouard Bustin, "Government Policy toward African Cult Movements: The Case of Katanga," in *African Dimensions,* ed. Mark Karp (Boston: Boston University Press, 1973), 115–19.

24 Conseil de province du Katanga (Comptes-rendus des séances), 1945, Congo Belge, Province d'Elisabethville, Agriculture et Colonisation, Annexe V, Amélioration de la santé de l'indigène par l'application d'une politique d'hygiène des villages, du logement, de l'alimentation, Réunion du 14 mai 1945; Conseil de province du Katanga (Comptes-rendus des séances), 1946, Province d'Elisabethville, Reorganisation territoriale de la province, 14 juillet 1946; Bustin, *The Lunda,* 158–81.

25 MRPCC, Secte Kitawala (renseignements généraux), Province d'Elisa-

bethville, District du Tanganika, Territoire de Kongolo, Beer de Laer, Rapport sur les activités de la secte Kitawala à Kongolo, 29 mai 1943; MRPCC, Province de Constermansville, Secretariat, no. 6483/Sec-Pers, Affaire Katuna Theo, 6 août 1943.

26 Conseil de province du Katanga (Comptes-rendus des séances), 1946, Etat d'esprit des populations indigènes, 11 octobre 1946; Conseil de province du Katanga (Comptes-rendus des séances), 1952 (summary statement), L'Exode rural dans les pays tropicaux; MRPCC, Affaire Katuna Theo.

27 Bustin, "Government Policy," 6; *Rapport sur l'administration du Congo Belge*, 1936, 9; AG, Kolwezi–AME Church.

28 JLVC, 438/113 TP, Le Chef de province, A. Maron, 14 novembre 1940, Elisabethville.

29 JLVC, Territoire de Malonga/Censure/Dilolo, A monsieur le procureur du roi à Elisabethville, 25 novembre 1940.

30 Ibid.

31 MRPCC, Beer de Laer, Rapport sur les activités de la secte Kitawala à Kongolo.

32 MRPCC, Secte Kitawala (renseignement généraux), Dossier du police au Katanga, territoire du Kongolo, Extrait du dossier administratif du nommé Kianza Djoni, 1937.

33 MRPCC, Secte Kitawala, Province d'Elisabethville, District du Tanganika, Secret-Sûreté publique, Rapport no. 2, Rapport sur les agissements du nommé Kulu Mupenda alias Kandeke Sandwe, propageant les doctrines du "Kitawala" en chefferie Benze du territoire d'Albertville, district du Tanganika, 8 mai 1937.

34 Fetter, *The Creation*, 173.

35 Bustin, *The Lunda*, 136.

36 Bustin, "Government Policy," 115.

37 Foster, *Class Struggle*, 20–45; Sholto Cross, "The Watchtower Movement in South Central Africa, 1908–1945" (D. Phil., Oxford University, October 1973), 8–10. See also E. P. Thompson, *The Making of the English Working Class* (New York: Vintage, 1967), 66–67.

38 Bustin, "Government Policy," 114; see also Karen Fields, "Charismatic Religion as Popular Protest: The Ordinary and the Extraordinary in Social Movements," *Theory and Society* 11, 3 (May 1982): 321–61.

39 The Watchtower unrest in Elisabethville, for instance, was largely a result of a series of boycotts against local merchants from 26 September to the end of November 1931. Cf. MRPCC, Rapport sur les agissement du nommé Kulu Mupenda; MRPCC, Secte Kitawala (handwritten notes), Tomo Nyirenda alias Mwana Lesa c.a.d. fils du Dieu.

40 It is more difficult to trace the early threads of Watchtower in the Tanganika-Moero District than in the Haut-Luapula District, primarily because the police and government surveillance of the movement in the former district was more episodic and perhaps inept than it was farther south. Until the end of the 1920s, there was only one major arrest and indictment of a Watchtower adept in Tanganika-Moero. The

indictment was handed down by the police tribunal at Albertville against one Lamazani, who was arrested for preaching sedition and transporting firearms in 1924–25. Lamazani escaped shortly before he was brought to trial and presumably returned to Tanganyika. However, 18 years later a police report for 7 July 1943 mentioned a middle-aged or "graying" Tanganyikan named Lamazani as being one of the chief lieutenants of Bushiri on the eve of the Masisi/Watchtower rising of 1944. "Assignation à prévenu (Lamazani)," *Journal administratif du Katanga*, Tribunal de Police (Albertville), 18 novembre 1923; MRPCC, Secte Kitawala (renseignements généraux), Province de Stanleyville, Territoire du Lubutu, P. Colente, Rapport no. 2 sur les agissements des relégués de la secte Kitawala en territoire du Lubutu, 25 octobre 1942; see also Cross, "The Watchtower Movement," 8.

41 The Kianza Djoni tendency of Watchtower acquired a following among the African soldiers of Force Publique stationed in Katanga during the Second World War. Many of the movement's followers in the military were from Kianza's home territory of Kongolo or from neighboring villages in the Tanganyika District (Tanganika-Moero before 1934) of Katanga. Although Kianza himself seemed not to have played a major role in the provincial insurrection of 1944, many of the soldiers who belonged to his movement provided some of the local leadership for the failed uprising, particularly in northern and western Katanga.

At least three noncommissioned African officers, Sergeant Mabonge Alphonse, Sergeant Kiembe Michel, and Limbo Mangeni, were on the fringes of the aborted insurrection and the Djoni tendency of Watchtower. All three were arrested with Kianza Djoni in July 1943; see MRPCC, Beer de Laer, Rapport sur les activités de la secte Kitawala à Kongolo; MRPCC, Secte Kitawala, handwritten notes; "Manono: R. 2169 Suite de jugement du janvier 1942," *Journal administratif du Congo*, 1945.

42 MRPCC, Rapport sur les agissements du nommé Kulu Mupenda.

43 Ibid.

44 Ibid.

45 Ibid.

46 Ibid.

47 Ibid.

48 Ibid.

49 Ibid.

50 MRPCC, Beer de Laer, Rapport sur les activités de la secte Kitawala à Kongolo.

51 Ibid.

52 Ibid.

53 MRPCC, Extrait du dossier administratif du nommé Kianza Djoni.

54 MRPCC, Beer de Laer, Rapport sur les activités de la secte Kitawala à Kongolo.

55 Ibid.

56 Ibid.
57 Ibid.
58 Ibid.
59 Ibid.
60 Ibid.
61 AG, B21, MOI/D 231, Grèves (chef de camp Moppe), 15 novembre 1941.
62 Ibid.; AG, B17, MOI/D 243, Grèves (Kipushi), 11 novembre 1941.
63 AG, Grèves (Moppe).
64 Ibid.
65 See George Shepperson, "Nyasaland and the Millennium," in *Millennial Dreams in Action*, ed. Sylvia Thrupp (New York: Schocken, 1970), 145; see also Shula Marks, *Reluctant Rebellion* (Oxford: Clarendon, 1970); TC/UM, 113, Sengier to Herbert Feis, 11 October 1941; AG, Grèves (Moppe).
66 JLVC, Congo Belge, Province d'Elisabethville, District du Lualaba, Territoire de Jadotville, No. 4111 S.P., Surveillance ligne de force: UMHK à Luishia, 25 septembre 1941, Jadotville.
67 Ibid.
68 AG, Grèves (Moppe).
69 Tshibangu, "La Situation sociale," 282.
70 NAUS, 855A.00/7-2345, no. 147, American Consulate General, Deposition of James Morrison of the American Presbyterian Congo Mission, Policy of the Belgian Congo Government towards the Indigenous Population (confidential), 1, 20 July 1945, Léopoldville.
71 JLVC, Union Minière du Haut-Katanga 12, 252/DG: 5763, A monsieur le gouverneur de la province (variations annuelles du coût d'un equipment de travailleur), 6 novembre 1941.
72 NAUS, Policy of the Belgian Congo Government; Tshibangu, "La Situation sociale," 282–87.
73 AG, A1, Administration générale, Rolus, Rapport sur la grève des travailleurs de l'Union Minière, février 1942; TC/UM, Sengier to Feis.
74 NAUS, Report to the Secretary of State, 20 July 1945.
75 TC/UM, 113, Sengier, Memorandum, 6 November 1940, 4.
76 AG, A10, MOI Elisabethville, Compte rendu de la séance tenue par la Commission de Revitaillment en viande, 18 juin 1943; AG, B5, d15/MOI, Taux salaires, 16 avril 1939.
77 JLVC, Variations annuelles.
78 The. annual report, for which Emile Rolus' *aide-memoire* was an addendum, assumed that the African workers were encouraged to strike by the publication of the parquet's investigation of the control and distribution of rations in the Lubumbashi camp. The report also said that real wages for all of the mining company's African workers did fall, despite the wage increases of 1938 and 1940, and that the company's attempt at mitigating the decline in wages by increasing the amount of rations issued to women and children had little or no effect on the

workers' standard of living. See AG, A1, Rapport annuel, 1942; see also AG, Rolus, Rapport sur la grève des travailleurs (1942); see n. 9.

79 Tshibangu, "La Situation sociale," 282–83.

80 AG, A1, Administration générale, 1256/b900, Camps des travailleurs, 18 janvier 1942.

81 Bates, *Rural Responses*, 34; Jewsiewicki, "Unequal Development," 321–23.

82 "Vie chère," *L'Essor du Congo* 5454 (4 avril 1944).

83 See Table 7.3; AG, Grèves (Kipushi).

84 AG, Grèves (Kipushi).

85 Ibid.

86 Tshibangu, "La Situation sociale," 294.

87 On 14 November 1941 Governor Maron sent a telegram to the governor-general in Léopoldville in which he drew rather ominous comparisons between the strikes at Manono and Kipushi. AG, Grèves (Kipushi); JLVC, Maron, Télégramme avion: Congo Léo, 14 novembre 1941, Elisabethville.

88 AG, Grèves (Kipushi).

89 Before the Second World War, a large portion of the smoked and fresh fish distributed to the company's workers was purchased from African fishermen and peddlers from Kasenga. After the war the provincial government, with the assistance of European retailers, suppressed this level of African entrepreneurship. See AG, Commission de Revitaillment; Conseil de province du Katanga (Comptes-rendus des séances), 1951, Annexe I, Questions A.I.M.O.I.: Recensement et identification des indigènes, 22 mars 1951, Elisabethville.

90 "Main-d'oeuvre indigène," *Rapport sur l'administration du Congo Belge*, 1946.

91 AG, Véntes aux indigènes — ventes à credit.

92 AG, B6, MOI no. 37, Rolus, Rapport sur les travailleurs indigènes, 11 décembre 1941.

93 TC/UM, 113, Sengier, Memorandum, 10 October 1941, New York, 7.

94 *Rapport sur l'administration du Congo Belge*, 1946, 8.

Chapter Eight. The Leviathan Collapsed and Rebuilt

1 NAUS, 855A.00/741, Friction between British and Belgians over the War Effort of the Congo (confidential), 31 January 1941, American Consulate, Léopoldville.

2 Quoted in Bustin, *The Lunda*, 247.

3 Tshibangu, "La Situation sociale," 282–87.

4 Duduri Ruhararamanzi, "La Grève des ouvriers noirs à l'UMHK" (Mémoire de licence, UNAZA, Lubumbashi, 1972), 60–71.

5 Tshibangu, "La Situation sociale," 283–84.

6 "Main-d'oeuvre indigène," *Rapport sur l'administration du Congo Belge*,

1946, 8–11; AG, B6, MOI no. 37, Rolus, Rapport sur les travailleurs indigènes, 11 décembre 1941.

7 AG, D6, Kw-6/C166-c, MOI, Kolwezi–AME Church, 8 avril 1939, Kolwezi; Bustin, *The Lunda*, 141.

8 AG, D6, C511-C6, Matricule KE 274 P/E: Sapoto Tshiniama, 23 avril 1944.

9 AG, A5, UMHK/Département MOI, Rapport sur la grève des travailleurs de l'Union Minière, 6 mars 1946.

10 AG, A1, 673/D-9001, Administration générale, 9 septembre 1940.

11 AG, Rapport sur la grève des travailleurs (1946); Tshibangu, "La Situation sociale," 283–84.

12 AG, A9, UMHK/Département MOI, Barème de salaires, 11 novembre 1941; JLVC, Congo Belge, Province d'Elisabethville, District du Lualaba, Territoire de Jadotville, No. 4111 S.P., Surveillance ligne de force: UMHK à Luishia, 25 septembre 1941, Jadotville.

13 TC/UM, 113, Sengier to G. C. Hutchinson (private correspondence), 19 November 1941; Tshibangu, "La Situation sociale," 276–80.

14 LCHI, Georges Lievens, Note historique sur le massacre de Lubumbashi, 1953; "La Grève de Panda," *L'Essor du Congo*, treizième année, no. 416 (7 décembre 1941): 1.

15 Tshibangu, "La Situation sociale," 303.

16 LCHI, Lievens, Note historique; LCHI, Georges Lievens, Lettre ouverte à Monsieur Rolus, 1954; Tshibangu, "La Situation sociale," 284.

17 LCHI, Lievens, Lettre ouverte; Tshibangu, "La Situation sociale," 284.

18 AG, Rapport sur la grève des travailleurs (1946); "La Tragédie de Panda," *L'Essor du Congo*, treizième année, no. 419 (10 décembre 1941): 1.

19 "La Tragédie de Panda," *L'Essor du Congo*.

20 AG, A1, Administration générale, Rolus, Rapport sur la grève des travailleurs de l'Union Minière, février 1942.

21 Ibid.

22 Ibid.; AG, B1, Département MOI, Aide mémoire fascicule, Classification des emplois remplis par les indigènes, mars 1946.

23 AG, Rapport sur la grève des travailleurs (1946).

24 "La Tragédie de Panda," *L'Essor du Congo*, 1; "Les grèves de Panda," *L'Essor du Congo*, treizième année, no. 414 (5 décembre 1941): 1.

25 Tshibangu, "La Situation sociale," 297.

26 LCHI, Lievens, Note historique.

27 Tshibangu, "La Situation sociale," 297.

28 Ibid.

29 LCHI, G. Montenez, handwritten notes (untitled), 28 septembre 1965; "Les Fusils et du gibier," *L'Essor du Congo*, douzième année (2 juin 1940): 1.

30 Tshibangu, "La Situation sociale," 299.

31 Conseil de province du Katanga (Comptes-rendus des séances), 1945, Congo Belge, Province d'Elisabethville, Agriculture et Colonisation, Annexe V, Amélioration de la santé de l'indigène par l'application d'une

politique d'hygiène des villages, du logement, de l'alimentation, Réunion du 14 mai 1945.

32 LCHI, Lievens, Note historique.

33 AG, Rolus, Rapport sur la grève des travailleurs (1942).

34 "La Grève de Lubumbashi," *L'Essor du Congo*, treizième année, no. 419 (10 décembre 1941): 1; LCHI, Emile Toussaint, handwritten notes (untitled), 2 janvier 1945.

35 LCHI, Mme Toussaint, Le Front de travail II/3, 2 janvier 1945.

36 Ibid.

37 LCHI, G. Montenez, handwritten notes.

38 LCHI, Lievens, Note historique; AG, Rolus, Rapport sur la grève des travailleurs (1942).

39 LCHI, Lievens, Note historique.

40 LCHI, Lievens, Lettre ouverte.

41 Ibid.

42 AG, Rolus, Rapport sur la grève des travailleurs (1942).

43 LCHI, Lievens, Lettre ouverte.

44 Ibid.

45 Gouverneur, *Productivity and Factor Proportions*, 79–82.

46 AG, d15/MOI, Taux salaires, 16 avril 1939.

47 Quoted in Bustin, *The Lunda*, 142.

48 AG, B21, MOI/301, Grèves (Kikole), 20 décembre 1941.

49 V. I. Lenin, *Two Tactics in Social Democracy* (Moscow: Progress Publishers, 1966), 176.

50 See Isaac Deutscher, *The Prophet Armed*, 3 vols. (New York: Vintage, 1965), 1: 125.

51 NAUS, 855A.00/762 PS/MO, no. 674, Mutiny in the Force Publique (Belgian Colonial Army), 6 March 1944, Léopoldville.

52 NAUS, 855A.00/761 PS/JB, no. 682, Mutiny in Force Publique (Belgian Colonial Army), 17 March 1944, American Consulate, Léopoldville.

53 See JLVC, District du Lualaba, 368/S.P., Incidents, Kolwezi, 10 janvier 1943 (confidentielle), 22 janvier 1943, Jadotville.

54 "Indiscipline et faineantise," *L'Echo du Kivu* (10 juillet 1942); "Un appel du governeur-général," *L'Essor du Congo*, no. 5053 (8 août 1942); see JLVC, C/1048, Monsieur le commissaire de district (Albertville), "CFL" Albertville, 1 février 1946, Albertville.

55 AG, Rapport sur la grève des travailleurs (1946).

56 In the original French the excerpt reads thus:

> Avec mille variante que l'on devine, le thème des revendications rencontre dans la brousse, le mécontentment des populations agricole. Celles-ci obéissent à la raison de plus fort, mais avec amertume. Partout l'espirit d'antipathie et de defiance gagne du terrain.
>
> L'indigène se detache de nous; il échappe de plus en plus à notre influence et à notre prestige. La physionomie du Congo change d'expression. La Belgique est en train de perdre son auréole Africain.

See NAUS, 855A.00/753, no. 654, Criticism by Apostolic Vicar of Belgian Government's War Policy of All-Out Production for the Congo, 26 January 1944, American Consulate, Léopoldville.

57 AG, Rapport sur la grève des travailleurs (1946).

58 NAUS, 855A.00/765, Despatch no. 699, Mutiny in Force Publique (account of rebellion by Mr. Daeleman, former officer in the Force Publique, in translation), 10 May 1944.

59 NAUS, 855A.00/763, Leyburn, Transmission of Eye-Witness Account of Insurrection in Belgian Congo, 6 April 1944, Cape Town; see also "Un étrange echo des grèves du Katanga," *L'Essor du Congo*, no. 5661 (16 décembre 1944).

60 NAUS, Leyburn, Transmission of Eye-Witness Account.

61 "Le Kasai devant la crise du cuivre," *L'Essor du Congo*, no. 5661 (16 décembre 1944).

62 NAUS, Mutiny in Force Publique, 10 May 1944; "Le Calendrier tragique des troubles recents du Kasai-Lomami," *L'Essor du Congo* (3 août 1944).

63 NAUS, Mutiny in Force Publique, 10 May 1944; NAUS, Leyburn, Transmission of Eye-Witness Account.

64 At least three noncommissioned African officers — Sergeants Mabonge Alphonse, Kiembe Michel, and Limbo Mangeni — were on the fringes of the aborted insurrection. They were also Watchtower adherents of the Djoni tendency. All three were arrested with Kianza Djoni in July 1943. See MRPCC, Secte Kitawala (renseignements généraux), Dossier du police au Katanga, territoire du Kongolo, Extrait du dossier administratif du nommé Kianza Djoni, 1937.

65 At Lubumbashi, for example, the clerks did convince a few factory operatives to join the planned insurrection. Without the consent of the military leaders, they convinced the factory workers to acquire arms and ammunition. Unaware of the fact that most of the military leadership of the insurrection had been arrested in the first week of May — primarily because the African mining clerks and other *évolué* leadership had not told them — this handful of men rose after a mining disaster and the second arrest of some of their erstwhile leadership. They were put down ruthlessly by the authorities. The municipal police reacted to the incident with a show of force that was completely out of proportion to the number of conspirators. A week after this isolated attempt at an armed uprising the rebellion was brought to a close in western Katanga. See MRPCC, Secte Kitawala (renseignements généraux), province d'Elisabethville, district du Tanganika, territoire de Kongolo, Beer de Laer, Rapport sur les activités de la secte Kitawala à Kongolo, 29 mai 1943; Bruce Fetter, "The Luluabourg Revolt at Elisabethville," *African Historical Studies* 2, 2 (1969): 137; for another illuminating discussion of the role of Union Minière workers in the failed insurrection, see Jean-Luc Vellut, "Le Katanga industriel en 1944: Malaises et anxiétés dans la société colonial," in *Congo Belge durant*

la Seconde Guerre Mondiale: recueil d'études, ed. Jean-Jacques Symoens and Jean Stengers (Bruxelles: Académie royale des Sciences d'Outre-Mer, 1983), 495–524.

66 MRPCC, Beer de Laer, Rapport sur les activités de la secte Kitawala à Kongolo.

67 "Les Mouvements de rébellion," *L'Essor du Congo* 17ème année, no. 5440 (18 mars 1944); NAUS, Leyburn, Transmission of Eye-Witness Account.

68 JLVC, Territoire Bukama, no. 831/S.P., Objet: Incidents s/w Prince Léopold (confidentielle), 29 avril 1944, Bukama.

69 NAUS, Mutiny in the Force Publique, 10 May 1944; "Les Mouvements de rébellion," *L'Essor du Congo.*

70 MRPCC, Extrait du dossier administratif du nommé Kianza Djoni.

71 Ibid.

72 JLVC, Incidents s/w Prince Léopold.

73 "Les Mouvements de rébellion," *L'Essor du Congo* (5 août 1944).

74 Fetter, "The Luluabourg Revolt," 273; "Les Mouvements de rébellion," *L'Essor du Congo,* 5 août 1944; see also Vellut, "Le Katanga industriel," 504–5.

75 "Les Mouvements de rébellion," *L'Essor du Congo,* no. 5842 (8 mai 1944).

76 NAUS, Mutiny in the Force Publique, 10 May 1944.

77 Ibid.

78 Ibid.

79 Ibid.

80 Ibid.

81 Ibid.; NAUS, Leyburn, Transmission of Eye-Witness Account.

82 "Le Calendrier tragique," *L'Essor du Congo.*

83 NAUS, Mutiny in the Force Publique, 10 May 1944.

84 Ibid.

85 "Les Mouvements de rébellion," *L'Essor du Congo* (5 août 1944).

86 NAUS, Mutiny in the Force Publique, 10 May 1944.

87 "La Grande Pitié," *L'Essor du Congo.*

88 "Le Calendrier tragique," *L'Essor du Congo.*

89 "Les Mouvements de rébellion," *L'Essor du Congo* (5 août 1944).

90 "La Grande Pitié," *L'Essor du Congo;* "A propos des mouvements de rébellion," *L'Essor du Congo,* no. 5495 (24 mai 1944).

91 Bustin, *The Lunda,* 119–22.

92 Ibid., 120–21 and 148.

93 "La Philosophie de la rébellion," *L'Essor du Congo.*

94 "L'Administration indigène," *L'Essor du Congo* (14 novembre 1944); Léopold Mottoulle, "Problèmes de la main-d'oeuvre indigène," *L'Essor du Congo* (5 août 1944).

95 "La Grand Pitié," *L'Essor du Congo.*

96 Mottoulle, "Problèmes de la main-d'oeuvre."

97 Conseil de province du Katanga, 1945, Amélioration de la santé de l'indigène.
98 Jean Sohier, *La Mémoire d'un policier belgo-congolais* (Bruxelles: Académie royale des Sciences d'Outre-Mer, 1974), 58–70.
99 AG, D22, Départment MOI, Apprentis et adolescents, 17 octobre 1950, Elisabethville.
100 Mottoulle, "Problèmes de la main-d'oeuvre."
101 AG, Apprentis et adolescents; "La Grand Pitié," *L'Essor du Congo.*
102 Bustin, *The Lunda,* 182–83.
103 On 18 November 1944 the situation had reached such a disturbing pitch that the governor-général of the Belgian Congo, Pierre-Paul Ryckmans, made a personal appeal over the radio to the Conseil de Government and the major employers to do something about the escalating level of indiscipline among the African workers. On the other hand, some quarters of government and industry felt that the problem of unrest had been fomented by the visible increase in the number of skilled and semi-skilled African workers. Further, it was suggested that the number of semiskilled and skilled African workers in strategic industries such as mining and the building trades be reduced, and that a legal code similar to the South African color bar be implemented in the Belgian Congo. See TC/UM, Sengier to Hutchinson, 26 February 1947; Conseil de province du Katanga, 1945, Amélioration de la santé de l'indigène.
104 Conseil de province du Katanga, 1945, Amélioration de la santé de l'indigène.
105 AG, B1, Département MOI, Instruction de référence no. 7, Engagements, classifications et promotion des travailleurs sortis des divers établissements scolaires, 12 octobre 1950, Elisabethville.
106 "Le Problème de l'élite congolaise," *L'Essor du Congo,* no. 5637 (18 novembre 1944); "Le Jury de qualification pour la main-d'oeuvre indigène," *L'Essor du Congo* (22 mars 1947).
107 Conseil de province du Katanga (Comptes-rendus des séances), 1951, Annexe I, Rapport sur le fonctionnement de l'organisation professionnelle indigène – exercice 1950, 69.
108 "Le problème de l'élite congolaise," *L'Essor du Congo.*
109 Conseil de province du Katanga, 1945, Amélioration de la santé de l'indigène.
110 "Le Jury de qualification," *L'Essor du Congo.*
111 Bustin, *The Lunda,* 217–36.
112 LCHI, Congo Belge, Gouvernement général, 2ème direction générale, Annexe à lettre no. 39.055 du décembre 1957.

Chapter Nine. Conclusion

1 NAUS, 855A.00/7-2345, no. 147, American Consulate General, Deposition of James Morrison of the American Presbyterian Congo Mission,

Policy of the Belgian Congo Government towards the Indigenous Population (confidential), 20 July 1945, Léopoldville.

2 NAUS, 855A.00B/12-1549, Dehoux encl. in Despatch no. 19, Governor General's Remarks Concerning Communist Infiltration in the Belgian Congo, 15 December 1949 (received 9 January 1950), American Consulate, Elisabethville.

3 See Ryckmans, *Dominer*, iii–vi; see also John Onwumelu, "Congo Paternalism: An Isolationist Colonial Policy" (Ph.D. dissertation, University of Chicago, 1966), 362.

4 See Thomas Hodgkin, *Nationalism in Colonial Africa* (New York: New York University Press, 1957), 48–56.

5 Crawford Young, *Politics in the Congo* (Princeton: Princeton University Press, 1963), 234.

6 N. Kajika, "Quelques aspects théoriques et méthodologiques d'une recherche en cours sur la vie travail et vie hors travail des mineurs de Kamoto," *Maadini*, quatrième trimestre, no. 4 (1974): 17 and 35.

7 Grevisse, *Le Centre extra-coutumier*, 237.

8 Fetter, *The Creation*, 164–65.

9 AG, B1, Département MOI, Aid memoire fascicule, Classification des emplois remplis par les indigènes, mars 1946.

10 Paul Baran, *The Political Economy of Growth* (New York: Monthly Review Press, 1968), 3–46.

11 Hans Gerth and C. Wright Mills, *Character and Social Structure* (New York: Harbinger Books, 1964), 236.

12 I, for instance, have learned a great deal from reading the works of historians of working people in other dependent and colonial societies, historians such as Jean Chesneaux and Ronald Suny. I have also benefitted from reading some of the more innovative recent works on workers in Europe and America. In the latter, the neighborhood, village, and workplace itself have come to replace or complement the trade union as the locus of working-class aspirations and protest. Such perspectives were especially helpful to me, since trade unions were illegal under Belgian colonial rule and have only recently become one of the institutions that Zairean workers can deploy against their employers. See Jean Chesneaux, *The Chinese Labor Movement, 1919–1927* (Palo Alto: Stanford University Press, 1967); Ronald Suny, *The Baku Commune* (Princeton: Princeton University Press, 1972); see also: Ira Katznelson and Aristide Zolberg, *Working Class Formation* (Princeton: Princeton University Press, 1986); Foster, *Class Struggle*; Rolande Trempé, *Les Mineurs de Carmaux* (Paris: Editions ouvrières, 1971); Montgomery, *Workers' Control*.

13 See, for example: Martin Legassick, "Gold, Agriculture, and Secondary Industry in South Africa: From Periphery to Sub-Metropole as a Forced Labor System," *The Roots of Rural Poverty in Central and Southern Africa*, ed. Robin Palmer and Neil Parsons (Berkeley: University of Cali-

fornia Press, 1977), 175–201; J. K. Rennie, "White Farmers, Black Tenants and Landlord Legislation: Southern Rhodesia 1890–1930," *Journal of Southern African Studies* 5, 1 (October 1978): 86–99; Charles van Onselen, "Black Workers in Central African Industry: A Critical Essay on the Historiography and Sociology of Rhodesia," in *Studies in the History of African Mine Labour in Colonial Zimbabwe*, ed. I. R. Phimister and C. van Onselen (Gwelo: Mambo Press, 1978), 80–102; Jewsiewicki, "La Contestation sociale"; Harold Wolpe, "Capitalism and Cheap Labour Power in South Africa: From Segregation to Apartheid," *Economy and Society* 1, 4: 425–55; Kubuya-Namulemba, "Regard sur la situation sociale."

14 See Colin Bundy, *The Rise and Fall of the South African Peasantry* (Berkeley: University of California Press, 1977); Perrings, *Black Mineworkers*; van Onselen, *Chibaro*; I. R. Phimister, "Capital and Class in Zimbabwe, 1890–1948," Henderson Seminar Paper No. 50 (Department of History, University of Zimbabwe), 6 October 1980, 23; Giovanni Arrighi, "Labour Supplies in Historical Perspective: A Study of the Proletarianization of the African Peasantry in Rhodesia," *Journal of Development Studies* 6, 3 (1970): 197–234; Terence Ranger, *The African Voice* (Evanston: Northwestern University Press, 1970).

15 For a stimulating discussion of this conceptual problem, see: Michael Burawoy, *The Politics of Production* (London: Verso Press, 1985), 209–45; G. Carchedi, *Problems in Class Analysis* (London: Routledge and Kegan Paul, 1983), vii–ix; Gouverneur, *Productivity and Factors Proportions*, 84–93; Poupart, *Facteurs de Productivité*;

16 See Jones, "Class Expression."

17 See AA, MOI no. 134 (3598), no. 1317, Antoine Sohier, Note de monsieur le procureur général, 26 novembre 1925, Elisabethville; "Le Personnel congolais, 237; Jewsiewicki, "Unequal Development," 317–44.

18 See Gordon Craig, *Germany, 1866–1945* (New York: Oxford University Press, 1978), 448–53; Carl P. Parrini, *Heir to Empire* (Pittsburgh: University of Pittsburgh Press, 1969), 142; Karl Polanyi, *The Great Transformation* (Boston: Beacon Press, 1957), 66 and 266; see also Mottoulle, "Contribution à l'etude du determinisme fonctionnel"; Fetter, L'Union Minière du Haut-Katanga."

19 See Roderick Aya, "Popular Intervention in Revolutionary Situations," in *Statemaking and Social Movements*, ed. Charles Bright and Susan Harding (Ann Arbor: University of Michigan Press, 1984), 318–19.

20 A good example of the self-serving tone of most such justifications is contained in the example below:

> Stabilization was above all an economic necessity for the Union Minière. For the native worker and for the native population in general, it was a benefit. Once placed in the service of the enterprise, the native ceased to be an anonymous

auxiliary; his willingness to work increased; he was better paid; and he lived better. He gave his labor willingly and without undue strain. He was pleased with his new existence. His personality developed and he acquired the dignity and conscientiousness of a true worker. (Toussaint, "Le Personnel congolais," 237)

21 Peter Richardson and Jean-Jacques Van Helten, "The Development of the South African Gold Mining Industry, 1895-1918," *Economic History Review* 37, 3 (August 1984): 331-8; F. A. Johnstone, *Class, Race and Gold* (London: Routledge and Kegan Paul, 1976).

22 See Leroy Vail and Landeg White, "The Struggle for Mozambique: Capitalist Rivalries, 1900-40," *Review* 3, 2 (Fall 1979): 253-55; AG, D8, no. 1309/d6, Transferts des travailleurs, 8 octobre 1937; NEC/SA, Testimony of Mr. Duncan M. Eadie, 6197-208, 2 April 1931, Durban; see also A. J. Beia, "Correspondance"; Higginson, "The Formation," 148.

Epilogue. New Battles, Old Terrain

1 Conseil de province du Katanga (Comptes-rendus des séances), 1951, Congo Belge, Province du Katanga, Service des A.I.M.O., Note sur l'organisation professionelle indigène — exercice 1951, 24-27.

2 NAUS, 855A.001/9-448 CS/A, Observations Regarding Loss of Libel Suit by Governor of the Katanga (restricted), 4 September 1948, American Consulate, Elisabethville.

3 Conseil de province du Katanga (Comptes-rendus des séances), 1951, Annexe I, Rapport sur le fonctionnement de l'organisation professionelle indigène — exercice 1950, 69.

4 Ibid., 69.

5 Ibid., 73-77.

6 Ibid., 211-23.

7 Ibid., 220-22.

8 Ibid., 223.

9 Ibid., 77-79.

10 Ibid., 73-75.

Bibliography

ARCHIVAL SOURCES

AA: Archives africaines

The records of the former Ministry of Colonies, the Repositoire de ancien Ministère des Colonies, in Brussels, Belgium, are cited as Archives africaines (AA) throughout the text. The records of the Bourse du Travail du Katanga, or the Office central du Travail du Katanga after 1927, compose the largest single fund of materials in the archives on African labor. Along with consular reports, correspondence between the Ministry of Colonies and the provincial administration, and depositions from the Office pour l'Inspection du Industrie et Commerce, these records provided the core of the primary evidence for the first three chapters.

AG: Archives gécamines

The personnel records of the mining company are an important part of the research that went into this work. Records on the basic characteristics of the African workforce are housed at the administrative seat of Générale des Carrières et MInes (Gécamines) in Lubumbashi, Zaire. Gécamines is the corporate entity created by the "Zaireanization" of the Union Minière du Haut-Katanga. Each major file, or *direction*, of the personnel records is preceded by an uppercase letter of the alphabet. For example, file A is organized around the records of the general administration of the mining company; file B is organized around troubleshooting areas for the mining company such as persistent strikes, work stoppages, abscondings, absenteeism, sabotage, theft, and so on; file C is concerned with recruitment in the main, although after stabilization some records concerning the overall disposition of the African workforce are housed in this *direction*; file D contains most of the documentation on the outlying mines, including the tin mines, from 1924 to 1940. These files are often further subdivided by a lowercase letter and a number. In other instances "MOI" (Main-d'Oeuvre indigène) and "Réunion" are used to indicate materials dealing with labor problems or administrative ones, if such materials are not in files A and B, respectively.

Archives of the Watch Tower Bible and Tract Society of Pennsylvania

While I have not personally consulted the records of this religious organization (nonmembers cannot normally acquire access to the archives), its administrators graciously sent me a large number of photocopied documents.

Most of these documents were either personal reminiscences of Congolese adherents from the 1930s and 1940s or correspondence between the Watch Tower society and various colonial officials. The archives are located in Brooklyn, New York.

BPRO: British Public Record Office
I consulted a number of diplomatic and consular reports from the British Public Record Office in London. The documents on deposit there can now be acquired on a selective basis on microfilm.

JLVC: Jean-Luc Vellut Collection
A large number of documents from the Jean-Luc Vellut Collection were used in the manuscript. This collection contains a vast number of official government documents generated by the former colonial government about the provinces of Kasai and Katanga, as well as a large fund of documents from the Union Minière and the other giant colonial trusts and missionary societies. All the documents are on microfiche and are housed at the University of Wisconsin–Madison and Université Louvain in Belgium.

LCHI: Lemarchand Collection, Hoover Institution on War, Revolution,
and Peace
A good portion of the police reports used in this work, particularly in chapter seven, were found in private collections in the United States. Many of these collections also contain a respectable fund of the private correspondence of some of the government officials and corporate executives closely associated with the Union Minière. One collection of documents, organized by René Lemarchand and housed at the Hoover Institution on War, Revolution, and Peace at Stanford University, Palo Alto, California, contains several autobiographical sketches of white trade union leaders at the Union Minière. One of these white trade unionists, Georges Lievens, wrote a brief narrative history of the African general strike, which is now a part of the collection. Additionally, the Lemarchand Collection also contains a great deal of material on the organization of the Belgian territorial administration in Ruanda-Urundi after the First World War. The collection also contains some of the unpublished notes for the manuscript sections of the censuses for Ruanda-Urundi from 1927 to 1933.

MRAC: Musée royal de l'Afrique centrale
I have examined a few files of territorial and district administration records that are housed in the archives of the Musée royal de l'Afrique centrale, Tervuren, Belgium. The majority of these records were given to the museum by private donors who, in the main, were former colonial administrators in the Belgian Congo. Most of these holdings are ethnographic studies of particular groups of people in the Congo. A few of them also attempt to sketch a brief political history of certain groups of people before the commencement of colonial rule.

MRPCC: Martin de Rycke Papers, Congo Collection

The police records used in the two sections on African Watchtower on the mines were taken almost exclusively from the Martin de Rycke Papers, which are housed in the Congo Collection at Michigan State University, East Lansing. The entire collection has only recently been indexed and catalogued with the aid of an expert librarian and archivist, Ms. O. Ezera. Most of the documents and correspondence in the papers have to do with the events in Kivu and Katanga between 1933 and 1944.

NAUS: National Archives of the United States

I have made use of materials in the Department of State section of the National Archives of the United States in Washington, D.C. Most of these records are concerned with the extraction and evacuation of strategic raw materials from Katanga during the Second World War.

Na Zim: National Archives of Zimbabwe

I had occasion to use the papers of H. G. Robins, which are housed in the National Archives of Zimbabwe, Harare, Zimbabwe. Robins was a prospector for Tanganyika Concessions Limited and probably one of the most prolific correspondents among the company's employees between 1906 and 1917.

TC/UM: Tanganyika Concessions/Union Minière

Another large fund of Union Minière records is that of Tanganyika Holdings Limited, 6 John Street, London, England. The actual archives are located in the subbasement of Empire House, London, England ECI. Most of the records housed there have to do with the technical and capital outlay problems of the Union Minière during the years when Tanganyika Concessions, the parent company of Tanganyika Holdings, was an important shareholder in the mining company.

TRCLD: Thomas Reefe Collection, Luba Documents

The Thomas Reefe Collection of documents on the Belgian Congo is on microfilm and deposited with the Center for Research Libraries' Cooperative Africana Microfilm Project (CAMP) in Chicago, Illinois. There are 11 reels, each of them representing the records of a given subregion of Shaba Province, Zaire, formerly Katanga Province, Belgian Congo.

GOVERNMENT SOURCES

Government reports and periodicals were extremely helpful in reconstructing the outlines of many of the important developments in Katanga from 1914 to 1949. The most important collections of government reports for this work were:

Annual Reports of Northern Rhodesia, 1923-29;

Documents parlementaires;
Native Economic Commission Reports for South Africa, 1931;
proceedings of Conseil de province du Katanga, or the Provincial Council of Katanga, 1923–56 (from 1917 to 1923 these reports were known as the proceedings of the Comité régional du Katanga);
Rapports annuels sur le Ruanda-Urundi, 1924–45;
Rapports de la Commission du Travail, reports drawn up by a body of government study groups created by the Belgian Ministry of Colonies to examine the African labor problem in the Belgian Congo from 1924 to 1931;
Rapports sur l'administration du Congo Belge, annual reports drawn up for the Belgian Parliament from 1907 to independence.

Most of these sources are available in their original printed form or on microfilm at many universities in the United States that have an emphasis on African or southern African studies. The University of California, Stanford University, Yale University, and Northwestern University are only a few. The only exceptions to this are the unpublished proceedings of the Conseil de province du Katanga. A complete set of these records is housed in the documents section of Olin Library at Cornell University. The most important government periodicals used were:

Bulletin administratif du Katanga, 1915–16
Bulletin agricole du Katanga, 1932–37
Journal administratif du Katanga, 1923–27
Journal officiel du Katanga, 1911–12
Rapport de la Commission du Travail, 1930–31
Rapport de la Commission pour l'Etude du Problème de la Main d'oeuvre, 1924–25
Revue administratif du Congo Belge, 1914–23
Revue juridique du Congo Belge, 1921–35

OTHER SOURCES

"A propos des mouvements de rébellion." *L'Essor du Congo,* no. 5495 (24 mai 1944): 1.
"L'Administration indigène." *L'Essor du Congo.* Paris: Editions Maspero, 1972.
Anderson, Ben. *Imagined Communities.* London: Verso, 1983.
"Un Appel du gouverneur-général." *L'Essor du Congo,* no. 5053 (8 août 1942): 1.
Arrighi, Giovanni. "Labour Supplies in Historical Perspective: A Study of the Proletarianization of the African Peasantry in Rhodesia." *Journal of Development Studies* 6, 3 (1970): 197–234.
"Articles demandes par le commerce du Congo." *Notre Colonie* 1e année, no. 6 (20 mars 1920): 39.

Austen, Ralph. *Northwest Tanzania under German and British Rule: Colonial Policy and Tribal Politics, 1889–1939.* New Haven: Yale University Press, 1973.

Aya, Roderick. "Popular Intervention in Revolutionary Situations." In *Statemaking and Social Movements,* edited by Charles Bright and Susan Harding, 318–27. Ann Arbor: University of Michigan Press, 1984.

Badhuin, Fernand. "Le Congo Belge." *L'Economiste français* (2 octobre 1926).

Badhuin, Fernand. "Le Boerenbond Belge." *Revue économique internationale* 22ème année 1, no. 1 (janvier 1930).

Baran, Paul. *The Political Economy of Growth.* New York: Monthly Review Press, 1968.

Bates, R. H. *Unions, Parties and Political Development.* New Haven: Yale University Press, 1971.

Bates, R. H. *Rural Responses to Industrialization.* New Haven: Yale University Press, 1978.

Baumer, Guy. *Les Centres indigènes extra-coutumier au Congo Belge.* Paris: Editions Montesforet, 1934.

Beach, D. N. *The Shona and Zimbabwe, 900–1850.* London: Heinemann, 1980.

Beia, A. J. "Correspondance." *Ngonga* (3 novembre 1934): 2.

Beling, W. A. *The Role of Labor in African Nation Building.* New York: Praeger, 1968.

Benoit, J. "Contribution à l'étude de la population active d'Elisabethville." *Bulletin du CEPSI,* no. 54 (septembre 1961): 57–72.

Birmingham, David. "The Date and Significance of the Imbangala Invasion." *Journal of African History* 6, no. 2 (1965): 143–52.

Boigelot, Andre. *Rapport sur l'hygiène des travailleurs noirs de mai 1918 à mai 1919.* Bruxelles: Presses de Vrament, 1920.

Botte, Roger. "Processus de formation d'une classe sociale africaine precapitaliste." *Cahiers d'études africaines* 14, no. 50, 4ème cahier (1974): 605–26.

Brassinne, Jacques. *Les Rapports secrets de la sûreté congolaise.* Bruxelles: Editions Arts et Voyages, 1973.

Buell, Raymond L. "Labor in the Congo." *The Nation* 127, no. 8287 (4 July 1928): 24–26.

Bundy, Colin. *The Rise and Fall of the South African Peasantry.* Berkeley: University of California Press, 1977.

Burawoy, Michael. "The Functions and Reproduction of Migrant Labor: Comparative Material from Southern Africa and the United States." *American Journal of Sociology* 81, 5 (March 1976): 1050–87.

Burawoy, Michael. *The Politics of Production.* London: Verso, 1985.

Bustin, Edouard. "Government Policy toward African Cult Movements: The Case of Katanga." In *African Dimensions,* edited by Mark Karp, 113–35. Boston: Boston University Press, 1973.

Bustin, Edouard. *The Lunda under Belgian Rule.* Cambridge: Harvard University Press, 1975.

"Le Calendrier tragique des troubles recents du Kasai-Lomami." *L'Essor du Congo* (3 août 1944): 1.

Carchedi, G. *Problems in Class Analysis.* London: Routledge and Kegan Paul, 1983.

Ceyssens, Rik. "Mutumbula. Mythe de l'Opprime." *Cultures et développement* 7, 3–4 (1975): 485–550.

Chandler, Alfred D. *The Visible Hand.* Cambridge: Belknap Press, 1977.

Chelepner, B. S. *Cent ans d'histoire sociale en Belgique.* Bruxelles: Editions Institut de Sociologie de Solvay, 1956.

Chesneaux, Jean. *The Chinese Labor Movement, 1919–1927.* Palo Alto: Stanford University Press, 1967.

Chomé, Jules. *Le Drame de Luluabourg.* Bruxelles: Editions de Remarques congolaises, 1960.

Chretien, J. P. "Une Revolte au Burundi en 1934." *Annales: economies, sociétés et civilisations* 25 (1970): 1678–717.

Cloward, Richard, and Frances Fox-Piven. *Poor People's Movements.* New York: Vintage, 1977.

"Considérations sur la main d'oeuvre indigène." *Notre Colonie* 10ᵉ année (décembre 1928).

Coquery-Vidrvitch, Catherine. *Le Congo au temps des grandes compagnies concessionaires, 1898–1930.* Paris: Mouton, 1972.

"Coup Attempt in Zaire." *New York Times,* 7 July 1975:1.

Craig, Gordon. *Germany, 1866–1945.* New York: Oxford University Press, 1978.

"Crimes et superstitions indigènes: La Secte des Bagabo." *Bulletin des jurisdictions indigènes et du droit coutumier congolais* 2ᵉ année, no. 11 (septembre 1934): 246–48.

Cross, Sholto. "A Prophet Not Without Honour." In *African Perspectives,* edited by Christopher Allen and R. W. Johnson, 171–84. London: Cambridge University Press, 1970.

Cross, Sholto. "The Watchtower Movement in South Central Africa, 1908–1945." D. Phil., Oxford University, October 1973.

Daye, Pierre. *L'Empire colonial Belge.* Bruxelles: Editions du Soir, 1923.

DeBauw, A. *Le Katanga: Notes le pays, see resources et l'avenir de la colonisation belge.* Bruxelles: Larcier et Cie, 1920.

"Decision Near on Disputed Aid to Zaire." *New York Times,* 21 January 1976: 1.

de Hemptinne, Felix, Monsignor. "La Politique indigène du gouvernement belge." *Congo. Revue générale de la colonie,* annexe II (juin 1928): 359–74.

de Heusch, Luc. *Le Roi ivre ou l'origine de l'etat.* Paris: Gallimard, 1972.

de Lanessan, J. L. "La Crise coloniale." *Revue économique internationale* 4ᵉᵐᵉ année 3, no. 4 (avril 1907).

Dellicour, Fernand. *Les Premières Années de la cour d'appel d'Elisabethville, 1910–1920.* Bruxelles: Editions Aurore, 1938.

de Marchovette, D'Orjo. "Notes sur les funerailles des Chefs Ilunga Kabale et Kabongo Kumwinda." *Bulletin des jurisdictions indigènes du droit coutumier congolais* 3ᵉᵐᵉ année (avril 1935).

Depelchin, Jacques Jean-Marie François. "From Pre-Capitalism to Imperialism: Social and Economic Formations in Eastern Zaire, 1880–1960 (Uvira Zone)." Ph.D. dissertation, Stanford University, 1974.

"Déracinés autour des grandes centres." *Congo. Revue générale de la colonie,* annexe II (juin 1924): 5.

de Schrevel, Michel. *Les Forces politiques de la décolonisation congolaise jusqu'à la veille de l'indépendance.* Louvain: Imprimerie M & L Symons, 1970.

Deutscher, Isaac. *The Prophet Armed.* 3 vols. New York: Vintage, 1965.

Dile, Jacques Kazadi wa. *Politiques et techniques de remuneration dans l'entreprise au Congo.* Kinshasa: Editions Lovanium, 1970.

Dupriez, Gerald. *La Formation du salaire en Afrique.* Leuven: Drukkerij Frankie, 1973.

Emmanuel, Arghiri. "White Settler Colonialism and the Myth of Investment Imperialism." *New Left Review* 73 (May–June 1972): 35–57.

"Les Emplois pour indigènes dans l'administration." *Ngonga* 1ère année, no. 20 (13 octobre 1934): 1.

"Un Étrange echo des grèves du Katanga." *L'Essor du Congo,* no. 5661 (16 décembre 1944): 1.

Fabian, Johannes. *Jamaa.* Evanston: Northwestern University Press, 1971.

Fabian, Johannes. "Popular Culture in Africa: Findings and Conjectures." *Africa* 48, 4 (1978): 315–34.

Fabian, Johannes. *Language and Colonial Power.* London: Cambridge University Press, 1986.

Fetter, Bruce. "The Luluabourg Revolt of Elisabethville." *African Historical Studies* 2, 2 (1969): 137–47.

Fetter, Bruce. "Elisabethville and Lubumbashi: The Segmentary Growth of a Colonial City." Ph.D. dissertation, University of Wisconsin–Madison, 1968.

Fetter, Bruce. "L'Union Minière du Haut-Katanga, 1920–1940: La Naissance d'une sous-culture totalitaire." *Cahiers du CEDAF* 9-10 (1973): 1–68.

Fetter, Bruce. "Zambia Watchtower at Elisabethville, 1931–1934: An Analysis of Personal and Aggregate Data." Paper presented at the African Studies Association Meeting, 1975.

Fetter, Bruce. "African Associations in Elisabethville, 1910–1935: Their Origins and Development." *Etudes d'histoire africaine* 2 (1976): 205–20.

Fetter, Bruce. *The Creation of Elisabethville.* Stanford: Hoover Institution Press, 1976.

Fetter, Bruce. "The Union Minière and Its Hinterland: A Demographic Reconstruction." *African Economic History* 12 (1983): 67–81.

Fields, Karen E. "The Ordinary and Extraordinary in Social Movement: Some Reflections on Charismatic Religion as a Mode of Popular Activism." Paper presented at the American Historical Association Meeting, New York, 27 December 1979.

Fields, Karen. "Charismatic Religion as Popular Protest: The Ordinary and the Extraordinary in Social Movements." *Theory and Society* 11, 3 (May 1982): 321–61.

Fields, Karen E. *Revival and Rebellion in Colonial Central Africa.* Princeton: Princeton University Press, 1985.

Foster, John. *Class Struggle and the Industrial Revolution.* London: St. Martin's Press, 1974.

Friedland, W. H. "Cooperation, Conflict and Conscription. TANU-TFL Relations, 1955–1964." In *Transition in African Politics,* edited by A. A. Castango, 136–70. New York: Praeger, 1967.

"Les Fusils et du gibier." *L'Essor du Congo,* douzième année (2 juin 1940): 1.

George, F., and J. Gouverneur. "Les Transformations Techniques et l'evolution des coefficients de fabrication à l'Union Minière du Haut-Katanga de 1910 à 1965." *Cultures et développement* 2, no. 1 (1969–70): 58–87.

Gerth, Hans, and C. Wright Mills. *Character and Social Structure.* New York: Harbinger Books, 1964.

Gould, David J. "From Development Administration to Underdevelopment Administration: A Study of Zairian Administration in the Light of the Current Crisis." *Cahiers du CEDAF* 6 (1978): 17–34.

Gouverneur, J. *Productivity and Factor Proportions in Less Developed Countries.* Oxford: Oxford University Press, 1971.

"La Grande Pitié du paysan indigène." *L'Essor du Congo* (23 septembre 1944): 1.

Gray, Richard, and David Birmingham, eds. *Pre-Colonial African Trade.* London: Cambridge University Press, 1970.

Green, James. *Grass-Roots Socialism.* Baton Rouge: Louisiana State University Press, 1978.

"La Grève de Lubumbashi." *L'Essor du Congo,* treizième année, no. 419 (10 décembre 1941): 1.

"Les Grèves de Panda." *L'Essor du Congo,* treizième année, no. 414 (5 décembre 1941): 1.

Grevisse, Fernand. *Quelques aspects de l'organisation des indigènes déracinés residant en territoire de Jadotville.* Anvers: Editions Institut colonial et Maritime, 1936.

Grevisse, Fernand. "Salines et saliniers indigènes du Haut-Katanga." *Bulletin du CEPSI* (Centre d'étude des problèmes sociaux indigènes, Elisabethville) 11 (1950): 270–350.

Grevisse, Fernand. *Le Centre extra-coutumier d'Elisabethville.* Bruxelles: Institut royal Colonial Belge, 1954.

Grillo, R. D. *African Railwaymen.* New York: Cambridge University Press, 1973.

Guebels, L. *Relations complète des travaux de la CPPI.* Elisabethville: CEPSI, 1953.

Gutkind, Peter. *An Emergent Urban African Proletariat.* Montreal: Centre for Developing Areas, 1975.

Gutkind, Peter. "The View from Below: The Political Consciousness of the Urban Poor in Ibadan." *Cahiers d'études africaines* 15, 1e cahier (1975): 3–35.

Gutman, Herbert. "Le Phénomène invisible: La Composition de la famille et du foyers noirs après la Guerre de Secession." *Annales: economies, sociétés et civilisations* 27ᵉ année, no. 45 (juillet-octobre 1972): 431–57.

Hance, William. *The Geography of Modern Africa.* New York: Columbia University Press, 1964.

Haywood, William D. *The Autobiography of Big Bill Haywood.* New York: International Publishers, 1966.

Haywood, William D., and Frank Bohn. *Industrial Socialism.* Chicago: Charles H. Kerr, 1911.

Heisler, Helmut. "The African Workforce of Zambia." *Civilisations* 21, 4 (1971): 425–35.

Heneaux-Depooter, Marie. *Misères et luttes sociales dans le Hainaut, 1860–1869.* Bruxelles: Editions Université libre du Bruxelles: , 1959.

Herfindahl, Orris. *Copper Costs and Prices: 1870–1957.* Baltimore: Johns Hopkins University Press, 1959.

Heyse, Theodore. *Le Régime du travail au Congo Belge.* Bruxelles: Editions Goemaere, 1924.

Higginson, John. "The Formation of an Industrial Proletariat in Southern Africa—the Second Phase, 1921–1949." In *Labor in the World Social Structure,* edited by Immanuel Wallerstein, 121–219. Beverly Hills: Sage Publications, 1983.

Hobsbawn, Eric. *Laboring Men.* New York: Vintage Press, 1964.

Hodgkin, Thomas. *Nationalism in Colonial Africa.* New York: New York University Press, 1957.

Horwitz, Ralph. *The Political Economy of South Africa.* London: Weidenfeld and Nicolson, 1967.

Iliffe, John. *Tanganyika under German Rule, 1905–1912.* London: Cambridge University Press, 1969.

"L'Impôt indigène et développement économique." *Notre Colonie* 21ᵉ année (15 novembre 1919).

"Indiscipline et faineantise." *L'Echo du Kivu* (10 juillet 1942): 1.

Jewsiewicki, Bogumil. "Notes sur l'histoire socio-economique du Congo." *Etudes d'histoire africaine* 3 (1972): 315–40.

Jewsiewicki, Bogumil. *Agriculture itinerante et economie capitaliste. Histoire des essais de modernisation de l'agriculture africaine au Zaire à l'époque coloniale.* 2 vols. Lubumbashi, Zaire: UNAZA, 1975.

Jewsiewicki, Bogumil. "Contestation sociale au Zaire. Grève administrative de 1920 (ex-Congo Belge)." *Africa-Tervuren* 2, 3-4 (1976): 57–67.

Jewsiewicki, Bogumil. "La Contestation sociale et la naissance du proletariat au Zaire au cours de la première moitié du xxᵉ siècle." *Revue canadienne des études africaines* 10, 1 (1976): 45–70.

Jewsiewicki, Bogumil. "The Great Depression and the Making of the Colonial Economic System in the Belgian Congo." *African Economic History* 4 (Fall 1977): 153–77.

Jewsiewicki, Bogumil. "Unequal Development: Capitalism and the Katanga

Economy, 1919–40." In *The Roots of Rural Poverty in Central and Southern Africa,* edited by R. Palmer and N. Parsons, 317–44. Berkeley: University of California Press, 1978.

Jewsiewicki, Bogumil. "Le Colonat agricole européen au Congo Belge, 1910–1960, problèmes politiques et économiques." *Journal of African History* 20 (1979): 559–71.

Jewsiewicki, Bogumil. "Zaire Enters the World System: Its Colonial Incorporation as the Belgian Congo, 1885–1960." In *Zaire: The Political Economy of Underdevelopment,* edited by Guy Gran, 29–54. New York: Praeger Publishers, 1979.

Jewsiewicki, Bogumil. "Political Consciousness among African Peasants in Colonial Zaire." *Review of African Political Economy* 19 (September–December 1980): 23–32.

Jewsiewicki, Bogumil. "Rural Society and the Belgian Colonial Economy." In *History of Central Africa,* Vol. 2, edited by David Birmingham and Phyllis Martin, 95–125. New York: Longman, 1983.

Jewsiewicki, Bogumil, and David Newbury, eds. *African Historiographies.* Beverly Hills: Sage Publications, 1986.

Jewsiewicki, Bogumil, Kilola Lema, and Jean-Luc Vellut. "Documents pour servir à l'histoire sociale du Zaire: Grèves dans le Bas-Congo (Bas-Zaire) en 1945." *Etudes d'histoire africaine* 5 (1973): 155–88.

Johnstone, F. A. *Class, Race and Gold.* London: Routledge and Kegan Paul, 1976.

Jones, Gareth Stedman. *Outcast.* London: Oxford University Press, 1971.

Jones, Gareth Stedman. "Class Expression versus Social Control?" *History Workshop* 4 (Autumn 1977): 163–71.

Jones, Gareth Stedman. *Languages of Class.* New York: Cambridge University Press, 1982.

"Le Jury de qualification pour la main-d'oeuvre indigène." *L'Essor du Congo* (22 mars 1947): 1.

Kajika, N. "Quelques aspects théoriques et méthodologiques d'une recherche en cours sur la vie de travail et vie hors travail des mineurs de Kamoto." *Maadini* 4 trimestre, no. 4 (1974): 17 and 35–36.

"Le Kasai devant la crise du cuivre." *L'Essor du Congo,* 5661 (16 décembre 1944): 1.

Kashamura, Anicet. *Culture et alienation en Afrique.* Conde-sur-Noireau, France: Edition du Cercle, 1972.

Katzenellenbogen, S. N. *Railways and the Copper Mines of Katanga.* London: Oxford University Press, 1973.

Katznelson, Ira, and Aristide Zolberg. *Working Class Formation.* Princeton: Princeton University Press, 1986.

Kayamba, Badye. "Capitalisme et déstructuration des sociétés lignagères dans l'ancien territoire de Sakania au Zaire (1870–1940)." Vols. 1 and 2. Thèse de doctorat, UNAZA, Lubumbashi, 1986.

Khang-Zulbal, K. "Histoire économique du district du Tanganika (1935–

1940)." Mémoire de licence, UNAZA, Lubumbashi, 1973.

Kindelberger, Charles. *The World in Depression, 1929–1939.* Berkeley: University of California Press, 1975.

Kubuya-Namulemba, Malira. "Les Associations féminines du Lubumbashi: 1920–1950." Mémoire de licence, UNAZA, Lubumbashi, 1972.

Kubuya-Namulemba, Malira. "Regard sur la situation sociale de la citoyenne lushoise d'avant 1950." *Likundoli* 2, 1 (1974): 63–71.

Kwitny, Jonathan. *Endless Enemies: The Making of an Unfriendly World.* New York: Congdon and Weed, 1984.

Lacroix, J. "Vers la sourverainté économique du Zaire, 1960–1970." In *L'Afrique d'indépendance politique à l'indépendance économique,* edited by J. Esseks, 176–94. Paris: Maspero, 1975.

Lambert-Culot, Marie-Claire. "Les Premières Années en Afrique du Comité special du Katanga." *Etudes d'histoire africaine* 3 (1972): 275–317.

Legassick, Martin. "Gold, Agriculture, and Secondary Industry in South Africa: From Periphery to Sub-Metropole as a Forced Labor System." In *The Roots of Rural Poverty in Central and Southern Africa,* edited by Robin Palmer and Neil Parsons, 175–201. Berkeley: University of California Press, 1977.

Lejeune, L. *Le Vieux Congo.* Bruxelles: Editions Gromaere, 1930.

Lekime, Fernand. *Katanga: Pays du cuivre.* Bruxelles: Editions Verviers, 1921.

Lemoine, Robert. "La Concentration des énterprises dans la mise en valeur du Congo." *Annales d'histoire economique et sociale* 6ème année, no. 29 (30 septembre 1934): 433–49.

Lenin, V. I. *Two Tactics in Social Democracy.* Moscow: Progress Publishers, 1966.

Leplae, Edmond. "Histoire et développement des cultures obligatoires de coton et de riz au Congo Belge de 1917 à 1933." *Congo. Revue générale de la colonie* 5, no. 5 (mai 1933).

Leroy-Beaulieu, Pierce Paul. *De la colonisation chez peuples modernes,* 5th ed., Vol. 1. Paris: Editions Guillaumin, 1902.

Lloyd, Trevor. "Africa and Hobson's Imperialism." *Past and Present* (April 1968): 435–57.

Lotar, Louis, "L'Immatriculation et l'ordre économique." *Congo. Revue générale de la colonie* (juin 1924): 364–71.

Lovens, Maurice. "La Revolte de Masisi-Lubutu (Congo Belge, janvier-mai 1944)." *Les Cahiers du CEFAF* 3-4: 1–154.

McNamara, Robert. "Les Crises des établissements humains." *Zaire-Afrique* 103 (mars 1976): 133–40.

Mahoney, Richard. *JFK: Ordeal in Africa.* New York: Oxford University Press, 1984.

Maila, Diambomba MuKanda. "L'Impact de l'industrie minière sur la structure dualiste de l'economie du Zaire." *Bulletin de Gécaminés. Industrie minière et developpement au Zaire* (1974): 79–83.

Malela, Mwabila. *Proletariat et conscience de classe au Zaire: Essai d'explica-*

tion de la proletariasation incomplète des salaires; L'Exemple des travailleurs de la ville industriel de Lubumbashi. Bruxelles: Editions Université libre de Bruxelles, 1973.

Marks, Shula. *Reluctant Rebellion.* Oxford: Clarendon, 1970.

Miller, Joseph. "Chokwe Trade and Conquest in the Nineteenth Century." In *Pre-Colonial African Trade,* edited by R. Gray and D. Birmingham, 175–201. London: Cambridge University Press, 1970.

Minon, Paul. "Quelques aspects de l'evolution recente du centre extra-coutumier d'Elisabethville." *Bulletin du CEPSI* 10, no. 3 (1951): 7–15.

Montgomery, David. *Workers' Control in America.* London: Cambridge University Press, 1979.

Moore, Barrington. *Injustice: The Social Basis of Obedience and Revolt.* White Plains, New York: M. E. Sharpe, 1978.

Morel, E. D. *Red Rubber: The Story of the Rubber Slave Trade in the Congo.* New York: Nassau Print, 1906.

Mottoulle, Léopold. "Mortalité infantile, mortinatalité et natalité: Mortinatalité et natalité chez les enfants des travailleurs Union Minière (camps industriels)." *Bulletin médical du Katanga* 7ème année, no. 1 (1920).

Mottoulle, Léopold. "Contribution à l'étude du déterminisme fonctionnel de l'industrie dans l'education de l'indigène Congolaise." *Bulletin de l'Institut royal colonial Belge* (1934): 210–15.

Mottoulle, Léopold. "Problèmes de la main-d'oeuvre indigène." *L'Essor du Congo* (5 août 1944): 1.

Mottoulle, Léopold. "L'Aspect social de l'attraction exercée par les centres urbains et industriels sur les populations Baluba du Congo Belge: Populations rurales de la province de Lusambo." *INCIDI* (1952): 301–8.

"Les Mouvements de rébellion." *L'Essor du Congo* 17ème année, no. 5440 (18 mars 1944): 1.

"Les Mouvements de rébellion." *L'Essor du Congo,* no. 5842 (8 mai 1944): 1.

"Les Mouvements de rébellion." *L'Essor du Congo* (5 août 1944): 1.

Mukendi, Wa Nsanga. "La Dynamique du développement ou l'instrument conceptuel de l'amenagement spatial." *Bulletin de Gécamines* (Maadini) 2e trimestre (1975): 1–15.

Mukendi, Wa Nsanga. "Le Gisment de manganese de Kisenge: Source de croissance de pauperisation." *Bulletin de Gécamines* (Maadini) 8, 4 trimestre (1975).

Mukendi, Wa Nsanga. "Africa's Natural and Mineral Resources and Neo-Colonialistic Land Use as a Process of Pauperization." Unpublished corporate address on behalf of the administration Générale Carrières et Mines (Gécamines).

Mukome, Mugeya. "Kalemie: Des origines à 1935." *Likundoli* 2 (1974): 10–14.

el-Murjebi, Hamed bin Muhammed. *Maisha ya Hamed bin in Muhammed el Murjebi yaani Tippu Tip Kwa maneno yake mwenyewe.* Dar es Salaam, Tanzania: East African Publishing House, 1966.

Mwendanga, M. K. "Occupation économique du district du Tanganyika (1935–1940) d'après les rapports annuels du Tanganyika-Moero." Mémoire de licence, UNAZA, Lubumbashi, 1972–73.

Noble, David F. *America by Design.* New York: Knopf, 1977.

O'Brien, Connor Cruise. *To Katanga and Back.* New York: Pantheon, 1964.

Onwumelu, John. "Congo Paternalism: An Isolationist Colonial Policy." Ph.D. dissertation, University of Chicago, 1966.

"Origine des centres indigènes." *Ngonga* 1ère ann8e, no. 15 (8 septembre 1934).

Palmer, Robin, and Neil Parsons, eds. *The Roots of Rural Poverty in Central and Southern Africa.* Berkeley: University of California Press, 1977.

Parpart, Jane L. *Labor and Capital on the African Copperbelt.* Philadelphia: Temple University Press, 1983.

Parrini, Carl. *Heir to Empire.* Pittsburgh: University of Pittsburgh Press, 1969.

Perham, Margery. *African Apprenticeship.* New York: Africana Publishing Company (Holmes and Meier), 1974.

Perrings, Charles. "Good Lawyers but Poor Workers: Recruited Angolan Labor in the Copper Mines of Katanga, 1917–1921." *Journal of African History* 18, 2 (1977): 237–59.

Perrings, Charles. *Black Mineworkers in Central Africa.* London: Holmes and Meier, 1979.

"La Philosophie de la rébellion." *L'Essor du Congo* (31 août 1944): 1.

Phimister, I. R. "Capital and Class in Zimbabwe, 1890–1948." Henderson Seminar Paper No. 50 (Department of History, University of Zimbabwe), 6 October 1980.

Phimister, I. R., and C. van Onselen, eds. *Studies in the History of African Mine Labour in Colonial Zimbabwe.* Gwelo: Mambo Press, 1978.

Phimister, I. R., and C. van Onselen. "The Political Economy of Tribal Animosity: A Case Study of the 1929 Bulawayo Location Faction Fight." *Journal of Southern African Studies* 6, 1 (October 1979): 1–44.

Picard, Edmond. *En Congolie.* Bruxelles: Paul Lacomblez, 1896.

Polanyi, Karl. *The Great Transformation.* Boston: Beacon Press, 1957.

Poupart, Robert. *Facteurs de productivité de la main-d'oeuvre autochtone à Elisabethville.* Bruxelles: Editions de l'Institut de Sociologie Solvay, 1960.

Poupart, Robert. *Première esquisse de l'évolution de au syndicalism Congo.* Bruxelles: Editions de l'Institut de Sociologie Solvay, 1961.

Price, Richard. "Theories of Labour Process Formation." *Journal of Social History* (Fall 1984): 91–110.

"Le Problème de l'élite congolaise." *L'Essor du Congo,* no. 5637 (18 novembre 1944): 1.

"Le Problème de la main-d'oeuvre agricole." *Centre Afrique* (6 mai 1943).

"Prohibition illimitée du permit du travail." *Le Matériel colonial* 22ème année, no. 106 (mars 1939).

Radosh, Ronald. "Corporatism. Liberal and Fascist as Seen by Samuel Gompers." *Studies on the Left* 3, no. 3 (Summer 1963): 67–77.

Ranger, T. O. *Revolt in Southern Rhodesia, 1896–97.* Evanston: Northwestern University Press, 1967.

Ranger, Terence. *The African Voice.* Evanston: Northwestern University Press, 1970.

Ranger, T. O. *Dance and Society in Eastern Africa*. Berkeley: University of California Press, 1975.

"Rapport de la commission pour l'étude du problème de la main-d'oeuvre au Congo Belge." *Congo. Revue générale de la colonie* (juin 1925): 1–2 (annexe).

"Renaissance de la rumeur sur les Batumbula." *L'Essor du Congo* (10 mars 19546): 1.

Renault, François. *Lavergerie, l'esclavage africain et l'Europe*. Paris: Editions Sacre, 1971.

Rennie, J. K. "White Farmers, Black Tenants and Landlord Legislation: Southern Rhodesia, 1890–1930." *Journal of Southern African Studies* 5, 1 (October 1978): 86–99.

"Reparation judiciaire." *L'Essor du Congo* (12 février 1937): 1.

Rey, Pierre Philippe. *Colonialisme, neo-colonialisme et transition au capitalisme*. Paris: Maspero, 1971.

Reyntjen, Dr. "La Rougeole dans les camps de l'Union Minière du Haut-Katanga. *Bulletin médical du Katanga* 12ème année, no. 2 (1935): 70–88.

Richards, Audrey. *Land, Labour and Diet in Northern Rhodesia*. London: Oxford University Press, 1934.

Richardson, Peter, and Jean-Jacques Van Helten. "The Development of the South African Gold Mining Industry, 1895–1918. *Economic History Review* 37, 3 (August 1984): 331–45.

Robert, M. "La Question minière." In *Politique économique du Congo: Rapport au Comité du Congres colonial*. Bruxelles: Editions Gromaere, 1924.

Roberts, Andrew. "Pre-Colonial Trade in Zambia." *African Social Research* (10 December 1970): 715–46.

Roberts, Andrew D. *A History of the Bemba*. Madison: University of Wisconsin Press, 1973.

Robinson, Ronald, and John Gallagher. *Africa and the Victorians*. London: St. Martin's Press, 1961.

Romaniuk, Anatole. *La Fécondité des populations congolaises*. Paris: Mouton, 1967.

Ruhararamanzi, Du Duri. "La Grève des ouvriers noirs à l'UMHK." Mémoire de licence, UNAZA, Lubumbashi, 1972.

Ryckmans, Pierre. *Dominer pour servir*. Bruxelles: Editions universelle, 1948.

Segaert, Henri. *Un Terme au Congo Belge, 1916–1918*. Sydney, 1918.

St. John, Christopher. "Kazembe and the Tanganyika-Nyasa Corridor, 1800–1900." In *Pre-Colonial African Trade*, edited by R. Gray and D. Birmingham, 202–28. London: Cambridge University Press, 1970.

Scott, James. *The Moral Economy of the Peasant*. New Haven: Yale University Press, 1976.

Scott, James. *Weapons of the Weak*. New Haven: Yale University Press, 1985.

Scott, Joan. *The Glassworkers of Carmaux*. Cambridge: Harvard University Press, 1974.

Sewell, William. "La Classe ouvrière de Marseille sous la Deuxième République." *Mouvement social* (juillet–septembre 1971): 27–66.

Shepperson, George. "Nyasaland and the Millennium." In *Millennial Dreams in Action*, edited by Sylvia Thrupp, 144–59. New York: Shocken, 1970.

Shepperson, George, and Thomas Price. *Independent African*. 2d ed. Edinburgh: University Press, 1958.

"La Situation industrielle en Belgique." *L'Economiste français* (1 avril 1888).

Snepp, Frank. *Decent Interval*. New York: Random House, 1978.

Sohier, Jean. *La Mémoire d'un policier belgo-congolais*. Bruxelles: Académie royale des Sciences d'outre-mer, 1974.

Steinberg, Maxime. "La Crise congolaise dans le parti ouvrier belge." In *La Deuxième internationale et l'Orient*, edited by G. Haupt and Madeline Reberioux, 105–35. Paris: Editions Cujas, 1967.

Stengers, Jean. *Combien le Congo a-t-il couté à la Belgique?* Bruxelles: Académie royale des Sciences Coloniales, 1957.

Stengers, Jean. *Belgique et Congo: L'Elaboration de la Charte coloniale*. Bruxelles: Renaissance du Livre, 1961.

Stengers, Jean. "Léopold II et la rivalité franco-anglaise en Afrique, 1882–1884." *Revue belge de philologie et d'histoire* 47 (1969): 425–79.

Stengers, Jean, and Jean-Jacques Symoens. *Le Congo Belge durant la Second Guerre Mondiale, recueil d'études*. Bruxelles: Académie royal des Sciences d'outre-mer, 1983.

Stenmans, Alan. *La Reprise du Congo par la Belgique*. Bruxelles: Renaissance du Livre, 1949.

Sternstein, Jerome. "The Strange Beginnings of American Economic Penetration of the Congo." *African Historical Studies* 3, 2 (1969): 189–203.

Stockwell, John. *In Search of Enemies*. New York: W. W. Norton, 1978.

Sundiata, I. K. "The Mores of Expansion, 1837–1914." *Presence africaine* 2ᵉ trimestre, no. 70 (1969): 60–65.

Suny, Ronald. *The Baku Commune*. Princeton: Princeton University Press, 1972.

Taussig, Michael. *The Devil and Commodity Fetishism in South America*. Chapel Hill: University of North Carolina Press, 1980.

Tempels, Placide. *La Philosophie bantoue*. Paris: Editions presence africaine, 1959.

Thompson, E. P. *The Making of the English Working Class*. New York: Vintage, 1967.

Thompson, E. P. "Le Charivari anglais." *Annales: economies, sociétés et civilisations* 27ᵉ année, no 2 (mars–avril 1972): 285–312.

Thornton, John K. *The Kingdom of Kongo*. Madison: University of Wisconsin Press, 1983.

Toussaint, E. "Le Personnel congolais: Les Besoins de main-d'oeuvre; les moyens employés pour y fair face." In *UMHK*, 230–43. Monograph series. Bruxelles, 1952.

"La Tragedie de Panda." *L'Essor du Congo*, treizième année, no. 419 (10 décembre 1941): 1.

Trempé, Rolande. *Les Mineurs de Carmaux*. Paris: Editions ouvrières, 1971.

Trotsky, Leon. *The History of the Russian Revolution*, Vol. 1. London: Sphere Publications, 1972.

Tshibangu, Kabet Musas. "La Situation sociale dans le ressort administratif de Likasi (ex-territoire de Jadotville) pendant la guerre." *Etudes d'histoire africaine* 6 (1974): 275–331.

Tshibangu, Kabet Musas. "L'Impact socio-économique de la grande crise économique mondiale des années 1929–1935 sur l'ancien Haut-Katanga industriel." Vols. 1 and 2. Thèse de doctorat, UNAZA, Lubumbashi, 1986.

Ulrich-Wehler, Hans. "Bismarck's Imperialism." *Past and Present* 48 (August 1970): 119–55.

UMHK: 1906–1956. 2d ed. Bruxelles, 1957.

L'Union Minière du Haut-Katanga. Monograph series. Bruxelles: L. Cuypers, 1954.

Union Minière du Haut-Katanga. Memoire. Bruxelles, 1957.

Uzoigwe, G. N. "The Kyanyangire Rebellion: Passive Revolt against British Overrule." In *War and Society in Africa*, edited by Bethwell Ogot, 179–214. London: Cass Publishers, 1972.

Vail, Leroy, and Landeg White. "The Struggle for Mozambique: Capitalist Rivalries, 1900–40." *Review* 3, 2 (Fall 1979): 243–75.

Valkeneer, G. "Centre d'Essais de Cultures maraichères et vivières à Kiniama en territoire de Sakania." *Bulletin du CEPSI* 13 (1950): 74–79.

Vandervelde, Emile. "Contre la politique colonial." *Le Peuple* (18 novembre 1908): 2.

Vandewalle, F., Colonel, and Jacques Brassinne. *Les Rapports secrètes de la sûreté congolaise.* Bruxelles: Editions Arts et Voyages, 1973.

Vanhove, J. *Histoire du Ministère des Colonies.* Bruxelles: Académie royale des Sciences d'outre-mer, 1968.

van Onselen, Charles. *Chibaro.* London: Pluto Press, 1976.

van Onselen, Charles. "Black Workers in Central African History: A Critical Essay on the Historiography and Sociology of Rhodesia." In *Studies in the History of African Mine Labour in Colonial Zimbabwe*, edited by I. R. Phimister and C. van Onselen, 80–102. Gwelo: Mambo Press, 1978.

van Onselen, Charles. *New Nineveh* and *New Babylon*, Vols. 1 and 2 of *Studies in the Social and Economic History of the Witwatersrand, 1886–1914.* London: Longman, 1982.

van Onselen, Charles. "The Witches of Suburbia: Domestic Service on the Witwatersrand, 1890–1914." In *Studies in the Social and Economic History of the Witwatersrand, 1886–1914*, Vol. 2, 50–59. London: Longman, 1982.

Vansina, Jan. *The Children of Woot.* Madison: University of Wisconsin Press, 1978.

Vansina, Jan. *Introduction à l'ethnographie du Congo.* Bruxelles: Edition CRISP, 1966.

Vansina, Jan. *Kingdoms of the Savannah.* Madison: University of Wisconsin Press, 1971.

Varbeke, Felix. "Du régime de la main-d'oeuvre." *Revue générale de la colonie* 2, no. 2 (juillet 1921).

Vellut, Jean-Luc. *Guide de l'étudiant en histoire du Zaire.* Lubumbashi: Editions Mont Noir, 1974.

Vellut, Jean-Luc. "Le Royaume du Cassange et les reseaux luso-africaines." *Cahiers d'études africaines* 15, 1ᵉ Cahier (1975): 367–82.

Vellut, Jean-Luc. "Rural Poverty in Western Shaba." In *The Roots of Rural Poverty in Central and Southern Africa*, edited by Robin Palmer and Neil Parsons, 294–316. Berkeley: University of California Press, 1977.

Vellut, Jean-Luc. "Le Katanga industriel en 1944: Malaises et anxiétés dans la société coloniale." In *Le Congo Belge durant la Seconde Guerre Mondiale: recueil d'études*, edited by Jean Stengers and Jean-Jacques Symoens, 495–523. Bruxelles: Académie royale des Sciences d'Outre Mer, 1983.

Vellut, Jean-Luc. "Mining in the Belgian Congo." In *History of Central Africa*, Vol. 2, edited by David Birmingham and Phyllis M. Martin, 126–62. New York: Longman, 1983.

Verhaegen, Benoit, ed. *Rebellions au Congo*. 2 vols. Bruxelles: Editions CRISP, 1969.

"Vie chère." *L'Essor du Congo* 5454 (4 avril 1944): 1.

Vinocur, John. "Zaire's Capital Puts on a Sunday Look for Visitors." *New York Times*, 11 October 1982: 4.

Wauters, A. J. *Histoire politique du Congo Belge*. Bruxelles: Editions Van Fleteren, 1911.

Weiss, Herbert. *Politics and Protest in the Congo*. Bruxelles: Editions CRISP, 1968.

Weissman, Stephen A. *American Foreign Policy in the Congo, 1960–1964*. Ithaca: Cornell University Press, 1974.

Wills, A. J. *An Introduction to the History of Central Africa*. London: Oxford University Press, 1965.

Wilmet, J. *La Repartition de la population dans la depression des rivières Mufuvya et Lufira (Haut-Katanga)*. Liege: Fonds nationales de Recherche scientifique, 1961.

Wilson, Godfrey, and Monica Wilson. *The Analysis of Social Change*. London: Cambridge University Press, 1968.

Wolpe, Harold. "Capitalism and Cheap Labour Power in South Africa: From Segregation to Apartheid." *Economy and Society* 1, 4 (1972): 425–55.

"Work at Tenke Is Suspended." *New York Times*, 6 March 1976: 1.

Yav, Andre. *Vocabulaire de ville de Elisabethville*. Edité par les agents anciennes domestiques aux communes de Elisabethville, Elisabethville, 1965.

Young, Crawford. *Politics in the Congo*. Princeton: Princeton University Press, 1963.

"The Zaire Bailout." *Forbes* (1 December 1975): 19.

Index

Sabotage, 96–98
Sakabinda, 139
Sakadi, 21
Sakania, 9
Sakayongo, 8
Salesians, 73, 74, 247n62
Salt, 22–23
Sampwe, 164
Sandoa, 48
Sankuru, 8, 131
Saulu Auguste, 133
"Schoolmasters," 136, 137
Schroeven, Jean, 70, 148–50 *passim*, 257n7
Scientific management, 11, 88, 91, 92
Second World War: as a catalyst for a change in African workers' aspirations, 4; as a watershed for African trade unionism, 11; impact of Anglo-American and German rearmament on UMHK, 162–63; creation of provincial censor, 167; as a factor in the provincial uprising, 198; as a factor in worker protest, 211; impact on relations between European foremen and African workers, 213
Secret police. *See* Sûreté
Segaert, Henri, 24, 82, 83
Senegalese, 80
Senga Albert, 133
Sengier, Edgar, 56, 178, 184
Sesame, 260n60
Shaba, 3. *See* Katanga
Shangulowe, 147
Shikutu wa Bruxelles. *See* Workers' lodges
Shikutu wa Bwango. *See* Workers' lodges
Shikutu wa Kabinda. *See* Workers' lodges
Shinkolobwe, 132, 220
Shituru, 189
Shoemaking factories, 88
Sisson, John, 68
Skilled workers: in non-metallurgical trades, 88, 95, 107; aspirations of, 144–48 *passim*; participation in worker protests, 165–67 *passim*, 189–91 *passim*
Sleeping sickness. *See* Diseases
Smallpox. *See* Diseases
Smugglers, 82
Social assistants, 89, 131

Social control, 119–20
Social engineering, 223–24n6
Societé Elisabethville-Katanga, 147. *See also* Voluntary associations
Societé général de Belgique, 8
Sogechim, 218–19
Sohier, Antoine, 76, 104, 130–31
Sokoni, 119
Songye, 6, 23–24
Southern Rhodesia, 7
Spanish influenza, 35
Squatters, 140–44, 263n62
Stabilization: economic justification of, 121; as a corporate rubric, 215; as a descriptive term, 215–16; origins of the term, 216; as a management concept, 277–78n20
Star of the Congo Mine, 31, 124
Stock market, 111, 112
Strikes: of underground workers at Prince Léopold, 92; of underground workers at Busanga, 166; peasant support of, 177; management's perception of, 182, 187–88; government's perception of, 193–97; during Second World War, 184–205 *passim*, 214–15; of contract workers at Likasi, 235n80
Strythagen, Raoul, 105–7 *passim*
Sûreté, 69, 113–14, 116, 170, 245n38
Swahili, 138, 176, 192
Swahili merchants, 6, 24

Tambwe Janvier, 171. *See also* Watchtower sects
Tanganika-Moero (District of), 23, 29, 44–46 *passim*, 205
Tanganyika Concessions Limited, 8, 19, 44
Tanzania, 5
Taxation, 20, 22, 25, 101–2, 135–36, 167
Taylor, Fredrick Winslow, 88
TCL. *See* Tanganyika Concessions Limited
Technology: as an outgrowth of UMHK's social policy, 91; shortcomings, 92
Tempels, Placide, 12, 229n40
Temps de campagnes, 98
Tenke-Dilolo, 132
Tenke-Dilolo railroad. *See* Railway

DATE DUE

ILL			
1560 4847			
2/10/06			

WITHDRAWN

DEMCO 38-296